Application of Mandatory Rules
in the Private International Law of Contracts

Kerstin Ann-Susann Schäfer

Application of Mandatory Rules in the Private International Law of Contracts

A Critical Analysis of Approaches in Selected Continental and Common Law Jurisdictions, with a View to the Development of South African Law

PETER LANG
Frankfurt am Main · Berlin · Bern · Bruxelles · New York · Oxford · Wien

Bibliographic Information published by the Deutsche Nationalbibliothek
The Deutsche Nationalbibliothek lists this publication in the Deutsche Nationalbibliografie; detailed bibliographic data is available in the internet at http://dnb.d-nb.de.

Cover Design:
Olaf Glöckler, Atelier Platen, Friedberg

ISBN 978-3-631-55176-9

www.peterlang.de

To my parents

Acknowledgement

This book is based on a thesis for the degree of Doctor of Philosophy at the University of Cape Town, South Africa. Research was done for my thesis during my stay as a postgraduate student at the University of Cape Town. Court decisions and academic literature up until 2000 have been taken into account. The thesis was finished later, back in Germany, in 2002 and was admitted to the degree Doctor of Philosophy in Public Law in 2003.

I wish to acknowledge my sincere gratitude to my supervisor, Professor Thomas W. Bennett, for his assistance and advice at all stages during the course of writing the thesis. It was his idea to write a comparative study on this particular topic. His criticism and advice during the discussion of the different drafts of the thesis have conspicuously contributed to the present work. Finally, I need to thank him for his invaluable help in adding the finishing touch to the style of writing and language. Thanks are also due to Ms Linda van de Vijver for her significant editorial assistance.

Furthermore, I am very grateful to my dear parents Helge Schäfer and Dr. Volker Schäfer, and to my friends Janine Sänger, Sven Alberding, Dr. Thomas Possel and Rasmus Elsner for their invaluable support and encouragement.

Kerstin Schäfer

Table of Contents

Chapter 5: Foreign internationally mandatory rules 135

Chapter 1
Introduction and preliminary matters

This thesis is a comparative examination of the application of mandatory rules in the area of the private international law of contracts.[1] As will be seen during the course of this study, and as will be briefly noted in the following introductory remarks, this question arises in a number of situations. It prompts fundamental issues that have been debated for many years by academics all over the world. Some of the problems are still not fully settled.

I The Problem: Application of mandatory rules in the conflict setting

The overriding question that has to be addressed is under what circumstances are mandatory rules to be applied in the private international law of contracts. How do these rules relate to the ordinary choice of law process? Are the rules superseded by the forum's choice of law rules for contracts, or do they deserve special consideration? The relationship between the rules of private international law that provide for the application of the law of a specified legal system, and rules of a mandatory nature that claim application to the transaction is a controversial matter.

The general rule in the private international law of contracts is that the 'proper law' governs most aspects of the contract. If the forum's choice of law rules lead to a foreign legal system, the foreign law is rendered applicable, within the scope of reference of the forum's conflict rules. This application of the foreign law includes application of its mandatory legislation to the exclusion of the *ius dispositivum* and the *ius cogens* of the forum and also to the exclusion of a potentially otherwise applicable law.[2] This approach is generally true of all the countries that will be examined, whether the foreign law is determined by a choice of law of the contracting parties (subjective choice of law), or by the forum's choice of law rules, in the absence of a choice by the parties (objective choice of law).[3] Thus a statute or a common law rule does not normally apply to a contract, unless it forms part of the proper law.[4]

---

1 The application of mandatory rules in other areas of private international law, eg law of torts or family law, will not be considered. For the application of mandatory rules as a means of stopping evasion in the area of family law, see Fawcett CLJ (1990) 44 et seq. For corresponding problems in international commercial arbitration, see Schiffer *Normen* (1989); Ungeheuer *Beachtung* (1996).

2 Compare Philip *Recent Provisions* 241, 242.

3 Philip *Contract Conflicts* 81, 92, 93; id *Recent Provisions* 241, 242 states: 'If the application of mandatory rules of the law of the forum were always preserved one might well

However, in respect of the application of mandatory rules, this is not the end of the matter. There are many circumstances in which the mandatory rules of a law other than the proper law should be applied, or at least considered or taken into account. The application can be based on *special choice of law rules* providing for the application of mandatory rules of a law other than the proper law.[5] Alternatively, a mandatory rule can be applicable without a separate and prior choice of law rule indicating its applicability, because it determines *its own scope of application*. In this case, the mandatory rule has an implied or express *unilateral conflict rule* attached to it, which indicates its international scope. Furthermore, the courts have taken into account mandatory rules of a law other than the proper law, on the basis of *policy considerations* or the forum's *ordre public*.

The application of the mandatory rules of a law other than the proper law therefore constitutes an exception to the general rule that the proper law of the contract governs most aspects of the contract.

II Historical background: From Savigny and the 'liberal state' to the modern welfare state of the 20th century

The application of the proper law was always subject to exceptions. The founder of today's traditional choice of law method,[6] the German academic writer Savigny (1779-1861) had already excluded rules of a strictly mandatory, compelling nature from the normal choice of law process: 'Gesetze von streng positiver, zwingender Natur, die wegen ihrer Natur zu jener freien Behandlung ... nicht geeignet sind'.[7] Savigny's 'connecting system' or 'allocation technique'

---

do without private international law'. However, with regard to the principle of party autonomy this result is not always accepted. For the difference between incorporation and party reference, see later in Chapter 2. In South Africa the legal situation is still unsettled, see Forsyth *Private International law* 278 et seq, 299 and later under Chapter 2, VI, 1.

4 Or unless it is a procedural one of the forum, cf Dicey & Morris *Conflict of Laws Vol 1/ 12th /13th ed* 21, 22.

5 Eg arts 3(3), 5(2) and 6(1) of the Rome Convention, which are discussed in Chapter 2, I, 1, 2

6 The choice of law rules of private international law of contracts in England, Germany and Switzerland, and in the Rome Convention are based on this traditional allocation technique, see Sonnenberger *FS Rebmann* 819; Kropholler *IPR* § 3 I; Lipstein Rec des Cours 135 (1972 I) 99, 163, 194, 195 et seq. This is also true of South African Roman-Dutch private international law, see Forsyth *Private International Law* 5 et seq, 43, 44, 57 et seq.

7 'Laws of a strictly positive, mandatory nature that are due to their nature ... not suitable for such a liberal treatment': Friedrich Karl von Savigny *System des heutigen römischen*

(*Anknüpfungsmodell*) consisted of multilateral conflict rules indicating the law applicable to the transaction.[8] The system was based on the principle of the *formal equality and interchangeability of legal systems*, and was neutral in that the substantive law rules were not considered. Savigny contended that *international uniformity of decision* would be achieved by his method.[9] In respect of mandatory rules based on moral reasons, or the public well being (*publica utilitas*), that had a political, police or economic character, he held that the *formal equality and interchangeability of legal systems* was not given and that 'each state appears for itself as conclusive'.[10] Savigny's approach was that these rules were of an abnormal nature and would diminish with the natural legal development of nations.[11]

Savigny's forecast was incorrect: Contrary to his prediction, during the last century, modern states have increasingly regulated private relationships.[12] The so-called 'liberal state' (*Liberalstaat*) that left its citizens to control their own legal relations has slowly but surely been replaced by the 'welfare state' or 'social state' (*Sozialstaat*), that aims to intervene actively in private relationships in the economic and social interests of the community.[13] Alongside the growing amount of economic dirigisme, mandatory legislation based on socio-political intentions to protect groups of individuals has been enacted to an ever greater degree.[14] Rules intended to protect or promote policies of the State

---

Rechts Vol VIII (1849) 33 et seq; cf Kropholler *IPR* § 3 II; Anderegg *Ausländische Eingriffsnormen* 1 - 2; Kreuzer *Ausländisches Wirtschaftsrecht* 8.

8 In order to select the appropriate legal system Savigny examined the legal relationship and asked where its 'proper and natural seat' was to be found: the so called '*centre of gravity approach*', Savigny *System des heutigen Römischen Rechts* Vol VIII 108; Triebel ICLQ 37 (1988) 935; Forsyth *Private International Law* 6, 43 - 44; Kropholler *IPR* § 3 I.

9 Savigny *System des heutigen Römischen Rechts* Vol VIII 23 et seq; Kropholler *IPR* § 3 I; Kreuzer *Ausländisches Wirtschaftsrecht* 7, 8; Forsyth *Private International Law* 46, 60, 61.

10 Savigny *System des heutigen Römischen Rechts* Vol VIII 36. Foreign mandatory rules of this kind remained therefore inapplicable; cf Kreuzer *Ausländisches Wirtschaftsrecht* 8, 9.

11 Savigny *System des heutigen Römischen Rechts* Vol VIII 38. However this approach must be seen against the background of the legal reality of the liberal state in the 19 century. For an overview, see Basedow RabelsZ 52 (1988) 9, 13 et seq.

12 Kreuzer *Ausländisches Wirtschaftsrecht* 9; also see Hartley *Contract Conflicts* 111 et seq; Lipstein *Conflict of Public Laws* 357, 360; Philip *Recent Provisions* 241, 242.

13 Basedow RabelsZ 52 (1988) 8,16 calls it 'mixed economy'; Sonnenberger *FS Rebmann* 819, 820; Voser 7 Am Rev Int'l Arb 319 Lexis-Nexis (3) of 38; Kren ZVerglRWiss 88 (1989) 48, 49; Keller *FS Vischer* 175, 176; Vischer Rec des Cours 142 (1974 II) 1, 21; Hartley *Contract Conflicts* 111 et seq.

14 See Kreuzer *Ausländisches Wirtschaftsrecht* 9; Erauw *International Contracts* 71 et seq, Hartley *Contract Conflicts* 111 et seq. For example, see the recent directives of the EU in the branch of consumer protection, Junker IPRax 1998, 65 et seq.

based on social, economic or political considerations are, for example, rules on anti-trust practices, import and export prohibitions, exchange control regulations and price control regulations. Examples of mandatory legislation intended to protect individuals are rules protecting the weaker contracting parties, such as consumers or employees.[15] Trade restrictions are also examples of mandatory legislation. They do not serve protectionist goals of economic or social policy, but they do pursue interests of a security nature, or may exert political pressure on foreign countries, for example, by means of embargoes. Such restrictions may also endeavour to prevent the loss of cultural treasures or to protect the environment.[16]

The issue of mandatory rules in private international law is rendered important by the increase in the number of rules that intervene in the private relationship in order to advance the interests of the state. These rules may affect relationships between individuals either by requiring action, making a particular provision obligatory, or prohibiting certain conduct or a specific provision in a contract.[17] All these rules are binding and do not permit any derogation.[18] Often the state interest in upholding these rules is of such importance that the provision is designed to apply irrespective of the law that governs the contract according to the 'normal' choice of law rules. They are therefore exceptions to the normal choice of law rules.[19] In England they are known as '*overriding statutes*' or '*directly applicable statutes*'.[20] Elsewhere they are referred to as '*lois de police*' or '*lois d'application immédiate*' or '*Eingriffsnormen*'.[21]

Along with this trend of increasing state intervention in private relations, international trade between private parties has increased.[22] But not only did international commercial agreements become more and more common, cross-border selling of goods and services to non-professionals expanded. In addition, the growth of multilateral corporations and free movement within the European Union, for example, has led to the international mobility of workers.[23] An

---

15 Also see Hartley (1979) 4 ELR 236, 238; id *Contract Conflicts* 111; Cheshire & North's *Private International Law/12th ed* 469, */13th ed* 575; Philip *Recent Provisions* 241, 242.

16 Basedow RabelsZ 52 (1988) 9, 16.

17 Cf Hartley (1979) 4 ELR, 236, 237.

18 Cf Lipstein *Öffentliches Recht* 39, 42, 43.

19 Philip *Recent Provisions* 241, 242; Dicey & Morris *Conflict of Laws Vol 1/12th ed* 21, 23, */13th ed* 21, 22; cf the published article of Hartley Rec des Cours 266 (1997) 345 et seq.

20 Cheshire & North's *Private International Law/12th ed* 497, */13th ed* 578; Dicey & Morris *Conflict of Laws Vol 1/12th ed* 21 – 25, */13th ed* 21, 22.

21 Cf Dicey & Morris *Conflict of Laws Vol 1/12th /13th ed* 21, 22; on further designations, Chapter 3.

22 Cf Kreuzer *Ausländisches Wirtschaftsrecht* 9.

23 See Morse *Contract Conflicts* 143, 144.

international contract may have connections not only with one country, but also with another, and the latter's mandatory legislation may also claim application. Hence, the parties are often faced with mandatory rules of the *lex fori*, the *lex causae* and a third country, with which the contract may have a certain connection. The third country may be, for example, the place of performance, the place where the contract was concluded, the habitual residence, or the place of business.[24]

The crucial question is how these mandatory rules relate to the traditional multilateral choice of law rules in private international law. Are they subject to the ordinary choice of law process (and thus can only be applied if they form part of the applicable law) or do they deserve special treatment? It has often been argued that the applicability of these norms cannot be determined by means of the traditional allocation technique. Instead, these rules fall outside the scope of reference of the normal multilateral conflict rules and deserve special choice of law considerations.[25]

While 'directly applicable statutes' of the *lex fori* are generally applied according to their own terms, despite a foreign proper law of the contract, problems arise with regard to foreign *lois d'application immédiate*. The treatment of these rules in the private international law of contracts has long been a subject of controversy amongst continental European lawyers. In fact, it is regarded as one of the most controversial issues in the modern international law of contracts world wide.[26]

In Germany and Switzerland the academic debate started over 50 years ago with the innovative approach of Wilhelm Wengler, who was the founder of today's *Special Connection Theory* (*Sonderanknüpfungstheorie*).[27] Since then, the controversy has continued unabated, and has led to an immense amount of academic contributions about this issue.[28]

---

24 Lipstein *Conflict of Public Laws* 357, 365 et seq.

25 For the different approaches, see infra Chapter 4, I, and Chapter 5, I.

26 Kreuzer *Ausländisches Wirtschaftsrecht* 10.

27 Wengler ZVerglRWiss 54 (1941) 168 et seq; also Zweigert RabelsZ 14 (1942) 283 et seq.

28 This is true for many Continental European countries, such as France, Italy, Austria etc, for references, see MünchKomm/Martiny Art 34 Schrifttum; Schurig RabelsZ 54 (190) 217, 218 footnote *; id *Lois* footnote 1; Sonnenberger *FS Rebmann* 819, 821 N 8; Baum RabelsZ 53 (1989) 152 footnotes *, 3, 4; Schäfer *FG Sandrock* 37 footnote 2.

In the United Kingdom the discussion concerning the application of 'directly applicable rules' of foreign states started later, during the negotiations of the Rome Convention. This may be due to the fact that English law outside the Rome Convention does not distinguish between the application of mandatory rules and public policy. The principle of mandatory rules overriding the normal choice of law process has in fact been introduced by the Rome Convention into English conflict of laws.[29] However, the problem is well known in English law and is often referred to within the notion of public policy and the essential validity or illegality of a contract.

III Party autonomy and mandatory rules

The question of the application of mandatory rules has arisen in the context of party autonomy, alongside the issue of the application of *lois d'application immédiate* in private international law. The tendency to grant the contracting parties a nearly unlimited freedom to choose a law to govern their transaction (party autonomy) has increased the importance of mandatory rules in the private international law of contracts.

The traditional requirements of a valid choice of law, such as an objective connection between the contract and the chosen law, or the reasonable or legitimate interest of the contracting parties in their choice, have been abandoned. The parties may choose a law that is completely unconnected with the transaction, and mandatory rules have therefore become a modern tool to restrict such freedom of choice.[30] Particularly with a view to protecting the weaker contracting party, freedom of choice has been limited by the application of mandatory rules of the law otherwise applicable, had the parties not made their choice. Policy considerations of the substantive law are thus extended into the field of conflict of laws. [31]

This approach indicates a change from the traditional choice of law method that was 'neutral' in determining the applicable law, in that it did not refer to values in substantive laws or to the result of its application.[32] This trend is reflected in

---

29 Apart from a few legislative directions, cf Jackson *Contract Conflicts* 59, 70; Cheshire & North's *Private International Law/12th ed* 137, 496, */13th ed* 132, 575.

30 Cf Lorenz RIW 1987, 569 et seq; Dicey & Morris *Conflict of Laws Vol II/12th ed* 1213, 1215 et seq, */13th ed* 1216, 1219 et seq.

31 For details, see Chapter 2.

32 See North *Private International Law Problems* 141, 142; Morse ICLQ 42 (1992) 1, 2; Erauw *International Contracts* 71, 72.

the Rome Convention, which deals with mandatory rules in a conceptually new manner.

IV Recent legislative approaches

The academic discussions have been stimulated by politically explosive court decisions, for example, the '*Pipeline-embargo*' case,[33] a decision of a Dutch court. This case concerned the much disputed embargo measures of the United States of America on the construction of a Russian gas-pipeline. These measures were intended by the United States government to apply extra-territorially, but were firmly rejected by the United Kingdom and the European Community.[34] Academics were also challenged by recent statutory approaches that provide for the application of (internationally) mandatory rules in certain choice of law rules, particularly the Rome Convention of 19 June 1980.[35]

The Rome Convention is of considerable interest because it contains a number of conflict rules that deal differently with the application of mandatory rules. Furthermore, the Convention was drafted by legal experts of many European countries and therefore reflects modern tendencies and approaches. The objective of the Rome Convention - the harmonisation of the conflict rules in the European member states - was ultimately confined to contractual obligations.[36] The Convention's conflict rules entered into legal force on 1 April 1991. They thus form the present basis of the private international law of contracts of its European member states.[37]

---

33 Arr-Rechtsbanks' Gravenhage (Den Haag) 17.9.1982, RabelsZ 47 (1983) 141 et seq. For a useful discussion of this case, see Basedow RabelsZ 47 (1983) 147 et seq.

34 The objections were so strong that the British Government invoked the 'Blocking' Protection of Trading Interests Act 1980, Chapter 11 and ordered the British companies concerned not to comply with the United States embargo, cf Lowe RabelsZ 52 (1988) 157, 179, 182; id GYBIL 27 (1984) 54, 67 et seq; see as well the articles of Vagts, Kuyper, Meessen and Basedow in GYBIL 27 (1984) 28 - 141.

35 Other statutory approaches are the Convention on the Law Applicable to Agency of 1978; Act, Doc Law Haye 13 Sess 1976 I 42 (cf Art 16); the Trust Convention, Act, Doc Law Haye 15 Sess 1984 I 25 (cf art 16 (2)); the Bretton Woods Agreement (IMF) (cf art VIII (2) (b)).

36 Compare a more detailed approach, Morse (1998) 2 YB Eur L 107; North *Contract Conflicts* 1, 4 et seq; Williams ICLQ 35 (1986) 1 et seq.

37 The Rome Convention opened for signature in Rome on 7 December 1981, after the deposit of the seventh instrument of ratification, art 29 Rome Convention. This requirement was eventually fulfilled by the United Kingdom; see BGBl II 1991 II 872. Currently the Rome Convention is in force in 15 Member States of the EU, such as the

The Rome Convention refers to mandatory rules in several provisions, four of which are relevant to this study: Articles 3 (3), 5 (2), 6 (1) and 7 (1) and (2).[38] These four conflict rules result in an 'irregular' application of mandatory rules, despite the proper law of the contract.[39] They are all somehow 'exceptions' to the general rule that the forum's conflict rules lead to the application of a foreign law including its rules of a declaratory nature and the mandatory rules under exclusion of the rules of the lex fori or another foreign law.[40] However, although all of these conflict rules deal with mandatory rules, they differ substantially from each other in respect of their structure, the type of mandatory rule referred to, and the effect given to it. The four provisions will be discussed during the course of this study within different structural contexts, depending on how they affect mandatory rules.

The parties' freedom of choice pursuant to art 3 (1) of the Convention is limited by arts 3 (3), 5 (2) and 6 (1) of the Convention, which provide for the application of the mandatory rules of the legal system that would govern in the absence of a choice of law of the parties.[41] Article 3 (3) deals with the situation of a purely domestic contract, while arts 5 (2) and 6 (1) contain special conflict rules for consumer and employment contracts.[42] With regard to consumer and employment contracts, the Rome Convention reflects the modern trend of extending the substantive law's protection of the weaker contracting party into the field of conflict of laws.[43] In this context, party autonomy is limited by mandatory rules.

The effect of art 7 (1) and (2) of the Convention is greater than that of the other provisions. These two provisions serve not only as a limitation of party autonomy; they also override the choice of law process in the absence of

---

United Kingdom, Germany, France, Italy, Spain, Belgium, Denmark, Netherlands, Greece, Austria, Portugal, Sweden, Finland, Luxembourg, Ireland.

38 Art 9 (6) of the Rome Convention is also concerned with mandatory rules, but this provision falls beyond the scope of this study.

39 Schurig RabelsZ 54 (1990) 217, 220; Mäsch *Rechtswahlfreiheit* 19, 20; Morris *Statutes* 187, 200, 201 with regard to overriding statutes.

40 See Schurig RabelsZ 54 (990) 217, 220; Philip *Recent Provisions* 241, 242.

41 See Junker IPRax 1989, 69, 70; Reithmann/Martiny/Martiny *Internationales Vertragsrecht* Rn 96.

42 With regard to arts 5 and 6 of the Convention, Morse ICLQ 41 (1992) 1, 6, 14; with regard to the German arts 29 and 30 EGBGB, Schurig RabelsZ 54 (1990) 217, 220; Junker IPRax 1989, 69, 71.

43 See North *Private International Law Problems* 141, 142; Morse ICLQ 42 (1992) 1, 2; Erauw *International Contracts* 71, 72.

a choice of law, and thus limit the scope of the *lex causae* in general.[44] Article 7 (2) allows for the application of the mandatory rules of the *lex fori* if they are *internationally mandatory*, i.e. applicable irrespective of the law applicable to the contract. Article 7 (1) is concerned with internationally mandatory rules of a third country that is neither the proper law of the contract nor the *lex fori*, but has a close connection with the situation. While arts 5 (2) and 6 (1) refer to the mandatory rules of the 'otherwise applicable law', art 7 (1) might refer to any foreign legal system with which the situation is closely connected.

Article 3 (3) defines mandatory rules as rules 'which cannot be derogated from by contract', and thus refers to mandatory rules in a *domestic or wider sense*.[45] This type of mandatory rule is also dealt with in arts 5 (2) and 6 (1). Article 7, however, refers to *internationally* or *conflict mandatory rules*; mandatory rules in a domestic sense do not fall within the scope of art 7. Internationally mandatory rules are rules that are not only mandatory in their domestic or national setting, but also apply to the case regardless of the proper law of the contract.[46] Thus, art 7, on the one hand, and arts 5 (2), 6 (1) and 3 (3), on the other, are concerned with *different types* of mandatory rules.

Furthermore, arts 5 and 6 are limited in their scope of application to mandatory rules that serve the protection of the consumer or worker,[47] while art 7 is not limited to a certain type of rule.[48] These differences are essential and will inform the basic structure of this study.

Only on rare occasions has a national legislature regulated the issue of mandatory rules in private international law. The new Swiss Private International Law Act of 18 December 1987 (hereafter referred to as the Swiss IPRG), which entered into legal force on 1 January 1989,[49] is one of these rare

---

44 Cf for this distinction Cheshire & North's *Private International Law/12th ed* 499, */13th ed* 578; Schurig RabelsZ 54 (1990) 217, 220; Philip *Contract Conflicts* 81, 94 -108.

45 Cheshire & North's *Private International Law/12th ed* 498, */13th ed* 578; other expressions used are: mandatory rules in a *national sense* or *simple mandatory rules*.

46 Cf Lorenz RIW 1987, 569, 578; Jackson *Contract Conflicts* 59, 66 'conflict mandatory rules'; Philip *Contract Conflicts* 81, 100 'internationally mandatory'.

47 Morse ICLQ 41 (1992) 1, 8; Hartley Rec des Cours 226 (1997) 341, 371; Junker IPRax 1989, 69, 71.

48 Delimitation problems arise concerning the scope of applicability of the different provisions, see Martiny IPRax 1987, 277, 278; Junker IPRax 1989, 69, 73, 74; Reithmann/Martiny/Limmer *Internationales Vertragsrecht* Rn 395; Morse ICLQ 41 (1992) 1, 10 footnote 45.

49 'Bundesgesetz über das Internationale Privaterecht' (IPRG), (Swiss) BBl 1988 I 5; for a translated text of the Act, see Karrer and Arnold *Switzerland's Private International Law Statute*.

enactments. It has attracted international attention and is therefore worth examining.[50]

The Swiss IPRG contains three provisions that are relevant to mandatory rules. Article 13 concerns the scope of reference of the conflict rules to the foreign legal system.[51] Article 18 enables the court to apply Swiss internationally mandatory rules, regardless of the proper law of the contract, and art 19 is concerned with internationally mandatory rules of a third country.

Furthermore, Switzerland has enacted special conflict rules to protect the economically weaker party, particularly the consumer (art 120) and the employee (art 121). These rules restrict freedom of choice by means of a technique that differs from that of the Rome Convention. The issue of which of these techniques is more favourable will be discussed.

V Definition of different kinds of mandatory rules

To lay the foundations for a discussion and analysis it is necessary to clarify first the meaning of the term 'mandatory rules'. In general it is clear that the expression refers to rules that do not permit any derogation by contract. Nevertheless, the expression deserves further scrutiny, since it includes different kinds of mandatory rule that have to be distinguished from each other.[52] These rules differ in the following respects:

(1) Their nature as mandatory rules in a domestic or international sense,
(2) Their origin, viz. the enacting country,
(3) Their classification as rules of a public or private law nature, and
(4) Whether the rule is applied as a rule or considered as *factum*.

---

50 Cf the comparison of the provisions of the Rome Convention with those of the Swiss IPRG Philip *Recent Provisions* 241 et seq.

51 The crucial question is whether art 13 of the IPRG determines that the internationally mandatory rules of public law of the *lex causae* are applicable for the sole reason that they belong to the proper law of the contract, cf Schnyder *Das neue IPRG* 29 et seq; Vischer RabelsZ 53 (1989) 438, 441 et seq.

52 The RC refers to mandatory rules in the following provisions: articles 3 (3), 5 (2), 6 (1), 7 (1), (2) and 9 (6). But even though the same expression 'mandatory rules' is used in these provision, the rules to which they refer are different in nature.

All these distinctions will be dealt with during the course of this study.[53] It is therefore useful to clarify their meaning in advance.

1 Mandatory rules in a domestic sense or international sense

Mandatory rules can be classified as mandatory on *different levels*. The first level or type is the mandatory rule in a *domestic sense.*[54] This type is also referred to as mandatory in a *wide sense* or *simply mandatory*. These rules are compulsory in a domestic setting, but are subject to the normal rules of private international law. The Rome Convention refers to this type of rule in art 3 (3) and defines mandatory rules as rules 'which cannot be derogated from by contract'.

Mandatory rules in a domestic sense have to be distinguished from another type of rule that is *internationally mandatory*. The latter, in addition to the criterion that it 'cannot be derogated from by contract', must claim application irrespective of the law governing the contract. Although these rules are generally called *internationally mandatory* rules (*international zwingende Normen*),[55] they are also known as '*interventionist rules*' (*Eingriffsnormen*),[56] '*conflicts*' mandatory rules,[57] mandatory rules in a '*narrower sense*',[58] 'overriding statutes', *lois d'application immédiate*, or 'directly applicable statutes'.

These rules have been described as being '*more*' mandatory than the mandatory rules in a domestic sense.[59] The parties cannot exclude them by contract in a domestic setting, nor can they exclude them by choosing another law as the proper law. These rules determine their own scope of application since they have an express or implied unilateral conflict rule attached to their substantive content.[60]

---

53 A further distinction can be drawn based on the effect given to mandatory rules. This distinction follows also from the nature of the mandatory rule as domestic or internationally mandatory and is considered in this study's choice of structure, cf Chapter 2 with Chapters 3, 4, 5, 6.

54 Cheshire & North's *Private International Law/12th ed* 498, */13th ed* 578.

55 North *Contract Conflicts* 3, 19.

56 Schurig RabelsZ 54 (1990) 217, 220, 221; Vischer RabelsZ 53 (1989) 439 et seq.

57 Jackson *Contract Conflicts* 59, 66.

58 Cheshire & North's *Private International Law/12th ed* 498, */13th ed* 578.

59 Schurig RabelsZ 54 (1990) 217, 220; Junker IPRax 1989, 69, 73; De Boer RabelsZ 54 (1990) 24, 57 speaks of 'super-mandatory' rules.

60 Hartley Rec des Cours 266 (1997) 345, 346.

2 The country of origin

Another important distinction is a *spatial criterion*. Do the rules emanate from the forum, the proper law, or a third country, which is neither the forum nor the proper law? It is broadly accepted that the internationally mandatory rules of the *lex fori* override the normal choice of law rules, but there are differences in reasoning and methodology.[61] Difficulties arise with defining and determining whether the rule in question is internationally mandatory. The forum has to identify such rules and provide proof as to whether they have an overriding effect on the situation in question. Mandatory rules are not only contained in statutes, but also in the common law and international Conventions.[62]

Mandatory rules in a domestic sense are in general applicable if they belong to the proper law.[63] But different approaches exist with regard to the application of internationally mandatory rules.[64] In this regard the continental distinction between public and private law must be mentioned, because internationally mandatory rules are often rules of a public law nature.[65] It has been questioned whether public law rules fall within the scope of the ordinary conflict rules or whether they are excluded from the normal choice of law process and subjected to another system of conflict of laws.[66]

The application of mandatory rules of a third country, which is neither the *lex fori* nor the proper law of the contract, is the real subject of dispute.[67] The question is whether and how these rules can be applied or considered by the court of the forum.

3 Private law or public law

A distinction can be drawn between internationally mandatory rules belonging to private and public law. This distinction is relevant in Germany and Switzerland in determining the applicability of internationally mandatory rules.

---

61 Cf Hartley Rec des Cours 266 (1997) 345, 369; Cheshire & North's *Private International Law/12th ed* 499, */13th ed* 577, 578.

62 Dicey & Morris *Conflict of Laws Vol I/12th / 13th ed* 22, 23; Lasok & Stone *Conflict of Laws* 374, 375.

63 Cf Becker RabelsZ 60 (1996) 691, 697.

64 Cf MünchKomm/Sonnenberger Einl Rn 34.

65 Cf Philip *Recent Provisions* 241, 242.

66 Schäfer *FG Sandrock* 37, 48, 49; Philip *Recent Provisions* 241, 242, 243.

67 Cf Schäfer *FG Sandrock* 37; Schurig Rabelsz 54 (1990) 217, 234; Dicey & Morris *Conflict of Laws Vol II/12th ed* 1242, */13th ed* 1245.

4 Application as law or consideration as fact

A differentiation can be drawn between the application of mandatory rules as 'law', and the consideration of mandatory rules as 'facts' within the operative facts of the substantive law of the *lex causae*. This differentiation has been developed with regard to foreign internationally mandatory rules. In effect, the consideration takes place at *different levels*: at the conflict of law level and at the level of substantive law. It is held that the application of a foreign rule as *law* is possible, if rendered applicable by a choice of law rule. Otherwise a foreign rule can only be given effect by considering it as a *fact* within the substantive rules of the *lex causae*. The provisions of the proper law taking cognisance of the apparently factual effects of the foreign mandatory rule may be those of illegality, public policy, *boni mores*, impossibility of performance, or the doctrine frustration. It will be seen during the course of this study that this distinction is of fundamental relevance for academic approaches and court decisions. However, the distinction is questionable, and the question of whether it is in fact justified in conflict of laws will be discussed.

VI Determination and limitation of the scope of examination

1 A comparative study

The purpose of this study is to present, compare and critically analyse approaches to the application of mandatory rules, whether academic, case law or statutory. I will discuss England and Germany, as representatives of the two main legal traditions, common and civil law. Reference will also be made, however, to Switzerland and South Africa.

Compared to other countries, where academics and courts could slowly adjust their private international law to the increase in international trade and the global economy, South African private international law is undeveloped. The law is still ill prepared for the country's connections with the rest of the world, which have greatly increased since the political revolution of the 1990s. The modern South Africa, which now participates in the new global economy, presents its lawyers and courts with new problems in private international law of contracts, and some of these problems will necessarily concern the application of foreign and South African mandatory rules to international contracts. In particular, the question of the application of mandatory rules in the private international law of contracts is still immature.[68]

---

[68] This was true at least until the year 2000, cf Forsyth *Private International Law* 278, 298.

Parliament has done much to reform the Roman-Dutch rules of private international law - legislation has been passed to regulate family law, succession, domicile, and enforcement of judgements - the question of legislating in the area of contract has not been broached. Thus, South African private international law of contracts will, at least for the immediate future, consist of Roman-Dutch common law rules, apart from a few statutory exceptions for particular contractual contexts.[69]

The comparison and critical analysis of the various approaches of the countries under investigation will show similarities and differences and reveal their advantages and disadvantages according to general principles of choice of law and practical needs. The purpose of this analysis is to propose a suitable approach for South African private international law. The submitted approach, however, may be equally suitable to other countries the private international law of which is based on the traditional allocation technique. The approach attempts to provide guidelines to courts that are confronted with litigation concerning international contracts. Furthermore, the discussion and analysis of the differing approaches, and the proposed solution itself, may contribute to the discussion amongst academics.[70]

A comparative study on a broad topic such as the application of mandatory rules in international law of contracts needs to be limited. This can be done in two ways. The study could limit itself to a certain field in which the application of mandatory rules arises, for example, the role of mandatory rules as a restriction of party autonomy in the private international law of contracts, or the problem of the application of internationally mandatory rules of a third country despite the proper law of the contract. Alternatively, the study could focus on a smaller number of legal systems. The present author has adopted the latter approach. Because of the difficulty and scope of the topic (which addresses various and fundamental questions of private international law), it is believed to be preferable to concentrate on a detailed presentation and analysis of the approaches in a few representative legal systems. Most aspects and fields in which the question of application of mandatory rules arises can thus be addressed.

---

69 See Forsyth *Private International Law* 274 et seq; Edwards *Conflict of Laws* para 472 refers to the Bills of Exchange Act 34 of 1964, s 70, the Insurance Act 27 of 1943, s 63 (1) and the Carriage of Goods by Sea Act 1 of 1986, s 1 as examples of statutes containing conflict rules in their particular contractual context.

70 Cf for the academic discussion in South Africa Forsyth *Private International Law* 301 et seq; Spiro XVII CILSA (1984) 197 et seq; Viejobueno XXII CILSA (1993) 172 et seq; Neels 1191 TSAR 694 et seq; Edwards *Conflict of Laws* para 469; cf also the extensive study of Van Rooyen *Die Kontrak* (1972).

Furthermore, rather than examining many approaches in a superficial manner, this thesis will analyse the academic approaches and the court decisions in detail. In order to evaluate the advantages and disadvantages of the various approaches and solutions of academics and the courts, the critical analysis will be based on certain criteria that are of fundamental value in orthodox conflict of laws: decisional harmony, comity of nations, the principle of unity of law relating to contracts, predictability and certainty in law, the need for choice of law considerations, multilateral conflict rules versus *unilateralism*, and so on.

2 The choice of countries

The legal situation in Germany has been chosen as representative of the civil law tradition because the academic writing in the relevant area is highly developed. It was the German academic Wilhelm Wengler who in 1941 initiated the long standing debate about the application of internationally mandatory rules in the private international law of contracts.[71] Since then many academics have made proposals about how to combine these rules with the ordinary choice of law process.[72] It is submitted that these approaches deserve more attention in the English speaking world than they have been given in the past. The German courts have also found solutions that are of particular interest.

England has been chosen as representative of the common law legal tradition because interesting cases have arisen since the 1920s regarding the application of mandatory rules, and the courts have developed relatively firm principles. The English position, with its merits and demerits, is always highly relevant to South African private international law, too.[73]

71 Wengler ZVerglRWiss 54 (1941) 168 et seq.

72 There has always been a lively exchange of academic approaches in Germany, Switzerland and Austria, the three German-speaking nations concerning private international law questions. The academic discussion in Switzerland and Austria is heavily influenced by German approaches, cf for Switzerland: Voser *Lois d'application immédiate* (1993) and Erne *Vertragsgültigkeit* (1985); cf for Austria: Reichelt ZfR 29 (1988) 82 et seq; Czernich/Heiss *EVÜ* Art 7 Rn 2, 30, 50. However, similar approaches can also be found in other continental European countries, such as France, Italy or the Netherlands. For a short comparative survey of the question of application of internationally mandatory rules, see: Honsell/Vogt/Schnyder/Mächler-Erne art 13 Rn 25 et seq, art 18 Rn 24 et seq, art 19 Rn 34, Lehmann *Zwingendes Recht* 76 et seq (France), 103 et seq (Italy), 117 et seq (Netherlands), cf for the Netherlands Schultz RabelsZ 47 (1988) 267 et seq; De Boer Rabelsz 54 (1990) 24 et seq both with references.

73 Traditionally, in matters of private international law, South African authors and courts have referred to English case law, cf Chapter 2, VI, 1 and Chapter 6, I.

The legal situation in the other major common-law jurisdiction, the United States of America is, however, of little use in developing a solution for a private international law of contracts that is based on the traditional allocation technique.[74] This is due to the following factors. Firstly, the different states do not necessarily have the same conflict rules. Not only may each state have its own particular conflict rules, but it may also follow different methods to solve the choice of law problem.[75] There are interesting academic approaches, such as Cavers's '*rules of preference*',[76] Currie's '*governmental interest analysis*',[77] or Leflar's '*better rule of law-approach*',[78] reflecting the 'American conflict revolution'.[79]

---

74 Although for instance some SA authors refer to US solutions, they do so in a very general and restrictive manner, cf Spiro XVII CILSA (1984) 197 referring to the basic provisions of the American Law Institute's Second Restatement of the Conflict of Laws. However, Forsyth *Private International Law* 5, 54, 61 makes it clear: The American methods for solution of the choice of law problem are not for export to South African private international law.

75 Courts rely on various methods: the 'centre of gravity', 'governmental interest', 'comparative impairment' method (refining Currie's doctrine), the Second Restatement of Conflict of Laws and the 'most significant relationship' or Leflar's 'better law approach'. Others refer to the 'vested rights' approach or simply apply the *lex fori*, cf Kay Mercer L Rev 34 (1983) 521, Appendix 591 - 592; Vischer Rec des Cours 232 (1992 I) 9, 64; see as well Peterson *Moderne amerikanische IPR Theorie* 77, 84. Furthermore, relevant cases for this study, particularly concerning the question of application of third countries' internationally mandatory rules, are few and not so significant. Most court decisions in the United States in the field of conflict of laws concern private international law of torts rather than contract, cf Reese Am J Comp L 30 (1982) 135, 139. For some recent court decisions, see Vischer Rec des Cours 232 (1992 I) 9, 66 et seq; also see Jayme IPRax 1986, 46 et seq.

76 Cavers *The Choice of Law Process* 114 et seq; id Harv L Rev 47 (1933 - 1934) 173 et seq, 192 et seq; cf on Cavers' approach Forsyth *Private International Law* 55; Lipstein Rec des Cours 135 (1972 I) 99, 157 et seq.

77 Currie *Selected Essays on the Conflict of Laws*; cf as well Lando Am J Comp L 30 (1982) 19, 24; Forsyth *Private International Law* 55 et seq; Lipstein Rec des Cours 135 (1972 I) 99, 154 et seq; Guedj Am J Comp L 39 (1991) 661, 681 et seq; Vischer Rec des Cours 232 (1992 I) 9, 48.

78 Leflar *American Conflicts Law* 193 - 195, 205 - 219; id NY UL Rev 41 (1966) 267 et seq; see on Leflar's approach Siehr Am J Comp L 30 (1982) 37, 47 et seq.

79 There are further important theories, such as Ehrenzweig's 'lex fori' approach. For these authors and a general representation of American theories, see Forsyth *Private International Law* 53 et seq; Lipstein Rec des Cours 135 (1972 I) 99, 143 et seq; Cheshire & North's *Private International Law/12th ed* 31 et seq; Vischer Rec des Cours 232 (1992 I) 9, 44 et seq; Kegel *FS Beitzke* 551 et seq; Vitta Am J Comp L 30 (1982) 1 et seq. The Second Restatement on the Conflict of Laws combines traditional conflict values with the modern American theories, Vischer ibid 57 et seq; Lando Am J Comp L 30 (1982) 19, 28.

However, the concern of these approaches is not exactly the concern of the present study.[80] These approaches certainly do refer to the application of mandatory rules, but only indirectly.[81] The crucial point, however, is that the American theories in general depart from Savigny's traditional allocation technique which consists of (multilateral) choice of law rules connecting a certain legal relationship with an appropriate legal system. American theories question the merits of the traditional choice of law process and the results obtained by mechanically connecting a private relationship to one geographical area.[82] They propose an alternative choice of law method, which in general focuses 'on the substantive rules and their underlying policies in order to determine whether they apply to a specified issue.'[83]

As far as conflict of laws of contracts is concerned, the modern American solutions to the choice of law problem were not accepted in European countries.[84] Nor have the American theories had any impact on the South

---

80 For an interesting comparison of American theories and the doctrine of *lois d'application immédiate* or *lois de police*: Guedj Am J Comp L 39 (1991) 661 et seq.

81 The purpose of these approaches is not to clarify the relationship between the ordinary choice of law process and the application of certain mandatory legislation, but rather to create a new choice of law process differing to the traditional allocation technique. Thereby the limits of the operation of particular rules to a particular case are determined by interpretation of the rules themselves, their policies, and governmental interests. Often this process will be predominantly based on mandatory rules because mandatory rules - more than rules of a declaratory nature - express policies and governmental interests and sometimes determine their spatial scope, cf Guedj Am J Comp L 39 (1991) 661; Lando Am J Comp L 30 (1982) 19, 22 et seq.

82 Vitta Am J Comp L 30 (1982) 1; Peterson *Moderne amerikanische IPR-Theorie* 77, 81.

83 Cf Guedj Am J Comp L 39 (1991) 661; also see Forsyth *Private International Law* 5, 53 et seq; Vitta Am J Comp L 30 (1982) 1 'But all of the modern theories have in common a critical attitude towards mechanical choice of law rules and the desire to make conflict law more responsive to the demands of substantive policies'; Lando Am J Comp L 30 (1982) 19, 22 et seq; Cheshire & North's *Private International Law/12th ed* 31, */13th ed* 24.

84 See Lando Am J Comp L 30 (1982) 19, 25; Siehr Am J Comp L 30 (1982) 37, 40: 'To date however there is no "Americanization" of European private international law. My impression is that there are two main explanations. The first pertains to general methodological divergences, the second reflects independent development in Europe similar to developments in the United States.' Also see ibid at page 67 et seq; Cheshire & North's *Private International Law/12th ed* 31, 38, */13th ed* 30, 31. Only a few European academics, in Germany and the Netherlands, in the late 1960s and early 1970s, influenced by the American conflict of law system and theories, rejected the traditional choice of law system of Savigny as a whole. They proposed that the conflict issue should be resolved on the basis of social values, and policy interests should infiltrate the conflict rules. However, these approaches were not generally accepted, cf Junker IPRax 1998, 65, 67; Erauw *International Contracts* 71, 73; Keller *FS Vischer* 175, 179 et seq; Zweigert RabelsZ 37 (1973) 437, 443 - 445; Vischer Rec des Cours 142 (1974 II) 1, 52 et seq.

African private international law.[85] To the contrary, the American approaches were expressly rejected as methods for the choice of law process and were held to be not for export.[86] Hence, the private international law of contracts in England, Germany, Switzerland, South Africa, and the provisions of the Rome Convention are based on the traditional allocation technique.[87]

The adherence to Savigny's traditional solution to the choice of law problem and the rejection of the 'modern' American theories (as choice of law method) does not mean that the traditional choice of law rules cannot and should not be refined, or that special choice of law considerations are sometimes required. The traditional process has already undergone notable refinement.[88] Particularly in the field of protecting the weaker contracting party, there is a trend towards new choice of law rules that take cognisance of substantive values and the applicable substantive law.[89] In principle this refinement can be reached by the choice of law techniques of alternative or cumulative connecting factors, or even the so-called escape clauses.[90] Thus, the traditional choice of law rules 'once rigid, blind and impartial, [are] now increasingly sensitive to preconceived material results and open to expectations.'[91]

Furthermore, the application of internationally mandatory rules in the private international law of contracts requires special choice of law considerations during the orthodox choice of law process.[92] As will be seen during the course of this study, the traditional allocation technique needs to be supplemented by more result- and policy-orientated choice of law criteria.[93] Apart from this refinement (and supplementation) of Savigny's allocation technique, however, this thesis is based upon the traditional conflict method.

---

85 Forsyth *Private International Law* 5, 53, 54, 61.

86 See Forsyth *Private International Law* 5, 53, 54, 61; Lipstein Rec des Cours 135 (1972 I) 99, 157, 163; Lando Am J Comp L 30 (1982) 19, 25; Siehr Am J Comp L 30 (1982) 37, 67 et seq.

87 Sonnenberger *FS Rebmann* 819; Kropholler *IPR* § 3 I; Lipstein Rec des Cours 135 (1972 I) 99, 163, 194, 195 et seq, Cheshire & North's *Private International Law/12th ed* 21, et seq, 38, 39; Forsyth *Private International Law* 5 et seq, 43, 44, 57 et seq.

88 Vischer Rec des Cours 232 (1992 I) 9, 93 et seq; Vitta Am J Comp L 30 (1982) 1, 9 et seq; De Boer RabelsZ 54 (1990) 24, 25 et seq; Guedj Am J Comp L 39 (1991) 661.

89 See Erauw *International Contracts* 71, 72; De Boer RabelsZ 54 (1990) 24, 25 et seq; compare as well Vitta Am J Comp L 30 (1982) 1, 9 et seq.

90 De Boer ibid 24, 25 et seq; Guedj ibid 661; Vischer ibid 108, 116 et seq.

91 De Boer ibid 26.

92 Guedj ibid 661; Vischer ibid 73, 100, 155 et seq; Lando Am J Comp L 30 (1982) 19, 32.

93 See later Chapters 3, 4, 5, 6; cf the article of Guedj ibid 661 et seq comparing American theories with the theory of the *lois de police*.

The solution stipulated in the EEC Convention on the Law Applicable to Contractual Obligations on 19 June 1980 (Rome Convention) will be fully discussed. The reason for this is that the Convention reflects modern trends in conflict of laws and represents the present statutory conflict rules for contracts in many countries.[94]

Furthermore, reference to the Rome Convention is required because this study concentrates to a large extent on the legal situation in Germany and England, and the conflict rules in the field of contractual obligations in both countries are now based on the provisions of the Rome Convention. On 1 September 1986 the Law of a Reform (New Enactment) of Private International Law of 25 July 1986 entered into force in Germany.[95] The international law of contractual obligations is governed by arts 27 to 37 of the introductory law of the Civil Code (Einführungsgesetz zum Bürgerlichen Gesetzbuch, EGBGB amended) and is thereby statutorily regulated for the first time. The old private international law (EGBGB old version) contained no conflict rules about contract law; the rules were developed in a typical common law manner.[96]

The new articles 27 to 37 are based on provisions of the Rome Convention that were incorporated in the EGBGB.[97] The Convention thus entered into force in Germany before the Rome Convention itself came into legal force.[98] Germany has signed and ratified the agreement, subject to the proviso that the provisions of arts 1 to 21 of the Convention do not apply directly in German national law. Nevertheless, the principle of uniform interpretation applies (art 36 EGBGB,

94 Furthermore, the Convention is considered for instance by South African academics as a useful persuasive source for their private international law of contracts, cf Edwards *Conflict of Laws* para 361 footnote 15.

95 'Gesetz zur Neuregelung des Internationalen Privatrechts', BGBl I 1142.

96 Triebel ICLQ 37 (1988) 935, 936; Soergel/von Hoffmann Rn 17 vor Art 27; Lorenz RIW 1987, 569.

97 'Gesetz zu dem Übereinkommen vom 19.6.1980 über das auf vertragliche Schuldverhältnisse anwendbare Recht' of 29 July 1986, BGBl II 809.

98 But rather then incorporating it as a statutory appendix to the Civil Code, Germany incorporated the most important provisions of the Convention into the German national law. The mentioned articles were thus adjusted to German terminology; Sandrock RIW 1986, 841, 842; Triebel ICLQ 37 (1988) 935, 936. For a text of the Convention provisions following their incorporation into the German code (EGBGB), see RabelsZ 50 (1986) 663, 673 - 678. This was strongly criticised by German writers and it is doubted whether Germany has fulfilled its obligation to incorporate the Convention properly because the provisions have been slightly modified and adapted to national legislation. Some provisions were thus even omitted and some of the provisions were separated and put in the general part (such as rules on formalities art 9 RC = art 11 EGBGB and public policy art 16 RC = art 6 EGBGB), cf MPI RabelsZ 47 (1983) 595, 602 et seq, 665 et seq, 673 et seq; Lando CMLR 24 (1987) 154, 162 et seq.

incorporating art 18 of the Convention). The provisions of the EGBGB originating from the Convention must therefore be interpreted in such a way that the goal of uniformity of law with other Contracting States remains protected.[99] For the purposes of this study it will be sufficient to present and analyse the relevant mandatory rules in the context of the corresponding provisions of the Rome Convention.[100]

The United Kingdom ratified the Rome Convention and implemented it in the Contracts (Applicable Law) Act 1990 (1990 Act), in force from 1 April 1991.[101] The Act incorporates the text of the Rome Convention (subject to two reservations) in Schedule 1. By incorporating the text of the Convention in a Schedule the Convention was given the force of law.[102] The 1990 Act applies to contracts concluded after 1 April 1990.[103] Since then the common law rules on choice of law in contract have, for the most part, been substituted by the rules of the Rome Convention.[104] This study directly refers to the relevant provisions of the 1990 Act dealing with mandatory rules are as the conflict rules of the Rome Convention. It also investigates academic approaches and case law solutions prior to the Rome Convention.

Finally, a few remarks need to be made about the author's decision to examine the legal situation in Switzerland. This was done because the Swiss national legislature has enacted special conflict rules dealing with the application of internationally mandatory rules.[105] This is indeed an unusual event.[106] The

99 cf Sandrock RIW 1986, 841, 842; Soergel/von Hoffmann Rn 16 vor art 27. For criticism, see Lando CMLR 24 (1987) 154, 162 with regard to the scope of art 36 which refers only to the chapter on contractual obligations, although some provisions of the Rome Convention, such as the rules on formalities and public policy, are transformed into rules in the general part of the EGBGB. Martiny ZEuP 1995, 67, 73 is critical, too. The interpretation has to be *autonomous* and must consider the *wording* of the provisions of not only one contracting state; for details: Martiny ibid 72; Kropholler *IPR* § 52 I 2.

100 Arts 27 (3), 29 (2), 30 (1) and 34 EGBGB. Furthermore, there is art 11 (4) EGBGB which is based on art 9 (6) Rome Convention. However, these provisions fall beyond the scope of this study. For these provisions, see Reithmann/Martiny/Limmer *Internationales Vertragsrecht* Rn 564 et seq.

101 S I 1991 No 707; see Dicey & Morris *Conflict of Laws Vol II/12th ed* 1187, */13th ed* 1195.

102 For other techniques to give this force of law to international conventions see Morris *Statutes* 187, 188.

103 1990 Act, Sched 1, art 17.

104 See only Dicey & Morris *Conflict of Laws Vol II/12th ed* 1187, */13th ed* 1195.

105 Switzerland is not a member of the EU and thus not a member of the Rome Convention.

106 Therefore, Switzerland was chosen instead of Austria, for instance, which incorporated the Rome Convention into its law on 1 December 1998, cf Czernich/Heiss *EVÜ*.

Swiss national solution therefore deserves attention and might well constitute a good foundation for the development of a suitable approach.

The presentation of the South African legal situation needs no further explanation, since one purpose of this study is to propose a solution for the application of mandatory rules in South African private international law of contracts, which is lacunose. However, it is submitted that the proposed approach is equally suitable for other countries' private international law of contract if and in so far these laws are based on a traditional allocation technique.

3 The contexts of application of mandatory rules in the private international law of contracts

This study addresses both contexts in which the question of application of mandatory rules in private international law of contracts arises: The relatively recent development of restricting party autonomy by the application of mandatory rules of the otherwise applicable legal system, and the problem of application of the so-called *lois d'application immédiate*, directly applicable statutes, or *Eingriffsnormen*.

With regard to the restriction of party autonomy, mainly the provisions of the Rome Convention will be discussed, since the issue is addressed by the Convention's conflict rules. However, other means of limiting party autonomy by, for example, the doctrine of evasion of law, will also be presented, and compared in order to propose a suitable approach for South African private international law.

The question of the application of directly applicable rules is of a more general nature and broader in scope, since these rules do not only serve to restrict party autonomy. They may also claim application in situations where the proper law is objectively determined by the forum's choice of law rules, in the absence of a choice of law by the parties. These rules in effect limit the scope of the proper law. They may emanate from the proper law, or the *lex fori*, or a third legal system. New statutory conflict rules, academic approaches, and the court practice of the countries under investigation will be discussed. The solutions and approaches will be critically analysed and compared. Finally, a proposal will be submitted regarding how these rules can be combined with the ordinary choice of law process. It is hoped that this proposal will constitute a solution for South African courts and lawyers dealing with this difficult and complex issue and form a useful contribution to the growing academic discussion.

In order to limit the scope of this study, choice of law rules concerning the formal validity of a contract, even though they may refer to mandatory rules, for instance, art 9 (6) of the Rome Convention, are not discussed. Furthermore, the Bretton Woods Agreement is not discussed at length. This Agreement contains a special rule in art VIII (2) (b) that provides for the application of the foreign exchange control regulations of member states, despite the proper law of the exchange contract. This rule has its own peculiarities, and the discussion thereof is beyond the limits of this dissertation.

VII Structure of this study

A comparison between different legal systems (the common-law system and the civil-law system) does not easily lend itself to a unified structure.[107] This is because reference is necessary to statutory solutions, together with case law and academic approaches; in some countries the academic attempts to find a solution are almost endless, while in other countries the academic contributions concentrate on a discussion of the court decisions. Therefore, the representation of jurisprudence and academic approaches of the countries under investigation may differ in length and depth.

Essential aspects of this study are the question of application of mandatory rules in different contexts, and the presentation and critical comparative analysis of the legal situation in the different countries. Therefore, the author has decided not to devote one chapter to each country. In order to avoid repetition, a representation according to the effect and use of mandatory rules and their structural context in private international law is preferable. There are two structural contexts: party autonomy and the problem of application of directly applicable statutes, in which the question of application of mandatory rules arises. The purpose and effect given to mandatory rules in these two contexts differ substantially.

Based on this differentiation, the study commences with an examination of the application of mandatory rules serving to limit party autonomy, and a comparison of the different solutions of the countries under investigation (Chapter **2**). Chapters **3**, **4**, and **5** address the problem of application of internationally mandatory rules, which is broader in scope and effect. The application of internationally mandatory rules of the *lex fori* despite the proper

[107] It has therefore been argued that it is better to compare only closely related legal systems, for example, the continental civil-law systems. Nevertheless, it has also been argued that the differences between the common-law and the civil-law systems should be reconciled, cf Beitzke RabelsZ 48 (1984), 623, 626.

law of the contract and foreign internationally mandatory rules will be discussed separately. The different solutions and approaches of case law, the legislature, and academic writers will be presented, critically analysed, and compared. A proposal for the application of internationally mandatory rules in South African private international law of contracts is submitted in Chapter **6**.

Chapter 2
Party autonomy and mandatory rules

Party autonomy in substantive private law is the freedom of the parties to choose the rules that will govern their contractual relationship. In private international law it is the freedom of the parties to choose the law of a country to govern their relationship.[1] Although party autonomy in private international law is to some extent the counterpart to substantive party autonomy,[2] there are nevertheless differences.[3] The latter is limited by the *ius cogens* of a national legal system, ie, the contracting parties are free only with regard to the dispositive rules.[4] The former, however, displaces the dispositive rules and the *ius cogens* (mandatory rules) of the objective proper law, together with those of the lex fori, in favour of the mandatory provisions of the chosen law. [5]

This effect of party autonomy has, however, not always been accepted. In the past academic authors said that party autonomy in international contracts should be restricted to *ius dispositivum*.[6] This so-called 'secondary choice of law' or 'incorporation of foreign law' ('*materiellrechtliche Verweisung*') means that the choice of law refers to the foreign *ius dispositivum* alone, and accordingly cannot replace the mandatory rules of the law that would be applicable in the absence of the parties' choice. Nowadays, however, the concept of party autonomy as 'primary choice' or 'party reference',[7] indicating the legal system that applies to the contract to the exclusion of the mandatory rules of the

---

1 Firsching/von Hoffmann *IPR* 382; Rinze (1994) JBL 412; Leible JBJZRW 1995, 245, 246.

2 See Sandrock/Steinschulte *Handbuch* Rn A 5; Firsching/von Hoffmann *IPR* 195; von Bar *IPR* Bd II 308; Morse YB EurL (1982) 107, 116; Lando Rec des Cours 189 (1984 VI) 229, 301.

3 Cf Junker IPRax 1993, 1, 2; von Bar *IPR* Bd II 309; De Boer RabelsZ 54 (1990) 24, 41; Rinze (1994) JBL 412, 413; Siehr in *FS Keller* 485, 486; Leible JBJZRW 1995, 245, 246.

4 Firsching/von Hoffmann *IPR* 382; Junker IPRax 1993, 1, 2.

5 Firsching/von Hoffmann *IPR* 382; Lando CMLR 24 (1987) 159, 170; De Boer RabelsZ 54 (1990) 24, 41; Junker IPRax 1993, 1, 2 states that 'had the choice of law of the parties not the effect of replacing the mandatory rules of the otherwise applicable law, it would not be interesting.'

6 This was advocated in earlier times by German academics, but has been rejected by German courts; for references, see Lando CMLR 24 (1987) 159, 177 et seq; Münch-Komm/Martiny Art 27 Rn 7.

7 The expressions 'party reference' and 'incorporation of foreign law' are used by Lando CMLR 24 (1987) 159, 169; id *Contracts* s 25; for the distinction, see Forsyth *Private International Law* 275, 276; De Boer RabelsZ 54 (1990) 24, 41, 42.

otherwise applicable legal system, is broadly accepted.[8] Indeed, it forms the primary connecting factor for choice of law in contract.[9]

Despite its acceptance as 'primary choice', party autonomy has never been granted in an unlimited manner. Academics and courts have developed differing principles to limit the parties' choice of law, such as the doctrine of evasion of law,[10] the restriction of choice to a limited number of legal systems,[11] the requirement of an objective connection with the chosen legal system, in addition to a clause specifying the choice of law,[12] and the restriction of the effect of the choice by the application of mandatory rules of the otherwise applicable law.[13] Most of these limitations concern the question of whether certain mandatory rules should be applied despite the fact that the parties have chosen another law to govern their transaction.

I Party autonomy and its limitations by the application of mandatory rules under the Rome Convention

The freedom to choose the applicable law is statutorily laid down in art 3 (1) of the Rome Convention (art 27 (1) EGBGB).[14] In terms of the Rome Convention party autonomy itself is at first sight unrestricted.[15] In particular, the facts of the case do not need to have any connection with the chosen law. Thus, the choice of a 'neutral law' (ie one that has no objective connection with the contract) is permitted.[16] Furthermore, a certain recognisable interest of a party in the appli-

---

8 MünchKomm/Martiny Art 27 Rn 13, 14; Junker IPRax 1993, 1, 2; for the English position, see the notorious decision in *Vita Food Products Inc v Unus Shipping Co Ltd* [1939] AC 277, [1939] 1 All ER 513 (PC); Dicey & Morris *Conflict of Laws Vol II/12th ed* 1211 et seq, */13th ed* 1216 et seq.

9 See Kropholler *IPR* §52 II; see also Junker IPRax 1993, 1; Firsching/von Hoffmann *IPR* 195; for details of the historical developments, see Püls *Parteiautonomie* (1995).

10 See below Chapter 2, V.

11 See below Chapter 2, III.

12 This restriction means that the choice of a 'neutral' law is not permitted. It used to be very common, notably in Germany and Switzerland, as well as other countries.

13 See section I, below.

14 Art 3 (1) of the RC states that 'a contract shall be governed by the law chosen by the parties.'

15 Party autonomy is neither prohibited nor restricted in the sense that only certain legal systems can be chosen. On these limitations, see Junker IPRax 1993, 1, 4 and the solution of the Swiss legislative concerning consumer and employment contracts, infra section III.

16 Morse YBEurL (1982) 107, 122; MünchKomm/Martiny Art 27 Rn 20; Rinze (1994) JBL 412, 415, 416; for the English position prior to the Rome Convention, see Dicey & Morris *Conflict of Laws Vol II/12th ed* 1213, */13th ed* 1217, 1218 and the leading case *Vita Food Products Inc v Unus Shipping Co Ltd* [1939] AC 277, at 290.

cation of the chosen law is not presupposed.[17] Nevertheless, party autonomy is in fact *not* absolutely unlimited. Although the freedom to choose a foreign law may not be restricted in the sense that the choice is invalid,[18] the effect of the choice or the scope of the chosen law may be restricted by the *application of mandatory rules* of a law other than the chosen law.[19]

1 Article 3 (3) of the Rome Convention: Purely domestic contracts

Article 3 (3) of the Rome Convention limits party autonomy in *purely domestic contracts* by declaring the mandatory rules of this law applicable, despite the choice of the parties. The article provides as follows:

> The fact that the parties have chosen a foreign law, whether or not accompanied by the choice of a foreign tribunal, shall not, where all the other elements relevant to the situation at the time of the choice are connected with one country only, prejudice the application of rules of the law of that country which cannot be derogated from by contract, hereinafter called mandatory rules.

Party autonomy itself is not excluded in purely domestic contracts, but the effect of the choice of law is limited in so far as the choice of law cannot preclude the application of the mandatory rules of the legal system with which the contract is solely connected.[20] This provision was the result of a compromise between differing opinions of the delegations. Some delegations, including that of Germany,[21] insisted that the parties were not entitled to make a valid choice of law, whereas other delegations, notably that of the United Kingdom, were opposed to such a limitation.[22]

---

[17] Firsching/von Hoffmann *IPR* 382, 383; Kropholler *IPR* § 40 IV.

[18] See Junker IPRax 1993, 1, 4; Lorenz RIW 1987, 569; however, see below Chapter 2, V the doctrine of evasion according to which a choice of law is rendered invalid; also see below for the solution of Swiss private international law.

[19] Lorenz RIW 1987, 569, 570; Rinze (1994) JBL 412, 419 et seq; see also Jackson *Contract Conflicts* 59, 63 et seq; Philip *Contract Conflicts* 81, 94 et seq; Dicey & Morris *Conflict of Laws Vol II/12th ed* 1215, */13th ed* 1219.

[20] MünchKomm/Martiny Art 27 Rn 71; Reithmann/Martiny/Martiny *Internationales Vertragsrecht* Rn 96; Dicey & Morris *Conflict of Laws Vol II/12th ed* 1215, */13th ed* 1219.

[21] According to many legal systems, including that of Germany, a choice of foreign law was permitted only for international contracts, cf Lando CMLR 24 (1987) 159, 164, 181; id Rec des Cours 189 (1984 VI) 229, 286; Junker IPRax 1989, 69, 70; Sandrock RIW 1987, 841, 846; MünchKomm/Martiny Art 27 Rn 13 et seq.

[22] Report on the E.E.C. Convention by *Giuliano/Lagarde* in North *Contract Conflicts* 372; also see Hartley Rec des Cours 266 (1997) 341, 366.

a International contracts versus purely domestic contracts

The rule that party autonomy is not excluded in purely domestic contracts follows indirectly from arts 1 (1) and 3 (3) of the Rome Convention. According to art 1 (1), the Convention applies 'in any situation involving a choice between the laws of different countries'. Thus, in purely domestic contracts, the Convention is not applicable. However, it follows from art 3 (3) of the Convention that the choice of law of the parties is itself enough to render the contract 'international' in the sense of art 1.[23]

Article 3 (3) restricts the choice of law in purely domestic contracts, but at the same time presupposes a valid choice of law.[24] Nevertheless, in Germany it is disputed whether the limitation of choice of law as laid down in art 3 (3) has the effect of making the *choice of law* to the foreign law an *incorporation* of foreign law.[25] If it did, party autonomy in purely domestic contracts would be reduced to the choice of foreign dispositive rules, without any possibility of displacing the mandatory legislation of the country with which the contract is solely connected, except for the choice.[26] According to this point of view, the freedom of choice of foreign law is limited to 'international contracts'.[27]

This was, in fact, the traditional doctrine in German conflict of laws: The choice of law was restricted to international contracts or matters. In *purely domestic contracts* the parties' *reference* to another law was invalid. The parties were free, however, to *incorporate* foreign *ius dispositivum* into their contract.[28]

The counter opinion argues that the choice of law itself is not invalidated by the provisions of the Rome Convention, not even in purely domestic contracts.[29] Rather art 3 (3) limits the effects of the choice.[30]

The advocates of both approaches justify their points of view by referring to a statement in the report of *Giuliano/Lagarde* that art 3 (3) is the result of a

---

23 MünchKomm/Martiny Art 27 Rn 17, 18; Hartley Rec des Cours 266 (1997) 341, 366, 367; Lando CMLR 24 (1987) 159, 164, 181; Philip *Contract Conflicts* 81, 94.

24 MünchKomm/Martiny Art 27 Rn 18, 71 et seq; Mäsch *Rechtswahlfreiheit* 94.

25 MünchKomm/Martiny Art 27 Rn 79; Junker IPRax 1989, 69, 70; Schurig RabelsZ 54 (1990) 217, 221 et seq; Sandrock RIW 1986, 841, 846; Lorenz RIW 1987, 569.

26 MünchKomm/Martiny Art 27 Rn 13 et seq, 79; Sandrock RIW 1987, 841, 846.

27 Junker IPRax 1989, 69, 70; Sandrock RIW 1987, 841, 846; for an interpretation from the Swiss point of view, see Von Overbeck *Contract Conflicts* 269, 271, 272.

28 Junker IPRax 1989, 69, 70; Sandrock RIW 1987, 841, 846; MünchKomm/Martiny Art 27 Rn 13 et seq; see Von Overbeck *Contract Conflicts* 269, 271, 272 for Switzerland.

29 Lorenz RIW 1987, 569; Junker IPRax 1989, 69, 70 with further references.

30 Lorenz RIW 1987, 569, 575 calls it '*Inhaltskontrolle*' instead of '*Abschlußkontrolle*'.

compromise between the delegations.[31] In the present author's opinion, however, the fact that the provision is a result of a compromise clearly supports the latter point of view, namely, that the issue is not the validity of the choice of law in so far as only incorporation of foreign law is permitted, but that party autonomy is limited by modifying the effects of the choice. However, the dispute is of a more theoretical nature since the result of both opinions is identical.[32]

b Requirements for purely domestic contracts

A contract is a purely domestic contract when all relevant elements of the contract, despite the choice of a foreign law (and a foreign tribunal), are connected with one country only (art 3 (3)).[33] The kinds of connections or circumstances that are sufficient to found an international contract are not defined in art 3 (3), and commentators on the Convention have unanimously held that *any* connection is not sufficient. Purely *incidental* connections with another state are disregarded and do not render art 3 (3) applicable, whereas any *substantial* connection with another country that is relevant to the legal transaction at issue does.[34] Examples of substantial connections are the place of performance, habitual residence, or the place of business of a party.[35] In general, substantive connections to another country are those which are of relevance for the objective connection in art 4 Rome Convention.[36] In cases where no substantial connection to another country exists, the parties are bound to the mandatory legislation of the country with which the contract is solely connected, despite the choice of law.

---

31 Junker IPRax, 1989, 69, 70; Lorenz RIW 1987, 569.

32 Schurig RabelsZ 54 (1990) 217, 222; but see Lorenz RIW 1987, 569, 575; Junker IPRax 1989, 69, 70.

33 MünchKomm/Martiny Art 27 Rn 77; Rinze (1994) JBL 412, 420.

34 Schurig RabelsZ 54 (1990) 217, 223; Lorenz RIW 1987, 569, 575; Droste *Begriff* 95; Mäsch *Rechtswahlfreiheit* 97, 98; MünchKomm/Martiny Art 27 Rn 78; Kaye *The New Private International Law* 166; Hartley Rec des Cours 266 (1997) 341, 366 et seq.

35 MünchKomm/Martiny Art 27 Rn 78; Soergel/von Hoffmann Art 27 Rn 91; Mäsch *Rechtswahlfreiheit* 100; BGH 26.10.1993 RIW 1994, 154, 155. Whether the place of contracting can constitute such a substantial connection is debatable, cf Lorenz RIW 1987, 569, 575; MünchKomm/Martiny Art 27 Rn 78; Droste *Begriff* 95; Jayme IPRax 1990, 220, 222; Mäsch *Rechtswahlfreiheit* 103 et seq.

36 MünchKomm/Martiny Art 27 Rn 78; see similar Lorenz RIW 1987, 569, 575 who advocates that all the connections used in the conflict rules of the Rome Convention (arts 27 - 37 EGBGB) are sufficient; Mäsch *Rechtswahlfreiheit* 104.

c Mandatory rules in the sense of article 3 (3) of the Rome Convention

Article 3 (3) defines mandatory rules as 'rules which cannot be derogated from by contract'. The definition is based on whether, under the legal system of which it forms a part, the rule in question is mandatory in a domestic context.[37] In principle, the Convention is referring to all mandatory rules of a national legal system: No distinction is made between statutory and common law rules, nor is the definition restricted to a certain kind of mandatory legislation.[38] These rules are also defined as mandatory rules in a *domestic or wider sense*.[39] Article 3 (3) refers to mandatory rules in the domestic sense, as well as internationally mandatory rules.[40]

It has been disputed for some time whether mandatory EU legislation is applicable to contracts where the parties have chosen the law of a non-member state as the governing law, while the contract is substantially connected to EU member states alone.[41]

Finally, it should be noted that many authors submit that mandatory rules in the domestic sense are not mandatory within the context of art 3 (3), if they are restricted to domestic cases where no foreign law is chosen.[42]

---

37 Hartley Rec des Cours 266 (1997) 341, 368; Morse YB EurL (1982) 107, 123; Junker IPRax 1989, 69, 74; MünchKomm/Martiny Art 27 Rn 74, 75.

38 In contrast to arts 5 (2) and 6 (1) Rome Convention where it is disputed whether they refer only to certain kinds of protective mandatory rules; MünchKomm/Martiny Art 27 Rn 73; Droste *Begriff* 139; for examples of mandatory rules of the UK and Germany, see Rinze (1994) JBL 412, 420.

39 Cheshire & North's *Private International Law/12th ed* 498, */13th ed* 576; other expressions used are *mandatory rules in a national sense* or *simply mandatory rules*.

40 Reithmann/Martiny/Limmer *Internationales Vertragsrecht* Rn 456; Morse YB EurL (1982) 107, 123; Dicey & Morris *Conflict of Laws Vol II/12th ed* 1240, */13th ed* 1243. In Germany it is questionable whether mandatory rules of public law that serve predominantly economic interests of the enacting country fall within the scope of art 3 (3), see Droste *Begriff* 140; Lehmann *Zwingendes Recht* 219; MünchKomm/Martiny Art 27 Rn 74; Reithmann/Martiny/Limmer *Internationales Vertragsrecht* Rn 456; cf Philip in *Contract Conflicts* 81, 96, 97. This general problem is dealt with in the context of the applicability of internationally mandatory rules Chapter 3, 4, 5.

41 Some authors advocate an application of art 3 (3) Rome Convention by analogy, cf Lando CMLR 24 (1987) 159, 181; Kropholler *IPR* § 40 IV, 3; others argue that in respect of art 20 Rome Convention EU law cannot be treated as equivalent to national law; the mandatory EU law is superior and applies directly, if it claims application, cf MünchKomm/Martiny Art 27 Rn 76; see also Junker IPRax 1998, 69, 70 et seq.

42 Morse YB EurL (1982) 107, 123; Dicey & Morris *Conflict of Laws Vol II/12th ed* 1216; Philip *Contract Conflicts* 81, 95; cf, however, Jackson *Contract Conflicts* 59, 65, 66.

d Article 3 (3) Rome Convention as a multilateral conflict rule

Article 3 (3) contains a multilateral conflict rule concerning the application of mandatory rules. Thus, the reference to mandatory legislation might result in application of the rules of the lex fori or those of a foreign legal system.[43] However, the reference is restricted to those mandatory rules emanating from the country with which the contract is solely connected, despite the choice of law. This would correspond with the objectively applicable law as determined by the conflict rules in the absence of a choice of law. Mandatory rules of yet another legal system cannot be rendered applicable on the basis of art 3 (3).

2 Limitation of the parties' choice in order to protect the weaker contracting party

Articles 5 and 6 of the Rome Convention lay down special choice of law rules applicable to certain consumer contracts, and to all individual employment contracts. Thus, with a view to protecting the socio-economically weaker party, arts 5 and 6 derogate from art 3 (1), by making the mandatory rules of a law other than the chosen proper law applicable for the weaker parties' benefit. Articles 5 and 6 also derogate from art 4, by specifying a different rule for the ascertainment of the proper law in the absence of a choice.[44] For this study the derogation from art 3 is relevant only when *party autonomy is restricted by the application of mandatory rules of a law other than the chosen law*.[45]

a Background and purpose of articles 5 and 6 of the Rome Convention

Article 5 (2) of the Rome Convention (and the corresponding art 29 (2) EGBGB) concerning consumer contracts and art 6 (1) of the Rome Convention (art 30 (1) EGBGB) concerning employment contracts are designed to limit the effects of a choice of law made by the parties. Such a choice of law cannot deprive the consumer or the employee of the protection afforded to him by the

---

43 MünchKomm/Martiny Art 27 Rn 75; Reithmann/Martiny/Limmer *Internationales Vertragsrecht* Rn 382; Rinze (1994) JBL 412, 420; Soergel/von Hoffmann Art 27 Rn 85.

44 See the *Report* of Giuliano/Lagarde in *Contract Conflicts* 379 et seq; Morse YB EuL 2 (1982) 107, 134; Lasok/Stone *Conflict of Laws* 380, 384; Cheshire & North's *Private International Law/12th ed* 495, */13th ed* 575; von Bar *IPR Bd II* 313; Junker IPRax 1998, 65, 67, 68; for consumer contracts, it is the law of the consumer's habitual residence, although it is generally not the consumer who must effect the characteristic performance of the contract; for employment contracts, it is the law where the employee habitually performs his work or where the place of business in which he is engaged is situated.

45 For a general scrutiny of this conflict rule, see Morse ICLQ 41 (1992) 1 et seq; id YBEurL 2 (1982) 107 et seq; id *Contract Conflicts* 143 et seq; Hartley *Contract Conflicts* 111 et seq; Schurig RabelsZ 54 (1990) 217, 220; Junker IPRax 1989, 69, 71.

mandatory rules of the law of the country that would be applicable in the absence of a choice.[46]

These provisions allow for the protection of the weaker contracting party at the level of conflict of laws.[47] Thus, the trend in domestic law of an ever increasing number of mandatory rules, that, through considerations of social policy, intervene in the private legal relationship, is extended into the field of international law.[48] This is a relatively new development in the field of conflict of laws which, according to the traditional point of view, is 'neutral' in the sense that makes no reference to the values enshrined in potentially applicable rules of substantive law.[49] According to the traditional point of view, the role of the national law is to decide whether certain groups of society are disadvantaged and in need of special protection. Such social policies should not intrude into the traditional choice of law process.[50]

This is not the place to discuss in detail the conflict revolution that changed this approach. Influenced by American theories such as Currie's *governmental interest analysis* approach[51] or Leflar's '*better law*' approach,[52] pertinent questions have been raised about the values and merits of the traditional choice of law process.[53] According to several modern schools of thought, the conflict process should be resolved not only on basis of the traditional territorial locality, but also on the basis of social values.[54] Based on these policy

---

46 Morse ICLQ 41 (1992) 1, 6, 14; Schurig RabelsZ 54 (1990) 217, 220; Junker IPRax 1989, 69, 71.

47 Morse ICLQ 41 (1992) 1, 2; Erauw *International Contracts* 71, 72; North *Private International Law Problems* 142; Dicey & Morris *Conflict of Laws Vol II/12th ed* 1286, */13th ed* 1285.

48 Von Bar *IPR Bd II* 313; Keller in *FS Vischer* 175 et seq; Morse ICLQ 41 (1992) 1, 2; Erauw *International Contracts* 71, 72; Kropholler *IPR* § 52 V; North *Private International Law Problems* 130; details about this development in national and international law can be found in Junker IPRax 1998, 65, 66; Kren ZVerglRWiss 88 (1989) 48 et seq; see already Vischer Rec des Cours 124 (1974 II) 1, 21.

49 See Erauw *International Contracts* 71, 72; Morse ICLQ 41 (1992) 1, 2; North *Private International Law Problems* 141 et seq; Junker IPRax 1998, 65, 66.

50 Junker IPRax 1998, 65, 66; North *Private International Law Problems* 141 et seq.

51 See the articles in Currie *Selected Essays*.

52 Leflar *American Conflicts Law* 193 - 195, 205 - 219; id NY UL Rev 41 (1966) 267 et seq.

53 And the results obtained by mechanically connecting the private relationship with one geographical area. For a representation of this development, see Keller *FS Vischer* 175, 178 et seq; Erauw *International Contracts* 71, 72; Junker IPRax 1998, 65, 67; also see North *Private International Law Problems* 141, 142; Vischer Rec des Cours 124 (1974 II) 1, 67.

54 Influenced by the American theories, few academics in some European countries, such as Germany and the Netherlands, in the late 1960s, early 1970s rejected Savigny's choice of

considerations, various solutions have been proposed to resolve the conflict between the weaker party's need for protection and the traditional conflict process.[55]

With regard to party autonomy it was argued that the protection granted by national mandatory legislation to the weaker contracting party would be frustrated if the parties (in particular the stronger contracting party) were permitted to circumvent those protective mandatory rules, simply by choosing another law to govern the contract.[56] Additionally, it has been pointed out that the policies and interests in international trade differ from those in international employment and consumer contracts. Whereas unrestricted freedom to choose the law to govern a transaction in international trade has its merits, these are regarded as fictitious for employment and consumer contracts. The weaker party is faced with the alternative of adhering to the terms set by the stronger party or of not contracting at all.[57] In this context a Neuhaus' famous statement is relevant: 'Party autonomy loses - just like in domestic law - its sense, if it becomes the rule of the stronger one over the weak.'[58] Articles 5 and 6 serve to elevate the protection of the weaker party in the contractual relationship to the level of conflict of laws.

---

law system as a whole. They were not accepted in Europe, however; see Junker IPRax 1998, 65, 67; Erauw *International Contracts* 71, 73; Keller *FS Vischer* 175, 179 et seq; Zweigert RabelsZ 37 (1973) 437, 443 - 445; Vischer Rec des Cours 142 (1974 II) 1, 52 et seq. American theories have had no impact on South African private international law, but have expressly been rejected as a choice of law method; see Forsyth *Private International Law* 53, 54, 61.

55 See, for instance, von Hoffmann RabelsZ 38 (1974) 396, 407 et seq who proposed that rules based on socio-political considerations of protecting the weaker party of a contract should be interpreted as internationally mandatory and subjected to a special connection. Others were in favour of considering the social values already within the ordinary choice of law process by changing the connecting factors, see Kropholler RabelsZ 42 (1978) 634, 636; Keller *FS Vischer* 175, 179 et seq. Lando Rec des Cours 189 (1984 VI) 229, 298 et seq proposes that party autonomy in weaker party contracts should be prohibited.

56 Von Hoffmann RabelsZ 38 (1974), 396, 399 et seq; Vischer Rec des Cours 124 (1974 II) 1, 28, 40, 42 et seq; Kropholler RabelsZ 42 (1978) 634, 366, 656; Keller *FS Vischer* 175, 184 et seq; Hartley *Contract Conflicts* 111, 112, 113.

57 Cf Lando Rec des Cours 189 (1984 VI) 229, 300; id *Contracts* ss 77 et seq.

58 Neuhaus *Grundbegriffe* 172 'Die Parteiautonomie verliert - wie auch im materiellen Recht - ihren Sinn, wenn sie zur Herrschaft des Stärkeren über dem Schwachen wird'; a similar statement is: 'Wo im materiellen Recht die Privatautonomie zugunsten zwingender Vorschriftenten zum Schutze einer Partei eingeschränkt sei, verliere die Anknüpfung an den Parteiwillen im IPR ihre Berechtigung', for further references Junker IPRax 1998, 65, 67.

b Article 5 (2) of the Rome Convention

Article 5 (2) provides as follows:

> Notwithstanding the provisions of article 3, a choice of law made by the parties shall not have the result of depriving the consumer of protection afforded to him by the mandatory rules of the law of the country in which he has his habitual residence;
>
> - if in that country the conclusion of the contract was preceded by a specific invitation addressed to him or by advertising, and he had taken in that country all the steps necessary on his part for the conclusion of the contract, or
> - if the other party or his agent received the consumer's order in that country, or
> - if the contract is for the sale of goods and the consumer travelled from that country to another country and there gave his order, provided that the consumer's journey was arranged by the seller for the purpose of inducing the consumer to buy. [59]

Article 5 (2) is designed to limit the effects of a law made by the parties, pursuant to art 3, where the contract is a consumer contract in the sense of art 5 (1). Therefore, art 5 does not invalidate the choice of law in a consumer contract, but declares that if any of the three conditions set out in art 5 (2) are present, the choice of law will not result in the consumer being deprived of the protection afforded to him by the mandatory rules of his country of habitual residence. Thus, party autonomy is in principle permitted; it is only the *effect* of

---

[59] The corresponding art 29 (1) EGBGB reads 'Bei Verträgen über die Lieferung beweglicher Sachen oder die Erbringung von Dienstleistungen zu einem Zweck, der nicht der beruflichen oder gewerblichen Tätigkeit des Berechtigten (Verbrauchers) zugerechnet werden kann, sowie bei Verträgen zur Finanzierung eines solchen Geschäfts darf eine Rechtswahl der Parteien nicht dazu führen, daß dem Verbrauer der durch die zwingenden Bestimmungen des Rechts des Staates, in dem er seinen gewöhnlichen Aufenthalt hat, gewährte Schutz entzogen wird, (1) wenn dem Vertragsschluß ein ausdrückliches Angebot oder eine Werbung in diesem Staat vorausgegangen ist und wenn der Verbraucher in diesem Staat die zum Abschluß des Vertrages erforderlichen Rechtshandlungen vorgenommen hat, (2) wenn der Vertragspartner des Verbrauchers oder sein Vertreter die Bestellung des Verbrauchers in diesem Staat entgegengenommen hat oder (3) wenn der Vertrag den Verkauf von Waren betrifft und der Verbraucher von diesem Staat in einen anderen Staat gereist ist und dort seine Bestellung aufgegeben hat, sofern diese Reise vom Verkäufer it dem Ziel herbeigeführt worden ist, den Verbraucher zum Vertragsschluß zu veranlassen.'

the choice of law of the parties that is limited by the application of mandatory rules of a law other than the chosen law.[60]

(1) Conditions of article 5 (2) of the Rome Convention

Article 5 is restricted in its scope of application and does not cover all consumer contracts. A contract falls within art 5 if it is 'a contract the object of which is the supply of goods or services to a person ("the consumer") for a purpose which can be regarded as being outside his trade or profession, or a contract for the provision of credit for that object'.[61] Thus, art 5 is applicable only if the *personal conditions* of the contracting parties are fulfilled, viz. one party acts as consumer outside his trade or profession, while the seller or supplier acts in the course of his trade or profession.[62] Article 5 applies to contracts for the supply of services and goods, which includes the provision of credit in relation to contracts with these objects.[63]

Additionally, the circumstances under which the contract was concluded must fulfil any of the three conditions set out in art 5 (2).[64] Each condition serves to establish a sufficiently close connection (prior to or during the conclusion of the contract) to the country of the consumer's habitual residence to merit the application of the mandatory rules of that country.[65] The conditions have been criticised for causing definition and distinction problems.[66] In general, because of the conditions laid down in art 5 (2), the scope of application of the article is

60 MünchKomm/Martiny Art 29 Rn 33; North *Private International Law Problems* 131; Hartley *Contract Conflicts* 111, 125.

61 Art 5 (1) RC; for these and further conditions, see MünchKomm/Martiny Art 29 Rn 5 et seq; Morse ICLQ 41 (1992) 1, 3 et seq; id YBEurL 2 (1982) 1, 134 et seq; Reithmann/ Martiny/Martiny *Internationales Vertragsrecht* Rn 715 et seq.

62 It is disputed whether art 5 applies to contracts where both parties act outside their professions, see Morse ICLQ 41 (1992) 1, 3, 4; Hartley *Contract Conflicts* 111, 125; Reithmann/Martiny/Martiny *Internationales Vertragsrecht* Rn 716; MünchKomm/ Martiny Art 29 Rn 5 et seq; Rinze (1994) 412, 422; Lorenz RIW 1987, 569, 576.

63 Contracts of carriage and contracts for the supply of services where the services are to be supplied to the consumer exclusively in a country other than that in which he has his habitual residence, art 5 (4) RC; for details about the covered and excluded kind of contracts: MünchKomm/Martiny Art 29 Rn 5 et seq; Morse ICLQ 41 (1992) 1, 3, 4, 5; Reithmann/Martiny/Martiny *Internationales Vertragsrecht* Rn 733.

64 For these conditions, see Morse ICLQ 41 (1992) 1, 6, 7; id YBEurL 2 (1982) 1, 135.

65 See von Hoffmann IPRax 1989, 261, 263; Morse YBEurL 2 (1982) 107, 135.

66 These problems will not be discussed in the context of this study. For an account, see Morse ICLQ 41 (1992) 1, 3 et seq; Rinze (1994) JBL 412, 422 et seq; von Hoffmann IPRax 1989, 261, 267; MünchKomm/Martiny Art 29 Rn 3, 5 et seq.

narrower than its heading 'consumer contracts' would suggest.[67] If none of the conditions of art 5 are met, party autonomy under art 3 (1) remains unaffected.[68]

(2) Mandatory rules in the sense of article 5 (2) of the Rome Convention

Article 5 (2) is structured in an multilateral manner in that it refers not only to mandatory rules of the lex fori, but also to foreign mandatory rules, if the consumer's country of habitual residence is a foreign country.[69] However, the (special) reference is restricted to the mandatory rules of the consumer's country of habitual residence, viz. the objective proper law. Mandatory rules in this provision are used in the definitional sense of art 3 (3), viz. mandatory rules in a domestic or wider sense. It is not required that the rule be internationally mandatory and applicable, regardless of which law is applicable to a contract.[70]

However, within the context of art 5, only those mandatory rules that serve to protect the weaker contracting party, the consumer, are referred to.[71] It is disputed whether the nature of these mandatory rules must therefore be delimited: Is reference being made to those rules expressly concerned with consumer protection, or to all mandatory rules that actually serve to protect the consumer in the specific situation?[72] The wording and the context of the provision favour a restrictive interpretation.[73] It cannot be denied, however, that in a particular case other mandatory rules might also serve the interests and protection of the consumer. Furthermore, it is difficult to distinguish mandatory rules concerning consumer protection from those rules of a more general character.[74]

---

67 MünchKomm/Martiny Art 29 Rn 3; North *Private International Law Problems* 130, 131.

68 In the absence of a choice, art 4 applies to determine the proper law, cf Morse ICLQ 41 (1992) 1, 9, 10.

69 MünchKomm/Martiny Art 29 Rn 36; Philip *Contract Conflicts* 81, 98; Rinze (1994) JBL 412, 422.

70 Morse ICLQ 41 (1992) 1, 8; Dicey & Morris *Conflict of Laws Vol II/12th /13th ed* 1290; Jackson *Contract Conflicts* 59, 65.

71 Reithmann/Martiny/Martiny *Internationales Vertragsrecht* Rn 739; Morse YBEurL 2 (1982) 107, 136.

72 For a discussion Mäsch *Rechtswahlfreiheit* 44 et seq; Morse YB EurL 2 (1982) 107, 136; id ICLQ 41 (1992) 1, 8.

73 See Morse Yb EurL 2 (1982) 107, 136; id ICLQ 41 (1992) 1, 8; Dicey & Morris *Conflict of Laws Vol II/12th/13th ed* 1290; Soergel/von Hoffmann Art 29 Rn 29; for further references, see Mäsch *Rechtswahlfreiheit* 43.

74 Cf Mäsch *Rechtswahlfreiheit* 44 et seq; von Bar *IPR Bd II* 324; MünchKomm/Martiny Art 29 Rn 35; Droste *Begriff* 212 et seq.

Examples of mandatory rules in the field of consumer protection can be found particularly in law that has been harmonised by EC legislation. Examples include Directive 87/102 on consumer credits,[75] Directive 85/577 on consumer protection,[76] Directive 90/314 on package holiday tours,[77] and Directive on Unfair Contract Terms,[78] that resulted in an alteration of § 12 of the General Terms and Conditions of Trade Act.[79] Other German examples are the provisions of the General Terms and Conditions of Trade Act[80] and the provisions on travel contracts.[81] Examples from English law include the provisions of the Consumer Credit Act 1977[82] and those of the Unfair Contract Terms Act 1977.[83]

(3) The relationship between the chosen law and the mandatory rules of the law of the consumer's country of habitual residence

The relationship between the chosen law and the mandatory rules of the law of the consumer's country of habitual residence is not entirely clear.[84] In principle it is accepted that the mandatory protective rules of the consumer's country of habitual residence do not automatically displace the chosen law, whether they are more favourable than the chosen law or not.[85] The purpose of art 5 (2) is to prevent the consumer being deprived, by a choice of law, of the protection that the law of the country of his habitual residence would afford him. This law defines the *minimum protection* available, but it does not necessarily define the maximum protection, since the purpose of this provision is not to prevent the

---

75 [1987] O J L 42/48 as amended by Directive 90/88 [1990] O J L 61/14; cf the German Verbraucherkreditgesetz; see MünchKomm/Martiny Art 29 Rn 4.

76 See especially art 6 of the Directive on contracts negotiated away from business premises [1985] O J L 61/31, which was implemented in Germany by the Haustürwiderrufsgesetz, see MünchKomm/Martiny Art 29 Rn 4; von Hoffmann IPRax 1989, 261, 268.

77 [1990] O J L 158/59.

78 See art 6 (2) Directive 93/13 [1993] O J L 95/29.

79 AGBG 9.12.1976, BGBl I, 3317 as amended 19.7.1996, BGBl I, 1013; however, since art 12 AGBG is an unilateral conflict rules it overlaps with art 5 (2) Rome Convention, see Junker IPRax 1989, 65, 70 et seq; MünchKomm/Martiny Art 29 Rn 4, 48.

80 MünchKomm/Martiny Art 29 Rn 36; Droste *Begriff* 214; Mäsch *Rechtswahlfreiheit* 52.

81 §§ 651 et seq BGB, for further examples, see MünchKomm/Martiny Art 29 Rn 36.

82 Cf Dicey & Morris *Conflict of Laws Vol II/12th ed* 1297, 1298, */13th ed* 1296, 1297; Hartley *Contract Conflicts* 111, 118; Rinze (1994) JBL 412, 420 for further examples.

83 For a discussion, cf Dicey & Morris *Conflict of Laws Vol II/12th ed* 1296, 1297, */13th ed* 1295, 1296; for the Unfair Terms in Consumer Contracts Regulations 1999 see Dicey & Morris *Conflict of Laws Vol II/13th ed* 1299 et seq.

84 Morse YBEurL 2 (1982) 107, 136 et seq; Dicey & Morris *Conflict of Laws Vol II/12th /13th ed* 1290; Junker IPRax 1989, 69, 71; MünchKomm/Martiny Art 29 Rn 37.

85 Morse YBEurL 2 (1982) 107, 137; Kaye *The New Private International Law* 213; Junker IPRax 1989, 69, 71; MünchKomm/Martiny Art 29 Rn 37.

consumer from gaining *greater* protection under the chosen law.[86] Consequently, this provision necessitates a comparison of the protective mandatory rules of the chosen law and those of the law of the consumer's country of residence; the law that is more favourable to the consumer prevails.[87]

It can therefore be concluded that the chosen law will apply to the extent that it does not conflict with any relevant mandatory rules of the law of the country of habitual residence. Furthermore, art 5 (2) allows the consumer to rely on the mandatory rules of the law of his country of residence, if they are more favourable to him than the chosen law; or he may rely on the chosen law, if it is more favourable to him than the mandatory rules of the law of his country of habitual residence.[88]

Difficulties arise in ascertaining which set of protective rules is most favourable to the consumer. Most authors agree that the consumer is not permitted to rely cumulatively on *both* the mandatory rules of his habitual residence *and* the rules of the chosen law.[89] It is believed that selecting the best consumer protection rules from each law, on a *'pick and choose'* basis, would be an incorrect course to follow (the so-called '*Rosinentheorie*'). The policy of art 5 (2) is that the consumer should not be deprived of the minimum protection of the law of his habitual residence, but if the chosen law offers him greater protection it is reasonable to let him to rely on it. In this case, however, the law of his country of habitual residence has no further part to play, as there is no reasonable justification for giving the consumer 'double protection'.[90]

The problem of determining the *object* of the comparison remains, with most authors assuming that a comparison of the legal systems as a whole is inade-

---

86 Morse YBEurL 2 (1982) 107, 136; Dicey & Morris *Conflict of Laws Vol II/12th ed* 1291, */13th ed* 1290; Junker IPRax 1989, 69, 71; MünchKomm/Martiny Art 29 Rn 37; Kropholler *IPR* § 52 V 3; von Bar *IPR Bd II* 324.

87 MünchKomm/Martiny Art 29 Rn 37, 38; Kropholler *IPR* § 52 V; von Bar *IPR Bd II* 324; Dicey & Morris *Conflict of Laws Vol II/12th ed* 1291, */13th ed* 1290.

88 Morse YBEurL 2 (1982) 107, 136, 137; Dicey & Morris *Conflict of Laws Vol II/12th /13th ed* 1290; MünchKomm/Martiny Art 29 Rn 37, 38.

89 Morse YBEurL 2 (1982) 107, 136, 137; id ICLQ (1992) 1, 8, 9; Dicey & Morris *Conflict of Laws Vol II/12th /13th ed* 1290; Kaye *The New Private International Law* 213; Junker IPRax 1998, 65, 67, 68; however, for a cumulative application, see Philipp *Contracts Conflict* 81, 99; Lorenz RIW 1987, 569, 577; Rinze (1994) JBL 412, 422.

90 Schurig RabelsZ 54 (1990) 217, 225; Junker IPRax 1989, 69, 71; Dicey & Morris *Conflict of Laws Vol II/12th /13th ed* 1290; Kaye *The New Private International Law* 213; MünchKomm/Martiny Art 29 Rn 37, 38.

quate to determine which one offers the consumer greater protection.[91] Ultimately, a comparison of certain single rules or sets of rules will occur (the so called '*Einzelvergleich*'). The court's examination will have to show which set of rules is more favourable to the consumer in a particular case, taking his expectations into account.[92]

c Article 6 (1) of the Rome Convention

In respect of employment contracts, art 6 (1) contains a provision that corresponds with art 5 (2) in its basic structure and purpose:[93]

> Notwithstanding the provision of article 3, in a contract of employment a choice of law made by the parties shall not have the result of depriving the employee of the protection afforded to him by the mandatory rules of the law which would be applicable under paragraph 2 in the absence of choice.[94]

Thus, once again, the parties are in principle free to select any law to govern their contract, but, the effect of their choice is limited in that the mandatory rules of an otherwise applicable law protecting the employee may still be applied.[95]

(1) Contracts subject to article 6 of the Rome Convention

In contrast to art 5, art 6 covers all individual employment contracts and not merely those having a substantial connection with the country in which the employee lives.[96] Nevertheless, there is a problem concerning whether a contract is one of employment for the purpose of art 6. Commentators agree that

---

91 Schurig RabelsZ 54 (1990) 27, 225; Junker IPRax 1989, 69, 72; Lorenz RIW 1987, 569, 577.

92 Schurig RabelsZ 54 (1990) 217, 225; Lorenz RIW 1987, 569, 577; Junker IPRax 1989, 69, 71, 72.

93 For a detailed discussion of art 6: Morse in *Contract Conflicts* 143 et seq; id YBEurL 2 (1982) 107, 138 et seq; id ICLQ 41 (1992) 1, 11; Junker IPRax 1989, 69 et seq; MünchKomm/Martiny Art 30 Rn 1 et seq.

94 Section (1) of art 30 EGBGB is identical in wording 'Bei Arbeitsverträgen und Arbeitsverhältnissen darf die Rechtswahl der Parteien nicht dazu führen, daß dem Arbeitnehmer der Schutz entzogen wird, der ihm durch die zwingenden Bestimmungen des Rechts gewährt wird, das nach Abs. 2 mangels einer Rechtswahl anzuwenden wäre.'

95 MünchKomm/Martiny Art 30 Rn 10, 18; Junker IPRax 1993, 1, 5; Morse YBEurL 2 (1982) 107, 139; id ICLQ 41 (1992) 1, 14; Dicey & Morris *Conflict of Laws Vol II/12th ed* 1306, */13th ed* 1304, 1307; Rinze (1994) JBL 412, 424.

96 Lasok/Stone *Conflict of Laws* 384; Junker IPRax 1993, 1, 8.

the article covers only contracts entered into by individual employees, not collective agreements.[97] According to the *Giuliano/Lagarde* Report, art 6 applies to both valid individual employment contracts, as well as void contracts and de facto employment relationships, 'in particular those characterised by failure to respect the contract imposed by law for the protection of employees'.[98]

Whereas German academic writers have accepted that the meaning of an 'employment contract' in art 6 is to be determined with reference to art 18 of the Rome Convention,[99] English writers tend to apply the private international law technique of characterisation. This latter approach, however, then leads to the problem of deciding which law must be applied to determine the classification of the particular contract.[100]

(2) Mandatory rules in the sense of article 6 of the Rome Convention

Art 6 (1) is a multilateral conflict rule since it refers to mandatory rules of the law applicable to the contract under para (2). Thus, in the absence of a choice by the parties the lex fori or any foreign law can be the law applicable according to art 6 (2), and the mandatory rules of the designated law, be it the forum or a foreign law, are rendered applicable.[101] Mandatory rules in the sense of art 6 (1) appear to be the relevant rules of employment protection, defined in art 3 (3) as rules which cannot be derogated from by contract (mandatory rules in the wider or domestic sense). Such rules need not be internationally mandatory as well, although many of the relevant rules in the field of employment protection will be of this nature.[102] According to the *Giuliano/Lagarde* Report, mandatory rules in the sense of art 6 (1) are not only those relating to the contract of employment itself, but also rules 'concerning industrial safety and hygiene which are regarded in certain Member States as being provisions of public law'.[103]

---

97 Dicey & Morris *Conflict of Laws Vol II/12th ed* 1304, */13th ed* 1305; Morse ICLQ 41 (1992) 1, 13. 14.

98 Giuliano/Lagarde *Report* in *Contract Conflicts* 379, 380; the German wording of art 30 EGBGB in fact refers expressly to 'employment relationships', see MünchKomm/Martiny Art 30 Rn 7, 8.

99 Art 36 EGBGB, cf MünchKomm/Martiny Art 30 Rn 7.

100 Morse ICLQ 41 (1992) 1, 12, 13 who favours a classification according to the lex causae.

101 Rinze (1994) JBL 412, 424.

102 See Morse ICLQ 41 (1992) 1, 14; Junker IPRax 1993, 1, 6, 7.

103 In *Contract Conflicts* 379, 380.

According to many authors the reference is not restricted to mandatory rules that are designed to protect the weaker contracting party, viz. the employee.[104]

However, in Germany, because of the general dispute regarding the scope of reference of conflict rules, there is a strong tendency to exclude mandatory rules serving general economic and social-political purposes, and thus public interests of the state, from the scope of the proper law. According to this point of view, these rules fall within the scope of art 7 of the Rome Convention.[105] Employee protection rules, however, will be covered by art 6 irrespective of their private or public law nature.[106]

Examples of German mandatory protective rules can be found in the protection from unwarranted termination (Kündigungsschutzgesetz).[107] Examples of English mandatory rules can be found in the Employment Rights Act 1996 (s 204 (1), the Act replaces the Employment Protection (Consolidation) Act 1978 with its mandatory rules in ss 141 (1), (2), 153 (5)), the Equal Pay Act 1970 and the Law Reform (Personal Injuries) Act 1948.[108] Whether a rule is mandatory depends ultimately on the national law of which it forms part. It is therefore submitted by many authors that a mandatory rule, despite its applicability according to the conflict reference, should not be applied if the particular rule is not applicable to the situation.[109] An often quoted justification for this proposition was found in s 141 of the Employment Protection (Consolidation) Act 1978 declaring that the British legislation forbidding unfair dismissal does not apply to work done by those ordinarily outside Great Britain. Although the 1978 Act had been replaced by the Employment Rights Act 1996, a similar provision is found in its s 196 (2), (3).[110]

---

104 MünchKomm/Martiny Art 30 Rn 19; Droste *Begriff* 203 et seq; see, however, Morse YB EurL (1982) 107, 139; id ICLQ 41 (1992) 1, 16.

105 Of course this will raise problems of distinction, cf MünchKomm/Martiny Art 30 Rn 19; Droste *Begriff* 203; see also Kaye *The New Private International Law* 227.

106 Also see the Giuliano/Lagarde *Report* in *Contract Conflicts* 379; MünchKomm/Martiny Art 30 Rn 20; Droste *Begriff* 128, 202; but see Philip *Contract Conflicts* 81, 98 et seq.

107 MünchKomm/Martiny Art 30 Rn 22, 53 et seq for further examples.

108 Although the Court of Appeal in *Sayers v International Drilling Co NV* [1971] 1 WLR 1176 did not apply this Act to a contract governed by Dutch law, this is not a *contra dictio*, since the question was not whether the Act was mandatory but whether it was internationally mandatory; for further examples, see Kaye *The New Private International Law* 225, 226; Dicey & Morris *Conflict of Laws Vol II/12th ed* 1317, */13th ed* 1318 et seq.

109 Kaye *The New Private International Law* 229 et seq; Rinze (1994) JBL 412, 424; Morse YB EurL (1982) 107, 139, 140.

110 Kaye *The New Private International Law* 229 et seq; Morse YB EurL (1982) 107, 139, 140; id ICLQ 41 (1992) 1, 14, 15; For the 1996 Act, see Dicey & Morris *Conflict of Laws Vol II/13th ed* 1318 et seq.

(3) The relationship between the chosen law and the mandatory rules of the otherwise applicable law according to paragraph (2)

As in the case of art 5 (2), art 6 (1) does not result in the chosen law being automatically displaced by the mandatory rules of the law applicable in the absence of a choice. This will only occur if the employee is afforded inferior protection by the chosen law.[111] This interpretation conforms with the wording of art 6: '... shall not have the result of depriving of ....' It would be out of step with the policy of employment protection that underlies art 6 (1) for the employee to be restricted solely to the level of protection offered by the mandatory rules of the otherwise applicable law, whether these are better or worse than those available under the chosen law.[112]

Therefore, art 6 (1) necessitates a comparison of the protection afforded to the employee by the mandatory legislation of the chosen law and the law applicable in the absence of a choice: The *more favourable law* for the employee is to be applied (*Günstigkeitsvergleich*).[113] The mandatory rules of the applicable law, in the absence of a choice, are applicable, according to para (1), if and to the extent that they are more favourable to the employee in the particular situation. Thus, the mandatory protection legislation of the otherwise applicable law constitutes the *minimum protection standard*.[114]

As with art 5 (2), the 'more-favourable principle' (*Günstigkeitsprinzip*) creates difficulties in determining *what* is to be compared: Is it the whole legal system, or sets of protective rules, or only individual provisions? Most authors submit that art 6 (1) does not lead to a cumulative application of the mandatory rules of both the chosen law and the otherwise applicable law.[115] The employee is not permitted to *pick and choose* from the individual rules of each law, so as to enjoy maximum protection ('*Rosinentheorie*'). Accordingly, a mandatory rule of the otherwise applicable law that regulates the particular question at issue should either be applied in its entirety, if it is more favourable to the employee than the protection granted by the chosen law, or else not applied at all, if it offers less protection than the chosen law. Although there are also some authors who assume that the mandatory protective rules of both laws are to be applied

---

111 Morse in *Contract Conflicts* 143, 152; MünchKomm/Martiny Art 30 Rn 23.

112 Kaye *The New Private International Law* 228 et seq.

113 MünchKomm/Martiny Art 30 Rn 23; Junker IPRax 1989, 71 et seq; Dicey & Morris *Conflict of Laws Vol II/12th ed* 1307 et seq, */13th ed* 1308 et seq.

114 MünchKomm/Martiny Art 30 Rn 23; Giuliano/Lagarde *Report* in *Contract Conflicts* 379.

115 Dicey & Morris *Conflict of Laws Vol II/12th ed* 1307 et seq, */13th ed* 1309; Kaye *The New Private International Law* 229; Morse YB EurL (1982) 107, 140; id ICLQ 41 (1992) 1, 15 et seq; Junker IPRax 1989, 69, 71 et seq; MünchKomm/Martiny Art 30 Rn 23.

on a cumulative basis,[116] the former view seems more acceptable: There is no justification for offering the employee more protection if the contracting parties *did* make a choice of law than if they had *not* made a choice. The policy underlying art 6 (1) is to protect the employee being deprived of the protection afforded to him by the mandatory rules of the art 6 (2) law, and not to grant him double protection.[117] However, it is conceded that it is not an easy task for the judge to decide which set of mandatory rules is more favourable to the employee.[118]

d Application of Articles 5 and 6 of the Rome Convention by analogy

Articles 5 and 6 restrict party autonomy by reference to mandatory legislation for consumer and employment contracts alone. There are no special conflict rules in the Rome Convention or EGBGB to protect the weaker party in other contracts with a similar inequality of bargaining power. This position has been criticised and some academics have proposed that arts 5 and 6 should be applied by analogy to equivalent cases where there is an inequality of bargaining power.[119]

Additionally, with regard to consumer contracts, it has been held that article 5 is too restrictive. It does not apply if the conditions of paras (1) or (2) are not met, although there are situations where the consumer is in a position similar to that described in the article. It has therefore been proposed that art 5 should be applied by analogy to consumer contracts that are not by definition covered by the article, and to contractual circumstances that do not fulfil any of the three conditions of para (2).[120] This solution is based on the assumption that these

---

[116] Philipp *Contract Conflicts* 81, 99 et seq; Lorenz RIW 1987, 569, 577.

[117] See the frequently quoted example of Gamillscheg ZfA 14 (1983) 307, 338: Should a German employee who works in an Muslim country be granted the Friday as local weekly (religious) holiday and also the Sunday as a weekly holiday according to German employment law?

[118] Kaye *The New Private International Law* 228; MünchKomm/Martiny Art 30 Rn 26; Morse ICLQ 41 (1992) 1, 16.

[119] With regard to arts 5 and 6, see Lando CMLR 24 (1987) 159, 185; id Rec des Cours 189 (1984 VI) 229, 298 et seq; Hartley *Contract Conflicts* 111, 112; for a discussion: Rinze (1994) JBL 412, 424 et seq; Martiny ZEuP 1995, 67, 70 with further references; for the corresponding German provisions, see Lorenz RIW 1987, 569, 571, 572; Kohte EuZW 1990, 150, 156.

[120] See Reithmann/Martiny/Martiny *Internationales Vertragsrecht* Rn 724, 730; the so called '*Gran-Canaria-cases*' caused many disputes in Germany. For a detailed discussion of academic and case law approaches, see Mäsch *Rechtswahlfreiheit* 111 et seq; the problem of the *Gran-Canaria* cases was that the contracts had been concluded in Spain, but payment and performance was to take place in Germany. The contracts included a choice

articles establish a *general* principle of protection for the weaker party, and that arts 7 and 16 of the Convention do not provide sufficient protection for contracts falling outside the scope of arts 5 and 6.[121]

The counter-opinion rejects an application by analogy to other contracts. It is argued that arts 5 and 6 were deliberately intended to deal with two specific situations and that the signatories of the Convention did not regard it necessary to depart from the freedom of choice to protect the weaker party in other contracts.[122]

e Relationship of articles 5 and 6 to article 7 of the Rome Convention

Some of the employee and consumer protection rules are not only mandatory in the national or domestic sense, but also apply irrespective of the law otherwise applicable to the contract. In the areas of employment and consumer protection, German examples include the special employee protection rules of unfair dismissal of severely disabled persons (Schwerbehindertengesetz, §§ 15 et seq SchwbG) or mothers (Mutterschutzgesetz, § 9 MuSchG).[123] English examples are the Employment Right Act 1996 (s 204, the Act replaces the Employment Protection (Consolidation) Act 1978 (ss 140, 153 (5))[124] and the Unfair Contract Terms Act 1977 (s 27 (2)).[125]

In this regard, two questions have arisen. Firstly, can mandatory rules that serve (predominantly) the protection of the weaker contracting party be regarded as internationally mandatory in the sense of art 7 of the Convention? This appears to be a continental European issue, since this highly controversial question is

of law clause which specified Spanish law as the applicable law. Spanish law at that time had not transformed the EC-Directive 85/577 and thus there was no law giving the consumer the right of retraction in door-to-door selling (the legal situation in Spain changed in 1991). In Germany this right of retraction was offered in the Haustürwiderrufsgesetz . None of the three conditions in art 5 RC was fulfilled. The crucial question was how to protect the German consumer: Some courts applied art 3 (3), others applied art 5 by analogy, ultimately, art 7 (2) was held to be applicable.

121 Lorenz RIW 1987, 569, 571, 572; Kohte EuZW 1990, 150, 156.

122 For further arguments and references, see Rinze JBL (1994) 412, 425.

123 As well as, for example, § 12 of the Standard Contract Act 1976 (AGBG). Cf MünchKomm/Martiny Art 30 Rn 61, 73, 73a et seq for further examples.

124 Morse ICLQ 4 (1992) 1, 14 footnote 56; Dicey & Morris *Conflict of Laws Vol II/12th ed* 1316 et seq, */13th ed* 1318 with further examples.

125 Dicey & Morris *Conflict of Laws Vol II/12th ed* 1296 et seq, */13th ed* 1295 et seq.

not disputed in the United Kingdom.[126] This question is discussed in detail in the context of the application of internationally mandatory rules.[127]

Secondly, if one assumes that consumer and employee protection rules can fall within the scope of art 7, what is the relationship between arts 5, 6 and 7 of the Convention? Academic writers disagree about whether art 7 (in Germany and the United Kingdom only art 7 (2)) can be applied in fields which are generally covered by arts 5 and 6.[128]

The relationship of these provisions is complicated by the fact that the norms are different in structure and content. While arts 5 and 6 are multilateral conflict rules for consumer and employment contracts and contain an alternative connection of mandatory rules through the 'more-favourable principle', art 7 (2) refers only to the rules of the forum state and concerns a special connection of internationally mandatory rules.[129] The relationship is relevant in cases where arts 5 and 6 refer to the applicability of foreign mandatory rules, while the internationally mandatory rules of the forum state that do exist are different and even less favourable than the other potentially applicable laws.[130]

Some authors argue that arts 5 and 6 provide exclusive rules which balance the interests involved, and are thus lex specialis to the general clauses of art 7. However, with regard to the kind of contract that is by definition not covered by arts 5 and 6, an application of the forum's internationally mandatory protection rules is possible.[131]

Others maintain that art 7 has priority.[132] This proposition is supported by the argument that the special connection by means of art 7 systematically prevails

---

126 See Morse ICLQ 41 (1992) 1, 10, 16, 17; Dicey & Morris *Conflict of Laws Vol II/12th ed* 1240, 1241, */13th ed* 1290, 1295 et seq.

127 Infra under Chapter 3, II.

128 Eg Junker IPRax 1998, 65, 69 et seq; Kaye *The New Private International Law* 214 et seq; Rinze JBL (1994) 412, 428, 429; Morse ICLQ 41 (1992) 1, 10, 16, 17; Lasok/Stone *Private International Law* 385.

129 Junker IPRax 1993, 1, 9; Reithmann/Martiny/Martiny *Internationales Vertragsrecht* Rn 744.

130 Staudinger/Magnus Art 34 Rn 30; Morse ICLQ 41 (1992) 1, 16, 17.

131 BT-Drucks 10/504, 83; BGH 26.10.1993 RIW 1994, 154, 157; BGH RIW 1997, 875; 878; von Hoffmann IPRax 1989, 261, 264, 266; Reithmann/Martiny/Limmer *Internationales Vertragsrecht* Rn 428; Lorenz IPRax 1994, 429, 431; Lasok/Stone *Private International Law* 383 et seq; Roth RIW 1994, 275, 277; id *Schnyder/Heiß/Rudisch* 35, 48, 49; Leible JBJZRW (1995) 245, 263; similar Mäsch *Rechtswahlfreiheit* 163.

132 Morse ICLQ 41 (1992) 1, 10, 16, 17; Dicey & Morris *Conflict of Laws Vol II/12th ed* 1295, */13th ed* 1294; Rinze JBL (1994) 412, 429; Junker IPRax 1993, 1, 7, 9; Lorenz RIW

over the normal choice of law rules and follows also from the wording of art 7 (2): 'Nothing in this Convention shall restrict ...'[133] The aforementioned differences in the structure of the provisions justifies the application of art 7 in fields incidentally covered by arts 5 and 6.[134] Internationally mandatory rules under Art 7 (at least those of para (2)) take precedence over the mandatory rules under arts 5 and 6, whereas the mandatory rules under art 5 and 6 take precedence over the mandatory rules of the chosen law, if and to the extent that they are more favourable.[135]

Some advocates of this latter approach restrict their own result by proposing a consideration of the particular interests pursued by arts 5 and 6. Article 7 (2) should be interpreted in the light of the goal to protect weaker parties under arts 5 and 6. Hence, the international mandatory provisions are inapplicable if the foreign rules are more favourable.[136]

f Concluding remarks

Articles 5 and 6 are innovative conflict rules that offer a high level of protection for the weaker party and have no direct counterpart in English and German conflict of laws prior to the Rome Convention.[137] These legal systems had no special multilateral choice of law rule designed to identify the law applicable to consumer or employment contracts and to achieve consumer and employee protection.[138] In the past, freedom of choice of law was recognised in principle, without any special limitations by means of a general conflict rule aimed at protecting the weaker party.[139]

1987, 569, 580; Staudinger/Magnus Art 34 Rn 36; Reithmann/Martiny/Martiny *Internationales Vertragsrecht* Rn 746; Droste *Begriff* 218 with references.

133 See Junker IPRax 1993, 1, 9; Droste *Begriff* 218; Rinze JBL (1994) 412, 429.

134 Rinze JBL (1994) 412, 429.

135 Rinze JBL (1994) 412, 429; Lorenz RIW 1987, 569, 580.

136 Staudinger/Magnus Art 34 Rn 34, 36; Lorenz RIW 1987, 569 580; Kaye *The New Private International law* 214, 215; Dicey & Morris *Conflict of Laws Vol II/12th ed* 1297, */13th ed* 1295; for a parallel discussion regarding the relationship between arts 3(3), 5, 6, see Rinze JBL (1994) 412, 421.

137 Dicey & Morris *Conflict of Laws Vol II/12th ed* 1286, 1302 et seq, */13th ed* 1285, 1303, 1304; Morse ICLQ 41 (1992) 1, 2.

138 Dicey & Morris *Conflict of Laws Vol II/12th ed* 1286, 1302, */13th ed* 1285, 1303, 1304; Anton *Private International Law* 344; Morse ICLQ 41 (1992) 1, 2, 11; Jackson *Contract Conflicts* 59, 70; Lando CMLR 24 (1987) 159, 172, 178; Junker IPRax 1993, 1 et seq.

139 Dicey & Morris *Conflict of Laws Vol II/12th ed* 1286, 1302, */13th ed* 1285, 1303; MünchKomm/Martiny Art 30 Rn 2; Morse *Contract Conflicts* 143, 150; Lando *Contracts* ss 32, 42, 43.

Nevertheless, possible limitations of party autonomy could result from the *principle of evasion of law* (*fraus legis*) if the choice of a foreign law was intended to circumvent important mandatory rules (of the forum).[140] In addition, certain individual mandatory rules of the lex fori were held to be applicable, despite a foreign lex causae, on the basis of public policy or because of their internationally mandatory character.[141] However, these approaches were of a unilateral nature since they concerned only the rules of the forum and not those of another foreign country.[142] In Germany, employee protection rules of a public law nature were subject to the principle of territoriality, and therefore applied irrespective of the proper law designated by the ordinary conflict rules.[143]

II Restriction of party autonomy under the Swiss IPRG

Under the Swiss IPRG party autonomy is statutorily laid down in art 116 (1) of the IPRG. In principle, the parties have a wide freedom to choose any law without limitations, such as the need for a reasonable interest in or an objective connection with the chosen law.[144] However, party autonomy is restricted to international contracts, and is limited in respect of consumer and employment contracts (arts 120 (2), 121 (1), (2) IPRG).

In contrast to the solution found by the drafters of the Rome Convention, where the effect of freedom of choice is limited by the application of mandatory provisions on the basis of the 'more-favourable principle', the Swiss legislature

---

140 *Vita Food Products v Unus Shipping* [1939] AC 277; North *Private International Law Problems* 111 et seq; Hartley *Contract Conflicts* 111, 113 et seq with reference to the Australian case *Golden Acres v Queensland Estates* [1969] St R Qd 378; for Germany, see MünchKomm/Martiny Art 27 Rn 10 et seq.

141 Hartley *Contract Conflicts* 111, 113 et seq with references; MünchKomm/Martiny Art 30 Rn 3; Lando *Contracts* ss 32, 43.

142 For instance, art 27 (2) of the Unfair Contract Terms Act 1977. See also ss 141, 153 (5) of the Employment Protection (Consolidation) Act 1978 as replaced by the Employment Right Act 1996 (s 204); the German Standard Contract Act of 1976; see Carter BYBIL 57 (1986) 1, 10 et seq; Dicey & Morris *Conflict of Laws Vol II/12th ed* 1286, 1302 et seq, */13th ed* 1318; Morse ICLQ 41 (1992) 1, 11. See the Scottish case *English v Donelly* 1959 SLT 2, 6, 7 where the Court of Session held that, despite the choice of English law as the proper law of the agreement, the Scottish Hire Purchase Act was nonetheless applicable.

143 See MünchKomm/Martiny Art 30 Rn 65, 66; Lando CMLR 24 (1987) 159, 178.

144 Von Overbeck *Contract Conflicts* 269, 271; Heini *FS Moser* 67, 68; the former case law had already abandoned the necessity of a *territorial connection* to the chosen legal system, BGE 91 II, 44 et seq; BGE 102 II 143, 145 et seq; for complete freedom of choice, see BGE 111 II 175, 180. However, a *reasonable interest* in the application of the chosen legal system was held to be necessary under pre-existing law; for a survey of pre-existing law, see Schwander *FS Keller* 473 et seq; Lando *Contracts* s 44.

adopted another approach to restricting party autonomy in order to protect the weaker contracting party: The choice is restricted to certain legal systems.

1 Domestic contracts

In contrast to the Rome Convention (art 3 (3)), the Swiss IPRG contains no special rule that limits party autonomy in situations where all other elements of the contract are connected with one country only, despite the choice of law. According to the predominant view in Switzerland, however, it follows indirectly from art 1 (1) of the Swiss IPRG that a choice of foreign law is possible only in international matters, viz. a contract or relationship that has connections with more than one legal system.[145] Hence, in purely domestic contracts the parties' freedom to choose the law applicable to their transaction is reduced to the *ius dispositivum* (incorporation), and the parties are not entitled to contract out of the *ius cogens* of the legal system in which the contract is wholly situated.[146]

2 Consumer contracts

Article 120 (1) and (2) of the IPRG provides as follows:

> (1) Contracts relating to the provision of ordinary goods and services intended for the personal or family use of the consumer and which are not associated with the professional or commercial activities of the consumer shall be governed by the law of the State in which the consumer is habitually resident:
>
> (a) If the supplier received the order in that State; or
>
> (b) If the conclusion of the contract was preceded in that State by an offer or an advertisement and the consumer performed there the necessary act to conclude the contract; or
>
> (c) If the consumer was induced by the supplier to go abroad to place his order there.
>
> (2) A choice of law by the parties is precluded.

145 According to art 1 (1), the Swiss IPRG is applicable to international relationships or matters only; see Schnyder *Das neue IPR-G* 106; Vischer/von Platna *IPR* 175; von Overbeck *Contract Conflicts* 269, 272; critically Schwander *FS Keller* 473, 476 et seq.

146 Schwander *FS Keller* 473, 478; von Overbeck *Contract Conflicts* 269, 272.

Thus, party autonomy is excluded in respect of consumer contracts,[147] provided that there is an additional territorial factor connecting the transaction with the state in which the consumer habitually resides (conditions in para (1), (a) to (c)). The parties to a consumer contract are free to choose the law to govern their agreement if none of the conditions set out in para 1 of art 120 is fulfilled.[148]

3 Employment contracts

Article 121 constitutes a special choice of law rule for employment contracts. In para (3) it provides as follows:

> The parties of the contract can chose the law of the state where the employee has his habitual place of residence, or where his employer has his place of business, habitual residence or domicile.

Art 121 (3) limits party autonomy by restricting the possible choice to four legal systems: the residence of the employee, the employer's place of business, the employer's place of residence, or the employer's domicile.[149] The choice of law of other legal systems is thus excluded.[150]

III The Swiss solution of restricting party autonomy versus the favour principle of the Rome Convention

The Swiss solution of limiting party autonomy to protect the weaker party differs substantially from the solution adopted by the Rome Convention. Whereas the Swiss legislature has completely excluded party autonomy in respect of consumer contracts, the Rome Convention has maintained party autonomy, but restricted the effect of the choice of law by providing for the application of certain mandatory rules of the law where the consumer is habitually resident.[151] The exclusion of party autonomy under Swiss private international law is based on the principle that the consumer should be able to

---

147 Kren ZverglRWiss 87 (1988) 48, 55, 56; von Hoffmann J Cons Policy 15 (1992) 365, 369; Honsell/Vogt/Schneider/Brunner Art 120 Rn 52; additionally, art 120 contains the choice of law rule that, in the absence of a choice of the contracting parties, the consumer contract is governed necessarily by the law of the consumer's habitual residence, see Kren ZverglRWiss 87 (1988) 48, 61.

148 For the detailed conditions, see Honsell/Vogt/Schnyder/Brunner Art 120 Rn 27 et seq.

149 Kren ZverglRWiss 87 (1988) 48, 56; Honsell/Vogt/Schnyder/Brunner Art 121 Rn 42; Junker IPRax 1993, 1, 4.

150 Honsell/Vogt/Schnyder/Brunner Art 121 Rn 42.

151 Kren ZVerglRWiss 87 (1988) 48, 57; von Hoffmann JConsPolicy 15 (1992) 365, 369; Junker IPRax 1993, 1, 7.

rely on the application of the legal system with which he is familiar.[152] The Swiss IPRG does not necessitate a comparison of the protection offered to the consumer by the chosen legal system and the otherwise applicable law, as is required by the favour principle.[153]

The radical solution of the Swiss legislature has been strongly criticised by academic writers.[154] It has been argued that the exclusion of party autonomy goes beyond its protective purpose, as the law of the habitual residence of the consumer may provide less protection than the law of another country.[155] It has also been suggested that completely excluding the freedom of the contracting parties to choose the proper law of their contract creates the impression that the contracting parties are minors.[156]

However, the Swiss solution has the advantage of constituting a relatively clear rule that can be easily applied by judges, since it does not require a complex comparison of different domestic laws.[157] Furthermore, it is not necessary to determine which domestic consumer-protection mandatory laws have to be compared.[158]

Despite the aforementioned differences, there are similarities between the Swiss IPRG and the Rome Convention with regard to the circumstances under which a limitation of party autonomy is reasonable. The sole fact that the consumer is habitually resident in a country does not justify the application of the law or the mandatory provisions of the relevant country. There must be a further contact between the transaction and that country.[159]

With regard to employment contracts, the Swiss solution does not exclude party autonomy totally but limits the choice to four legal systems. In contrast, art 6 (1) of the Rome Convention only limits the effect of party autonomy by means of the favour principle, and thus ensures, as a minimum protection, the application of mandatory rules of the law of the country in which the employee habitually carries out his work.

---

152 Junker IPRax 1993, 1, 7.

153 Kren ZverglRWiss 87 (1988) 48, 57; Erauw *International Contracts* 71, 84.

154 See von Hoffmann J Cons P 15 (1992) 365, 369; Kren ZverglRWiss 87 (1988) 48, 69; *positive* von Overbeck *Contract Conflicts* 269, 272 et seq.

155 Cf von Hoffmann J Cons P 15 (1992) 365, 369, Schnyder *Schnyder/Rudisch/Heiss* 57, 61; Heini *FS Moser* 67, 75.

156 Lorenz RIW 1987, 569, 571; Kren ZverglRWiss 87 (1988) 48, 69.

157 Schnyder *Schnyder/Heiss/Rudisch* 57, 61.

158 Schnyder *Schnyder/Heiss/Rudisch* 57, 61.

159 Von Hoffmann J Cons P 15 (1992) 365, 372; Erauw *International Contracts* 71, 84.

The Swiss solution was criticised for granting the employer the right to determine the law, by choosing the law of his domicile to the disadvantage of the employee.[160] Once a legal system has been chosen in accordance with art 121 (3) of the IPRG, no further protection is offered. It has been argued that the intention of protecting the weaker party cannot be fulfilled by limiting the legal systems that can be chosen, without a consideration of the material content of the domestic rules and the result of their application. It might well be that another law, which cannot be chosen according to art 121 (3) of the IPRG, offers the employee more protection.[161] On the other hand, in contrast to the Rome Convention, there is no need to determine and compare the protective mandatory provisions of different legal systems.

IV Internationally mandatory rules

Party autonomy under the Rome Convention and under the Swiss IPRG is limited by the internationally mandatory provisions of the forum, which are applicable regardless of the chosen proper law of the contract (art 7 (2) of the Rome Convention, art 18 of the IPRG). Party autonomy is also limited by the application or consideration of mandatory laws of legal systems other than the lex causae and the lex fori (art 7 (1) of the Rome Convention, art 19 of the IPRG).[162] Finally, the parties' choice of law is limited by the courts' refusal to apply certain rules of the chosen law because of their public law nature (at least in Germany and Switzerland)[163] and of the public policy of the forum.

However, the application of internationally mandatory rules does not mainly serve to limit party autonomy, but rather limits the scope of the proper law in general. Thus, these rules may 'intervene' in the domain of proper law in cases where the proper law has been determined by the parties' choice, as well as where the proper law has been indicated objectively by the conflict rules of the forum in the absence of a choice.[164] These provisions are dealt with separately in later chapters.[165]

---

160 Junker IPRax 1993, 1, 5; von Overbeck *Contract Conflicts* 269, 274.

161 Heini *FS Moser* 67, 75 with examples and references.

162 Morse YB EurL (1982) 107, 124; Dicey & Morris *Conflict of Laws Vol II/12th ed* 1216, 1217, */13th ed* 1221; MünchKomm/Martiny Art 27 Rn 8; Lorenz RIW 987, 569, 572; Heini *FS Moser* 67, 73 et seq; Siehr *FS Keller* 485, 505 et seq.

163 See infra Chapter 5, I, 2, II, 1.

164 Its strongest effect is still the limitation of the scope of the chosen law, since party autonomy is the primary connecting factor in international law of contracts, cf Lorenz RIW 1987, 569, 572; Coester ZVerglRWiss 82 (1983) 1, 9, 27.

165 See Chapters 3 and 4 infra.

V Evasion of Law (*fraus legis)*

The principle of *evasion of law* needs to be examined in the context of limitation of freedom of choice and the application of mandatory rules.[166]

1 The doctrine of *fraus legis*

The doctrine of *fraude á la loi* in the field of conflict of laws was developed in French family law.[167] Whereas it has found acceptance in the Latin countries in particular, elsewhere 'the fraus legis doctrine is applied only rarely and with certain reluctance'.[168] In Germany the doctrine is known in substantive and private international law and is accepted, subject to strict conditions.[169] In South African private international law the doctrine is also well known and in principle accepted,[170] but cases in point are rare.[171] Although it has often been stated that English private international law has no doctrine of evasion of law, it has nevertheless been recognised as a problem in some areas of law, and has lead to a number of anti-evasion measures.[172]

The general principle of evasion of law covers situations where persons, in order to avoid the *jus cogens* of the normally applicable legal system, 'act ... to create artificial connecting factors which attract to them or their transaction some other system as governing law'.[173] This manipulation of connecting

166 Cf Lando CMLR 24 (1987) 159, 182; id Rec des Cours 189 (1984 VI) 229, 290 et seq; Forsyth *Private International Law* 282; MünchKomm/Martiny art 27 Rn 10, 11; Knüppel *Zwingendes Recht* 39 et seq.

167 See Vischer *Connecting Factors* s 90.

168 Vischer *Connecting Factors* s 92 with references; see also Forsyth *Private International Law* 108.

169 See Firsching/von Hoffmann *IPR* 243; Raape/Sturm *IPR Bd I* 326 et seq.

170 The principle is widely accepted by the old authorities, Huber *De Conflictu Legum* 8, 13; Voet *De Statutis* 9.2.9 excipe 3; Van der Keessel *Praelectiones* 125 - 127; as well as academic writers, Van Rooyen *Die Kontrak* 172 et seq; Forsyth *Private International Law* 107 et seq, 248 et seq, 282.

171 See the famous case concerning a marriage, *Pretorius v Pretorius* 1948 (4) SA 144 (O), and more recently, *Kassim v Ghumran & another* 1981 Zimbabwe LR 227; for further references, see Forsyth *Private International Law* 248 et seq. It appears that there is no case in the law of contract.

172 See Fawcett 49 CLJ [1990] 44 et seq; for instance, the enactment of the anti-evasion provision: sec 27 (2) (a) of the Unfair Contracts Terms Act; also see the dictum of Lord Wright in the leading case *Vita Food Products v Unus Shipping* [1939] AC 277, at page 290 that the intention of the contracting parties must be 'bona fide and legal'.

173 Forsyth *Private International Law* 107; also see Raape/Sturm *IPR Bd I* 326: '...arglistig eine Anknüpfung zu verwirklichen, um die unerwünschten Normen des an sich maßgeblichen Rechts auszuschalten und statt ihrer die günstigeren eines anderen Rechts zum

factors can occur in many ways. For example, the parties may change their nationality, habitual residence or domicile, or place of contracting, thus changing the applicable law, and avoiding certain mandatory rules. The abuse of freedom of choice may indeed be regarded as fraudulent evasion.[174]

If the manipulation of connecting factors has been in *fraudem legis*, the manipulated connecting factor will not operate and the normally (ie without the fraudulent manipulation of a connecting factor) applicable legal system will apply. With regard to mandatory rules, the principle of evasion can thus lead to an application of mandatory rules of the normally applicable law instead of those of the law that the parties intended to apply.[175] The conditions for fraudulent evasion are, firstly, that the change through manipulation of a connecting factor must be effective, and, secondly, the change must be effected with the intention to avoid the application of mandatory rules of the otherwise applicable law.[176] Thirdly, the intention to avoid a law must be viewed as reprehensible by the forum.[177] Such disfavour may result from either the content and importance of the evaded rule, or from the motives for or circumstances of the avoidance.[178] This criterion, based on value considerations, is essential since it distinguishes *avoidance* of the law from *evasion* of the law.[179]

Zuge kommen zu lassen...'; Firsching/von Hoffmann *IPR* 243; Vischer *Connecting factors* ss 90 et seq.

174 See Firsching/von Hoffmann *IPR* 243, 246 - if the parties to a purely domestic contract conclude the contract abroad for the sole purpose of creating an international contract, thus allowing them to choose the applicable law in order to avoid the jus cogens of the sole connection country; MünchKomm/Martiny Art 27 Rn 10; Fawcett 49 CLJ [1990] 44, 48 et seq; Lando Rec des Cours 189 (1984 VI) 229, 290 et seq with regard to weaker party contracts; Forsyth *Private International Law* 282.

175 See Vischer *Connecting factors* s 91; Raape/Sturm *IPR Bd I* 331; Forsyth *Private International Law* 107. There is some disagreement about whether the doctrine of *fraus legis* is to be regarded as a special aspect of public policy, or an independent ground for nullifying the contract. In the latter case, it would be a concrete example of abuse of rights, or justified by the defence of the authority of the law. According to Vischer *Connecting factors* s 91 it is due to this legal basis of *fraus legis* that only fraudulent evasion of the lex fori and not of the law of a foreign country is usually sanctioned.

176 According to Raape/Strum *IPR Bd I* 328 the intention must also be malicious; Firsching/von Hoffmann *IPR* 243; Vischer *Connecting Factors* s 91.

177 Raape/Strum *IPR Bd I* 330; Firsching/von Hoffmann *IPR* 243; see similar North *Private International Law Problems* 112 concerning a fraudulent choice.

178 Firsching/von Hoffmann *IPR* 243; Schurig *FS Ferid* 375, 400 et seq; see similar North *Private International Law Problems* 112 concerning a fraudulent choice.

179 See on this criterion Schurig *FS Ferid* 375, 400 et seq.

2 Evasion of law as limitation of party autonomy?

With regard to freedom of choice and the application of mandatory rules in the international law of contracts, the crucial question about evasion of law is whether a choice of law that was *intended* to *evade* the *ius cogens* of the otherwise applicable law may be invalidated by the doctrine of *fraus legis*.[180]

In the leading English case *Vita Food Products v Unus Shipping*,[181] the parties to a shipping contract had chosen English law as proper law. This choice was upheld by the Privy Council despite the fact that the contract had no connection to England. *Lord Wright* indicated that such a connection was not essential and stated that:

> Where there is an express statement by the parties of their intention to select the law of the contract, it is difficult to see what qualifications are possible, provided the intention expressed is *bona fide* and *legal,* and provided there is no reason for avoiding the choice on the ground of *public policy.*'[182]

This dictum could theoretically prevent all cases of evasion of the law,[183] but, disputes have arisen as to the content of these limitations, since the dictum itself does not indicate under what conditions a choice is *male fide* and not legal.[184] Lord Wright's limitations did not apply to the facts of the case and the parties were thus permitted to evade the Hague Rules. Furthermore, as far as the present author is aware, the choice of contracting parties has never been invalidated by an English court because it was *male fide* and not legal.[185]

---

180 Lando CMLR 24 (1987) 159, 182; id Rec des Cours 189 (1984 VI) 229, 290 et seq; Forsyth *Private International Law* 282.

181 [1939] AC 277, for the facts of the case North *Private International Law Problems* 111.

182 At page 290.

183 Fawcett 49 CLJ [1990] 44, 48; similar Lando Rec des Cours 189 (1984 VI) 229, 290.

184 For the problem of defining the content, see North *Private International Law Problems* 112 et seq; Kaye *The New Private International Law* 52; Dicey & Morris *Conflict of Laws Vol II/11th ed* 1172; Cheshire & North's *Private International Law/11th ed* 453, 454; Collier *Conflict of Laws* 147.

185 See Fawcett 49 CLJ [1990] 44, 48; Dicey & Morris *Conflict of Laws Vol II/11th ed* 1172; in general the Australian case *Golden Acres Ltd v Queensland Estates Pty Ltd* [1969] Qd R 378, 384 is referred to in this context; where a choice of law was struck down on the basis that it 'was made for the specific purpose of avoiding consequences of illegality which would or might have followed if Queensland law applied'. The Court of Appeal applied the Queensland legislation as an overriding statute of the forum. Cf Hartley Rec des Cours 266 (1997) 341, 404; North *Private International Law Problems* 113, 114.

The problem of evasion of law as a limitation on freedom of choice is that in principle there can be no doubt that any choice of law clause will always have the effect of avoiding the otherwise applicable law.[186] It is contradictory to give the parties unrestricted freedom to choose the applicable law (and to avoid mandatory legislation of the otherwise applicable legal system) and at the same time to strike down a choice of law because it is evasive.[187] The crucial question is therefore determining when the accepted intention of the parties to avoid a law becomes an unacceptable evasion.[188] No clear guidance is given, apart from the very general statement that 'avoidance only becomes evasion where the reason for, or the circumstances of, the choice are not acceptable in the eyes of the forum'.[189] It is broadly accepted that the mere intention of the parties to avoid mandatory legislation is not sufficient to disregard the choice of law on the basis of *fraus legis*.[190]

In Germany and Switzerland, it is held that the choice of law cannot itself be *evasive*, subject, however, to the condition that the contract is an international one, viz. apart from the choice of law, it is not wholly located within only one country.[191] The choice of a law unconnected with the contract (*neutral law*) is held to be acceptable, since the parties may have legitimate reasons for submitting their contract to a neutral legal system, provided that the contract has connections with more than one legal system.[192]

Prior to the Rome Convention (art 3 (3)), it was a matter of debate in English law whether a connection to the chosen law was needed and whether a choice of law in purely domestic contracts was permitted. Statements indicate that the common law would have regarded a choice of an unconnected legal system as

186 If the chosen law does not correspond with the objectively determined proper law.

187 See Knüppel *Zwingendes Recht* 41; Raape/Sturm *IPR Bd I* 332; similar Fawcett 49 CLJ [1990] 44, 51; Keller/Siehr *IPR* 383 et seq.

188 Cf similar North *Private International Law Problems* 112; Fawcett 49 CLJ [1990] 44, 50.

189 North *Private International Law Problems* 112; Schurig *FS Ferid* 375, 399 et seq.

190 MünchKomm/Martiny Art 27 Rn 10; Lando Rec des Cours 189 (1984 VI) 229, 293.

191 See Knüppel *Zwingendes Recht* 41; Raape/Sturm *IPR Bd I* 332 with references; this was not the case in RG 21.9.1899 RGZ 44, 300; Keller/Siehr *IPR* 383; MünchKomm/ Sonnenberger Einl Rn 689; MünchKomm/Martiny Art 27 Rn 10 states that *fraus legis* might apply in extreme situations without giving any guidance.

192 MünchKomm/Martiny Art 27 Rn 10, 11; Lando Rec des Cours 189 (194 VI) 229, 286 et seq; id *Contracts* ss 43, 44 with references. The parties may want to submit their contract to the law of the country that dominates the market, or to a legal system which is well developed or well suited to the type of contract, or they may wish to refer to a law which they have used in earlier transactions.

valid, even in purely domestic contracts, based on the assumption that the parties might have reasonable grounds for their choice of another law.[193]

However, it has been submitted that a choice of law may be struck down as evasive if it leads to unfairness or is against national interests.[194] In this case, the doctrine of evasion cannot be based upon the fraudulent manipulation or creation of a connecting factor (eg changing the place of residence, or going abroad to change the place of concluding a purely domestic contract, so that an international contract is created), but upon the fraudulent *abuse* of party autonomy.[195] In a case where avoidance leads to unfairness it is typically only one party to the contract who seeks to evade the law. Where one party is in the stronger economic position there is a risk of no 'genuine' agreement on the choice of the applicable law, since there is often no real freedom of choice for the weaker party.[196] In these cases evasion of law may be objectionable and the doctrine of *fraus legis* may operate as a justified restriction of the parties' freedom to choose the applicable law.[197] Where evasion operates against the national interest, it is held to be objectionable because the content of the law and its underlying policy are being thwarted.[198]

---

193 See Dicey & Morris *Conflict of Laws Vol II/12th ed* 1213, 1214, 1215, */13th ed* 1218; more cautious North Private *International Law Problems* 114 and Carter BYBIL 57 (1986) 1, 10 et seq; critically Cheshire & North's *Private International Law/11th ed* 453, 454.

194 Cf Fawcett 49 CLJ [1990] 44, 51 et seq; similar North *Private International Law Problems* 112 et seq; Lando Rec des Cours 189 (1984 VI) 229, 293 with regard to weaker party contracts.

195 On this distinction, see Coester-Waltjen *FS Lorenz* 297, 316 et seq; Schurig *FS Ferid* 375, 402 et seq; MünchKomm/Sonnenberger Einl IPR Rn 697.

196 Lando Rec des Cours 189 (1986 VI) 229, 294; Fawcett 49 CLJ [1990] 44, 52.

197 Fawcett 49 CLJ [1990] 44, 51, 52. According to Lando an application of the *fraus legis rule* may be justified in weaker party contracts if and to the extent that 'the choice of law by the parties would violate a strong public policy of the otherwise applicable law, and ... the choice is not supported by legitimate interests of international trade', cf id Rec des Cours 189 (1984 VI) 229, 293.

198 Fawcett 49 CLJ [1990] 44, 53 refers to recent anti-evasion provisions such as sec 27 (2) (a) Unfair Contract Terms 1977 or the Carriage of Goods by Sea Act 1971, implementing the Hague-Visby Rules, compare *The Hollandia* [1983] AC 565, 572, 573.

3 Evasion of law under the Rome Convention

Another question arises about the extent to which the doctrine of *fraus legis* can possibly be applied under the Rome Convention regime.[199] As was seen above, the Convention does not contain a *fraus legis* limitation on the parties' freedom of choice, but uses another concept to limit party autonomy: The effect of choice of law is limited by the application of mandatory rules of a law other than the chosen law. In contrast to the doctrine of *fraus legis*, the Convention uses objective criteria to determine under what circumstances and conditions a choice of law is restricted, such as in consumer, employment or purely domestic contracts, or through the application of internationally mandatory rules.[200] The intention of the contracting parties to avoid certain mandatory rules is irrelevant.

Nevertheless, the issue was considered by the drafters, as evidenced by arts 3 (3), 5 (2) and 6 (1) of the Convention which prevent the evasion of mandatory rules of the otherwise applicable law.[201] Party autonomy is to be restricted predominantly on the basis of these statutory conflict rules.[202] There will be little room for invoking the *fraus legis* doctrine under these circumstances. Particularly because the Convention provides for a nearly unfettered freedom of choice, no local connection is required nor is a legitimate interest of the contracting parties necessary. However, the Convention does not eliminate evasion.

The Convention has been criticised for not providing adequate protection to some groups of weak parties. Thus, it might be possible to restrict party autonomy in extreme situations on the basis of the evasion doctrine, if the weaker party is not granted protection under the rules of the Convention.[203] However, the strict conditions of the principle of evasion must be fulfilled. In particular, the manipulation or fraudulent use of a connecting factor must be made with the intention to avoid mandatory rules of the otherwise applicable legal system, and the motives of at least one contracting party and the circumstances of the evasion must be reprehensible in the eyes of the forum.[204]

199 Cf Lando CMLR 24 (1987) 159, 182 et seq; id Rec des Cours 189 (1984 VI) 229, 292.

200 Lando CMLR 24 (1987) 159, 182 et seq; id Rec des Cours 189 (1984 VI) 229, 292; MünchKomm/Sonnenberger Einl IPR Rn 695.

201 See Lando CMLR 24 (1987) 159, 182 et seq.

202 See only MünchKomm/Martiny Art 27 Rn 10, 11.

203 Lando CMLR 24 (1987) 159, 183; id Rec des Cours 189 (1984 VI) 229, 293; MünchKomm/Martiny Art 27 Rn 10; Coester-Waltjen *FS Lorenz* 297, 315 et seq.

204 For details about consumer contracts falling outside the scope of art 5, see Coester-Waltjen *FS Lorenz* 297, 317 et seq.

4 Conclusion and remarks

In conclusion, it can be stated that the doctrine of evasion of law as a limitation of party autonomy has a fairly minor role to play in the private international law of contracts.[205] In general the doctrine of evasion cannot apply if the parties enjoy unfettered freedom of choice of law. It would be contradictory to allow unrestricted party autonomy and at the same time to invalidate a choice of law as evasive. Thus, where a local connection with the chosen legal system or a legitimate interest is not necessary for a valid choice, the intention of the contracting parties to evade thereby the *ius cogens* of the otherwise applicable legal system should not render their choice fraudulent.

However, where the contracting parties manipulate or create a connecting factor, the doctrine of evasion applies and may invalidate a choice of law. An example of such manipulation is going abroad to change the place of concluding a purely domestic contract, so that an international contract is created, which permits the choice of a foreign legal system as the proper law. For the choice of law to be invalidated, the choice must also have been made for the sole purpose of avoiding otherwise applicable mandatory legislation.[206]

Besides this example, the application of the *fraus legis* doctrine to the parties' choice of law is extremely vague, and no clear guidance is given. It might apply to situations where the stronger contracting party 'dictates' to the weaker party the application of a certain law, thereby intending to circumvent restrictive mandatory protection rules. But, the difficulties of determining whether the contracting parties *intend* to evade the *ius cogens* of the otherwise applicable legal system remain.

Additionally, the doctrine bristles with difficulties of definition: Under what circumstances is such an evasion reprehensible and accordingly not acceptable? Such value considerations will largely depend on the importance of the policies pursued by the evaded law.[207]

---

[205] MünchKomm/Sonnenberger Einl Rn 689, 708, 709; Knüppel *Zwingendes Recht* 41 et seq.

[206] Under the Rome Convention the intention of the parties might be to avoid the application of art 3 (3) and thus the application of mandatory rules of the sole connection country.

[207] Cf Schurig *FS Ferid* 375, 399 et seq. Evasion of law has to be distinguished from the application of internationally mandatory rules, which are applicable irrespective of the law governing the contract and independent of the intentions of the contracting parties, although their application is in the interest of the enacting state, cf Dicey & Morris *Conflict of Laws Vol II /11th ed* 1172; MünchKomm/Sonnenberger Einl IPR Rn 695; the Australian case *Golden Acres Ltd v Queensland Estates Pty Ltd* [1969] Qd R 378, 384.

It is the present author's opinion that in the interests of certainty the scope of the *fraus legis* doctrine should be limited to extreme and obvious cases.[208] The doctrine is too uncertain in scope and definition.[209] In addition, *fraus legis* depends on the motives or intentions of the parties, not objective criteria.[210] Finally, it should be mentioned that the small number of reported cases where the doctrine was considered were concerned with evasion or avoidance of the forum's law. To the knowledge of the present author there are no reported cases where a choice of law was invalidated as being *fraudem legis* because of an intention to evade a foreign law.[211]

It is submitted that restriction of party autonomy through the application of mandatory rules under certain conditions is preferable. The use of objective criteria and the development of firm conflict rules promote certainty in law, uphold the expectations of the contracting parties, and are independent of the motives of the parties. Nevertheless, there might be extreme cases where the *fraus legis* doctrine is reasonable. Furthermore, in countries where a system of choice of law rules limiting party autonomy does not exist, the principle might serve as a useful means of pursuing certain substantive law policies, such as protection of the weaker contracting parties, or even state interests, as expressed in mandatory statutes, provided that the fraudulent motives of the contracting parties can be proved.

VI Proposal for South African private international law of contracts on the limitation of party autonomy

In this section it will be discussed whether the South African private international law of contracts should adopt a relatively wide concept of party autonomy, whereby the application of mandatory rules of the otherwise applicable legal system limits the effect of a choice of law, as in the Rome Convention, or whether another means of limiting party autonomy is preferable. The present legal situation in South Africa concerning party autonomy and its limitations in international contracts will be discussed, followed by a proposal

---

208 Forsyth *Private International Law* 282; Coester-Waltjen *FS Lorenz* 297, 318; Schurig *FS Ferid* 372, 403.

209 Forsyth *Private International Law* 282; detailed Fawcett 49 CLJ [1990] 44, 54, 58 et seq.

210 Fawcett 49 CLJ [1990] 44, 58, 59.

211 See North *Private International Law Problems* 113; Vischer *Connecting Factors* s 91; for references of decided cases, Raape/Sturm *IPR Bd I* 331 et seq; in *Golden Acres Ltd v Queensland Estates Pty Ltd* [1969] Qd R 378 the evaded law was both the otherwise applicable legal system and the lex fori.

that the concept of limiting the freedom of choice by application of mandatory rules should be adopted.

1 Party autonomy and its limitations under present South African private international law of contracts

The legal position of party autonomy and its limitations in South African private international law of contracts is to some extent unclear.[212] In particular, it is uncertain whether a choice of law by the parties can appoint an entire body of foreign law to govern the contract, thereby excluding even the *ius cogens* of the otherwise applicable legal system, or whether the choice of law can replace only to a certain degree the *ius dispositivum* (incorporation).[213]

The Roman Dutch authorities, J Voet and Van der Keessel, restricted the freedom of the parties to choose the law applicable to their transaction to the *ius dispositivum* alone.[214] Court judgments, however, indicate an affinity for the acceptance of unlimited party autonomy.[215] One such example is the case of *Guggenheim v Rosenbaum*[216] where the court held that in 'our law the proper law of the contract is the law of the country which the parties have agreed or intended … shall govern it'. A further example is *Improvair (Cape) v Establissements Neu*[217] where the court stated that if there is an express choice, 'there is usually no difficulty in finding that the agreed system constitutes the proper law of the contract'. Finally, in *Laconian Maritime Enterprises Ltd v Agromar Lineas Ltd,*[218] Booysen J stated '[the fact] that our law recognises party autonomy in respect of the proper law of a contract seems clear. Thus where the parties have expressly or impliedly (or tacitly) agreed upon a governing law our courts would give effect to the intention of the parties'.[219]

---

212 For details about this, see Forsyth *Private International Law* 278 et seq; Edwards *Conflict of Laws* par 461; Van Rooyen *Die Kontrak* 67 et seq.

213 See Forsyth *Private International Law* 278 et seq; Edwards *Conflict of Laws* para 461.

214 J Voet *Commentarius* 1.4 App 18 - 22; Van der Keessel *Praelectiones* 143 - 145; see Forsyth *Private International Law* 278.

215 See *Standard Bank of SA Ltd v Efroiken and Newman* 1924 AD 171 at 185-6; *Berman v Winrow* 1943 TPD 213 at 216; *Guggenheim v Rosenbaum (2)* 1961 (4) SA 21 (W) at 31 A; *Pretorious & another v Natal South Sea Investment Trust Ltd* 1965 (3) SA 410 (W) at 417C-H; *Improvair (Cape) v Establissements Neu* 1983 (2) SA 138 (C) at 145 B; *Laconian Maritime Enterprise Ltd v Agromar Lineas Ltd* 1986 3 SA 509 (D) at 525 G.

216 1961 (4) SA 21 (W) at 31 A.

217 1983 (2) SA 138 (C) at 145 B.

218 1986 (3) SA 509 (D).

219 At 525.

However, it has been shown by Van Rooyen,[220] and is stressed by other South African academics,[221] that the courts have never actually had to rule on the limits of the freedom of the parties, in particular whether a rule of the *ius cogens* of the otherwise applicable law can be replaced by a foreign law chosen by the parties. It is noted by these authors that most cases have either centred on rules of the *ius dispositivum*, or the chosen law was also the law which would be applicable in the absence of the parties' choice.[222]

It has been suggested that one of the clearest cases where the *ius cogens* has been at issue was *Commissioner of Inland Revenue v Estate Greenacre*.[223] The case concerned the application of the South African Death Duties Act 29 of 1922 to a marriage agreement. The settlement in question was made by a South African domiciliary, since deceased, in favour of English domiciliaries, and English law had expressly been chosen. The issue before the court was whether the statute's scope of application extended to the settlement even though another law applied by virtue of the chosen proper law of the contract. The court held that the essence of the settlement was English law, in other words, the proper law, and the otherwise applicable law was South African law, but ruled that the settlement did not constitute a *donatio inter vivos* and therefore no death duties were payable.[224] Although the case does not deal explicitly with the *ius cogens*, Mathews AJP stated that:[225]

> The parties could not by contract declare that no provision thereof should render any party thereto liable to obligations … imposed by any union Statute … But the court is entitled to examine the deed to ascertain what were the obligations … and the court can only do that by ascertaining the English law: If the trustees (under the settlement) had … to enforce the covenants this Court would have had to interpret the contract according to the law of England. For example, if interested parties had taken proceedings in Natal to have the deceased's covenant on any ground, this Court would have determined such a matter by the law of England ...

---

220 Van Rooyen *Die Kontrak* 67 et seq.

221 Forsyth *Private International Law* 279, 280; Edwards *Conflict of Laws* para 361; id *'Proper Law' Doctrine* 38, 52, 53.

222 Forsyth *Private International Law* 279, 280; Van Rooyen *Die Kontrak* 67 et seq.

223 1936 NPD 225; see Forsyth *Private International Law* 279, 280; Van Rooyen *Die Kontrak* 69 et seq.

224 Forsyth stresses that the case is in fact concerned with an interpretation of the South African Act as internationally mandatory legislation which is applicable regardless of the proper law of the contract, id *Private International Law* 280.

225 At 229.

In other words, the judge maintains that the parties have chosen English law to govern the contract regardless of whether it is challenged 'on any ground'. Therefore, the South African law is not available as a means of challenging the contract. Consequently, the case provides *obiter* support for the concept of party autonomy in the sense that the otherwise applicable mandatory rules are excluded.[226]

Thus, one can agree with Forsyth that, *de lege lata*, it is not clear as to whether the parties can avoid the *ius cogens* of the otherwise applicable legal system by means of a choice of law. Dicta in case law, however, seem to suggest that the parties' choice may have that effect.[227]

Most academic writers in South Africa seem to favour a wide concept of party autonomy that excludes the *ius cogens* of the otherwise applicable legal system. In other words, the parties' freedom to choose the legal system that will apply to their transaction should not be reduced to an incorporation of facultative norms.[228] This approach is justified by the following considerations: It promotes certainty, lowers transaction costs, avoids the sometimes difficult task of determining the law applicable by reference to various factors, protects justified expectations, and ensures predictability of results and convenience. Furthermore, it serves the parties' need for freedom of contract. The parties might have a reasonable interest in choosing a legal system that has no connection to the contract. The reasons for parties choosing a 'neutral' law could be that the law does not favour either party, it is well developed or dominant in their business field, or the parties are familiar with the law as they have used it before.[229] However, with regard to the limits on the contracting parties' freedom of choice, the academics' approach becomes carefully vague.

Edwards states that the *ius cogens* may allow for the application of mandatory rules to the particular contract. In theory, the degree to which party autonomy and the applicable choice of law may depart from the *ius cogens* of the otherwise applicable legal system is dependent on the 'common law or statute or international Convention prevailing in the *rechtskring* under conside-

---

226 See Forsyth *Private International Law* 280.

227 Forsyth *Private International Law* 280; see also Edwards *Conflict of Laws* para 361.

228 Forsyth *Private International Law* 280; Edwards *Conflict of Laws* para 361; Van Rooyen *Die Kontrak* 72, 73; Viejobueno XXVI CILSA (1993) 172, 190; critically Spiro XVII CILSA (1984) 197 et seq. It seems, however, that Spiro refers to application of (internationally mandatory) public laws of other laws to show that the choice of foreign law does not automatically exclude the *ius cogens* of other laws.

229 See Forsyth *Private International Law* 278, 280; Edwards *Conflict of Laws* para 361 footnote 12.

ration'.[230] He refers to the dictum of Lord Wright in the *Vita Food* case: Contractors are free to select a system with which their contract has no factual connection, provided that the choice is *bona fide*, *legal* and not contrary to *public policy*. He argues that this approach will be authoritative in the domestic courts. However, with regard to South African private international law, he seems to favour the adoption of the *civil law doctrine of evasion* to combat attempts to evade *ius cogens*, where the evasion reflects unfairness in the bargaining position of the contracting parties or is opposed to the national interest.[231] With regard to 'statutes' he refers in particular to mandatory provisions that apply irrespective of the proper law,[232] and with regard to international conventions he refers to the imperative provisions of the Bretton Woods Agreement or the Rome Convention.[233]

Van Rooyen proposes that the effect of party autonomy should be limited by the application of mandatory rules of other legal systems if and to the extent that the *ius cogens* rules claim applicability ('aanspraak maak op gelding'). He maintains that the loss of certainty does not outweigh the disadvantage of not applying the rule.[234] He appears to be referring to internationally mandatory rules that claim application regardless of the proper law of the contract.[235]

Forsyth does not support Van Rooyen's view. He favours a limitation on the doctrine of party autonomy based upon distinctions such as that between 'international or local contracts'. He also favours a limitation of party autonomy in 'weak party' contracts, where the choice of law dictated by the economically stronger part would frustrate the purpose of national mandatory provisions enacted for the protection of the weaker party.[236] It is, however, not quite clear whether party autonomy would be excluded in these contracts, or whether only the effect of the choice would be limited in the sense that parties cannot contract out of the protective *ius cogens* of the otherwise applicable legal system. A further limitation of party autonomy can result from the application of public policy and internationally mandatory rules of the forum and, in very limited

230 Edwards *Conflict of Laws* para 361.

231 Edwards *Conflict of Laws* para 361 footnote 13.

232 Edwards *Conflict of Laws* para 361 footnote 14: for instance, he confirms s 1 (1) (a) of the Carriage of Goods by Sea Act of 1986 that provides that the Hague Visby rules have a mandatory effect in SA.

233 Edwards *Conflict of Laws* para 361 footnote 15. The Rome Convention is held to be a fruitful persuasive source for SA private international law.

234 Van Rooyen *Die Kontrak* 40 et seq, 72, 73, 232; according to Van Rooyen the doctrine of evasion should be limited to formalities, ibid 172 et seq; Forsyth *Private International Law* 281.

235 See also Forsyth *Private International Law* 281, 300 footnote 162.

236 Forsyth *Private International Law* 281.

cases, the rules of a third legal system.[237] Furthermore, Forsyth refers to the doctrine of *fraus legis* as a limitation on the parties' freedom of choice. However, since the scope of the doctrine is uncertain, he advocates the limitation of its application to exceptional cases, to allow for considerations of certainty in law.[238]

To summarise: It can be stated that although South African courts until now have not had to rule on the limits of the freedom of choice, *obiter dicta* in court decisions indicate that South African courts will in principle allow the parties to choose a law to govern their transaction, thereby replacing not only *ius dispositivum* but also the *ius cogens* of the forum state and of the otherwise applicable law. South African academics do not restrict party autonomy to an incorporation of foreign law but favour the acceptance thereof as primary choice. However, there is uncertainty about the limitations on freedom of choice.

2 Proposal

The different solutions proposed by South African authors to restrict party autonomy, and the conflict rules limiting party autonomy in the countries under investigation, as discussed above, are the result of very similar policy considerations. These include the protection of the weaker party in contractual issues, and the need to favour the national interest. As was discussed above,[239] these considerations emanate from a trend during the last century in the domestic law of many countries to intervene increasingly in the private relationship, and to limit party autonomy by enacting mandatory provisions to protect the weaker contracting parties from abuse.[240] All the provisions discussed on the limitation of choice of law in contracts purport to extend this policy to the level of conflict of laws. It is submitted, that for considerations of

[237] The difference towards *Van Rooyens*' approach seems to lye in the willingness to take into account *ius cogens* of legal systems other than the lex fori or lex causae.

[238] Forsyth *Private International Law* 282; see also Van Rooyen *Die Kontrak* 172 et seq who restricts the doctrine to formalities.

[239] See supra Chapter 2, I, 2, a; for SA, see Forsyth *Private International Law* 280, 281; Edwards *Conflict of Laws* para 361 footnotes 13 and 14.

[240] Or to protect national social or economic interests, such as restrictions on the import and export of goods, exchange control regulations, laws for the protection of cultural heritage, etc. Whereas these rules are in general held to be directly applicable statutes of the forum states, and are thus applied regardless of the proper law of the transaction, whether chosen by the parties or objectively determined, the category of rules that protects the weaker party does not necessarily fulfil these criteria. The applicability of mandatory rules of the forum, the lex causae, or even another legal system which claims application regardless of the proper law is dealt with in the following chapter.

certainty and predictability South Africa should also develop statutory or common law conflict rules in this area.

This can be achieved either by excluding party autonomy completely in respect of certain contracts, as Switzerland has done with regard to consumer contracts, or by limiting party autonomy to certain legal systems, as Switzerland has done with regard to employment contracts, or by limiting the effect of the choice by providing mandatory rules of the law which would have been applicable in absence of a choice, as provided in the Rome Convention.[241] The crucial question in this study is the examination of whether the restriction of party autonomy by means of mandatory rules[242] offers an appropriate solution for South African private international law.

With regard to the limitation of party autonomy in order to protect the weaker contracting party, the problem of restricting the effect of the choice of law by the application of certain mandatory rules of the otherwise applicable law is the difficulty of determining and delimiting the mandatory protection rules of the legal systems, both those of the chosen law and those of the otherwise applicable legal system. In addition, comparing the protective rules of the legal systems is a difficult task. Articles 5 and 6 of the Rome Convention do not indicate whether the comparison should be concerned with particular provisions, or with a group of norms, or with the legal system as a whole; in other words, whether the comparison should be concrete or abstract.

The original aim of the 'more-favourable principle' was to guarantee minimum protection to the weaker party. According to arts 5 (2) and 6 (1) of the Rome Convention, the minimum protection standard was that granted by the law which is applicable in the absence of a choice. However, applying the most protective rules of the chosen law and the otherwise applicable law to a consumer contract on a 'pick and choose' basis can lead to the undesirable result of the consumer in international contracts being afforded greater protection than in a domestic contract, where only one system of law is applicable. This problem does not arise where the freedom to choose the applicable law is completely excluded or is restricted to particular legal systems for certain contracts. In these cases, either the parties cannot contract out of the otherwise applicable legal system, or they can freely choose between a small number of legal systems.

241 Junker IPRax 1993, 1, 4; Kren ZverglRWiss 87 (1988) 48, 55; Hartley *Contract Conflicts* 111, 113; see arts 5 (2), 6 (1) RC, arts 120, 121 IPRG.

242 Arts 3 (3), 5 (2) and 6 (1) RC.

However, the advantage of limiting only the *effect* of the choice of the parties by providing for the application of mandatory laws of other legal systems is that party autonomy itself is not restricted. Party autonomy, with all its merits, is thereby preserved as a connecting factor in the international law of contracts. Furthermore, the favour principle provides far-reaching protection for the consumer and the employee, because he is not restricted to the law of his habitual residence (that might offer him even less protection than the chosen law). Lastly, it offers a broader freedom to the contracting parties to determine the applicable legal system and allows them to predict their obligations and rights.

The major disadvantages of the restriction on the freedom of choice itself are as follows: Either the parties cannot contract out of the otherwise applicable legal system, even though the chosen law might offer greater protection for the weaker party, or the stronger contracting party may be permitted to choose at least the less protective law of the enumerated legal systems. This runs counter to the policy on which the limitation of free choice is based. Therefore, the limitation of the effect of the choice, rather than the limitation of the choice itself, or the restriction of the choice to a small number of legal systems, is the preferable option in restricting party autonomy.

In contrast to the 'more-favourable principle', the doctrine of *fraus legis* does not offer sufficient protection for the weaker party. It has been shown that the doctrine is of doubtful value in the international law of contracts - which is the true domain of party autonomy. Apart from its vagueness and the difficulties that arise because of its dependence on the subjective *intention* of the contracting parties, it is of minor relevance in areas where party autonomy and not only incorporation of foreign law is permitted. This is because one of the major effects of party autonomy is that the contract is subjected to the chosen law, including its *ius cogens*, with the exclusion of those rules of the otherwise applicable law.

To apply the doctrine of evasion to cases where 'unfairness' is alleged, it would have to be shown that (1) certain mandatory rules of the otherwise applicable law are evaded by the choice of law; (2) the choice was made with the intention to circumvent these rules; and (3) the intention to avoid the *ius cogens*, and the circumstances and effect of the choice are reprehensible in the eyes of the forum. This process of evaluation is extremely vague and it has been shown above that no clear guidance is provided. The doctrine of evasion thus leads to uncertainty, and also cannot offer sufficient protection to the weaker party in international law, since it depends on vague and subjective criteria.

For these reasons, it is submitted that South Africa should adopt the 'favour principle' as a means of limiting the parties' freedom to choose the applicable law in weaker party contracts. For this purpose the choice of law rules in arts 5 and 6 of the Rome Convention could be adopted. They are well established in European countries and they offer appropriate protection to consumers and employees.

Nevertheless, it must be conceded that the favour principle also has disadvantages: Difficulties arise in determining which sets of rules are to be compared and in deciding which law offers the greater protection. It will be necessary for the judge to examine both the rules of the law of the consumer's habitual residence and the rules of the chosen law in order to decide which law is more favourable.

The Rome Convention has been criticised for offering only partial protection for certain contracts. It is argued that there are other kinds of contract, where one party is typically in a weaker bargaining position, that are not afforded special protection under the Convention.[243] To protect the weaker party from abuse by the stronger party it is possible to create special statutory or common law conflict rules for other contracts where one party is typically in the weaker bargaining position so that the stronger party cannot avoid the national protection afforded to the weaker party via a favourable choice of law. Such special choice of law rules should take into account and balance the interests of the contracting parties of the special type of contract and find appropriate connecting factors.

Alternatively, it is also possible to create a general, broad choice of law rule that ensures the protection of the weaker party. Such a choice of law rule might read as follows:

> A choice of law made by the parties in contracts where one party is typically in the weaker bargaining position shall not have the result of depriving the weaker party of the protection afforded to him by the mandatory rules of the otherwise applicable law.

It must be remembered, however, that special protection on the level of conflict of laws is not always justified in 'weaker party' contracts, nor is a restriction of party autonomy in *any* situation in an international setting reasonable.[244] For each international contract, the protection of the weaker party has to be care-

243 Lando Rec des Cours 189 (1984 VI) 229, 292, 293; id CMLR 24 (1987) 159, 183.

244 See for instance art 5 (2) RC where party autonomy is limited when there is a special connection to the country of the consumer's habitual residence.

fully balanced with the need for the contracting parties' freedom of choice. Special protection for the weaker party should be provided only where strong social and political policy considerations demand such protection, even at the level of conflict of laws, and where these policy considerations were frustrated by allowing the parties the freedom to choose another law to govern their contract.

Chapter 3
Internationally mandatory rules

The previous chapter dealt with the limitation of party autonomy by the application of mandatory provisions. It has thus been seen that, in various contexts, mandatory rules play a major role when applying the principle of party autonomy. The examination, however, focused on a relatively new trend in the private international law of contracts: While the parties' freedom to choose the applicable law is unlimited, special conflict rules have been created that limit the *effect* of the choice of law by the application of mandatory rules of the objectively applicable law. Mandatory rules have thus become a modern tool to limit party autonomy. Although, as was seen these special conflict rules reflect a change from the traditional allocation technique, which was neutral and blind, towards a more result-selecting process, they still operate within traditional choice of law techniques. The technique of 'alternative connection' or 'optional connection' to a legal system (or to certain rules) based on the so-called 'more-favourable principle', is well known to conflict lawyers.[1]

The following chapters, by contrast, are concerned with the question of when 'internationally mandatory rules' are applied in the international law of contracts by the court of the forum state: In what circumstances and on what juristic basis? This is an issue that is older in origin, broader in scope, and has a stronger effect on the choice of law process than the one discussed in the previous chapter.

In probably all legal systems there are certain rules of substantive law that, in view of their special nature and purpose, claim application regardless of the law applicable according to the normal choice of law rules, and are thus exceptions to the normal choice of law rules.[2] As has already been noted in the Introduction, Savigny, founder of today's traditional allocation technique, became aware of this phenomenon and excluded certain mandatory rules from his multilateral choice of law system. He held that due to their special nature and substantive content these rules are opposed to the principle of interchangeability of laws, which is the very basis of his multilateral choice of law system.[3]

---

1 Cf Vischer Rec des Cours 232 (1992 I) 13, 116 et seq.

2 See also Vischer Rec des Cours 232 (1992 I) 13, 153, 162; Philip *Recent Provisions* 241, 242; Dicey & Morris *Conflict of Laws Vol I/12th ed* 21, 23, */13th ed* 16. 21; Hartley Rec des Cours 266 (1997) 341, 346, 347; Schwander *IPR AT* 329.

3 Savigny *System des heutigen Römischen Rechts Vol VIII* 32; for criticism of this argument, see Schurig RabelsZ 54 (1990) 217, 229; see more detailed Chapter 1.

Conflict lawyers and judges in many countries maintain that the application of internationally mandatory rules deserves special treatment in private international law.[4] Some have held that these rules fall outside the scope of private international law, or at least outside the scope of the reference of the ordinary conflict rules, and are thus exceptions to the ordinary choice of law process. Others have advocated the development of a separate, additional choice of law system that will indicate under what circumstances internationally mandatory rules are to be applied. Yet others restrict themselves to the application of the ordinary conflict rules, thus submitting internationally mandatory rules to the ordinary choice of law process, with the proviso that internationally mandatory rules of another law may still be applied or taken into account, regardless of the proper law.

Furthermore, the application of these rules creates problems not only with regard to party autonomy and its limitations, but also in cases where the applicable law has been determined by the forum's conflict rules, in the absence of a choice of law. These rules are intended to override the ordinary choice of law process and may consequently limit the scope of the proper law in general.[5] Thus, it is evident that the application of internationally mandatory rules touches on the most basic methodical foundations of private international law.[6]

How to treat these norms in the private international law of contracts, and how to integrate them with the ordinary rules on choice of law, is an extremely controversial and difficult task, one that has been disputed in Continental Europe for more than 60 years.[7] The problem has therefore been labelled the

---

4 See, for instance, Schurig RabelsZ 54 (1990) 217, 220, 226, 229; Lorenz RIW 1987, 569, 579; Drobnig RabelsZ 52 (1988) 1, 3; Basedow RabelsZ 52 (1988) 8 et seq; MünchKomm/Sonnenberger Einl Rn 34 et seq; Vischer Rec des Cours 232 (1992 I) 13, 153 et seq; Hartley Rec des Cours 266 (1997) 341, 346; most of the approaches will be dealt with in Chapter 5, I.

5 Schurig RabelsZ 54 (1990) 217, 220; Lorenz RIW 1987, 569, 572; Fawcett 49 CLJ [1990] 44, 58; Cheshire & North's *Private International Law/12th ed* 499, */13th ed* 578.

6 Drobnig *FS Neumayer* 159, who states that the 'special connection' of 'interventionist norms' affects the methodical foundations of private international law; Vischer also states that 'the dichotomy between the normally applicable law and "lois d'application immédiate" is a fact', cf id Rec des Cours 232 (1992 I) 13, 162, 166; Voser *Lois d'application immédiate* 1 et seq, 50 et seq; De Boer RabelsZ 54 (1990) 24, 61; in contrast, see Schurig RabelsZ 54 (1990) 217 et seq. According to him this results from a misunderstanding of the choice of law system of private international law, which he holds is necessarily open to new developments, and may be altered or broadened by the creation of new choice of law rules, taking into account the different interests involved.

7 See the early approaches of Wengler ZVerglRWiss 54 (1941) 168 et seq; Zweigert RabelsZ 14 (1942) 283 et seq; for the parallel tendency in the Netherlands at that time,

'darling of the topics',[8] the 'last frontier of Conflicts Law',[9] and the 'battleground of the opinions'.[10]

As far as English law was concerned the principle of mandatory rules overriding the choice of law process was introduced by the Rome Convention. Under the pre-existing case law, no distinction was made between the application of mandatory rules and public policy.[11] Nevertheless, the problems surrounding the application of internationally mandatory rules were well known and were dealt with under the notions of public policy, illegality, essential validity, or with reference to certain English statutory rules (overriding statutes).[12]

As a result, there is a large body of academic writing about this issue. Particularly in the 1980s, during and after the Rome Convention negotiations, large numbers of academic studies were generated.[13] Despite the debates and

---

see Schultzs RabelsZ 47 (1983) 267 et seq with references; Lipstein Rec des Cours 135 (1972 I) 99, 204 describes it as the 'interplay between ordinary rules of Private International law and unilateral self-limiting rules of domestic law'.

8 Lorenz RIW 1987, 569, 578.

9 Junker JZ 1991, 699.

10 Schurig RabelsZ 54 (1990) 217, 234.

11 See, for instance, Hartley Rec des Cours 266 (1997) 341, 346 footnote 4; Jackson *Contract Conflicts* 59, 70; Cheshire & North *Private International Law/12th ed* 137, 496.

12 See the cases of *Grell v Levy* (1864) 10 CB (NS) 73; *Boissevain v Weil* [1950] AC 327; [1950] 1 All ER 728; *Foster v Driscoll* [1929] 1 KB 470 (CA); *Regazzoni v KC Sethia* [1958] AC 301; cf Lipstein ICLQ 26 (1977) 884 et seq; id Rec des Cours 135 (1972 I) 99, 195, 204 et seq; Collins ICLQ 25 (1976) 35, 49; Fawcett 49 CLJ [1990] 44, 57; Dicey & Morris *Conflict of Laws Vol II/11th ed* 1170 et seq; Jackson *Contract Conflicts* 59, 62.

13 See amongst others Anderegg *Ausländische Eingriffsnormen* (1989); Basedow RabelsZ 47 (1983) 147 et seq; id RabelsZ 52 (1988) 8 et seq; id GYB Int L 27 (1984) 109 et seq; Baum RabelsZ 53 (1989) 152 et seq; Coester ZverglRWiss 82 (1983) 1 et seq; Coing WM 1981, 810 et seq; Drobnig *FS Neumayer* 159 et seq; id RabelsZ 52 (1988) 159 et seq; Erne *Vertragsgültigkeit* (1985); Forsyth *The role of public law* 94 et seq; Gamillscheg ZfA 14 (1983) 307 et seq; Hartley *Foreign Public Laws* 13 et seq; id (1979) 4 ELR 236 et seq; Heini ZSR 100 I (1981).65 et seq; Hentzen RIW 1988, 508; Jackson *Contract Conflicts* 59; Junker IPRax 1989, 69 et seq; Kegel *FS Seidl-Hohenveldern* 243 et seq; id *The Rôle of Public Law* 29 et seq; Kleinschmidt *Anwendbarkeit* (1985); Knüppel *Zwingendes Recht* (1988); Kratz *Ausländische Eingriffsnorm* (1986); Kreuzer *Schlechtriem/Leser* 89 et seq; id *Ausländisches Wirtschaftsrecht* (1986); Lehmann *Zwingendes Recht* (1986); id ZRP 1987, 319 et seq; Lipstein Rec des Cours 135 (1972 I) 99 et seq; id *Conflict of Public Laws* 357; id *Conflict of laws and public law* 38 et seq; id *Öffentliches Recht* 39 et seq; id ICLQ26 (1977)884 et seq; Lorenz RIW 1987, 569 et seq; Mann *FS Beitzke* 607; id *FS Wahl* 139; id Rec des Cours 132 (1971 I) 107 et seq; Martiny IPRax 1987, 277 et seq; Mülbert IPRax 1986, 142; Philip *Contract Conflicts* 81 et seq; id *Recent Provisions* 241; Radtke ZVerglRWiss 84 (1985) 325 et seq; Schubert RIW 1987,

the fact that at least in Germany and Switzerland 'the "claims" are marked out and the drafts are presented',[14] the issue is still controversial and unsettled.[15] Decided cases on the topic are relatively rare. Nevertheless, cases will arise, especially, given the tendency of the modern welfare state to intervene to an ever increasing extent into private relationships and judges will have to solve the dichotomy between the normal choice of law process and mandatory rules claiming application to the transaction.[16]

Over time, rules claiming application regardless of the governing law have been variously labelled by academic authors. In Germany and Switzerland they have usually been discussed under the term '*Eingriffsnorm*' ('interventionist rule'), which was created by Neuhaus.[17] Even today this is the predominant designation,[18] along with the characterisation as 'internationally mandatory rules' (*international zwingende Bestimmungen*). The expressions '*lois d'application immédiate*' ('rules of immediate application') and '*lois de police*', developed by French scholars,[19] are well known in most countries. Other scholars have labelled the norms '*selbstbegrenzte*' ('self-limited') or '*selbstgerechte Sachnormen*' ('self-righteous rules of substantive law').[20] Some authors use the

---

729; Schurig *Lois* 55 et seq; Siehr RabelsZ 52 (1988) 41 et seq; Schwander *Lois* (1975); Sonnenberger *FS Rebmann* (1989) 819 et seq; Vischer RabelsZ 53 (1989) 438 et seq.

14 See Junker JZ 1991, 699, 700.

15 Recent publications include Becker *Theorie* (1991); Becker RabelsZ 60 (1996) 691 et seq; Busse ZVerglRWiss 95 (1996) 386 et seq; Droste *Begriff* (1991); Hartley Rec des Cours 266 (1997) 341 et seq; Leible JBJZRW 1995, 245 et seq; Mäsch *Rechtswahlfreiheit* (1993); Mentzel *Sonderanknüpfung* (1993); Morscher *Rechtssetzungsakte* (1992); Schäfer *FG Sandrock* 37 et seq; Schiffer ZVerglRWiss 90 (1991) 390 et seq; Schurig RabelsZ 54 (1990) 217 et seq; Remien RabelsZ 54 (1990) 431et seq; Zimmer IPRax 1993, 65 et seq; Vischer Rec des Cours 232 (1992 I) 13, 150 et seq; Voser *Lois d'application immédiate* (1993); Ungeheuer *Beachtung* (1995).

16 In the field of international arbitration, too, the arbitrator is increasingly confronted with the application of internationally mandatory rules, see Voser 7 Am Rev Int'l Arb 319 (1996), LEXIS NEXIS p 3 of 38.

17 *Die Grundbegriffe des IPR* (1962) 58; but see Siehr RabelsZ 52 (1988) 41, 42 who mentions that the term Eingriffsnorm emanates from Neumayer *Internationales Verwaltungsrecht* IV (1936) 244 et seq.

18 Kreuzer *Schlechtriem/Leser* 89, 90; Coester ZVerglRWiss 82 (1983) 1, 4; MünchKomm/ Martiny Art 34 Rn 9; Siehr RabelsZ 52 (1988) 41 et seq; Schurig RabelsZ 54 (1990) 217, 228; Busse ZVerglRWiss, 95 (1996) 386, 388; Droste *Begriff* 4; Lorenz RIW 1987, 569, 578; Kropholler *IPR* § 3 II 1; Schubert RIW 1987, 729 et seq; Erne *Vertragsgültigkeit* 4; Ungeheuer *Beachtung* 5.

19 They originate from Phocion Francescakis *La théorie du renvoi* 4; id Rev dir int priv proc 3 (1967) 691, 695, see Voser *Lois d'application immédiate* 1; also see Lipstein ICLQ 16 (1977) 884, 896.

20 Kegel *Die selbstgerechte Sachnorm* 51, 53.

term '*politische und wirtschaftspolitische Gesetze*' ('political and politico-economic laws') or simply '*öffentliche rechtliche Normen*' ('public law rules').[21] Others allocated the internationally mandatory rules to the so-called '*internationale öffentliche Recht*' ('*Public Conflict of Laws*' or '*International Public Law*')[22] or to the '*internationale Verwaltungsrecht*' ('*International Administrative Law*').[23] More recently, these norms were discussed as part of a new branch of law, the '*Wirtschaftskollisionsrecht*' ('*International Commercial Law*').[24] In the United Kingdom, they are dealt with under the designation 'public laws',[25] 'overriding statutes',[26] or mandatory provisions in *a conflict sense*, in contrast to mandatory rules in *a domestic sense*.[27] As a result of the wide-ranging negotiations that led to the Rome Convention, the term 'internationally mandatory rules' became more common among signatories to the Rome Convention.[28]

Article 7 (1) and (2) of the Rome Convention contains provisions dealing with the application of internationally mandatory rules, despite the proper law of the contract. Similar provisions can be found in arts 18 and 19 of the Swiss IPRG. Article 7 (2) of the Rome Convention and article 18 of the Swiss IPRG enable the forum state to apply its own *lois d'application immédiate*. Article 7 (1) of the Rome Convention and article 19 of the Swiss IPRG concern the application or consideration of internationally mandatory rules of *third* countries, despite the proper law of the contract. In addition, art 13 (3) of the Swiss IPRG

---

21 Schiffer *Normen* 28; Morscher *Rechtssetzungsakte* 3; see for further designations Kreuzer *Schlechtriem/Leser* 89, 91; Schurig *Lois* 55, 56 et seq.

22 BGH 17.12.959 BGHZ 31, 367, 370 et seq; BGH 18.2.1965 BGHZ 43, 162, 165; BGH 16.4.1975 BGHZ 64, 183, 188 et seq; Kegel *The Rôle of Public Law* 29 et seq; Mann Rec des Cours (1971-I) 115, 118, 119.

23 Kegel *IPR* § 1 VII 1. B), § 2 IV, § 23; MünchKomm/Sonnenberger Einl Rn 5, 38, 355 et seq; Mann Rec des Cours (1971-I) 115, 120.

24 Schubert RIW 1987, 729, 731; Schnyder *Wirtschaftskollisionsrecht* (1990); see Drobnig, Basedow, Siehr RabelsZ 52 (1988) 1 et seq, 8 et seq; 41 et seq.

25 Cf Lipstein *Conflict of laws and public law* 38, 40 et seq; Forsyth *The role of public law* 94 et seq.

26 Morris *Statutes* 187 et seq; Dicey & Morris *Conflict of Laws Vol I/12th ed* 21 et seq, */13th ed* 16, 21 et seq; Cheshire & North's *Private International Law/11th ed* 466 et seq, */13th ed* 579.

27 Jackson *Contract Conflicts* 59 et seq; also see Kaye *The New Private International Law* 242 et seq who distinguishes between contract-mandatory rules, half- and full-conflict-mandatory rules. For a distinction between mandatory rules in a wider and narrower sense, or internationally and domestically mandatory, cf Hartley Rec des Cours 266 (1997) 341, 345; Cheshire & North's *Private International Law/12th ed* 498, */13th ed* 578.

28 See Droste *Begriff* 143; Staudinger/Magnus Art 34 Rn 55; MünchKomm/Martiny Art 34 Rn 7, 9; Reithmann/Martiny/Martiny *Internationales Vertragsrecht* Rn 387; Hartley Rec des Cours 266 (1997) 341, 346; North *Contract Conflicts* 3, 19; Philip *Contract Conflicts* 81, 82.

provides for the scope of application of the proper law, as indicated by the normal choice of law rules, and thus to some extent regulates the question of the applicability of internationally mandatory rules arising from the proper law of the contract, an issue that is not expressly regulated in the Rome Convention.

Both these approaches will be explained, compared and discussed.

I The application of internationally mandatory rules: Three issues

The general proposition in conflict of laws is that the normal choice of law rules (be they the subjective choice of law of the parties or the objective conflict rules) refer to the applicable legal system, including its mandatory legislation, thereby replacing - within the scope of the relevant conflict rule - the *ius dispositivum* and the *ius cogens* law of the forum state and the otherwise applicable law.[29]

There are exceptions to this general rule. Depending upon the country in which the rules originate three issues must be examined when considering internationally mandatory rules:[30]

(1) Do the internationally mandatory rules of the forum state intrude into the foreign *lex causae* and override the normal choice of law process?

(2) Are all mandatory rules belonging to the proper law applicable, for the sole reason that they belong to the proper law? In other words, the scope of reference of the normal conflict rules to the proper law of the contract is at issue. The applicability of internationally mandatory rules of a public law nature or rules that serve the public interests of the foreign enacting state, has been heavily debated in Switzerland and Germany, as well as in other continental Europe countries.

(3) The main subject of controversy is whether internationally mandatory rules of a *third* legal system, which is neither the *lex causae* nor the *lex fori*, can and should be considered or applied: the situation envisaged in art 7 (1) of the Rome Convention and art 19 of the Swiss IPRG.

---

[29] Amongst others MünchKomm/Martiny Art 34 Rn 24; Dicey & Morris *Conflict of Laws Vol I* 21; Philip *Recent Provisions* 241, 242, 244; id *Contract Conflicts* 81, 92, 93.

[30] For this differentiation, see MünchKomm/Martiny Art 34 Rn 2, 3, 19 et seq; Staudinger/Magnus Art 34 Rn 1, 13 et seq; Anderegg *Eingriffsnormen* 7 et seq; Radtke ZVerglRWiss 84 (1985) 325, 332; Busse ZVerglRWiss 95 (1996) 386, 390 et seq.

These three issues will be examined as follows: The application of internationally mandatory rules of the forum state will be discussed in Chapter **4**, and the application or consideration of foreign internationally mandatory rules in Chapter **5**.

The following section describes the characteristics of internationally mandatory rules and the problems of identifying and distinguishing them.

II Characterising, identifying and distinguishing internationally mandatory rules

One of the major difficulties with internationally mandatory rules is identifying them distinguishing them from rules that are mandatory only in a domestic setting.[31] Two aspects can be identified: a *formal* aspect meaning the peculiarity of the rules overriding the choice of law process by claiming application (whatever the proper law according to the normal conflict rules) and a *material* aspect meaning their content. The material aspect is of particular interest where the statute does not expressly indicate the international reach of a mandatory rule. If this meaning has to be deduced from an interpretation of the statute, then the material aspect becomes all important as the formal aspect does not assist with identifying the rule as international.[32]

Generally speaking English academics do not set out to distinguish internationally mandatory rules from those that are mandatory only in a domestic setting. They usually restrict themselves to a statement that the former are not so much concerned with settling disputes between the parties, but rather represent the interests and policies of the state, ie seek to protect either groups or the national economic system.[33] Examples provided are rules designed to protect the weaker party of a contract, such as consumers or employees, or rules that are

---

[31] Vischer Rec des Cours 232 (1992) 13, 154, 157 et seq; De Boer RabelsZ 54 (1990) 24, 61; MünchKomm/Sonnenberger Einl 35 et seq; see also Fawcett 49 CLJ [1990] 44, 60.

[32] MünchKomm/Sonnenberger Einl Rn 45, 46; MünchKomm/Martiny Art 34 Rn 92; Staudinger/Magnus Art 34 Rn 54; Cheshire & North's *Private International Law/12th ed* 499 et seq, */13th ed* 578 et seq.

[33] See Hartley ELR 4 (1979) 236, 238 et seq; Fawcett 49 [1990] 44, 60; Jackson *Contract Conflicts* 59, 60, 65, 66; Morris *Statutes* 187 et seq describes simply the term overriding statute (at 194) and gives examples (200 et seq); also see Forsyth *The Role of public law* 94 et seq; Cheshire & North's *Private International Law/12th ed* 496 et seq, */13th ed* 578 et seq; Plender *Contracts Convention* 9.11 et seq; for a critical approach, see Mäsch *Rechtswahlfreiheit* 142 footnote 83; cf, however, Lipstein ICLQ 26 (1977) 884, 897, 898 and id *Conflict of Laws and public law* 38, 40 et seq for an attempt to identify these rules as 'public law rules'.

based on socio- or economic-political considerations, such as exchange control regulations, price control regulations, rules on antitrust practices, or import and export restrictions.[34] Hartley suggests that this approach may be because the distinction between mandatory rules that are applicable only as part of the proper law and those that apply regardless of the applicable law is 'fairly new in the private international law systems of the English speaking world'.[35]

In contrast, German and Swiss academics have tried for a long time to define those mandatory rules that claim application regardless of the proper law of the contract (thus requiring special consideration during the choice of law process).[36] Unlike England, where it is broadly accepted that the mandatory rules of the proper law are applicable no matter whether international or domestic, and no matter whether of a private or public law nature, many German and Swiss authors have assumed that certain rules do not fall within the scope of reference to the foreign law. They therefore have had to define which rules these are.

Finding a uniform all-embracing definition has, however, proved to be an extremely difficult task, because a universal definition is expected to cover many different kinds of rules.[37] Furthermore, the whole discussion lacks clarity since terms appear to have different meanings: On the one hand, too many terms have been used for the same phenomenon, and, on the other, the same term has been chosen for different meanings. A good example is the German and Swiss designation '*Eingriffsnorm*' ('*interventionist norm*'). Some authors restrict this designation to rules that serve interests that go beyond those of the parties, others use the term in a broader sense, including the socio-politically motivated rules that serve the interests of the contracting parties.[38]

---

34 Hartley (1979) 4 ELR 236, 238; Cheshire & North's *Private International Law/12th ed* 496, 499 et seq; */13th ed* 576 et seq; Fawcett 49 CLJ [1990] 44, 46; Dicey & Morris *Conflict of Laws Vol I/12th /13th ed* 21 et seq.

35 Hartley Rec des Cours 266 (1997) 341, 346 footnote 4; Hartley himself states that these rules 'serve purposes outside the traditional ambit of contract law'.

36 See the representation of the different German approaches in MünchKomm/Martiny Art 34 Rn 9 et seq; Schurig RabelsZ 54 (1990) 217, 226 et seq; Mäsch *Rechtswahlfreiheit* 135 et seq; for Switzerland Voser *Lois d'application immédiate* 58 et seq.

37 Reithmann/Martiny/Limmer *Internationales Vertragsrecht* Rn 389.

38 Voser *Lois d'application immédiate* 63; MünchKomm/Martiny Art 34 Rn 13; von Hoffmann IPRax 1989, 261 et seq; Staudinger/Magnus Art 34 Rn 60.

It has been proposed that interventionist norms should be discussed *in the original sense* and in *a wider sense*.[39] This distinction has its merits because it differentiates on the basis of the meaning of the term 'interventionist norm'. Nevertheless, the creation of new designations for the same phenomenon and the imprecise treatment of settled definitions are unfortunate. It leads to uncertainty in an area of law that is already necessarily vague and indefinite.

Lastly, it must be borne in mind that a general definition must cover rules that have their origins in different legal systems - the *lex fori*, the *lex causae* and a third country - and that the interest of the forum in applying these rules differs according to their origin. These differences, however, should not be allowed to obstruct the development of a general and uniform definition. Such an achievement would serve the choice of law objective of *uniformity of result* and *decisional harmony*.[40] Therefore, the question of a universal criterion for definition or classification has to be separated from the question of whether and how a certain statutory or common law rule is applied by the court of the forum state. The latter question remains one that is to be settled by the forum's conflict rules.[41]

1 The *formal* criterion: Internationally mandatory rules as unilateral conflict rules

Article 7 (1) and (2) of the Rome Convention and arts 18 and 19 of the Swiss IPRG refer to internationally mandatory rules by providing that the rule of the enacting country must be applied regardless of the law applicable to the contract.[42] From a choice of law perspective, these rules claim application irrespective of the proper law. Some authors state that these rules contain a so-called '*conflict legal application or interventionist order or command*' ('*Kollisionsrechtlicher Eingriffsbefehl oder Anwendungsbefehl*') for application.[43] However, this does not mean that these rules apply without any prior choice of law rule indicating their application, as the designation *lois*

---

39 Voser *Lois d'application immédiate* 64; Vischer RabelsZ 53 (1989) 438, 440, 445; Anderegg *Ausländische Eingriffsnormen* 3 et seq, 143 et seq.

40 Staudinger/Magnus Art 34 Rn 55.

41 Staudinger/Magnus Art 34 Rn 55, 114; MünchKomm/Sonnenberger Einl Rn 58. The question of when and under what circumstances foreign internationally mandatory rules are applied or given effect to will be investigated in Chapter 5.

42 MünchKomm/Martiny Art 34 Rn 6, 7; Reithmann/Martiny/Limmer *Internationales Vertragsrecht* Rn 390; Soergel/von Hoffmann Art 34 Rn 12; Jackson *Contract Conflicts* 59, 66; North *Contract Conflicts* 3, 19; Schwander *IPR AT* 252; Vischer Rec des Cours 232 (1992) 13, 154, 168, 169.

43 Cf Lorenz RIW 1987, 569, 578; Junker IPRax 1989, 69, 73; Vischer Rec des Cours 232 (1992) 13, 156, 157.

d'application immédiate would suggest.[44] The 'application order' is a unilateral conflict rule that is attached to the substantive law rule determining its scope or reach. In other words, the substantive law rule has to be intellectually complemented by a unilateral conflict rule, which then determines under what conditions the rule is applicable.[45]

The specific feature of this kind of attached unilateral conflict rule is that it indicates under what circumstances a particular substantive law *rule* is applicable, rather than specifying when the legal *system* of which it forms part is applicable to a certain legal question.[46] The attached unilateral conflict rule can arise from an express term of the substantive rule or, alternatively, if the rule does not express a spatial ambit, from an interpretation of the rule. The substantive rule then has an implied unilateral conflict rule.[47] Thus, generally speaking, internationally mandatory rules are not subject to the ordinary conflict rules. Their scope of application is determined by means of their special unilateral choice of law rule, irrespective of the law applicable according to the normal rules of private international law.[48]

However, the formal classification does not assist in identifying what kinds of rules override the choice of law rules if the rule does not contain an express term indicating its scope of application and the spatial ambit therefore has to be determined by considering the purpose of the statute.[49] Determining the scope by interpreting a statute is extremely difficult and is described as being akin to the process of creating new legislation.[50]

---

44 See Vischer Rec des Cours 232 (1992) 13, 156; Schurig *Lois* 55,63; for a contrasting opinion, see Morse *Public Policy* England - 17.

45 See Vischer Rec des Cours 232 (1992) 13, 156; for details, see Schurig *Kollisionsnorm* 57 et seq; id *Lois* 55, 63 et seq; see also Hartley Rec des Cours 266 (1997) 341, 347, 348; this in fact corresponds with the English description of overriding statutes, see Morris *Statutes* 187, 194, 200 et seq; Forsyth *The Role of Public law* 94, 96 et seq; Lipstein ICLQ 26 (1977) 884 et seq, 900.

46 Vischer Rec des Cours 232 (1992) 13, 156; Hartley Rec des Cours 266 (1997) 341, 347; Forsyth *The role of public law* 94, 97. According to Schurig this distinction is a false one: Any choice of law refers to rules of law, some to a bound set of rules, some to singular provisions, id *Lois* 55, 61 et seq.

47 Amongst others Hartley Rec des Cours 266 (1997) 341, 348.

48 Hartley Rec des Cours 266 (1997) 341, 348.

49 Schurig RabelsZ 54 (1990) 217, 228; Staudinger/Magnus Art 34 Rn 56; also see the examination by Vischer Rec des Cours 232 (1992) 13, 157 et seq.

50 Coester ZVerglRWiss 82 (1983) 1, 17; Lorenz RIW 1987, 569, 578; also see Vischer Rec des Cours 232 (1992) 13, 155 and Forsyth *The role of public law* 94, 96.

2 The *material* criterion: The purpose of the rule

In general, internationally mandatory rules are rules that intervene into private relationships, either by requiring action, by making a particular provision obligatory, or by prohibiting specified conduct. They thus serve the economic or socio-political interests of the enacting state, which are interests that go beyond the private interest of settling a dispute between the contracting parties.[51] In Germany and Switzerland, different solutions have been proposed to distinguish internationally mandatory rules from mandatory rules that are subject to the proper law of the contract.[52]

Before discussing the approaches, it must be noted that it is primarily the legislature's responsibility to attach a unilateral conflict rule to a rule or set of rules determining their territorial scope. Accordingly, all rules containing an express term indicating their territorial scope are internationally mandatory, if the conditions under which they claim application are fulfilled.[53]

a Time of enactment of the rule

Whether the rule existed already at the time the contract was concluded or whether it was enacted afterwards is irrelevant to the classification of a rule as internationally mandatory.[54]

b The distinction between public law and private law

It has been convincingly argued that the classification of a rule as being of a public or private law nature is unhelpful for distinguishing internationally

---

51 For instance, the definitions of Erne *Vertragsgültigkeit* 4, 12; Radtke ZverglRWiss 84 (1985) 325, 328; Hartley ELR 4 (1979) 236, 237; id Rec des Cours 266 (1997) 341, 346 rules that 'serve purposes outside the traditional ambit of contract law'; Schulte *Eingriffsnormen* 13 et seq, 18; Schiffer *Normen* 30, 31; Fawcett 49 CLJ [1990] 44, 60; Schäfer *FG Sandrock* 37, 39; for further references, see MünchKomm/Sonnenberger Einl Rn 39.

52 MünchKomm/Martiny Art 34 Rn 11; MünchKomm/Sonnenberger Einl Rn 35, 39 et seq; Voser *Lois d'application immédiate* 58 et seq.

53 See MünchKomm/Sonnenberger Einl Rn 45; Staudinger/Magnus Art 34 Rn 52; Vischer Rec des Cours 232 (1992) 13, 155.

54 This was proposed by Wengler RabelsZ 47 (1983) 248; but see Radtke ZVerglRWiss 84 (1985) 325, 328; MünchKomm/Martiny Art 34 Rn 17; Kreuzer *Ausländisches Wirtschaftsrecht* 10.

mandatory rules.[55] The public / private distinction emanates from the domestic law distinction in continental Europe, where public law is concerned with rules regulating the legal relationship between the state and the individual, while private law is concerned with the relationship between individuals.[56] This distinction has been transported by German and Swiss case law and by some academics into the realm of private international law. As a result, it has been generally held that private international law refers only to rules of private law. Public law rules fall out of the scope of the usual conflict rules and are subject to a different choice of law process, viz. they have to be connected separately.[57] The result of this approach is that the public law rules of the forum state will be always preserved whereas those of a foreign legal system, whether of the proper law or of a third legal system are in principle inapplicable.[58]

As will be seen in a later stage of this study, this approach has been rejected by most authors, and has been partly rejected or at least functionally modified by Swiss and German courts.[59] Although it is true that many internationally mandatory rules are public law rules, the distinction between public and private law is of no use in classifying internationally mandatory rules. The distinction has generally been rejected because the boundaries between public and private law are permeable and result from specific historical circumstances.[60] The distinction has already resulted in many difficulties in substantive law.[61] Moreover, the dichotomy between public and private law is based on the continental European peculiarity of a divided jurisdiction for administrative and

---

55 See MünchKomm/Sonnenberger Einl Rn 38; detailed von Bar *IPR Bd I* Rn 252 et seq; Siehr RabelsZ 52 (1988) 41, 75, 76, 91; MünchKomm/Martiny Art 34 Rn 11; Staudinger/Magnus Art 34 Rn 65.

56 In Germany, Switzerland and France this is a basic distinction in law, eg von Bar *IPR Bd I* Rn 252; the public/private law distinction is also well known in South Africa, see Cockrell 1993 *Acta Juridica* 227 et seq; for a comparison of this distinction in various countries, see Lipstein *Conflict of Laws and public law* 38 et seq; also see Philip *Contract Conflicts* 81, 88, 89.

57 Kegel *Die Rolle des Öffentlichen Rechts* 243 et seq; for Switzerland see Honsell/Vogt/Schnyder/Mächler-Erne Art 13 Rn 12; also see Philip *Contract Conflicts* 81, 85, 89.

58 Philip *Contract Conflicts* 81, 85.

59 See Voser *Lois d'application immédiate* 66; 68; MünchKomm/Martiny Art 34 Rn 11; for a differentiation, see the German Federal Supreme Court BGHZ 31, 367, 370; BGHZ 64, 183, 189 and the Swiss Federal Tribunal Court in BGE 80 II 53, 62.

60 MünchKomm/Martiny Art 34 Rn 11; Staudinger/Magnus Art 34 Rn 65; Lorenz RIW 1987, 569, 578; Radtke ZVerglRWiss 82 (1984) 325, 328; Busse ZVerglRWiss 95 (1996) 385, 388 et seq; also see Mäsch *Rechtswahlfreiheit* 135.

61 Busse ZverglRWiss 95 (1996) 385, 389.

civil disputes that is not found in other legal systems.[62] Internationally mandatory rules are of both a public and private law nature.[63]

Furthermore, such a distinction is not supported by the Giuliano/Largarde Report or by the German legislative reasons for art 34 EGBGB, the German equivalent of art 7 (2) of the Rome Convention.[64] In Switzerland the legislature has expressly rejected a differentiation based on the public or private law character of a rule by enacting art 13 (3) of the Swiss IPRG: The application of a foreign rule is *not excluded by the mere fact* that it is supposed to be of a *public law character.*[65]

c Interests and purposes pursued by the rule

Nevertheless, the distinction between public and private law has constituted the starting point of German and Swiss judgments. As a second step, however, the distinction has been refined to a more *functional* approach: Those public law rules that serve primarily the realisation of the economic and political interests of the state have to be distinguished from rules that predominantly serve the fair reconciliation of the interests of individuals.[66] The latter rules are applicable according to the principles of private international law, while the former are subject to public international law. If the former rules belong to the *lex fori*, they are in principle applicable, but if they emanate from a foreign legal system, they are inapplicable.[67]

---

62 Radtke ZVerglRWiss 82 (1984) 325, 328; Busse ZVerglRWiss 95 (1996) 385, 389; MünchKomm/Sonnenberger Einl Rn 5; Drobnig RabelsZ 52 (1988) 1, 3; Jackson *Contract Conflicts* 59, Forsyth *The role of public law* 94.

63 For examples, see Chapter 4, III.

64 BT-Drucks 10/504, 83; Lorenz RdA 1989, 220, 222; Kegel's opposing opinion (see in *Schlechtriem/Leser* 111 and *FS Seidl-Hohenveldern* 243, 275) that art 7 refers only to mandatory rules of a private law nature does not go conform with the wording of art 7 nor with the Report of *Giuliano/Lagarde* in *Contract Conflicts*, who give examples of both private and public law rules, such as rules on cartels, competition and restrictive practices, consumer protection and certain rules concerning carriage (on page 382); on this point of view, see MünchKomm/Martiny Art 34 Rn 11.

65 For a full explanation of art 13 of the Swiss IPRG, see Chapter 5, IV, 4.

66 Federal Supreme Court BGHZ 31, 367, 370 et seq; BGHZ 43, 162, 165; IPRespr 1962/63 Nr 163 (525); IzRspr 1964/65 Nr 56 (231); BGHZ 64, 183, 189; BGHZ 128, 41, 52; Federal Tribunal Court BGE 80 II 53, 61, 62; BGE 82 I 196, 197 et seq; BGE 95 II 109, 114; BGE 107 II 489, 492.

67 According to the German Federal Supreme Court the public law rules fall out of the scope of reference of the proper law; however, it has to be noted that with regard to those rules that serve private interests this conclusion is an interpretation of German academics. As will be seen later, one may easily interpret the German case law as stating that those rules serving the private interests of a third legal system are applicable.

The predominant academic opinion advocates, in accordance with the German and Swiss case law,[68] a demarcation that follows the *purpose and interest* pursued by a specific regulation. However, the pre-condition that the rule must be of a public law nature is abandoned. A mandatory rule can be classified as an '*interventionist norm*' (viz. internationally mandatory) if the rule intervenes in a private relationship in the *public interest, in particular, in the state's economic and political interest.* If the regulation predominantly serves to *reconcile the interests of the contracting parties*, it is subject to the general conflict rules and the proper law of the contract.[69] Thus, the 'private' or 'public' nature of a rule is not relevant to its classification as internationally mandatory, but its purposes and the interests pursued.[70] Some authors therefore classify these rules as *functionally* public law rules.[71]

Other authors attempt to distinguish interventionist norms from domestic mandatory rules by using the vague criterion of the rule's 'relevance to ordering society' ('*Ordnungsrelevanz*').[72] A rule is an *interventionist norm* if the legislature's intention in enacting the rule was to regulate the general economy and society.[73] In contrast, a 'neutral law' serves the interests of the contracting parties in settling the dispute.[74]

d Concluding remarks

In general it can be stated that there is unanimity that rules pursuing economic and state-political interests, such as import and export controls, exchange control and currency regulations, and antitrust law, are internationally

---

68 See the previous footnotes.

69 MünchKomm/Martiny Art 34 Rn 12; Kropholler *IPR* § 3 II, § 52 VIII 1; Radtke ZVerglRWiss 84 (1985) 325, 328; Staudinger Magnus Art 34 Rn 57; Schiffer *Normen* 30, 31; Anderegg *Ausländische Eingriffsnormen* 88; Schubert RIW 1987, 729, 731; Kratz *Ausländische Eingriffsnorm* 1; Sandrock/Steinschulte *Handbuch* A Rn 88, 89; Vischer RabelsZ 53 (1989) 438, 440, 445; cf also the recent cases BAG 24.8.1989 IPRax 1991, 407, 411; BAG 29.10.1992 IPRax 1994, 123, 128; for criticism, see Schurig RabelsZ (1990) 217, 228; Mäsch *Rechtswahlfreiheit* 136; Lorenz RIW 1987, 569, 579.

70 *Direction of the impact of law* (Stoßrichtung des Gesetzes), cf MünchKomm/Martiny Art 34 Rn 12.

71 Voser *Lois d'application immédiate* 63; Schiffer *Normen* 30, 31.

72 Rehbinder JZ 1973, 151, 156 'social, economic- and company order private law'; Sonnenberger *FS Rebmann* 819, 823 et seq; MünchKomm/Sonnenberger Einl Rn 34, 39 et seq; Drobnig RabelsZ 52 (1988) 1, 3; Basedow RabelsZ 52 (1988) 8, 12, 18 et seq; Voser *Lois d'application immédiate* 58, 62 et seq.

73 See Basedow RabelsZ 52 (1988) 8, 18; for criticism, see Mäsch *Rechtswahlfreiheit* 142.

74 Voser *Lois d'application immediate* 58 et seq; MünchKomm/Sonnenberger Einl Rn 36.

mandatory rules.[75] However, a '*grey zone*' of rules has a '*double function*' and serves both the interests of the contracting parties and those of the state.[76] In particular, the socio-politically motivated rules of a private law nature - for example, rules that protect tenants, consumers and employees - are problematic.[77] One opinion is that these socio-politically motivated rules are internationally mandatory rules in the sense of art 7 of the Rome Convention and of arts 18 and 19 of the Swiss IPRG.[78] Others exclude these rules from the category of internationally mandatory rules, since they predominantly serve the fair reconciliation of the interests of the parties.[79]

The existence of this '*grey zone*' illustrates the weakness of the approaches discussed above. Frequently, from either starting point (distinction with reference to the purpose and interests pursued by the rule or with reference to its *Orndungsrelevanz*) the same rule is either considered as a rule that exclusively serves the reconciliation of the parties' interests or as a rule that also serves the public interest.[80]

Under present law, the question of definition is connected with the need to distinguish the scope of art 7 of the Rome Convention and arts 18 and 19 of the IPRG from special conflict rules dealing with employment and consumer contracts.[81] This is evidenced by the fact that the protection of tenants is frequently regarded as internationally mandatory, while consumer protection is

---

75 Amongst all MünchKomm/Sonnenberger Einl Rn 47; MünchKomm/Martiny Art 34 Rn 10; Vischer Rec des Cours 232 (1992) 13, 157 et seq; Schubert RIW 1987, 729, 730 et seq; Voser *Lois d'application immédiate* 58 et seq; Soergel/von Hoffmann Art 34 Rn 3.

76 Mäsch *Rechtswahlfreiheit* 135 et seq; MünchKomm/Sonnenberger Einl Rn 8 et seq; Voser *Lois d'application immédiate* 62, 63.

77 For details Chapter 4, III, 2, a; MünchKomm/Sonnenberger Einl Rn 48; Kropholler *IPR* § 3 II 3.

78 Von Hoffmann RabelsZ 38 (1974) 407 et seq; Soergel/von Hoffmann Art 34 Rn 4; Firsching/von Hoffmann *IPR* 414 et seq; Busse ZverglRWiss 95 (1996) 385, 388, 392 N 22; Siehr RabelsZ 52 (1988) 42, 48; Schnyder *Wirtschaftskollisionsrecht* 10, 13; Erne *Vertragsgültigkeit* 6.

79 Radtke ZVerglRWiss 84 (1985) 325, 328, 329; Schubert RIW 1987, 729, 731; Schiffer *Normen* 30, 31; MünchKomm/Sonnenberger Einl Rn 48, 54, who distinguishes between those rules that serve predominantly or only the interests of the parties and those that also serve public interests; also see Vischer Rec des Cours 232 (1992) 13, 157 et seq; id RabelsZ 53 (1989) 438, 440, 445, Voser *Lois d'application immédiate* 58 et seq.

80 With regard to consumer and lessee protection, see Schubert RIW 1987, 729, 731 (only mandatory in a domestic sense) and, on the other hand, Anderegg *Eingriffsnormen* 94.

81 With regard to arts 5 and 6 RC, see Junker IPRax 1998, 65, 69; id IPRax 1993, 1 et seq; Martiny ZEuP 1995, 67, 84; for arts 120 and 121 Swiss IPRG, cf Vischer RabelsZ 53 (1989) 438, 449, 450, 458; id Rec des Cours 232 (1992) 13, 159; Schwander *IPR AT* 246; Voser *Lois d'application immédiate* 58 et seq.

held to be nationally mandatory, despite the fact that both types of protective rules pursue private interests - the protection of the weaker contracting party - and national interests.[82]

The general conclusion to be drawn from these difficulties is that no universal criterion can be found to delimit internationally mandatory rules from those that are mandatory in a domestic sense.[83] The current approaches simply provide guidelines. If a rule serves both public and private interests, it is a matter of degree as to which interests are *predominantly* served. The judge will have to interpret every provision with reference to its content, policy and the predominant interests. In addition, he will have to decide whether the interests pursued by the rule are of such importance that it must be applied regardless of the proper law of the transaction.

Recent statements omit a general definition of the content of the rule since it has been realised that a universal definition is not possible.[84] In order to determine whether a rule is internationally mandatory or mandatory in a domestic sense, authors refer to the formal criterion laid down in art 7 of the Rome Convention: the claim to apply irrespective of the law governing the contract. Internationally mandatory are therefore rules that contain a 'conflict legal interventionist order' or an attached (implied or express) unilateral conflict rule indicating their territorial scope.[85] It is submitted, however, that this definition *describes* the phenomenon, rather than providing useful criteria that indicate under what conditions a mandatory rule is internationally applicable.[86]

---

82 Cf Mäsch *Rechtswahlfreiheit* 135 et seq; MünchKomm/Sonnenberger Einl Rn 49; MünchKomm/Martiny Art 34 Rn 16; Sonnenberger *FS Rebmann* 819, 823; Voser *Lois d'application immédiate* 58 et seq.

83 Also see De Boer RabelsZ 54 (1990) 24, 61; MünchKomm/Sonnenberger Einl Rn 36.

84 Lorenz RIW 1987, 569, 578; id RdA 1989, 220, 222, 227; Busse ZVerglRWiss 95 (1996) 387, 389; Becker RabelsZ 60 (1996) 691, 693; Junker IPRax 1989, 69; 73; id JZ 1991, 699, 700 N 3; Taupitz BB 1990, 642, 649; von Bar *IPR Bd I* Rn 256 et seq.

85 Junker IPRax 1989 69, 73; Lorenz RIW 1987, 569, 578; Taupitz BB 1990, 642, 649.

86 For criticism see Schurig RabelsZ 54 (1990) 217, 228; Mäsch *Rechtswahlfreiheit* 143.

Chapter 4
Internationally mandatory rules of the lex fori

It is a well established rule in the private international law of all the countries under investigation that the internationally mandatory rules of the *lex fori* apply, regardless of the legal system that governs the transaction according to the normal conflict rules.[1] It has also been accepted that the application of directly applicable or overriding statutes is an exception to the general rule that a statute does not normally apply unless it is a procedural rule of the *lex fori* or unless it forms part of the proper law.[2] The reason for the application of the directly applicable rules of the forum state is the simple fact that a judge cannot, by relying upon party autonomy or the objective choice of law rules, disregard mandatory rules that are applicable to the situation in question and are intended to override the normal choice of law rules. The judge is bound by his sovereign.[3]

The reservation of the internationally mandatory rules of the forum is embodied in art 7 (2) of the Rome Convention and art 18 of the Swiss IPRG, provisions that no more than accept the pre-existing law. Under pre-existing law, however, the applicability of these internationally mandatory rules was based upon different structural or methodological reasoning. A discussion of these approaches follows.

I Methodological approaches

Under pre-existing law the application of the forum's internationally mandatory rules, despite a foreign proper law, was based either upon the forum's *ordre public*, or alternatively upon the overriding nature of a certain substantive law rule, or sometimes simply upon its nature as a public law rule.[4]

---

1 Lipstein *Conflict of Law and public law* 38, 46; id *Conflict of Public Laws* 357, 361, 364; Forsyth *The role of public law* 94, 95 et seq; Vischer Rec des Cours 232 (1992) 13, 155 et seq; id RabelsZ 53 (1989) 438, 445; MünchKomm/Martiny Art 34 Rn 89; Zweigert ZVerglRWiss 54 (1941) 173 et seq.

2 MünchKomm/Martiny Art 34 Rn 24; Dicey & Morris *Conflict of Laws Vol I/12th /13th ed* 21; Philip *Recent Provisions* 241, 242, 244; Morris *Statutes* 187, 200, 201.

3 See art 20 (3) Grundgesetz (Constitutional Law of the Federal Republic of Germany); MünchKomm/Martiny Art 34 Rn 89; Anderegg *Ausländische Eingriffsnormen* 3; Forsyth *The role of public law* 94, 95.

4 See in this regard Jaffey ICLQ 23 (1974) 1, 3, 15 et seq; Knüppel *Zwingendes Recht* 43 et seq; Schulte *Eingriffsnormen* 49 et seq; MünchKomm/Martiny Art 34 Rn 89; Hartley Rec

1 Positive function of *ordre public*

One possible reason for allowing a mandatory rule of the forum to intrude into a foreign *lex causae* is the *ordre public*.[5] This approach is based on the understanding that the *ordre public* has not only a broadly accepted negative function, viz. the refusal to apply foreign law in so far as the result of such application would be repugnant to the fundamental principles of the forum state, but also a so-called '*positive function*'. The positive function leads to application of the forum's mandatory rules despite a foreign *lex causae*.[6]

According to some academic authors internationally mandatory rules are *special statutory expressions of the ordre public*.[7] Similarly, in England overriding statutes have often been called *crystallised rules of public policy*.[8] However, it is not clear whether these authors are saying that the application is a result of the positive function of public policy, or whether they simply want to stress that in order to classify a certain rule as having an overriding effect the rules must pursue fundamental policies of the forum state. Forsyth states that 'the same wariness that attends the application of that principle [public policy] should attend the classification of a statute as overriding'.[9]

The designation as crystallised rules of public policy may also result from the fact that English law, outside the Rome Convention, did not distinguish between the public policy refusal and the application of mandatory rules.[10] Additionally, it seems that at least in the situation where a contract, valid under its proper law, violates English public policy, the application of the English public policy rule leads to the application of English law. Thus, even in

---

des Cours 266 (1997) 341, 351, 388; Honsell/Vogt/Schnyder/Mächler-Erne Art 18 Rn 4; Mann Rec des Cours 132 (1971 I) 109, 123 et seq.

5 Radtke ZVerglRWiss 84 (1985) 325, 330; MünchKomm/Martiny Art 34 Rn 89; Knüppel *Zwingendes Recht* 43 et seq; Raape/Sturm *IPR I* 200; Hartley Rec des Cours 266 (1997) 341, 351; Vischer Rec des Cours 232 (1992) 13, 165.

6 Firsching/von Hoffmann *IPR* 250; Kropholler *IPR* § 36 I; Knüppel *Zwingendes Recht* 43 et seq; Hartley Rec des Cours 266 (1997) 341, 351; Raape/Sturm *IPR I* 200 N 13; for details Schwander *Lois* 41 et seq.

7 See Raape/Sturm *IPR I* 212, 213; in particular *Mann* advocates to apply mandatory rules of the forum on the basis of the positive *ordre public*, id *FS Beitzke* 607, 611, 615. Cf for references MünchKomm/Martiny Art 34 Rn 89; Honsell/Vogt/Schnyder/Mächler-Erne Art 18 Rn 4; Schwander *Lois* 41 et seq.

8 Forsyth *The role of public law* 94, 100; Morris *Statutes* 187, 203; Dicey & Morris *Conflict of Laws Vol I/12th /13th ed* 24.

9 Forsyth *The role of public law* 94, 100.

10 Hartley Rec des Cours 266 (1997) 341, 346 Footnote 4; Jackson *Contract Conflicts* 59, 70.

situations where the negative function of public policy is applied to exclude foreign law that is repugnant to some fundamental policies of the forum state, the *lex fori* is applied because the foreign law is declared inapplicable.[11]

The public policy doctrine has been used to ensure the application of English mandatory common law rules regardless of a foreign proper law.[12] Accordingly, English courts have by reference to the doctrine of public policy refused to enforce contracts, although valid under their foreign proper law, on basis of the common law rules that champertous contracts,[13] contracts in restraint of trade[14] or contracts involving trading with the enemy[15] are illegal. One may also refer in this context to a certain group of decisions which have held, by reference to the notion of English public policy, that contracts that prejudice the good relations of the United Kingdom with foreign and friendly countries are illegal.[16]

The English attitude contrasts with German and Swiss law, where at least lip service is paid to the notion that the only consequence of applying the forum's *ordre public* is that the foreign law is not applied to the extent that it violates the notion of *ordre public*. The 'gap' resulting from the partial exclusion of the foreign law does not lead to application of the rules of the *lex fori.* Instead, it must be closed primarily by the means offered by the applicable foreign legal system or the choice of law technique of 'adaptation' ('*Anpassung*' or '*Angleichung*'). The latter is in Germany and Switzerland to solve the problem what law to apply to cases where at least two different legal rules apply

---

11 Morse *Public Policy* England - 10 and 17; cf also Hartley Rec des Cours 266 (1997) 341, 387, 388. This conclusion is often not expressly drawn, but it seems that it is too obvious to English authors to be stated. See the representation of the English public policy rule in Dicey & Morris *Conflict of Laws Vol I/12th ed* 88 et seq, */13th ed* 81 et seq and id *Vol II/12th ed* 1277 et seq, */13th ed* 1276; Cheshire & North's *Private International Law/12th ed* 128 et seq, */13th ed* 123 et seq, 583.

12 See Jaffey ICLQ 23 (1974) 1, 15 et seq; 18; see also, although less explicit, Morris *Statutes* 187, 201; Dicey & Morris *Conflict of Laws Vol I/12th /13th ed* 23; Hartley Rec des Cours 266 (1997) 341, 351.

13 *Grell v Levy* (1864) 10 CB (NS) 73; for details about this decision, see Morse *Public Policy* England - 64, 65; Hartley Rec des Cours 26 (1997) 341, 399 et seq.

14 *Rousillon v Rousillon* (1880) 14 Ch D 351; see on this case Morse *Public Policy* England - 64; Jaffey ICLQ 23 (1974) 1, 16.

15 *Dynamit A/G v Rio Tinto Co* [1918] AC 260, at 292, 294, see Morse *Public Policy* England - 64; Mann Rec des Cours 132 (1971 I) 109, 125; Cheshire & North's *Private International Law/12th ed* 132, */13th ed* 127.

16 See Cheshire & North's *Private international Law/12th ed* 131, 132, */13th ed* 127 with reference to *Foster v Driscoll* [1929] 1 KB 470, *Regazzoni v KC Sethia (1944) Ltd* [1958] AC 301 and other court decisions; the principle was referred to more recently in *Royal Boskalis Westminster NV v Mountain* [1999] QB 674; cf also Chapter 5, III, 2.

simultaneously to the same issue ('cumulation') or to cases where no law is applicable ('gap').[17]

Nevertheless, the positive function of public policy has been supported by some academics and has been occasionally invoked by judges to apply German mandatory legislation.[18] The Supreme Court of the German Reich for instance applied the German 'Hire Purchase Act' (Abzahlungsgesetz, AbzG, as now replaced by the 'Consumer Credit Act', VerbrKrG) as a result of the positive function of the *ordre public,* despite the proper law of the hire purchase contract being that of the Netherlands.[19] The Federal Supreme Court of Germany has also occasionally applied mandatory rules of the forum by means of the positive *ordre public*.[20]

2 '*Special connection*', '*lois d'application immédiate*', 'overriding statutes'

Alternatively, the forum's internationally mandatory rules have been applied despite a foreign proper law, on the basis of the characterisation of a rule as an overriding statute, as *lois d'application immédiate* or as an *interventionist norm* (*Eingriffsnorm*) by means of a '*special connection*' (*Sonderanknüpfung*).

This methodological approach has been referred to above in the context of identifying internationally mandatory rules and distinguishing them from the

---

17 Knüppel *Zwingendes Recht* 44 with further references to case law and literature; Sandrock/Steinschulte *Handbuch* Rn A 181; MünchKomm/Martiny Art 34 Rn 31; Kropholler *IPR* § 36 V; Schulte *Eingriffsnormen* 49, 51; sceptically, however, Firsching/von Hoffmann *IPR* 251; Keller/Siehr *IPR* 546, 457; Schwander *Lois* 43. In general, adaptation means that in cases of cumulation or gap, in order to avoid contradictions, the judge is permitted to (1) either alter or 'adapt' the substantive law rules (*materiellrechtliche Lösung*) or, (2) shift or alter the scope of application of certain conflict rules or create a new conflict rule for the situation in question (*internationalprivatrechtliche Lösung*). On the problem of adaptation, its content and possible solutions, see in general Kegel *IPR/7th ed* § 8; also see Bennett 105 III (1988) SALJ 444 et seq.

18 See footnote 7.

19 RG 28.3.1930 JW 1932, 591; Raape/Sturm *IPR I* 213. This decision has been criticised as extreme, it was seriously doubted that the non-application of the AbzG would infringe substantial principles of German law, cf Droste *Begriff* 20; Mann *FS Beitzke* 607, 612.

20 See the case law with regard to §§ 764, 762 German Civil Code (BGB) in terms of which certain wagering transactions are not binding; the BGH applied §§ 764, 762 despite the proper law of the contract on grounds of the *ordre public* BGH 25.5.1981 NJW 1981, 1898; but the BGH overruled precedents and would not apply the *ordre public* with regard to this norm BGH 26.2.1991 WM 1991, 576, for details Droste *Begriff* 18, 19; for references Sandrock/Steinschlute *Handbuch* Rn A 142; MünchKomm/Martiny Art 34 Rn 31.

domestic mandatory rules.[21] It is based on an assumption that every state has enacted certain rules that cannot be subordinated to the ordinary choice of law rules, but are applicable regardless of the proper law of a transaction.[22] When a rule does not expressly specify its territorial scope, the statute has to be interpreted to determine whether it was the intention of the legislature that the rule should be applied regardless of a foreign proper law.

This approach differs in method from the former solution, as the application of the mandatory rule in question is based upon its own express or implied claim to apply. It is called an overriding statute, *lois d'application immédiate*, or - with regard to the choice of law process - *special connection*, because these rules apply independently of the normal conflict rules; they are *leges specialis*.

Nevertheless, and importantly, according to this approach these rules form, at least in theory, part of the choice of law process for determining the applicable legal system, whereas the *ordre public* applies only *after* the choice of law process has been followed and the proper law has been determined.[23]

It needs to be reiterated at this point that, in theory, this approach does not result in the existence of a different, third, kind of rule, alongside the internal substantive law rules and the standard choice of law rules. It is no more than a synthesis of both rules: a rule of substantive law to which a unilateral choice of law rule is expressly or impliedly attached.[24] It is therefore not correct, as is sometimes maintained, that the *lois d'application immédiate* are immediately applicable, *without any* prior choice of law rule leading to their application.[25] They are applicable because they contain an '*interventionist-*' or '*application-order*'(*Eingriffs-* or *Anwedungsbefehl*), viz. an express or implied unilateral choice of law rule which overrides the standard choice of law rules.[26]

---

21 Supra under Chapter 3, II.

22 See Wengler ZVerglRWiss 54 (1941) 168 et seq. This approach is called 'Sonderanknüpfungstheorie', and was first developed with regard to the application of mandatory rules of the forum, but was later - initiated by Wengler - extended to foreign rules. See Chapter 5 I, 3. With regard to the rules of the forum, see Sandrock/Steinschulte *Handbuch* Rn A 142; Schwander *IPR AT* 239; Morris *Statutes* 187, 200 et seq; Lipstein ICLQ 26 (1977) 884, 887; Jaffey ICLQ 23 (1974) 1, 18 et seq.

23 Radtke ZverglRWiss 84 (1985) 325, 330 et seq; Schwander *IPR AT* 246.

24 Kropholler *IPR* § 13 V; but see also for a classification of statutes in three classes Forsyth *Private International Law* 11 et seq. One can do so but should keep in mind that this is simply a combination of a substantive rule and a choice of law rule.

25 Kropholler *IPR* § 13 V and Schurig *Lois* 55, 63 et seq. are very lucid in this sense.

26 Schurig *Lois* 55, 74; Mäsch *Rechtswahlfreiheit* 134; Coing WM 1981, 810, 812 N 9; Radtke ZVerglRWiss 84 (1985) 325, 329, 331; Vischer Rec des Cours 142 (1974 II) 1,

In England, Germany and Switzerland, courts have applied their own internationally mandatory rules on the basis of their claim to apply to the situation despite a foreign proper law.[27] Examples of internationally mandatory rules and relevant court decisions will be dealt with later in this chapter, since these internationally mandatory rules are under present law covered by art 7 (2) of the Rome Convention and art 18 of the Swiss IPRG.

Finally, it can be mentioned that rules of public law were occasionally applied in Switzerland and Germany, despite a foreign proper law, due simply to their mandatory public law nature.[28] The *principle of territoriality of public law* and the so-called *international public law*, according to which foreign public law rules are in principle inapplicable, will be dealt with later in this study.[29] With regard to the public law rules of the forum state claiming application to the private relationship in question, it is sufficient to state, very broadly, that this approach assumes that public law rules in general fall out of the scope of private international law and determine their own scope of application unilaterally.[30] At least methodologically, the application of a public law rule of the forum state conforms to the concept of a *special connection* or of the *lois d'application immédiate*, because the forum's rule is applied independently of the normal conflict rule, on the basis of its own unilateral claim to apply. This is based, however, upon the troublesome distinction between public and private law.[31]

19, 22; Siehr RabelsZ 46 (1982) 357 et seq; Honsell/Vogt/Schnyder/Mächler-Erne Art 18 Rn 4.

27 See Sandrock/Steinschulte *Handbuch* Rn A142 et seq; Droste *Begriff* 11 et seq; Dicey & Morris *Conflict of Laws Vol I/13th ed* 21 et seq; id *Vol II/12th ed* 1240 et seq, */13th ed* 1242 et seq; Jaffey ICLQ 23 (1974) 1, 18 et seq; for references to Swiss court decisions, see Schwander *Lois* 251 et seq; id *IPR AT* 239 et seq; Honsell/Vogt/Schnyder/Mächler-Erne Art 18 Rn 17.

28 With regard to the External Economic Relations Act (AWG) and the corresponding ministerial order (AWV) BGH 23.10.1980 RIW 1981, 194, 195. The provisions of the AWV were held to be *public law* and thus rendered a contract void despite its Swiss proper law. See Droste *Begriff* 15 et seq and Knüppel *Zwingendes Recht* 60, 61 for examples of the decisions of lower courts concerning the §§ 20 et seq of the Transport of Goods by Road Act (GüKG) and the underlying principle of territoriality and for decisions of the Federal Labour Court concerning the Employees' Representation Act (Betriebsverfassungrecht).

29 Cf Chapter 5, I, 2, II.

30 Kegel *IPR/7th ed* § 23; id *Die Rolle des öffentlichen Rechts* 243, 244 et seq; MünchKomm/Sonnenberger Einl Rn 355, 356.

31 For references, see Knüppel *Zwingendes Recht* 35 et seq; Morscher *Rechtssetzungsakte* 48, 50 et seq; Schulte *Eingriffsnormen* 26 et seq; see the discussion of MünchKomm/Sonnenberger Einl Rn 355 et seq; von Bar *IPR Bd I* 243 et seq; id *Bd II* 452.

3 Critical remarks

The approach of a special connection or *lois d'application immédiate*, according to which certain rules claim application regardless of the proper law and are applied according to their own terms, became established in art 7 (2) of the Rome Convention and art 18 of the Swiss IPRG.[32] This approach also results from the official Report of Giuliano/Lagarde that expressly refers to the theory of '*lois d'application immédiate*'.[33]

The application of internationally mandatory rules on the basis of their own express or implied claim to apply, in accordance with the theory of *lois d'application immédiate*, is to be preferred to the doctrine of a positive operation of the forum's *ordre public*. It may be true that the doctrine of the positive *ordre public* is the source of the concept of *lois d'application immédiate*.[34] However, the *ordre public* approach has been criticised, particularly because the doctrine has undergone a fundamental change and is held to be reserved primarily for the negative function: the exclusion of foreign law that would be repugnant to fundamental values and principles of the forum state.[35] Under present law the *ordre public* is expressly restricted to its negative function.[36] The application of mandatory rules of the forum is reserved by art 7 (2) of the Rome Convention and art 18 of the Swiss IPRG.[37]

Furthermore, internationally mandatory rules do not necessarily express such fundamentally ethical policies of the state that they can be characterised as rules

---

32 MünchKomm/Martiny Art 34 Rn 4; Schurig *Lois* 55, 58; Vischer RabelsZ 53 (1989) 438, 445 et seq; Schwander *IPR AT* 239 et seq; Siehr *FS Keller* 485, 505.

33 Giuliano/Largarde *Report* in *Contract Conflicts* 382.

34 Cf Vischer Rec des Cours 232 (1992) 13, 165; Honsell/Vogt/Schnyder/Mächler-Erne Art 18 Rn 4.

35 Knüppel *Zwingendes Recht* 44; Sandrock/Steinschulte *Handbuch* Rn A 181; MünchKomm/Martiny Art 34 Rn 31; 96; Firsching/von Hoffmann *IPR* 250; Vischer Rec des Cours 232 (1992) 13, 165; for international commercial arbitration, also see Voser 7 Am Rev Int' Arb 319, LEXIS-NEXIS, 4 of 38.

36 See art 16 RC and art 17 Swiss IPRG; MünchKomm/Martiny Art 34 Rn 31, 96; Vischer Rec des Cours 232 (1992) 13, 165.

37 It is unfortunate that art 18 of the Swiss IPRG uses the expression 'is reserved'. However, despite this wording, it is generally held that art 18 refers to the *lois d'application immédiate* which claim application irrespective of the proper law; see Schnyder *Das neue IPR* 34, 35; Schwander *IPR AT* 239 et seq.

of the *ordre public*. They often have a broader content, or are the consequence of economic dirigisme.[38]

II Article 7 (2) of the Rome Convention, article 18 of the Swiss IPRG

The reservation of the forum's internationally mandatory rules is statutorily laid down in art 7 (2) of the Rome Convention and art 18 of the Swiss IPRG. Article 7 (2) of the Rome Convention provides that:

> Nothing in this Convention shall restrict the application of the rules of the law of the forum in a situation where they are mandatory irrespective of the law applicable to the contract.[39]

Similarly, art 18 of the Swiss IPRG provides that:

> Provisions of Swiss law which, in view of their special objective, must be applied without regard to the law designated by this statute remain reserved.[40]

As was already stated, both provisions are based on the doctrine of *lois d'application immédiate* or the concept that certain mandatory rules claim application regardless of the proper law. These provisions simply stipulate statutorily what was well established under pre-existing law. As many authors have stated, even without such a statutory provision in the Convention or in the Swiss IPRG, the courts of the forum state would most probably have continued to apply their own mandatory rules to the extent that these rules claimed application.[41]

---

38 Cf MünchKomm/Martiny Art 34 Rn 96; Voser 7 Am Rev Int'l Arb 319, LEXIS-NEXIS, 4 of 38; Vischer Rec des Cours 232 (1992) 13, 165; Basedow RabelsZ 52 (1988) 8, 21, 22.

39 There is an awkward change in the wording in the German equivalent, art 34 EGBG. Instead of 'the rules of the law of the forum' it reads 'the rules of German law', 'Dieser Unterabschnitt (Art(s) 27 - 37 EGBGB) berührt nicht die Anwendung der Bestimmungen des deutschen Rechts, die ohne Rücksicht auf das auf den Vertrag anzuwendende Recht den Sachverhalt zwingend regeln'. For an interpretation in the multilateral sense of art 7 (2), see Droste *Begriff* 112 et seq.

40 'Vorbehalten bleiben Bestimmungen des schweizerischen Rechts, die wegen ihres besonderen Zweckes, unabhängig von dem durch dieses Gesetz bezeichneten Recht, zwingend anzuwenden sind.'

41 See Morse YB Eur L 2 (1982) 107, 144; Schwander *IPR AT* 239; North *Contract Conflicts* 3, 18, 19; Morse *Public Policy* England - 72; Cheshire & North's *Private International Law/12th ed* 499, */13th ed* 578; Dicey & Morris *Conflict of Laws Vol I/12th ed* 21 et

Neither provision stipulates any requirements for an application of the forum's mandatory rules, except that the rule in question must be 'mandatory irrespective of the law applicable to the contract' or 'in view of its special objective, must be applied without regard to the law designated by this statute'. Instead of providing a means of characterising internationally mandatory rules and stipulating the circumstances under which an application is reasonable, these rules proposing simply the existence of mandatory rules that override the ordinary conflict rules.[42] Both articles therefore have a declaratory character and have been called a '*blanket provision of the law*' (*Blankettnorm*)[43] or '*opening clause*'(*Öffnungsklausel*).[44] It is said that the application of these rules is not based upon art 7 (2) or art 18, but rather on the specific statute that contains an attached unilateral conflict rule determining its international scope.[45]

1 Domestic Contact

It is disputed whether, in addition to the characterisation of a rule as internationally mandatory, there must be a certain *connection with the forum*.[46] Many authors maintain that such a connection is necessary, because art 7 (1) of the Rome Convention and art 19 of the Swiss IPRG provide for a close connection, and even the invocation of the forum's *ordre public* requires a local connection with the forum.[47] However, this condition is not stipulated in art 7 (2) of the Rome Convention or in art 18 of the Swiss IPRG. It is for the internationally mandatory rule of the forum state to determine the spatial or territorial conditions under which it applies.[48]

---

seq; id *Vol II/12th ed* 1240, 1241; Sandrock RIW 1986, 841, 852; Honsell/Vogt/Schnyder/Mächler-Erne Art 18 Rn 3; Heini *FS Moser* 67, 73; MünchKomm/Martiny Art 34 Rn 89; Kropholler *IPR* § 52 VIII 1; von Bar *IPR I* 232; Soergel/von Hoffmann Art 34 Rn 13.

42 MünchKomm/Martiny Art 34 Rn 93; Mäsch *Rechtswahlfreiheit* 134 et seq; Coester ZVerglRWiss 82 (1983) 1, 11 et seq; also see the report of Giuliano/Lagarde in North *Contract Conflicts* 382 which refers to the *lois d'application immédiate*.

43 MünchKomm/Sonnenberger Einl Rn 56; Sonnenberger *FS Rebmann* 819, 825; also see Honsell/Vogt/Schnyder/Mächler-Erne Art 18 Rn 8; for criticism in this regard, see De Boer RabelsZ 54 (1990) 24, 58.

44 MünchKomm/Martiny Art 34 Rn 93; Roth RIW 1994, 273, 278.

45 MünchKomm/Martiny Art 34 Rn 91; Roth RIW 1994, 275, 277, 278.

46 Kropholler *IPR* § 52 VIII 1; Reithmann/Martiny/Limmer *Internationales Vertragsrecht* Rn 393; MünchKomm/Martiny Art 34 Rn 94, 100; Soergel/von Hoffmann Art 34 Rn 95; see Honsell/Vogt/Schnyder/Mächler-Erne Art 18 Rn 14.

47 Kropholler *IPR* § 52 VIII 1; Lorenz RdA 1989, 220, 227; MünchKomm/Martiny Art 34 Rn 100 with further references; Staudinger/Magnus Art 34 Rn 77.

48 Cf MünchKomm/Sonnenberger Einl Rn 56; Radtke ZVerglRWiss 84 (1985) 325, 331; also see Hartley 4 ELR (1979) 236, 241.

Generally, however, mandatory provisions will not be applicable to the factual situation if there is no domestic connection.[49] Especially in cases where the international scope of a rule results only from judicial interpretation of a statute, the courts should not extend the scope of a mandatory rule extra-territorially where there is no connection with the forum state.

2 Internationally mandatory rules

Neither article refers to mandatory rules in a domestic sense or simply mandatory rules. They refer only to internationally mandatory rules, viz. rules that must be upheld irrespective of the law applicable to the contract.[50] The peculiarities of these rules have been described above and what was said there is equally valid in respect of art 7 (2) and art 18. It is generally held that rules of both private and public law can be internationally mandatory rules,[51] and that statutory provisions as well as judge-made rules can be internationally mandatory.[52] In contrast to arts 5 and 6, art 7 of the Rome Convention and art 18 of the Swiss IPRG are general clauses and are therefore not limited to a certain kind of mandatory rule or to certain types of contracts.[53]

Still, the major difficulty is how to identify a rule as being internationally mandatory if the rule does not contain an express term indicating its territorial scope. It was seen above that, thus far, no universal criterion has been found to delimit these rules from mandatory rules in a domestic sense. The *interest approach*, according to which a rule is internationally mandatory if it predominantly serves public as opposed to private interests, is of no use with regard to protective rules that serve both public and private interests. The same is true for the *Ordnungsrelevanz* approach.

---

49 Radtke ZverglRWiss 84 (1985) 325, 331; Honsell/Vogt/Schnyder/Mächler-Erne Art 18 Rn 14; Kaye *The new Private International Law* 262.

50 Amongst all Reithmann/Martiny/Limmer *Internationales Vertragsrecht* Rn 387; MünchKomm/Martiny Art 34 Rn 7 et seq; Honsell/Vogt/Schnyder/Mächler-Erne Art 18 Rn 10; Vischer RabelsZ 53 (1989) 438, 445; North *Contract Conflicts* 3, 19; Philip *Contract Conflicts* 81, 82, 100; Morse YB Eur L 2 (1982) 107, 143.

51 Staudinger/Magnus Art 34 Rn 65; MünchKomm/Martiny Art 34 Rn 11; Jackson *Contract Conflict* 59, 60; Vischer RabelsZ 53 (1989) 438, 445, 446; Siehr RabelsZ 52 (1988) 41, 44; Honsell/Vogt/Schnyder/Mächler-Erne Art 18 Rn 13; Morscher *Rechtssetzungsakte* 89.

52 Lasok/Stone *Conflict of Laws* 374; Morse *Public Policy* England - 17, 18; Schwander *IPR AT* 240; cf for examples Kaye *The new Private International Law* 242 et seq; Dicey & Morris *Conflict of Laws Vol I/12th /13th ed* 23.

53 For the differences, see Martiny IPRax 1987, 277, 278; Junker IPRax 1989, 73, 74.

The judge is therefore still faced with the difficult task of identifying particular rules and determining their overriding effect. He has to establish whether the meaning and purpose of the law demand application to the situation in question, despite a foreign proper law. One indication may be that the intention of the legislature would be frustrated if the rule were not applied to the situation,[54] another may be that the rule must be applied without exception if its purpose is to be met.[55]

Notwithstanding the weaknesses of the above-mentioned approaches, they have nevertheless led to the development of useful guidelines for identifying internationally mandatory rules. It seems to be established that rules that intervene in private relationships and whose legislative purpose would be frustrated if they were not applied, can be classified as internationally mandatory if they also pursue the *economic and political interests* of the enacting country (interests *beyond* the private interests of the contracting parties). On the other hand, rules that serve *exclusively the fair reconciliation of the contracting parties and their interest in settling the dispute* are mandatory only in a domestic sense.

In general, most authors stress that an extensive application of the forum's mandatory rules, despite a foreign proper law, runs counter to the aim of decisional harmony, a fundamental principle in private international law and the major objective of the Rome Convention. Such application also runs counter to a bilateral system of conflict of laws.[56] Furthermore, an extensive application of mandatory rules jeopardises the principle of freedom of choice in private international law.[57] Bearing these issues in mind, the forum should interpret its rules restrictively, and apply its mandatory provisions with restraint.

---

54 With regard to the restriction to a choice of law of the contracting parties, see *Irish Shipping Ltd v Commercial Union Assurance Co plc* [1991] 2 QB 206, 220, 221 (CA); also see Dicey & Morris *Conflict of Laws Vol I/12th /13th ed* 21, 22.

55 Schwander *IPR AT* 243, 244; Schwander *Lois* 291.

56 Vischer states, that besides the content and purpose of the rule, the decision whether a rule is internationally mandatory should also include 'considerations proper to conflict of laws' and that in view of the international situation a 'restriction or modification of the scope' of the internationally mandatory rule may be necessary; see id Rec des Cours 232 (1992) 13, 158, 162 et seq; also see Schwander *IPR AT* 243, 244, 247; see generally for a restrictive application Reithmann/Martiny/Limmer *Internationales Vertragsrecht* Rn 387; Staudinger/Magnus Art 34 Rn 45; Morse YB Eur L 2 (1982) 107, 144; Philip *Contract Conflicts* 81, 102; Vischer Rec des Cours 232 (1992) 13, 158 et seq; Morscher *Rechtssetzungsakte* 54, 55; Vischer RabelsZ 53 (1989) 438, 446.

57 MünchKomm/Martiny Art 34 Rn 13 a; Vischer Rec des Cours 232 (1992) 13, 159.

3 Legal consequences

The legal consequence of art 7 (2) of the Rome Convention and art 18 of the Swiss IPRG is application of the internationally mandatory rule. In the choice of law process, this is a *special reference or connection.*[58] If the judge has identified a mandatory provision of the forum state that is applicable to the situation in question, he has to apply the rule, despite the foreign proper law.

Article 7 (2) and art 18 are obligatory, and do not grant the judge discretion in deciding whether effect is to be given to the forum's internationally mandatory rules.[59] However, the *legal consequences* will depend on the mandatory rule itself. For example, if the internationally mandatory rule sanctions an infringement that results in the transaction being null and void, the legal consequences flow directly from the rule. If on the other hand, the rule simply states a prohibition, without specifying the legal consequences of a violation, the consequences will flow indirectly from the substantive rules of the *lex causae.*[60]

III Examples of internationally mandatory rules of English, German and Swiss law

Some examples of internationally mandatory rules in German, English and Swiss law will be described in this section. The examples include references to those rules that include an express term indicating their territorial scope, as well as those rules where the claim to apply irrespective of the proper law has been determined by interpretation of the rule. With regard to the latter category, those rules that have *not* been characterised as internationally mandatory will also be examined.

1 Rules serving the state's economic and political goals

Internationally mandatory rules that serve the state's economic and political goals and intervene in private relationships include import and export restrictions, foreign exchange control regulations, currency regulations, and

---

58 Clearly Schwander *IPR AT* 532; Honsell/Vogt/Schnyder/Mächler-Erne Art 18 Rn 23; Knüppel *Zwingendes Recht* 198, 205; Staudinger/Magnus Art 34 Rn 48, 82.

59 MünchKomm/Martiny Art 34 Rn 54, 55, 58; Schwander *IPR AT* 245; Kaye *The new Private International Law* 262; Staudinger/Magnus Art 34 Rn 82.

60 MünchKomm/Martiny Art 34 Rn 58; Honsell/Vogt/Schnyder/Mächler-Erne Art 18 Rn 23; Staudinger/Magnus Art 34 Rn 82; *contra* Morscher *Rechtssetzungsakte* 93; Reithmann/Martiny/Limmer *Internationales Vertragsrecht* Rn 399.

anti-trust law (although the latter clearly also protects the private interest of freedom of competition).[61] The identification of these rules as internationally mandatory does not unduly burden the judge. In general, these rules are intended to override the ordinary choice of law rule and - within their territorial scope - claim application regardless of the proper law of the contract. These rules serve fundamental economic and political interests of the enacting state, and the intention of the legislature - be it only self-interested or political - would most probably be frustrated if they were not applied within their ambit.

a Foreign exchange control and currency regulations

Foreign exchange control regulations and currency regulations serve the economic and political interests of the enacting state and are generally held to be internationally mandatory and thus applied by the forum despite a foreign proper law.[62] These rules may stipulate that permission must be obtained from the relevant authority or may impose an obligation to notify in respect of contracts involving payment in a foreign currency or the borrowing of foreign currency. Without such permission contracts are usually illegal or at least provisionally invalid and unenforceable, irrespective of the proper law of the contract.[63]

In the notorious English case, *Boissevain v Weil*,[64] the House of Lords applied the Defence Regulations 1939, declared in terms of sec 3 (1) of the Emergency Powers (Defence) Act 1939, to a loan agreement between a British subject and a Dutch subject, both resident in Monaco during the war. The former subject borrowed a sum of French francs from the latter. It was agreed that the British subject would repay the loan after the war in pounds sterling. After the war the British subject failed to repay the money. The Dutch subject sued the British subject in England, but was unable to recover his money, because the House of

---

61 See Kegel *Rôle of Public Law* 29, 49; also see the enumeration of Reithmann/Martiny/Limmer *Internationales Vertragsrecht* Rn 405 et seq; MünchKomm/Martiny Art 34 Rn 63 et seq; Vischer Rec des Cours 232 (1992) 13, 157; Honsell/Vogt/Schnyder/Mächler-Erne Rn 16; Lipstein *Conflict of Laws and Public Law* 45, 46; Dicey & Morris *Conflict of Laws Vol I /12th /13th ed* 21 et seq.

62 See Reithmann/Martiny/Limmer *Internationales Vertragsrecht* Rn 420; MünchKomm/Martiny Nach Art 34 Anh II Rn 6 '*versteckte Kollisionsnorm*'; Morscher *Rechtssetzungsakte* 90, 91; Hartley Rec des Cours 266 (1997) 341, 420.

63 Reithmann/Martiny/Limmer *Internationales Vertragsrecht* Rn 419, 421; MünchKomm/Martiny Nach Art 34 Anh II Rn 6; Hartley Rec des Cours 266 (1997) 341, 420. Art VIII (2) (b) of the International Monetary Fund (IMF) contains a special choice of law rule for the application of mandatory rules of foreign currency regulations, but it is not applicable in respect of regulations of the forum.

64 [1950] AC 327; [1950] 1 All ER 728 (HL).

Lords held that the British Defence Regulations, in terms of which it was an offence for any British subject to borrow foreign currency without the consent of Treasury commission, applied to all British subjects, irrespective of the place of contracting and of the proper law of the agreement.[65]

In Germany the Federal Supreme Court ruled that a loan agreement between a German subject and a Swiss subject, governed by the law of Switzerland, was invalid because it infringed German foreign trade provisions. The parties had deliberately not requested the necessary permission from the German National Bank authority. The court applied the German provisions, due to their public law nature, despite the Swiss proper law.[66]

b Competition and Anti-Trust Law

Anti-trust law is another area where regulations are often internationally mandatory and apply regardless of the proper law of private agreements.[67] These rules intervene in private relationships in order to safeguard the public interest in freedom of competition as an institution. They also, however, serve to protect the individual's freedom of competition.[68]

In Germany the territorial scope of the Anti Trust Law is statutorily laid down in paragraph 130 (2) of the Anti Cartel Act (Gesetz gegen Wettbewerbs-beschränkungen, GWB.)[69] Paragraph 130 (2), sentence 1 of the GWB reads as follows:

> This law applies to all restraints of competition that have an effect in the territory where this law is applicable, even if they are instigated outside of that territory'[70]

Paragraph 130 (2) contains an *unilateral choice of law rule* that requires, under certain circumstances, a *special connection* of the provisions of the GWB and

---

65 For the facts of the case, see Hartley Rec des Cours 266 (1997) 341, 420, 421.

66 BGH 23.10.1980 RIW 1981, 194, 195.

67 For the UK, cf Dicey & Morris *Conflict of Laws Vol II/12th ed* 1241, */13th ed* 1243.

68 MünchKomm/Martiny Art 34 Rn 75; Sandrock/Steinschulte *Handbuch* Rn A 154. It is situated in the border area between private and public law, see Kegel *Rôle of Public Law* 29, 49; Vischer Rec des Cours 232 (1992) 13, 184, 185.

69 Anti Cartel Act, 27.7.1957 as amended on 26.8.1998, BGBl. I 2546; the provision was originally statutorily laid down in para 98 (2) GWB, however, was moved due to other amendments to para 130 (2) GWB.

70 'Dieses Gesetz findet Anwendung auf alle Wettbewerbsbeschränkungen, die sich im Geltungsbereich dieses Gesetzes auswirken, auch wenn sie außerhalb dieses Geltungsbereichs veranlaßt werden'.

thus determines under what circumstances the German anti-trust law is internationally mandatory.[71] The relevant criterion for the applicability of the GWB is thereafter the *effect of restraints of competition on the domestic market*, wherever they were instigated - the *effect principle* ('Auswirkungsprinzip').[72] Thus, if a cartel agreement affects the German market, the German anti-trust law is applicable, even where foreign restraint of competition is evident and governed by another law.[73]

It has been proposed that the unilateral conflict rule in § 130 (2) of the GWB should be converted into a multilateral conflict rule. This would result in a foreign anti-trust law being applied irrespective of the proper law if the foreign law forbids a certain performance by the debtor (restraint of competition) and this performance has an effect on the foreign market.[74]

In *Rousillon v Rousillon*[75] the agreement at issue had been concluded between a Swiss and a French party, both domiciled in France. In the agreement, which was governed by French law, the Swiss party had agreed not to compete with the French party in England. The contract was declared void since it violated the English common law rule on restraint of trade. The court regarded the English rule as a matter of public policy, and therefore applied the rule, despite the fact that the agreement was valid in terms of the foreign proper law.

In the European Union national anti-trust regulations are in most cases replaced by arts 81 and 82 (previously arts 85 and 86) of the Treaty of the European Community. These cartel provisions are not express conflict rules as in para 98 of the GWB. Nevertheless, because of the *purpose and wording* of the

---

71 MünchKomm/Martiny Art 34 Rn 75, 113; Reithmann/Martiny/Limmer *Internationales Vertragsrecht* Rn 412; Basedow RabelsZ 52 (1988) 8, 21; id NJW 1989, 627, 628; Sandrock/Steinschulte *Handbuch* Rn A 154; but see Mann *FS Beitzke* 607, 614 et seq who argues in accordance with his point of view (see Chapter 4, I, 1) that § 130 (2) GWB is simply a special rule of the *ordre public*.

72 The effect principle as used in § 130 (2) GWB is too broad and has to be concretised; the notion of *domestic effect* has to be 'delimited and put into specific terms' by means of the 'protective purpose of the GWB and of the special provisions that are to be considered in each case'; BGH 17.7.1973 NJW 1973, 1609, 1610 *Ölfeldrohre-decision* and BGH 29.5.1979 NJW 1979, 2613 *Organische Pigmente*; for further reference to case law and the effects principle, see Reithmann/Martiny/Limmer *Internationales Vertragsrecht* Rn 412; Sandrock/Steinschulte *Handbuch* Rn A 154; Basedow NJW 1989, 627, 628; Kegel *Rôle of Public Law* 29, 51.

73 See Kegel *Rôle of Public Law* 29, 50, 52 et seq.

74 This is disputed in MünchKomm/Martiny Art 34 Rn 75; MünchKomm/Sonnenberger Einl Rn 68; Basedow NJW 1989, 627, 632, 633; Kropholler *IPR* § 12 V.

75 (1880) 14 Ch D 351.

provisions, they are applicable, regardless of the proper law, to the extent that the cartel agreement in question has a competition-limiting effect on the Common Market.[76]

In contrast to other countries where anti-trust law is generally applied on the basis of implied or express unilateral conflict rules of the forum state, Switzerland has enacted a multilateral conflict rule. Article 137 (1) of the Swiss IPRG provides that:

> Claims on restraint of competition are governed by the law of the state in whose market the restraint directly effects the "damaged person".[77]

This conflict rule leads to a '*special connection*' of domestic as well as foreign mandatory anti-trust law. It was based on the assumption that competition serves the national market of each country and that restraint of competition must therefore be governed by the law of the state in whose market the claimant is directly affected.[78]

c Import and Export Restrictions and Embargoes

Foreign trade restrictions, such as import and export control regulations, are further examples of internationally mandatory rules.[79] Restrictions are imposed whenever national political aims cannot be otherwise fulfilled.[80] Usually, contracts concerning the import or export of certain goods are void or provisionally invalid, unless the contractors have obtained official permission.[81] These restrictions on foreign trade can serve quite different policies: economic,

---

76 For details, see Reithmann/Martiny/Limmer *Internationales Vertragsrecht* Rn 413 and Sandrock/Steinschulte *Handbuch* Rn A 156 et seq; Basedow NJW 1989, 627, 633 et seq; also see Dicey & Morris *Conflict of Laws Vol II/12th ed* 1241, */13th ed* 1244.

77 'Ansprüche aus Wettbewebsbehinderung unterstehen dem Recht des Staates, auf dessen Markt der Geschädigte von der Behinderung unmittelbar betroffen ist.'

78 Voser *Lois d'application immédiate* 40, 41; Schnyder *Wirtschaftskollisionsrecht* Rn 8 Footnote 33, Rn 56; Vischer Rec des Cours 232 (1992) 13, 184, 185; id RabelsZ 53 (1989) 438, 457.

79 Morscher *Rechtssetzungsakte* 90; Remien RabelZ 52 (1988) 431, 442; Lipstein *Conflict of laws and public law* 38, 46.

80 Soergel/von Hoffmann Art 34 Rn 18; Remien RabelsZ 52 (1988) 431, 442; see § 1(1) of the German AWG (External Economic Relations Act, 28.4.1961 BGBl 1961 I 481 as amended on 11.12.1996 BGBl I 1850); for Switzerland, see Morscher *Rechtssetzungsakte* 90, 91 footnote 30, art 1 BG für aussenwirtschaftliche Maßnahmen 25.7.1982 SR 946.201.

81 Soergel/von Hoffmann Art 34 Rn 23 et seq.

health, military-strategic or foreign policy purposes, or the protection of threatened animal species or the cultural property of a country.[82]

Apart from import and export restrictions, there are also measures that are designed to impose specific disadvantages on particular states, such as trade embargoes.[83] An embargo is a prohibition imposed by a state on those persons subject to its sovereignty that forbids the conclusion of certain legal transactions with persons in another state.[84] Such prohibitions lead to the invalidity of contracts, and override a foreign *lex causae* because they are internationally mandatory.[85] The English common law rule that contracts involving trade with an enemy are illegal may also fall within this category. In *Dynamit AG v Rio Tinto Co*[86] this rule was applied, based on English public policy, despite a foreign proper law.[87]

The national foreign trade law of European countries is to a large extent displaced in respect of third states by the foreign trade regulations of the European Union Law.[88] Protective provisions enacted by the European Community are connected independently of the *lex causae*, ie they apply regardless of the proper law of the contract.[89] International Conventions may also contain internationally mandatory trade restrictions.[90]

Examples of internationally mandatory rules may also be found in measures that serve to protect human health or animal and plant life. Examples include the

---

82 Remien RabelsZ 52 (1988) 431, 434 et seq; MünchKomm/Martiny Art 34 Rn 63; Soergel/von Hoffmann Art 34 Rn 19-53; see the examples given by Basedow GYBIL 27 (1984) 109, 112 et seq.

83 MünchKomm/Martiny Art 34 Rn 63; Reithmann/Martiny/Limmer *Internationales Vertragsrecht* 417.

84 MünchKomm/Martiny Art 34 Rn 63; Reithmann/Martiny/Limmer *Internationales Vertragsrecht* Rn 416 et seq; in general Remien RabelsZ 52 (1988) 431 et seq.

85 MünchKomm/Martiny Art 34 Rn 66; Remien RabelsZ 52 (1988) 431, 463, 464; Reithmann/Martiny/Limmer *Internationales Vertragsrecht* Rn 417; Sandrock/Steinschulte *Handbuch* Rn A 169; Morscher *Rechtssetzungsakte* 90, 91.

86 [1918] AC 292.

87 For similar cases, see Dicey & Morris *Conflict of Laws Vol II/13th ed* 1278 Footnote 39.

88 The competence to regulate this matter results from art 113 EC-Treaty, Reithmann/Martiny/Limmer *Internationales Vertragsrecht* Rn 418; MünchKomm/Martiny Art 34 Rn 65 et seq.

89 Sandrock/Steinschulte *Handbuch* Rn A 170.

90 The cornerstone of the world trade order is the General Agreement of Tariffs and Trade (GATT) 30.10.1947, now World Trade Organisation (WTO) 15.4.1994 in legal force in Germany and England. Although freedom of trade is established as basic principle, several exceptions exist which are the legal basis of many export and import restrictions, eg, the CoCom, cf Basedow GYBIL 27 (1984) 109, 113.

import restrictions of paragraph 47 (1) of the German Act regulating the transport of food and implements,[91] and the measures imposed for the protection of national treasures of artistic, historic or archaeological value.[92]

d Protection of landed property

Certain mandatory rules, particularly in Switzerland, focus on the protection of land.[93] For instance, arts 2 and 26 of the Acquisition of Landed Property by Foreigners Act (Bundesgesetz über den Erwerb von Grundstücken durch Personen im Ausland)[94] stipulate that the acquisition of landed property by foreigners is subject to the permission of the relevant authority. Contracts concluded without such permission are illegal regardless of their proper law.[95]

2 Protection of the weaker contracting party

Vischer states that '[i]t is debatable whether protective private law rules whose objective is the safeguarding of a party's position in a contract or other relationship may enter into the category of norms which are to be applied irrespective of the bilateral conflict rules ....'[96]

In England, however, it seems generally accepted by case law and academic authors that mandatory legislation that serves the socio-economic policy of protecting the weaker party of a contract can be characterised as internationally mandatory rule, even if the rule does not specify its territorial scope by an express term.[97] Conversely in Germany and Switzerland, it is disputed whether rules that serve to protect the weaker contracting party can be classified as internationally mandatory.[98] It is not an easy task to determine whether the rule

---

91 Lebensmittel- und Bedarfsgegenständegesetz, LMBG, 15.8.1974 BGBl. I 1945 with later amendments. § 47 (1) reads 'The "transfer" of food that does not comply with the German provisions into the territory of the Federal Republic of Germany is forbidden'; cf also Übereinkommen über den internationalen Handel mit gefährdeten Arten freilebender Tiere und Pflanzen, 3.3.1973 in force in Germany since 20.6.1976, BGBl 1 976 II 1237.

92 See Gesetz zum Schutz deutschen Kulturgutes gegen Abwanderung, 6.8.1955, as amended on 31.8.1990, BGBl II 889; for further examples: MünchKomm/Martiny Art 34 Rn 66 et seq, 86; Soergel/von Hoffmann Art 34 Rn 24-32, 51, 52.

93 Morscher *Rechtssetzungsakte* 90; Honsell/Vogt/Schnyder/Mächler-Erne Art 18 Rn 16.

94 16.12.1983 SR 211.412.41.

95 Morscher *Rechtssetzungsakte* 90.

96 Vischer Rec des Cours 232 (1992) 13, 157, 158.

97 See Dicey & Morris *Conflict of laws Vol I/12th ed* 24; id *Vol II/12th ed* 1241, 1317 et seq; */13th ed* 1243, 1294 et seq.

98 See Chapter 3, II, 2; Reithmann/Martiny/Limmer *Internationales Vertragsrecht* Rn 395 et seq; Staudinger/Magnus Art 34 Rn 29 et seq, 55 et seq.

in question pursues public interests, in particular state economic and political interests (and are therefore internationally mandatory), or whether the rule serves the fair reconciliation of interests of the contracting parties. (In the latter case, there is no 'special connection', and applicability depends on whether the rule belongs to the proper law or possibly on the 'favour principle'.) This distinction is much simpler in respect of regulations that are mainly of a public law nature and pursue interests beyond those of the private parties.[99]

The difficulties emanate from the fact that these rules usually serve both the interests of the contracting parties and the social-political interests of the state.[100] The protection of tenants, consumer protection and employee protection fall within this category (which is also called '*Sonderprivatrecht*', '*special private law*')[101] In contrast to other mandatory rules, their applicability depends on an assumed inequality of bargaining power; they do not apply in cases of contract parity.[102]

Special conflict rules (arts 5 and 6 of the Rome Convention and arts 120 and 121 of the Swiss IPRG) exist in the areas of consumer and employee protection. The controversy about the internationally mandatory nature of protective rules is therefore confused with the demarcation of the scope of the special conflict rules.[103] This unfortunate situation leads to a lack of clarity in discussion. It is often not clear whether and under what conditions protective rules are regarded as internationally mandatory, because it is not specified whether the rules are excluded in principle or simply because they are covered by special conflict rules.[104]

Consumer protection is the main subject of controversy in Germany. In contrast to the comprehensive regulation in art 6 of the Rome Convention, the consumer protection in art 5 of the Convention is restricted to certain types of contracts

99 In section 1 above.

100 Mentzel *Sonderanknüpfung* 13, 212; Reithmann/Martiny/Limmer *Internationales Vertragsrecht* Rn 397.

101 See especially Firsching/von Hoffmann *IPR* 414 , 415; Soergel/von Hoffmann Art 34 Rn 54; v. Hoffmann IPRax 1989, 261, 266; Leible JBJZRW (1995) 245, 261. But this list is not exhaustive, the protection of capital investors as well as insurance contracts can be added.

102 Soergel/von Hoffmann Art 34 Rn 54.

103 See for instance Kropholler *IPR* § 52 V 1 a; W Lorenz IPRax 1994, 429, 431; Vischer Rec des Cours RabelsZ 53 (1989) 13, 159; for a clear distinction, see Junker IPRax 1998, 65, 70.

104 See eg MünchKomm/Martiny Art 34 Rn 16 who states that 'it principally can be assumed that protective rules are mandatory private law which need not, but can fall in the category of the interventionist norms.'

and to limited circumstances.[105] This has led to an urgent search for an alternative method of protecting the consumer in international contracts.[106] If the legislature decides that the protective rule must be applied regardless of the proper law of the contract, the judge is bound by the will of his sovereign. The dispute can thus be reduced to a consideration of protective rules that do not contain an express term determining their international scope of application. The issue then is whether these rules can be internationally mandatory at all.[107] This question has become one of the most debated issues in the German law of international contracts. The main arguments will be presented in the following excursus.

a Excursus: Dispute about characterising protective private laws as internationally mandatory rules

According to one point of view, rules that protect the weaker contracting party cannot be classified as internationally mandatory rules in the sense of art 7 (2) of the Rome Convention and art 18 of the Swiss IPRG. Internationally mandatory rules are rules that serve only public interests, in particular state economic and socio-political interests that are situated outside the contractual relationship. Protective rules serve primarily the fair reconciliation of the interests of the contracting parties, when there is an inequality of power, and are thus subject to the ordinary conflict rules (and possibly also to the special conflict rules for consumer and employment contracts). They are thus applicable only if they belong to the proper law, or they may be applicable on the basis of the favour principle.[108]

The internationally mandatory character of a rule does not automatically follow from the fact that it protects the weaker contracting party, since the socio-political objective of consumer protection is pursued, as is the fair reconciliation of interests of the parties.[109] The ordinary conflict rules are based

[105] Reithmann/Martiny/Limmer *Internationales Vertragsrecht* Rn 395; Kropholler *IPR* § 3 II 3; MünchKomm/Martiny Art 34 Rn 16; Staudinger/Magnus Art 34 Rn 71; Junker IPRax 1993, 1, 8; Mäsch *Rechtswahlfreiheit* 126.

[106] Roth *Schnyder/Heiß/Rudisch* 35, 38, 39; Junker IPRax 1993, 1, 8.

[107] Sonnenberger *FS Rebmann* 819, 823; Schubert RIW 1987, 729, 731 Footnote 29, 30; see also Voser *Lois d'application immediate* 60; Roth *Schnyder/Heiß/Rudisch* 35, 42.

[108] Mankowsky RIW 1993, 453, 461; id IPRax 1994, 88, 94; id RIW 1995, 364, 368; Sonnenberger *FS Rebmann* 819, 822, 823; Radtke ZVerglRWiss 84 (1985) 325, 328; Schubert RIW 1987, 729, 731; Kleinschmidt *Anwendbarkeit* 278 et seq; similar BAG 24.8.1989 BAGE 63, 17, 32; BAG 29.10.1992 IPRax 1994, 123, 128; Voser *Lois d'application immediate* 59.

[109] MünchKomm/Sonnenberger Einl Rn 49; Anderegg *Ausländische Eingriffsnorm* 87; Schubert RIW 1987, 729, 731; Radtke ZVerglRWiss 84 (1985) 324, 328.

on private interests and thus also cover protective laws: It is a matter for the legislator of the proper law to grant adequate protection to the weaker party.[110]

Some of the advocates of this approach exclude all 'special private law rules',[111] while others demand that the rule in question pursues an additional public interest (a 'plus'),[112] or at least that it serves 'mainly' public interests.[113] Such an additional interest is affirmed especially with regard to lessee protection, while with regard to consumer protection it is rejected.[114]

According to this approach a rule that is internationally mandatory cannot fall under arts 5 and 6 of the Rome Convention, and, conversely, a protective rule that falls within the scope of arts 5 and 6 cannot be internationally mandatory. In other words, a rule cannot simultaneously serve interests that are predominantly private *and* interests that are predominantly public. One or other interest must prevail. The object of the normal connection cannot be the object of a special connection, since both connections are based on and pursue different and incompatible goals.[115]

The counter-opinion espouses an extension of the group of rules that can qualify as internationally mandatory rules.[116] The reason for this approach is the

---

110 Sonnenberger *FS Rebmann* 819, 822, 823; Mankowsky IPRax 1994, 88, 94; Anderegg *Ausländische Eingriffsnorm* 80, 92: (1) the interest of the contracting parties to enforce their contract and (2) the fair reconciliation of their aims and (3) interests of legal security.

111 Schubert RIW 1987, 729, 731; Kleinschmidt *Anwendbarkeit* 278 et seq; similar Radtke ZVerglRWiss 84 (1985) 325, 328.

112 MünchKomm/Sonnenberger Einl Rn 50.

113 Anderegg *Ausländische Eingriffsnorm* 93 et seq.

114 Anderegg *Ausländische Eingriffsnorm* 93, 94; MünchKomm/Sonnenberger Einl Rn 49, 50; Voser *Lois d'application immédiate* 59, 61; for criticism, see Mäsch *Rechtswahlfreiheit* 139.

115 Mankowsky RIW 1993, 453, 460; id IPRax 1994, 88, 94, 95; id RIW 1996, 8; id RIW 1995, 364, 368; Voser *Lois d'application immédiate* 51et seq; Sonnenberger *FS Rebmann* 819, 823.

116 Von Hoffmann IPRax 1989, 261, 263, 266; Soergel/von Hoffmann, Art. 34 Rn 4, 54 et seq; id J Cons Policy 15 (1992) 365, 377; Roth RIW 1994, 275, 277; id *Schnyder/Heiß/Rudisch* 35, 43; Lorenz RIW 1987, 569, 578, 580; Erne *Vertragsgültigkeit* 6; Lorenz IPRax 1994, 429, 431; Leible JbJZRW (1995) 245, 261; Siehr RabelsZ 52 (1988) 41, 48; Jayme IPRax 1995, 234, 236. This approach corresponds with a proposal made by *von Hoffmann* 1974 where he suggested a '*special connection*' of these protective norms. The starting point of the special connection of the social protective norms is whether the rule demands application. No matter how strong the state's intention, application of the rule is restricted by the 'international policy' which consists of (1) the degree of contact the legal relationship has with the enacting state and (2) the

'*double function*' of these norms, since socio-political mandatory provisions that protect the weaker contracting party also pursue socio-political interests, and have a market-adjusting effect, which serves interests beyond those of the contracting parties.[117] It is accurately not possible to fix the boundaries between economic-political interests or the interests of the contracting parties.[118] The existence of arts 5 and 6 of the Rome Convention and arts 120 and 121 of the Swiss IPRG does not exclude the applicability of internationally mandatory rules of the forum state protecting consumers or employees by means of art 7 of the Rome Convention and art 18 Swiss of the IPRG, respectively.[119]

Most of the academic statements do not exclude the '*special private law rules*' per se from the scope of art 7 of the Rome Convention and art 18 of the Swiss IPRG.[120] They do, however, restrict the possibility of a rule having an international mandatory character to situations where the international scope is either expressly determined or the purpose and the legislative policy behind a rule justifies such a conclusion.[121] If there is any doubt, the rule is not internationally mandatory.[122] Particularly in the controversial field of consumer protection, a clear determination of whether a rule is internationally mandatory remains elusive.[123]

As a result of these latter approaches the relationship of arts 5 and 6 of the Rome Convention to art 7 (2) has to be clarified. On this 'second level' it is disputed whether arts 5 and 6 are *lex specialis* to art 7 (2) with regard to the types of contract they concern,[124] or whether art 7 (2) prevails over arts 5 and

material reconcilability with international common understanding, id RabelsZ 38 (1974) 415 et seq.

117 Reithmann/Martiny/Limmer *Internationales Vertragsrecht* Rn 398; Mentzel *Sonderanknüpfung* 13; Leible JBJZRW (1995) 245, 261.

118 Mäsch *Rechtswahlfreiheit* 138; MünchKomm/Martiny Art. 34 Rn 79; Reithmann/Martiny/Limmer *Internationales Vertragsrecht* Rn 397; Leible JBJZRW (1995) 245, 261.

119 Soergel/von Hoffmann Art 34 Rn 54; Roth *Schnyder/Heiß/Rudisch* 35, 41, 42; Honsell/Vogt/Schnyder/Mächler-Erne Art 18 Rn 12, 16; Schwander *IPR AT* 246.

120 MünchKomm/Martiny Art 34 Rn 16, 79a, Art 29 Rn 44; Art 30 Rn 70a; Lorenz RIW 1987, 560, 580; Reithmann/Martiny/Martiny *Internationales Vertragsrecht* Rn 744; id/Limmer Rn 397; Leible JBJZRW (1995) 245, 261; Junker IPRax 1993, 1, 9, 10; Staudinger/Magnus Art 34 Rn 36, 37; Lehmann *Zwingendes Recht* 219, 220; Kropholler *IPR* § 3 II, 3, § 52 V 1a.

121 Staudinger/Magnus Art 34 Rn 71; Kropholler *IPR* § 3 II 3, § 52 V 1a; Junker IPRax 1993, 1, 9, 10 'elementary protective norms'.

122 Leible JBJZRW (1995) 245, 261; Staudinger/Magnus Art 34 Rn 71.

123 For criticism, see Mäsch *Rechtswahlfreiheit* 127.

124 BT-Drucks 10/504, 83; BGH 26.10.1993 RIW 1994, 154, 157; Lorenz IPRax 1994, 429, 431; also see Roth RIW 1994, 275, 277; id *Schnyder/Heiß/Rudisch* 35, 38, 48.

6.[125] In Switzerland this question is certainly not as puzzling, since party autonomy is excluded with regard to consumer and employment contracts.

German case law is ambivalent about both questions: whether the protective rule can be internationally mandatory at all, and the relationship of arts 5 and 6 of the Convention to art 7 (2). Two leading cases of the Federal Labour Court seem to support the view that a rule can only be qualified as internationally mandatory rules in the sense of art 7 (2) if it pursues predominantly interests beyond those of the contracting parties. The Court held that certain rules protecting employees were not internationally mandatory, because the rules served mainly the fair reconciliation of the contracting parties.[126] However, in 1993 the Federal Supreme Court held,[127] with reference to the Giuliano/Lagarde Report, that it is in principle possible for consumer protection rules to be internationally mandatory. The Court did, however, not refer to the distinction proposed by the Federal Labour Court.[128] According to the Federal Supreme Court art 5 of the Rome Convention is *lex specialis*, with the result that mandatory consumer protection may be applicable to consumer contracts that fall outside the scope of art 5, despite the proper law of the contract.[129]

In conclusion, it can be stated that the dispute as to whether the '*special private law rules*' can be internationally mandatory in the sense of art 7 (2) of the Rome Convention and art 18 of the Swiss IPRG is complicated by the existence of special choice of law rules in arts 5 and 6 of the Convention.[130] However, this question should be separated from the general question about whether protective private law rules can be classified as internationally mandatory rules.

According to the Giuliano/Lagarde Report an exclusion of these protective rules is not justified, because consumer protection and transport law are expressly mentioned.[131] The same is true for the official reasoning of the German legislature.[132] In addition, there are a number of protective rules that include an express unilateral conflict rule that determines their international scope. In

---

125 Junker IPRax 1993, 1, 9; Lorenz RIW 1987, 569, 580; Droste *Begriff* 218, 219.

126 BAG 24.8.1989 BAG 63, 17, 32 (*Kanalfähren*); BAG 29.10.1992 IPRax 1994, 123, 128 (*Piloten*).

127 BGH 26.10.1993 RIW 1994, 154, 157; see Lorenz IPRax 1994, 429, 431.

128 Roth RIW 1994, 275, 277; Staudinger/Magnus Art 34 Rn 66.

129 BGH RIW 1997, 875, 878; BGH 26.10.1993 RIW 1994, 154, 157.

130 Junker IPRax 1998, 65, 69; id IPRax 1993, 1, 8, 9; id IPRax 1989, 69, 72 et seq; Mäsch *Rechtswahlfreiheit* 126, 129 et seq.

131 *Report* in *Contract Conflicts* 382; Roth *Schnyder/Heiß/Rudisch* 35, 43, 44.

132 BT-Drucks 10/504, 83 et seq; von Hoffmann IPRax 1989, 261, 264.

principle, it is therefore possible that protective rules are internationally mandatory.

In England it seems that authors are too willing to interpret a statute as an overriding statute for the sole reason that its policy is to protect the weaker party.[133] Nevertheless, rules that do not expressly determine their international scope should be only restrictively interpreted as overriding the choice of law rules. And, in the view of the present author the mere fact that these rules intend to protect the weaker party is insufficient to express a fundamental state policy that they must apply regardless of the proper law.

Hence, a protective rule should only be classified as internationally mandatory if it also serves public interests. Given the increasing tendency of modern welfare states to enact mandatory laws to protect the weaker party, an extensive application of these rules can disturb the bilateral system of conflict of laws and will run counter to fundamental principles, such as the principle of party autonomy.[134] In short, the concept of internationally mandatory rules has always been a rare exception to the ordinary conflict rules.

b Examples

The following examples of overriding statutes are from the fields of employment protection, consumer protection, lessee protection.[135]

---

[133] For instance Morse *Public Policy* England - 76 et seq with examples, such as the Consumer Credit Act 1974; concerning the Scottish Hire-Purchase Act, also see *English v Donelly* 1958 SC 494.

[134] Also see Vischer Rec des Cours 232 (1992) 13, 158 et seq.

[135] Other examples may stem from the protection of investors, such as The German Stock Exchange Act (BörsenG), 22.6.1896, as amended 1989, BGBl I 1989, 1412, that restricts the enforceability of claims under futures deals in certain circumstances; s 61 of the BörsenG is interpreted as internationally mandatory rules; cf MünchKomm/Martiny Art 34 Rn 76a; or the English Financial Services Act 1986, that in certain circumstances renders investment agreements unenforceable, Ss 5, 56 of the Act, cf Dicey & Morris *Conflict of Laws Vol II/12th ed* 1241, */13th ed* 1243, 1244. Another example is the law of transport: Cf *The Hollandia* [1983] AC 565. The case concerned a contract - expressly governed by Dutch law - to transport a machine from Scotland to the Dutch West Indies. The machine was damaged in a port in the Dutch West Indies. Under Dutch law, the Hague Rules would have been applicable, in terms of which the carrier's liability would have been much lower than under the Hague-Visby Rules. The House of Lords held that the Hague-Visby Rules (contained in a schedule to the Carriage of Goods by Sea Act 1971) have the force of law in the United Kingdom and are applicable irrespective of the governing law. This had previously been controversial, for references, see Morse *Public Policy* England - 87 Footnote 2; for details, see Dicey & Morris *Conflict of Laws Vol II/12th ed* 1217, 1240, */13th ed* 1221, 1243; also see *The Antares (Nos 1 and 2)* [1987] 1

(1) Employment protection

One well-known mandatory law that is explicitly international is the Employment Rights Act 1996 which provides in sec 204 (1) that for the purpose of this Act it is immaterial whether the law which governs any person's employment is the law of the United Kingdom, or of a part of the United Kingdom, or not. The Act does, however, contain provisions limiting its scope and the criteria defined in these provisions must be fulfilled before application of the Act is mandatory. According to sec 196 of the Act certain provisions do not apply when the employee ordinarily works outside Great Britain. Thus, the rules of the Act are internationally mandatory if the person ordinarily works in Great Britain, regardless of the proper law of the employment contract.[136]

Another well-known example is the Law Reform (Personal Injuries) Act 1948. Section 1 (3) of the Act protects injured employees from clauses that exempt the employee from liability. However, the Act is not expressly internationally mandatory and was not given overriding effect by the Court of Appeal in *Sayers v International Drilling Co.*[137] By contrast, in the Scottish case *Brodin v Seljan*,[138] the same provision was applied to an exemption clause contained in an employment contract, the proper law of which was Norway. The main difference in this case was that the accident took place in a Scottish port, and the employee sued the company for damages in Scotland.[139] Many authors, therefore, conclude that the provision on exemption clauses is internationally mandatory, provided that the injury occurs in England.[140]

Lloyd's Rep 424, 428 et seq; for further examples of English internationally mandatory rules in the field of international transport law, see Dicey & Morris *Conflict of Laws Vol I/12th /13th ed* 24, 25.

136 Dicey & Morris *Conflict of Laws Vol I/13th ed* 23, id *Vol II/13th ed* 1318; Cheshire & North's *Private International Law/13th ed* 579; cf for sec 153 (5) of the predecessor, the Employment Protection (Consolidation) Act 1978, Cheshire & North's *Private International Law/12th ed* 500.

137 [1971] 3 All ER 163 (CA). This case concerned a contract of employment between a Dutch company and an English employee on an oil rig in Nigerian waters. The contract contained an exemption clause restricting the employer's liability in the event of injury. Although this clause was void under the British Act, the court did not apply the Act. The objective proper law of the contract was held to be Dutch law, according to which the agreement was valid. Thus, the statute was held to be mandatory in only a domestic sense. For a detailed discussion, see Hartley Rec des Cours 266 (1997) 341, 413, 414.

138 1973 SC 213 (Outer House, Court of Session).

139 The Court held that sec 1 (3) of the Law Reform (Personal Injuries) Act 1948 was mandatory irrespective of the proper law of the contract, because the accident took place in Scotland.

140 Hartley Rec des Cours 266 (1992) 341, 415; Dicey & Morris *Conflict of Laws Vol II/12th /13th ed* 1317, 1318.

Other examples of express and implied internationally mandatory rules can be found in the Equal Pay Act 1970, the Sex Discrimination Act 1975 and the Race Relations Act 1976.[141]

In its leading case '*Kanalfähren*' (1989)[142] and the '*Piloten-decision*' (1992)[143] the Federal Labour Court (BAG) dealt with the application of German employee protection rules to contracts governed by a foreign law and thus developed principles according to which a mandatory rule can be classified as internationally mandatory.[144] The BAG held[145] that rules pursuing economic policy interests of the state, as well as social-political rules intended to protect the weaker party may be internationally mandatory irrespective whether they have a public or private law nature and stated that:

> For the classification it is crucial that the rule was enacted at least also in the public interest and not only in the interest of the contracting parties .... A public interest is indicated by aligned adjusting interference into private legal relations of economic and working life by prohibitions or permission reservations.....[146]

The BAG decided on basis of these principles that the general German dismissal protection regulations (§§ 1-14 Kündigungsschutzgesetz) and § 613 a of the German Civil Code (BGB) were not internationally mandatory, because they served mainly the fair reconciliation of the conflicting interests of employees and employers.[147]

---

141 For details, see Dicey & Morris *Conflict of Laws Vol II/13th ed* 1319, 1320.

142 BAG 24.8.1989 IPRax 1991, 407 et seq ('Kanalfähren').

143 BAG 26.10.1992 IPRax 1994, 123 et seq (Pilotenentscheidung); cf BAG 24.3.1992 NZA 1992, 1129.

144 In both cases a foreign law was the proper law of the contract by the choice of the parties, and in both cases the dismissal notice given to the employee was completely valid under the proper law, although invalid according to German law. The employees instituted an action against the terminations, relying on German provisions that offered protection from unwarranted termination. On these decisions, see Mankowsky IPRax 1994, 88 et seq; Roth RIW 1994, 275, 277 et seq; Magnus IPRax 1991, 382 et seq.

145 The court referred to the policy underlying the legislation of art 34 of the EGBGB (the German equivalent to art 7 (2) of the Rome Convention).

146 The court went on to state that 'they contrast to mandatory rules which serve above all the reconciliation of conflicting interests of the contracting parties...they are subject to the proper law of the contract....'; BAG 24.8.1989 IPRax 1991, 407, 410, 411; BAG 29.10.1992 IPRax 1994, 123, 128; cf Mankowsky IPRax 1994, 88, 94; but also Roth RIW 1994, 275, 278 who follows these principles in the field of labour law, but rejects them as general definition.

147 BAG 29.10.1992 IPRax 1994, 123, 128, 129; BAG 24.8.1989 IPRax 1991, 407, 411, § 613 a BGB protects the employee in cases where the business as a whole is transferred.

However, in the field of labour law many mandatory provisions pursue public interests and are thus held to be internationally mandatory.[148] Examples include the protection of mothers and severely disabled persons from unwarranted dismissal, and the protection of minors in employment.[149] The Swiss public labour law provisions in the 'Bundesgesetz über die Arbeit in Industrie, Gewerbe und Handel' are likewise internationally mandatory.[150]

(2) Consumer protection

Another well-known example of an English overriding statute is the Unfair Contract Terms Act 1977. The Act contains mandatory regulations that protect the consumer in many types of contracts.[151] Section 27 (2) stipulates that the provisions of the Act have effect notwithstanding any contract term that applies or purports to apply the law of some country outside the United Kingdom, provided that one of the conditions in the subsection is satisfied.[152] In Scotland[153] it has been held that the Hire Purchase and Small Debt (Scotland) Act 1932 applied to all contracts concluded in Scotland notwithstanding the fact

---

The German provisions were also not be applied on basis of the 'more-favourable principle', because the law that would have governed the contract without a choice of the parties (art 5 (2) RC), was the law chosen by the parties.

148 Reithmann/Martiny/Martiny *Internationales Vertragsrecht* Rn 1365; id/Limmer Rn 427, Junker IPRax 1993, 1,6, 7; BAG 24.8.1989 IPRax 1991, 407, 411.

149 Schwerbehindertengesetz; Mutterschutzgesetz, Reithmann/Martiny/Martiny *Internationales Vertragsrecht* Rn 1365, 1380, 1384, 1385; Kropholler *IPR* § 52 V 2; Junker IPRax 1993, 1, 6, 7.

150 From 13.3.1964 SR 822.11; Morscher *Rechtssetzungsakte* 91.

151 For further details, see Morse *Public Policy* England - 77; Dicey & Morris *Conflict of Laws Vol I/12th /13th ed* 23, 24 and id *Vol II/12th ed* 1296 et seq, */13th ed* 1295 et seq; Cheshire & North's *Private International Law/12th ed 500, /13th ed* 580.

152 These conditions are: (a) that the term appears to have been imposed wholly or mainly for the purpose of enabling the party imposing it to evade the application of the Act, or (b) that in the making of the contract one party contracted as consumer and was then habitually resident in the UK, and the essential steps necessary for the making of the contract were taken there.

153 *English v Donelly* 1958 SC 494, the statute's overriding nature was defined by interpretation. The court stated that 'the Act is a piece of social legislation designed for the protection of certain persons, i.e. members of the public who hire articles through companies ... Hence it follows that the test for the applicability of the Act, which under section 11 extends only to Scotland, is whether or not the contract was entered into in Scotland ..., irrespective of where the contract is ultimately completed or is to be executed ....'; also see the Australian decision *Kay's Leasing Corp Pty Ltd v Fletcher* (1964) 116 CLR 124; on which see Morse *Public Policy* England - 76; Hartley Rec des Cours 266 (1997) 341, 411 et seq.

that the contracting parties in this case had chosen the law of England to govern the hire-purchase agreement.

As has been explained, the question whether mandatory consumer protective rules without an express term indicating their international scope can qualify as internationally mandatory is disputed in Germany. Nevertheless, some consumer protective rules are expressly internationally mandatory. Most of them arise from unified EC law that has been transferred into national law. Some of the EC Directives contain '*annex conflict rules*' that unilaterally determine their scope of application in relation to 'third countries'.[154] In general these '*annex conflict rules*' contain a given standard that consumer protection is to be granted irrespective of the proper law provided the contract has a *close connection* with the countries of the member states.[155] One example is art 6 (2) of the Directive on Unfair Contract Terms (Richtlinie über mißbräuchliche Klauseln in Verbaucherverträgen 5.4.1993).[156] Paragraph 12 of the General Terms and Conditions of Trade Act (AGBG)[157] transfers the given standard of art 6 (2) of the Directive into German national law and leads to the applicability of the provisions of the AGBG despite the foreign proper law of the contract if 'the contract has a *close connection* to the territory of Germany'.[158] Thus, the rules of the Act are internationally mandatory, if the conditions of paragraph 12 are fulfilled.[159]

There is considerable dispute about whether the Act on the Right to Cancel Front Door Transactions (Haustürwiderrufsgesetz, HtWiG) and the Consumer

---

154 MünchKomm/Martiny Art 29 Rn 4; Junker IPRax 1998, 65, 70, 71. According to art 189 (3) EGV these 'annex conflict rules' are not choice of law rules, but contain the order to the Member states to adjust their own conflict rules to the standard of the Directive.

155 For the relationship to art 5 RC, see Junker IPRax 1989, 65, 70; MünchKomm/Martiny Art 29 Rn 4.

156 Directive 93/13 [1993] OJ L 95/29; printed in NJW 1993, 1838 et seq.

157 Gesetz zur Regelung des Rechts der Allgemeinen Geschäftsbedingungen 9.12.1976, BGBl I, 3317 as amended 19.7.1996, BGBl. I, 1013.

158 Section 2 determines a close connection '(1) if the contract was concluded because of a public offer or advertising or ... in the territory of the imposer and (2) the contract party has had his habitual residence in this territory while he expressed his will and the expression of will was given within the territory.' For delimitation problems, see Junker IPRax 1998, 65, 71; MünchKomm/Martiny Art 29 Rn 48.

159 Also see the unilateral conflict rule §8 of the Time-Sharing Act (TzWrG 20.12.1996 BGBl 1996 I, 2154-2175 which transfers the Directive from 26.10.1994 for the Protection of the Acquiring Party with regard to certain Aspects of Acquisition Contracts of Time Sharing of Property, art. 9 Directive 94/47 [1994] OJ L 280/83. Paragraph 8 TzWrG provides that German law is applicable if the property is situated in Germany even if the contract is governed by a foreign law.

Credit Act (Verbraucherkreditgesetz, VerbrKrG) can be interpreted as having an overriding effect.[160]

(3) Protection for tenants

In Germany and Switzerland, rules protecting tenants and tenant farmers are held to be mandatory regardless of the proper law, if the apartment or property is situated within Germany or Switzerland. Although the legal protection of tenants pursues both public interests and the fair reconciliation of the contracting parties,[161] the prevailing academic opinion and case law holds that these rules are internationally mandatory. This is because the legal protection of tenants is interwoven with public law provisions - regulation of the housing market.[162]

---

160 16.1.1986, BGBl I, 122 as amended 20.12.1996, BGBl I 2154, § 1 of the HtWiG contains a power of revocation; *pro* von Hoffmann IPRax 1989, 261, 268; Kohte EuZW 1990, 150, 153 Jayme IPRax 1990, 220, 222; *contra* Junker IPRax 1998, 1, 9; Mankowsky RIW 1995, 364, 368; Droste *Begriff* 169 et seq; MünchKomm/Sonnenberger Einl Rn 50; VerbrKrG 17.12.1990, BGBl. I 1990, 2840 as amended 20.12.1996, BGBl I, 2154; *pro* von Hoffmann, IPRax 1989, 271; Soergel/von Hoffmann Art 34 Rn 61; Kohte EuZW 1990, 150, 153; *contra* MünchKomm/Martiny Art 34 Rn 80; Droste *Begriff* 171 et seq.

161 Schubert RIW 1987, 729, 731argues therefore that these mandatory rules, and those which protect the consumer or employee, are not internationally mandatory.

162 Anderegg *Ausländische Eingriffsnorm* 94; MünchKomm/Sonnenberger Einl Rn 50; Vischer RabelsZ 53 (1989) 438, 446; Reithmann/Martiny/Limmer *Internationales Vertragsrecht* Rn 406; BAG 24.8.1989 IPRax 1991, 407, 411; Voser *Lois d'application immédiate* 61.

Chapter 5
Foreign internationally mandatory rules

The application of the forum's internationally mandatory rules despite the existence of a foreign proper law is well established. Whether *foreign* internationally mandatory rules are to be applied by the forum, however, is still problematic and unsettled. The forum's interests in applying foreign rules differ substantially from its interests in applying its own law. A judge is generally not bound by the rules of a foreign sovereign,[1] unless his own has directed him to do so by means of a statutory conflict rule,[2] an international Convention,[3] or the common law.[4]

Therefore, the question is whether *de lege lata* conflict rules referring to foreign internationally mandatory rules exist, or whether *de lege ferenda* it is possible and reasonable to develop special conflict rules regulating the applicability of internationally mandatory rules. Or whether, in the alternative, these foreign rules can justifiably be applied according to their own determined scope without any prior choice of law rule of the forum indicating their application?

In any event, it is clear that foreign internationally mandatory rules may affect private relationships. Contracts often have connections with a number of legal systems, in which mandatory legislation is enacted with marked effects on the contracts. Violation of the legislation may constitute a criminal offence and result in heavy penalties. It cannot be denied that these mandatory rules have a *factual* impact on parties' relationship. The question remains, however, whether the forum shall take account of the rules and their effects, which is a matter to be decided by the conflict of laws of the forum state.

As has already been noted, from the forum's point of view, foreign rules include those of the *lex causae*, as well as those of another foreign law, ie a *third* country. Where the conflict rules of the forum indicate that a foreign law is to govern the transaction, the question is whether *all* the mandatory rules of the proper law are automatically rendered applicable: both internationally and domestically mandatory rules, as well as the rules of private and public law. Do the conflict rules refer to private law only and not to rules that intervene in the private relationship in the public interest, or do they refer to the *lex causae* in its

---

1 The judge is bound only by his sovereign, see Lehmann *Zwingendes Recht* 18; Anderegg *Eingriffsnormen* 3; MünchKomm/Martiny Art 34 Rn 89.

2 Morscher *Rechtssetzungsakte* 49; Schubert RIW 1987, 729, 738.

3 For example, Art VIII (2) (b) of the Bretton Woods Agreement (IMF).

4 Schubert RIW 1987, 729, 738, 739.

entirety, including all its rules? The issue can be restated thus: Once the conflict rules have selected the relevant foreign legal system, what is their scope of reference within that system?[5]

With regard to the internationally mandatory rules of a third country that is neither the *lex fori* nor the *lex causae*, the question is whether these rules are to be applied and thus permitted to intrude into the contract, possibly rendering it illegal or unenforceable.[6] It is submitted that in this situation a further division needs to be made. As will be seen, in most decided cases, the contract was governed by the law of the forum state and the question was whether a foreign rule should be applied.[7] This is a *'false third country case'*, since there are in fact only two legal systems involved: the forum and a foreign law. In the '*true third country case'*,[8] the proper law is a foreign law and the internationally mandatory rule that intervenes in the legal relationship is of yet another foreign legal system: the third country.

Art 7 (1) of the Rome Convention allows a judge to give effect to third countries' internationally mandatory rules, under certain conditions and on a discretionary basis. However, this novel provision has been the subject of so much criticism that Germany and the United Kingdom entered a reservation (as they are entitled to do in terms of art 22).[9] Therefore, art 7 (1) is not in force in the United Kingdom and Germany. Switzerland, in contrast, has enacted a specific conflict of law provision permitting the consideration of third countries' internationally mandatory rules (art 19 of the Swiss IPRG).

The following examination of the application of foreign internationally mandatory rules in the countries under investigation commences with an exposition of the approaches of academic writers (section **I**), followed by case law solutions in Germany (section **II**) and the common law approach of the United Kingdom (section **III**). The solution of art 7 (1) of the Rome Convention and the impact of this rule on the pre-existing law in the United Kingdom and Germany is then examined (section **IV**). The investigation will be supplemented by consideration of the Swiss solution and a short survey of other legislative approaches.

---

5 Remien RabelsZ 54 (1990) 431, 461 et seq; Staudinger/Magnus Art 34 Rn 19 et seq; MünchKomm/Martiny Art 34 Rn 22, 24, 39 et seq.

6 Among others Lehmann ZRP 1987, 319, 320; Erne *Vertragsgültigkeit* 1 et seq.

7 MünchKomm/Martiny Art 34 Rn 23, 49; Drobnig *FS Neumayer* 159, 177; Dicey & Morris *Conflict of Laws Vol II* 1246, 1247; Morse *Public Policy* England - 70.

8 Lehmann *Zwingendes Recht* 12; MünchKomm/Martiny Art 34 Rn 23.

9 For England, see sec 2 (2) of the Contract (Applicable) Law Act 1990 which provides that art 7 (1) RC shall not have the force of law in England. Germany has not incorporated this article into its private international law Act, the EGBGB.

I Approaches of academic writers

There are various approaches to the interplay between foreign internationally mandatory rules and the normal conflict rules. In Germany and Switzerland (as well as in other continental European countries, such as France, Italy, Netherlands) authors debate whether and how those rules can be taken into account. In Germany there is a discrepancy between academic and case law solutions. The same was true of Swiss law prior to the IPR Reform 1989.[10] On the other hand, in England, most authors concentrate more pragmatically on an analysis of the case law.[11]

The following approaches are based on different basic understandings of the scope of reference of the normal conflict rules, and even of the function of private international law in general.[12] The academic proposals are concerned with the mandatory laws of both the *lex causae* and a third country, and usually the rules are examined in relation to each other.

1 '*Schuldstatutstheorie*' or '*Proper law doctrine*'

The advocates of the so-called '*Schuldstatutstheorie*' ('*proper law doctrine*' or '*Schuldstatuts-theory*') or '*Einheitsanknüpfung*'[13] ('*unity connection*'), including Mann and the Swiss academic Heini, submit that the normal conflict rules refer to the *lex causae* in its entirety.[14] Private international law is understood as a 'comprehensive' choice of law system whose normal choice of law rules refer to *all* the rules of the *lex causae* that are relevant to the issue, irrespective of

---

10 Busse ZverglRWiss 95 (1996) 386, 390, 394; Schurig RabelsZ 54 (1990) 217, 240 et seq; for Switzerland Erne *Vertragsgültigkeit* 12 et seq, 112 et seq; Morscher *Rechtssetzungsakte* 57 et seq.

11 However, some authors have expressed their opinions, and these will be referred to in this section. Eg, Lipstein *Conflict of laws and public law* 357; Mann Rec des Cours 132 (1971 I) 107, 157, 190.

12 See also Voser *Lois d'application immédiate* 50 et seq, 56.

13 For example, Kreuzer *Ausländisches Wirtschaftsrecht* 55; MünchKomm/Martiny Art 34 Rn 26.

14 Mann Rec des Cours 132 (1971-I) 107, 157 et seq; id *FS Wahl* 139 et seq; id *FS Beitzke* 607 et seq; cf recently Busse ZverglRWiss 95 (1996) 390, 414 et seq; for Switzerland Heini ZSR 100 (1981) 65 et seq; id BerGesVR 22 (1982) 37 et seq; in the past also Vischer *FG Gerwig* 167, 170, 171. However, Vischer abandoned his former point of view, and in 1974 proposed that the *lex causae* be applied in its entirety, as well as the rules of a third country by means of a special connection, id Rec des Cours 142 (1974 II) 1, 24. Today he supports the *Special Connection Theory* id Rec des Cours 232 (1992 I) 13, 165 et seq, 178 et seq; for references Erne *Vertragsgültigkeit* 112 et seq.

their public or private law nature.[15] Thus, the validity of a contract is governed exclusively and always by the proper law, and the proper law is applied 'as a whole, in its entirety, as it is in force'.[16]

They reject the '*principle of the non-applicability of foreign public law*', pointing out that public laws will not be '*directly*' applied in the sense that the forum would enforce a foreign state's exercise of sovereign power against citizens, in which case 'the state's jurisdiction to enforce its law *iure imperii* is in fact territorially limited'.[17] Rather, the concern in private international law is the '*indirect*' application of public prohibitions, with reference to their '*reflex effect*' or 'consequence' in private law and the private relationship.[18] Naturally, internationally mandatory rules, whether of private or public law, are subject to the forum's *ordre public* and, additionally, they will be inapplicable if the rule does not claim application in the concrete situation.[19] The *self-limitation* of these rules is thus respected. Internationally mandatory rules of a public or private law nature are thus always applicable if and to the extent that they belong to the proper law of the contract, and are rendered applicable by the choice of law rules of the forum, provided that they do not violate the forum's *ordre public*.

In terms of this theory, a third country's internationally mandatory rules are generally inapplicable, when the forum's conflict rules have referred to another law to govern the contract. Then the third country's rules have not been rendered applicable.[20] The only exception is where a conflict rule expressly orders the application of the law of a third country, such as Art VIII (2) (b) of the Bretton Woods Agreement (IMF).[21] However, a third country's internationally mandatory rules can be considered as '*facts*' within the domestic law

---

15 Mann Rec des Cours 132 (1971-I) 107, 157, 190; id *FS Wahl* 139, 146 et seq; Busse ZverglRWiss 95 (1996) 414, cf for a discussion Schäfer *FG Sandrock* 37, 41 et seq; Knüppel *Zwingendes Recht* 33 et seq.

16 Mann *FS Wahl* 139, 146; id Rec des Cours (1974 I) 107, 192.

17 Vischer Rec des Cours 232 (1992 I) 13, 151; Mann *FS Wahl* 139, 142.

18 Mann *FS Wahl* 139, 142 et seq; id Rec des Cours (1974-I) 107, 182, 192 et seq; cf also Vischer Rec des Cours (1992 I) 13, 150 et seq, Vischer, however, does not support the *Schuldstatuts-theory* any longer but favours the *Special Connection Theory*.

19 Mann *FS Wahl* 139, 141, 153, according to *Mann* this is a matter of substantive law and not for conflict of laws, critically Radtke ZverglRWiss 84 (1985) 325, 343 footnote 71 since the 'will' to apply is not a material element of the rule but conflict of laws element.

20 Mann *FS Beitzke* 607, 609 et seq; id *FS Wahl* 139, 159,160; id Rec des Cours (1974 I) 107, 157 et seq.

21 Mann *FS Beitzke* 607, 615.

rules of the *lex causae*.[22] As '*fact*' the violated foreign rule may be considered within the notion of *boni mores*[23] and can thus lead to invalidity of the contract if the latter is considered immoral, or may constitute the reason for impossibility of performance.[24]

Thus the crucial criterion for the question of whether (and how) foreign internationally mandatory rules are to be applied is whether the rule belongs to the proper law of the contract. A third country's rule is never applied but may be considered as 'fact' within the substantive law of the *lex causae*.[25]

As will be seen later in this study, the '*Schuldstatuts-theory*' was dominant in German case law until the 1950s. It was then abandoned by the Federal Supreme Court, at least with regard to the question of the applicability of internationally mandatory rules of a public law nature emanating from the proper law.[26] Swiss case law does not follow the *proper law doctrine*: Certain public law rules are in principle excluded from the scope of reference of the conflict rules and are thus inapplicable despite their belonging to the proper law of the contract.[27] German and Swiss courts have rejected - like the advocates of the proper law doctrine - a *direct application* of third countries' internationally mandatory rules on several grounds, but have taken these rules into account as '*facts*'.[28]

In England the dominant academic opinion and the courts' solution seem to correspond with the solution proposed by the advocates of the proper law doctrine: internationally mandatory rules are applicable as part of the *lex causae*. With regard to third countries' internationally mandatory rules the English position is more complex, as will be shown later. English courts have developed certain guidelines for taking these rules into account, but their juristic basis is uncertain.[29]

---

22 On the differentiation between application as rule and consideration as fact, see supra in Chapter 1,V, 4 and for criticism, see infra section 7, b.

23 The corresponding English rule would be English public policy.

24 Mann *FS Beitzke* 607, 608 et seq; id *FS Wahl* 139, 149; Heini ZSR 100 (1981) 65, 71; id BerDGesVR 22 (1982) 37, 46 et seq.

25 Mann *FS Wahl* 139, 160; Heini ZSR 100 (1981) 65, 83; cf Radtke ZverglRWiss 84 (1985) 332, 342.

26 Cf since 1959 BGH 21.12.1959 BGHZ 31, 367 et seq.

27 See the leading case BG 2.2.1954 BGE 80 II 53 et seq.

28 This will be discussed in detail later, see Chapter 5, II, 2, c.

29 The predominant point of view is that these rules are rules of English substantive law: Dicey & Morris *Conflict of Laws Vol II/12th ed* 1241, 1243 et seq, 1247, */13th ed* 1246 et seq, 1249, 1280 et seq; Cheshire & North's *Private International Law/12th ed* 518, 519, */13th ed* 585, 586, 600 et seq; Morse *Public Policy* England - 69 et seq, see Chapter 5, III, 2.

In contrast to England, where the proper law doctrine has found much academic support,[30] German and Swiss academic writers do not generally accept the approach.[31] However, it is partly supported in an altered form by advocates of the '*Combination Theory*' ('*Kombinationstheorie*').[32]

2 '*International Administrative Law*', '*Public Conflict of Laws*'[33]

The theory of '*International Public Law*' (*Internationales öffentliches Recht*) or '*International Administrative Law*' (*Internationales Verwaltungsrecht*) exists in direct opposition to the proper law doctrine. It was developed by Kegel[34] and has been accepted in German[35] and Swiss courts.[36]

The philosophy underlying this approach is that international private law refers to private law alone, not public law.[37] Public law rules do not promote justice between individuals, they promote the interests of the state, and are therefore subject to '*International Administrative Law*'[38] or '*Public Conflict of Laws*'.[39] The latter is understood as to consist of the national conflict rules that indicate which public law is to be applied.[40] Public conflict of laws is based on the

30 Dicey & Morris *Conflict of Laws Vol II/12th ed* 1241, 1243, 1247, */13th ed* 1243, 1244, 1248; Forsyth *The role of public law* 94, 105; Collier *Conflict of Laws* 206; Cheshire & North's *Private International Law/12th ed* 518 et seq, */13th ed* 600 et seq; Schäfer *FG Sandrock* 37, 41 footnote 21.

31 Nowadays Piehl RIW 1988, 841 et seq; Palandt/Heldrich Art 34 Rn 4 - 6; Busse ZverglRWiss 95 (1996) 414 et seq; Heini ZSR 100 (1981) 65 et seq; id BerDGesVR 22 (1982) 37 et seq.

32 Cf infra section 4; Siehr RabelsZ 52 (1988) 41 et seq; Knüppel *Zwingendes Recht* 84.

33 Or '*conflict of public laws*' (Öffentliches Kollisionsrecht) which is by no means the same as '*public international law*', see Mann Rec des Cours (1974-I) 107, 118. Some authors distinguish the *principle of territoriality* from the so called *Power Theory* as separate approaches, MünchKomm/Martiny Art 34 Rn 28, 29; Staudinger/Magnus Art 34 Rn 132, 136. In the present study, however, it is believed that the *Power Theory* is one aspect of the doctrine of *international administrative law*.

34 Soergel/Kegel*/11th ed* vor Art 7 Rn 395 et seq; Kegel/Seidl-Hohenfeldern *FS Ferid* 233, 236 et seq; Kegel *IPR/5th ed* § 2 IV, § 23; Kegel *FS Seidl-Hohenveldern* 243, 250 et seq.

35 For the German case law see Chapter 5, II; cf on the similarities between this approach and the German jurisdiction, cf Lehmann *Zwingendes Recht* 73; Coester ZVerglRWiss 82 (1983) 1, 2. Other academic writers who endorse Kegel's approach are Sandrock/Steinschulte *Handbuch* A Rn 184 et seq; Schäfer *FG Sandrock* 37, 48 et seq.

36 See Erne *Vertragsgültigkeit* 15, 16; BGE 80 II 53, 63; BGE 95 II 109, 114; BGE 107 II 489, 492.

37 Soergel/Kegel*/11th ed* vor Art 7 Rn 395; BGHZ 31, 370 et seq; BGHZ 64, 183, 188 et seq.

38 Sandrock/Steinschulte *Handbuch* A Rn 185; Kegel *Rôle of Public Law* 29, 31.

39 Kegel *FS Seidl-Hohenveldern* 243, 244.

40 Kegel *Rôle of Public Law* 29, 36.

'*principle of territoriality*' (*Territorialitätsgrundsatz*), namely, that public law in principle has no effect outside the territory of its legislating country. It follows that foreign public law is necessarily inapplicable in the forum state, regardless of whether the public law forms part of the proper law or a third country's law.[41] With regard to state intervention into private contracts, the *principle of territoriality* means that 'each state may encroach upon private rights in its territory and only there'.[42] Thus internationally mandatory public law rules of the proper law are not rendered applicable by the conflict rules of private international law, but are subject to the *International Public Law*, and accordingly do not have effect outside the territory of the enacting country.[43]

There are, however, exceptions to this general principle. Firstly, foreign public law is applicable if the foreign enacting state has the *power to implement* it or if the provision has *de facto already affected* the relationship.[44] The applicability of this exception will depend on the individual circumstances. Examples of the foreign state having the power to implement its mandatory rules are where a debtor resides within the enacting state, or where relevant property is situated within the foreign state.[45]

Secondly, Kegel holds that '*equality of interests*' may form an exception to the general inapplicability of foreign public law. If the foreign rule pursues interests that are equally protected in the forum state, foreign public law should be applied even though it serves foreign interests.[46] Examples can be found in bilateral treaties and international Conventions, such as art VIII (2) (b) of the IMF.[47] Having regard to equality of interests may well lead to a consideration of the foreign provision as fact within the substantive law rules, and render the contract void because of its immoral content or purpose. Alternatively, it is argued that the factual effects of the provision on a private relationship may be

---

41 Kegel *FS Seidl-Hohenveldern* 243, 246; Sandrock/Steinschulte *Handbuch* A Rn 184, 185; Schäfer *FG Sandrock* 37, 49; for the principle of territoriality, also see BGHZ 31, 370 et seq; BGHZ 64, 188 et seq.

42 Kegel *Rôle of Public Law* 29, 32.

43 Cf Soergel/von Hoffmann Art 34 Rn 3; Schäfer *FG Sandrock* 37, 49.

44 Sandrock/Steinschulte *Handbuch* A Rn 187 - 190; Schäfer *FG Sandrock* 37, 49; BGHZ 31, 367, 371.

45 Soergel/Kegel/*11th* ed vor Art 7 Rn 396 et seq; Schäfer *FG Sandrock* 37, 49.

46 German and Swiss courts have formulated a further exception to the dogma of non-applicability of foreign public law. If the foreign rule serves private and not economic state interests, it may be applied, BGHZ 31, 367, 371; BGHZ 64, 183, 190; BGE 80 II 53, 61 et seq; BGE 95 II 109, 114; cf Sandrock/Steinschulte *Handbuch* A Rn 193; Schäfer *FG Sandrock* 37, 49.

47 Kegel *Rôle of Public Law* 29, 36; Sandrock/Steinschulte *Handbuch* A Rn 191; Schäfer *FG Sandrock* 37, 49.

considered if they result in impossibility of performance or frustration of the contract.[48] This process is not an application of the foreign law, but simply its consideration as '*factum*': a so-called '*factual circumstance abroad*' (*Auslandssachverhalt*).[49]

3 '*Special Connection Theory*' or '*Theory of Special Point of Contact*'

At the outset it must be emphasised that there is no uniform *Special Connection Theory* (*Sonderanknüpfungslehre*). On the contrary, the theory is debated from different positions and given different nuances of meaning.[50] It is beyond the scope of this thesis to deal with all the manifestations of this theory in detail. Nevertheless, the *Special Connection Theory* seems to be relatively unexplored in the common law world, and the structural foundations of this theory and the main approaches need to be explained.[51]

The theory is similar to the theory of *International Public Law* in that it excludes all internationally mandatory rules, whether of the *lex causae* or of a third country, from the scope of reference of the normal choice of law rules. Internationally mandatory rules are therefore subjected to *special conflict rules* that are independent of the normal choice of law rules.[52] In contrast, however, to the theory of *International Public Law*, this result is not based on the principle that normal conflict rules cannot refer to public law, but rather on the notion that the connecting factors of the normal conflict rules for contracts are not

---

48 Schäfer *FG Sandrock* 37, 50; Kegel *FS Seidl/Hohenveldern* 243, 258, 273; id *Rôle of Public Law* 29, 55 et seq.

49 Kegel *Rôle of Public Law* 29, 46, 55 et seq; Schäfer *FG Sandrock* 37, 50 et seq.

50 Similarly Lehmann *Zwingendes Recht* 66; Radtke ZVerglRWiss 84 (1985) 325, 335. Authors who favour a *Sonderanknüpfung* include Wengler ZVerglRWiss54 (1941) 168 et seq; Zweigert RabelsZ 14 (1942) 183 et seq; Neumayer RabelsZ 25 (1960) 653, 654; Drobnig *FS Neymayer* 159 et seq; Sonnenberger *FS Rebmann* 819 et seq; MünchKomm/Sonnenberger Einl Rn 34 et seq, 58 et seq, 379 et seq; MünchKomm/Martiny Art 34 Rn 33 et seq; von Hoffmann RabelsZ 38 (1974) 396, 413 et seq; Soergel/von Hoffmann Art 34 Rn 86 et seq; Kreuzer *Ausländisches Wirtschaftsrecht* 81 et seq; Kropholler *IPR* § 52 IX; Schiffer *Normen* 173 et seq; Großfeld/Rogers ICLQ 32 (1983) 931 et seq; Schurig RabelsZ 54 (1990) 217 et seq; id *Lois* 55 et seq, Reithmann/Martiny/Limmer *Internationales Vertragsrecht* Rn 458 et seq; Mentzel *Sonderanknüpfung* 224 et seq; for Switzerland Vischer RabelsZ 53 (1989), 439 et seq; id Rec des Cours 232 (1992 I) 13, 265, 278 et seq; Erne *Vertragsgültigkeit* 147 et seq; Voser *Lois d'application immédiate* 69 et seq; Morscher *Rechtssetzungsakte* 55, 56, 88, 89; Schnyder *Wirtschaftskollisionsrecht* 30 et seq.

51 For details Mentzel *Sonderanknüpfung* 16 et seq; Knüppel *Zwingendes Recht* 52 et seq.

52 See Kreuzer *Schlechtriem/Leser* 89, 98; id *Ausländisches Wirtschaftsrecht* 59 et seq; Radtke ZVerglRWiss 84 (1985) 325, 334; for criticism, see Schiffer *Normen* 103 et seq.

suited to choosing foreign internationally mandatory rules,[53] and therefore cannot render these rules applicable.[54]

a '*Conflict of Economic Laws*' (*Wirtschaftskollisionsrecht*)

The special connection theories assume that the normal multilateral conflict rules of private international law are not appropriate as a means of reference to mandatory rules that pursue the economic and political interests of a foreign country. The traditional conflict rules have the purpose of identifying the spatially most suitable legal system.[55] The latter is determined by connecting factors, which are mainly about settling the parties' conflicting interests. These connecting factors include, in particular, an (express) choice of law but they also include such objective connecting factors as residence, domicile and place of performance.

Internationally mandatory rules serve state economic and political goals and the interests of the enacting country, which are not taken into account by the connecting factors of the general choice of law rules for contracts.[56] It is also argued that the multilateral conflict rules are based on the *principle of equality* and therefore the interchangeability *of legal systems*.[57] This equality and interchangeability, however, is no longer relevant and justified where a rule serves a state's economic and social-political interests.[58]

It is therefore argued that the question of when these state interests are to be taken into account by the application of international mandatory rules cannot be answered by the ordinary choice of law rules. Instead, the application of internationally mandatory rules that uphold state interests requires different conflict rules, taking into account the particular interests at stake.[59]

---

53 As well as those rules of the forum!

54 See Radtke ZVerglRWiss 84 (1985)325, 334, 338 et seq; Kreuzer *Ausländisches Wirt schaftsrecht* 82 et seq; id *Schlechtriem/Leser* 106 et seq; MünchKomm/Martiny Art 34 Rn 34; id/Sonnenberger Einl Rn 34; Vischer RabelsZ 53 (1989) 438, 441;Voser *Lois d'application immédiate* 50 et seq; Morscher *Rechtssetzungsakte* 55, 56, 88, 89.

55 MünchKomm/Sonnenberger Einl Rn 34.

56 Mentzel *Sonderanknüpfung* 39; Kreuzer *Ausländisches Wirtschaftsrecht* 81 et seq; Vischer RabelsZ 53 (1989) 438, 440 et seq; id Rec des Cours 232 (1992 I) 13, 179 et seq.

57 This principle is also well known in South African PIL, see Forsyth *Private International Law* 6.

58 Kreuzer *Schlechtriem/Leser* 89, 108; Schnyder *Wirtschaftskollisionsrecht* Rn 11; Basedow RabelsZ 52 (1988) 8, 9, 22; for criticism of this argument, see Siehr RabelsZ 52 (1988) 41, 88; Schurig RabelsZ 54 (1990) 217, 230; Schubert RIW 1987, 729, 738 et seq.

59 Sonnenberger *FS Rebmann* 819, 827; Kreuzer *Schlechtriem/Leser* 107, 108 et seq; id *Ausländisches Wirtschaftsrecht* 82; MünchKomm/Sonnenberger Einl Rn 34; Basedow

An independent and new system of conflict of laws concerning the applicability of internationally mandatory rules intervening in private contracts has to be created: the '*Conflict of Economic Laws*'.[60] It consists of unilateral mandatory rules of different legal systems, and an attempt at systematising their application and conditions for application.[61] However, this choice of law system is not a new branch of law, nor is it in itself conclusive. Rather, it is a systematisation of mandatory rules gathered from several areas of law that are important in international commerce. This quasi '*second*' conflict of laws system does not replace the traditional private international law, but supplements it and applies cumulatively. Its existence and growing importance is justified by increasing state interference in private relationships, a consequence of the change from the liberal state to the modern welfare state.[62] It is not yet conclusively established how the conflict rules have to be formulated, and under what conditions mandatory rules are applicable. In other words, what is the relevant connecting factor and are there other conditions that must be fulfilled?

b Does the special connection imply a return to unilateralism?

Does the '*special connection*' of internationally mandatory rules imply a return to the unilateral approach of the *statute theory* and thus a change of method?[63] In debating this question, the following two questions are often not clearly separated from each other.

One question is whether the foreign internationally mandatory rule is applied by the forum for the sole reason that it claims application, and whether the forum must establish which foreign law claims application to the transaction.[64] This approach would in fact imply a return to the unilateral approach. But this is by no means the dominant opinion amongst scholars. As will be seen later, the reason for taking foreign internationally mandatory rules into account is, according to most scholars, the existence of statutory or judge-made conflict

RabelsZ 52 (1988) 8, 9; Kropholler *IPR* § 52 IX; Hentzen RIW 1988, 508, 509; Vischer Rec des Cours 232 (1992 I) 13, 179 et seq; Radtke ZVerglRWiss 84 (1985) 325, 338.

60 Drobnig, Basedow and Siehr in RabelsZ 52 (1988) 1 et seq, 8 et seq, 41et seq; Remien RabelsZ 54 (1990) 431 et seq; Schnyder *Wirtschaftskollisionsrecht* (1990); Schubert RIW 1987, 729 et seq.

61 See Schnyder *Wirtschaftskollisionsrecht* (1990) and the articles of Drobnig, Basedow and Siehr in RabelsZ 52 (1988) 1 et seq.

62 Cf Chapter 1; Basedow RabelsZ 52 (1988) 8, 13 et seq; Schnyder *Wirtschaftskollisionsrecht* Rn 29.

63 For a short survey of the statute theory and the differences between it and the multilateral choice of law system as developed by Savigny, see Forsyth *Private International Law* 31 et seq, 41 et seq, 44.

64 Vischer Rec des Cours 232 (1992 I) 13, 168; also see Mentzel *Sonderanknüpfung* 58.

rules of the forum state, ie the forum decides autonomously which foreign rules are to applied.[65]

A separate question is whether there are parallels with the statute theory because the ordinary multilateral conflict rules consist of a category and a connecting factor that indicate the applicable legal system. In contrast to the normal conflict rules, the category of the 'new' conflict rules of economic law is not a legal relationship or a legal question, but certain mandatory rules. The statute theory also took groups of norms, rather than a legal relationship, as the starting point of the choice of law process.[66]

c Origins of the *Special Connection Theory*

The *Special Connection Theory* was founded by Wengler. He considered the scope of applicability of foreign mandatory laws independently of the proper law,[67] and suggested that mandatory laws should not only be applied if they belonged to the proper law of the contract. In addition, mandatory legislation of a *third* legal system should be applicable under certain conditions and after consideration of its own scope of applicability.[68] Wengler established the following conditions for the applicability of foreign mandatory rules:[69]

- The spatial scope of the rule must demand application (*örtlicher Geltungswille*).
- There must be a '*really close connection*' between the legal relationship and the enacting country. An example is the ability of the enacting country to implement its rule because it is the country where a contract is to be performed. A state acts '*ultra vires*' and cannot expect an application of its mandatory rules by another state if it declares its provisions to be extraterritorially applicable, even if there is no or only a minor link.
- The provision must not violate the *ordre public* of the forum.[70]

---

65 See Siehr RabelsZ 52 (1988) 41, 84; Staudinger/Magnus Art 34 Rn 12; MünchKomm/Martiny Art 34 Rn 99; Schubert RIW 1987, 729, 734 et seq.

66 Siehr RabelsZ 52 (1988) 41, 71, 72; Mentzel *Sonderanknüpfung* 56 et seq; for criticism, see Schurig RabelsZ 54 (1990) 217, 230.

67 Wengler ZVerglRWiss 54 (1941) 168 et seq.

68 Ibid 168, 182.

69 Ibid 168, 183, 185, 187.

70 Ibid 168, 197. Wengler later completed his approach with the criterion of mutuality or reciprocity, viz a state that has enacted mandatory rules that it wants to be applied regardless of the proper law of the contract should mutually apply those of another country. Cf RabelsZ 47 (1983) 215, 248; Lehmann *Zwingendes Recht* 68.

Zweigert adopted Wengler's approach and concretised it to prohibitive regulations that render performance illegal.[71] He amplified the criterion of the '*close connection*' to consideration of the '*international typical interests*' of states where the rules shall be applied.[72] Mandatory provisions that render performance illegal do not infringe typical international interests and are thus applicable by means of a special connection *if the movement of assets leading to performance occurs either wholly or in part within the territory of the country that has enacted them*.[73]

Both Wengler and Zweigert argue that the '*special connection*' process is based on the overall objective in conflict of laws of achieving an internationally uniform result, ie *decisional harmony*.[74] As was previously explained, each state on its own determines the scope of applicability of certain mandatory provisions that pursue important state interests. Consequently, in order to reach the same result wherever litigation takes place, the forum has to apply the internationally mandatory rules of a foreign enacting state. Furthermore, Wengler and Zweigert emphasise the need to respect the interests of foreign states.[75] However, neither author explains why these norms require a special connection, nor do they explain the nature of the difference between a special connection and the traditional allocation technique.

---

71 Zweigert RabelsZ 14 (1942) 283 et seq; Lehmann *Zwingendes Recht* 69; Radtke ZVerglRWiss 84 (1985) 325, 335.

72 Zweigert RabelsZ 14 (1942) 283, 291.

73 Zweigert RabelsZ 14 (1942) 283, 290 - 295; Zweigert distinguishes '*règles sympathiques*' and '*règles hétérogènes*'; cf also Schulte *Eingriffsnormen* 123, 127; Radtke ZVerglRWiss 84 (1985), 325, 336.

74 About this principle in South African PIL, see Forsyth *Private International Law* 60.

75 Wengler ZVerglRWiss 54 (1941) 168, 181; Zweigert RabelsZ 14 (1942) 283, 287 - 290; with regard to comity in South African PIL, see Forsyth *Private International Law* 38 et seq, 58, 59.

d Further developments

Various other attempts have been made to develop criteria for a special connection of foreign mandatory provisions.[76] The different approaches can be classified in four groups:

(1) One applies foreign internationally mandatory rules according to their claim of application (*Unilateralisation*). The advocates of this approach, however, stress that it is still for the forum to decide whether foreign mandatory rules will be applied, and excessive claims of applicability are restricted by controlling the content of the foreign mandatory rules.[77]

(2) Others propose that foreign internationally mandatory rules should be applied if corresponding mandatory provisions of the forum state are applicable despite the proper law of the contract (*Bilateralisation*).[78]

(3) Most academic authors argue that the spatial criterion of a *close connection* between the situation and the enacting state is the real reason for a special connection.[79]

(4) Recent statements emphasise that the reason for a special connection is the *interest of the forum* in the application of the foreign rule. Thus some authors refer exclusively to the forum's interest in the application of the foreign rule while others combine this criterion with the spatial criterion of a close connection.[80]

Generally, the above conditions and reasons for a special connection are combined in some form. This makes it extremely difficult to identify a clear division between the different 'approaches', and each may therefore be interpreted as a separate attempt to specify the conditions of a special connection.[81] Disagreement about the concrete formulation of the conflict rules,

---

76 For the following classification, see Kreuzer *Ausländisches Wirtschaftsrecht* 62 et seq; Reithmann/Martiny/Limmer *Internationales Vertragsrecht* Rn 459.

77 Von Hoffmann RabelsZ 38 (1974) 396, 413 et seq; Soergel/von Hoffmann Art 34 Rn 89 et seq; Vischer Rec des Cours 232 (1990 I) 13, 168 et seq.

78 For references,see Kreuzer *Ausländisches Wirtschaftsrecht* 62 footnote 206.

79 Wengler ZVerglRWiss 54 (1941) 168, 185 et seq; MünchKomm/Martiny Art 34 Rn 99 et seq; also Großfeld/Rogers ICLQ 32 (1983) 931, 944.

80 See especially Kreuzer *Ausländisches Wirtschaftsrecht* 92 et seq; but also MünchKomm/ Sonnenberger Einl Rn 58 et seq, 379 et seq; Sonnenberger *FS Rebmann* 819, 833; the shared values approach of Großfeld/Rogers ICLQ 32 (1983) 931, 939, 943 et seq; Erne *Vertragsgültigkeit* 206.

81 Similar Reithmann/Martiny/Limmer *Internationales Vertragsrecht* Rn 458.

the relevant connecting factors, and the conditions under which foreign internationally mandatory rules should be applied by means of a special connection is a result of two factors: the absence of normative guides and the variety of possibly relevant mandatory provisions.[82]

In general, instead of using general conflict rules (with necessarily vague and indefinite conditions) for all types of internationally mandatory rules, there is a trend towards a greater differentiation in conflict rules and connecting factors for internationally mandatory rules. The differentiation depends on the legal field to which the internationally mandatory rule belongs, for example, a special connection for anti-trust law or foreign trade law.[83]

Alongside this trend, the debate has led over the past years to a fruitful conclusion that the elements of a (general) conflict rule are to be interpreted more specifically, making differentiation possible. The *Special Connection Theory* has also been given a principled base, which it lacked in the early approaches of Wengler and Zweigert.[84]

e Double functionality of contracts

The dogmatic foundation of the need for a special connection is the fact that states intervene increasingly in private relationships, which has consequences for the conflict of laws process. As elaborated by some academics, one of whom is Kreuzer,[85] the basis of the special connection is an understanding that a contract does not exclusively concern the interests of the contracting parties. In the modern welfare state, contracts are simultaneously objects and instruments of the governmentally guided economy, a phenomenon that is referred to as the '*double functionality*' of contracts in economic law.[86] Kreuzer eg speaks of the '*micro-function*' of a contract (the fair reconciliation of the interests of the contracting parties) and its '*macro-function*' (the economic system of a state).[87]

---

[82] MünchKomm/Sonnenberger Einl Rn 35; MüchKomm/Martiny Art 34 Rn 25; Kreuzer *Schlechtriem/Leser* 89, 98; id *Ausländisches Wirtschaftsrecht* 62; Sonnenberger *FS Rebmann* 819, 831.

[83] Radtke ZVerglRWiss 84 (1985) 325, 338; Sonnenberger *FS Rebmann* 819, 831; Kreuzer *Schlechtriem/Leser* 89,110.

[84] See Kreuzer *Schlechtriem/Leser* 89, 108 et seq; Mentzel *Sonderanknüpfung* 31, 38; Schiffer *Normen* 151 et seq.

[85] Kreuzer *Ausländisches Wirtschaftsrecht* 82 et seq; id *Schlechtriem/Leser* 89, 106; Rehbinder JZ 1973, 152 et seq.

[86] Kreuzer *Ausländisches Wirtschaftsrecht* 82 et seq; id *Schlechtriem/Leser* 89, 106; Rehbinder JZ 1973, 152 et seq; Mentzel *Sonderanknüpfung* 38 et seq; Voser *Lois d'application immédiate* 51 et seq; Schnyder *Wirtschaftskollisionsrecht* Rn 29.

[87] Kreuzer *Schlechtriem/Leser* 89, 106 et seq; id *Ausländisches Wirtschaftsrecht* 83.

As has been noted, the ordinary conflict rules for contracts are based on a concept that considers the contract to be an instrument for the fair reconciliation of the interests of the contracting parties. The relevant connecting factors (party autonomy and objective factors, such as the characteristic performance) focus only on private interests (*micro-function*) and do not take into account the interests of states in regulating their economic and social system (*macro-function*). A disparity between the double functionality of contracts in substantive law and the international law of contracts becomes evident if one assumes that the normal conflict rules refer to one legal system entirely and exclusively.[88]

The strict adherence to the notion of the normal conflict rules covering all rules of the designated legal systems leads to skewed results. The objective connecting factor of the closest connection, which is presumed to be the law of the country where the party who is to effect the characteristic performance resides, would, for instance, exclude the exchange control regulations of the country of the pecuniary debtor.[89] A further example is that it could lead to the application of an export ban enacted by the state of the seller, but could ignore an import ban enacted by the state of the buyer.[90]

The same is true for the subjective connecting factor: the freedom of choice of law. In most countries parties are allowed to choose a neutral law, one with which the transaction might not have any connection apart from the choice of law itself. Is it reasonable to apply this legal system in its entirety, including its economic and state-political legislation, and to ignore those rules of the legal system with which the contract is objectively most closely connected? It seems difficult to justify the application of the economic legislation of the neutral law and at the same time to exclude the latter country's law, although this country might have a strong interest in the matter.

For the reasons given, internationally mandatory rules that pursue the state's economic and social-political interests and serve the functioning of an economic and social system do not fall within the scope of reference of the normal conflict rules, but have to be connected separately. It is argued, in relation to third countries' internationally mandatory rules, there is no justification for preferential treatment of the rules of the proper law simply because the normal conflict rules refer to the legal system from which they emanate.[91]

---

88 Kreuzer *Schlechtriem/Leser* 89, 107; id *Ausländisches Wirtschaftsrecht* 82; Mentzel *Sonderanknüpfung* 39; Voser *Lois d'application immédiate* 52.

89 Cf Kreuzer *Ausländisches Wirtschaftsrecht* 83.

90 Cf Vischer Rec des Cours 232 (1990 I) 13, 160.

91 Voser *Lois d'application immédiate* 53; Vischer Rec des Cours 232 (1992 I) 13, 184.

f Elements of a conflict rule for a special connection

Despite the many aspects of disagreement, the different approaches to a special connection have four propositions in common:[92]

- The provision referred to must be *internationally mandatory*.
- All the *conditions* for the application of the provision must be fulfilled.
- There must be a *sufficiently close connection* between the enacting country and the factual situation or legal relationship.
- The *content* of the provision and its *legal consequence* must be *compatible* with the legal system of the forum.

These four conditions are more or less comprehensively referred to as essential conditions for a special connection, although the sequence of the criteria and their content may differ slightly. They will be examined more extensively below.

g Internationally mandatory rule

The first condition for a special connection is that the foreign mandatory rule must claim application regardless of the proper law of the contract. The difficulties with the definition of rules that are internationally mandatory, and thus subject to a special connection, have already been scrutinised.[93] This issue became one of the most problematic tasks of the *Special Connection Theory*.

It is not quite clear whether the internationally mandatory character of a rule is to be determined by the foreign enacting state or by the forum.[94] It should at least be for the enacting state to determine under what conditions the rule claims application. However, with regard to the general definition as to what type of rule falls outside the scope of reference of the normal conflict rules, and has to be connected separately, it might be unrealistic to expect a forum state to adopt a foreign definition of an internationally mandatory rule, although this clearly would promote decisional harmony.

---

92 For instance Lorenz RIW 1987, 569, 581 et seq; MünchKomm/Martiny Art 34 Rn 98 et seq; Kreuzer *Schlechtriem/Leser* 89, 98; Schubert RIW 1987, 729, 734; for further references, see Schäfer *FG Sandrock* 39, 45; Radtke ZVerglRWiss 84 (1985) 325, 335.

93 See supra, Chapter 3, II.

94 *Foreign state* Lorenz RIW 1987, 569, 581; Magnus/Staudinger Art 34 Rn 12; *forum* MünchKomm/Martiny Art 34 Rn 9; MünchKomm/Sonnenberger Einl Rn 34; Voser *Lois d'application immédiate* 57.

It has to be reiterated at this point that, according to the predominant opinion, the claim of a foreign rule to apply is neither the only condition for a special connection nor a sufficient *reason* for a special connection.[95] In short, foreign internationally mandatory rules are not applied simply because they claim application. There is no principle in public international law that requires the forum state to apply the law of a foreign country. On the contrary, the application of foreign law is exclusively a matter for each legal system to determine on its own. Therefore, foreign internationally mandatory laws are applied or considered by the forum only to the extent that the conflict of laws of the forum so requires.[96]

Some of the academic authors, however, tend towards a unilateral approach and allow the foreign law to determine its own sphere of application.[97] But these authors also require that further criteria be fulfilled, such as an interest of the forum, international interests, and/or a close connection, and these criteria serve as limitations on the foreign rule's claim to apply. In effect, the forum state has the power to determine whether the foreign rule's claim to apply is reasonable and justified.[98]

The prevailing opinion, on the other hand, understands the condition of the foreign mandatory law's claim of application as a final exclusionary criterion that must be fulfilled. A foreign internationally mandatory rule is - although applicable according to choice of law principles of the forum state - not applied if it does not claim to be applicable in the situation.[99]

---

95 MünchKomm/Martiny Art 34 Rn 99; Kreuzer *Ausländisches Wirtschaftsrecht* 91, 92; MünchKomm/Sonnenberger Einl 58 et seq, 379 et seq; see also Vischer Rec des Cours 232 (1990 I) 13, 168 footnote 363; Schiffer *Normen* 159, 160.

96 Siehr RabelsZ 52 (1988) 41, 65, 84; MünchKomm/Martiny Art 34 Rn 99; Coester ZVerglRWiss 82 (1983) 1, 8 et seq; MünchKomm/Sonnenberger Einl Rn 34; Schubert RIW 1987, 729, 734; Mentzel *Sonderanknüpfung* 228 et seq; Schurig RabelsZ 54 (1990) 217, 231; Erne *Vertragsgültigkeit* 96, 97; see also Lipstein *Conflicts of Public Laws* 357, 358 et seq; Philip *Recent Provisions* 241, 248.

97 Vischer Rec des Cours 232 (1990 I) 13, 168; Soergel/von Hoffmann Art 34 Rn 89, 92; von Hoffmann RabelsZ 38 (1974) 413; see also Kropholler *IPR* § 3 II.

98 Soergel/von Hoffmann Art 34 Rn 89 et seq; Philip *Recent Provisions* 241, 249.

99 See MünchKomm/Martiny Art 34 Rn 99; MünchKomm/Sonnenberger Einl Rn 63. Kreuzer *Ausländisches Wirtschaftsrecht* 90 stresses that the reference to the foreign rule is not a reference to substantive law that does not consider the will to apply. Also see Siehr RabelsZ 52 (1988) 41, 71, 72. In this regard, also see the differing bilateral approach that applies foreign mandatory rules in the circumstances in which the forum's internationally mandatory rules apply.

The *Special Connection Theory* as developed by Wengler and Zweigert has sometimes been interpreted as similar to unilateralism, or as expressing a unilateral way of thinking.[100] The criticism was that the claim of application of the foreign law is the wrong connecting factor.[101] But this conclusion does not follow from Wengler's article. Although often not clearly expressed, according to Wengler and most advocates of this theory, it is the forum that decides which foreign law may be applied. From the point of view of the forum, the relevant criteria for the decision are a *sufficient close connection* or the *forum's interest* in application of the foreign rule.[102] The misunderstanding might be a result of the fact that the classification of a foreign rule as internationally mandatory has unfortunately been placed at the beginning of the choice of law process.[103] However Wengler made it clear that:

> It shall be permitted to start with a sentence *which should logically be the last*, but which is easier to understand: the foreign mandatory law is applied in so far as it claims application.[104]

To avoid the continual confusion, *Sonnenberger* has suggested that the sequence of conditions should be changed: (1) interest of the forum in applying the foreign rule, (2) specification of the connecting factor, (3) claim of application of the foreign rule.[105]

h Close connection

The foreign rule's claim to apply regardless of the proper law is a necessary, but not sufficient, condition for a special connection. Further conditions must justify its application and most of the academic authors speak of *close connection* as a criterion.[106]

---

100 Eg Anderegg *Ausländische Eingriffsnormen* 129 et seq; Mentzel *Sonderanknüpfung* 57 et seq; Schurig *Lois* 55, 67; Schubert RIW 1987, 729, 734 et seq; *contra* Schiffer *Normen* 159 et seq; critical also Vischer Rec des Cours 232 (199 I) 13, 168 footnote 363; on the general debate, see supra section 3, b.

101 Coester ZverglRWiss 82 (1983) 1, 5, 29; Schurig *Lois* 55, 66; Schubert RIW 1987, 729, 743 et seq.

102 Similar Schiffer *Normen* 159 et seq; Bar *IPR Bd I* 234; MünchKomm/Sonnenberger Einl Rn 58, 379.

103 Also see Schiffer *Normen* 160.

104 Wengler ZverglRWiss 54 (1941) 168, 183.

105 MünchKomm/Sonnenberger Einl Rn 58 et seq, 379 et seq; cf also Voser 7 Am Rev Int'l Arb 319, Lexis-Nexis 26 et seq of 38 - **(1)** close connection, **(2)** international mandatory nature of a rule, **(3)** content of the mandatory rule.

106 MünchKomm/Martiny Art 34 Rn 99 et seq; Neymayer BerGesVR 2 (1958) 35 et seq; see also *Zweigert* and *Wengler* supra under section 3, c; Schiffer *Normen* 176 et seq; Erne

In contrast to the earlier approaches that attempted to find a unified solution for all kinds of foreign internationally mandatory rules and for all types of contracts, the prevailing opinion is that special criteria for a close connection are to be developed with particular reference to the type of mandatory rule and contract in question. This is because of the realisation that a special connection is not possible by the use of only one general conflict rule that comprehensively covers all kinds of internationally mandatory rules. Rather the type of contract and the kind of rule must be differentiated.

Generally, the criterion of a close connection is concretised by specifying certain spatial, personal or functional characteristics that depend on the type of contractual relationship and subject matter of the mandatory provision itself.[107] A sufficiently close connection that depends on the rule in question and the factual situation can, for instance, be the *situs*, if assets or property are disposed of within the enacting country. Other examples include the effect on the market for application of an anti-trust law, the movement of value as a relevant criterion for foreign exchange regulations, the place of business, habitual residence, and nationality.[108] The choice of law of the contracting parties, however, is usually not sufficient.[109]

i Control of the content, 'shared values'

Finally, a *control of the content* of the internationally mandatory rule is necessary: The content and the legal consequences of the rule must be somehow compatible with the legal system of the forum.

This 'quality check'[110] can be located within the *ordre public* of the forum. It could result in an ordinary public policy exclusionary rule that refuses to apply a rule, after the choice of law process has been already followed, and the foreign mandatory rule has been rendered applicable by the forum's conflict rules.[111] Most of the authors, however, tend to favour '*a kind of ordre public*

Vertragsgültigkeit 190 et seq; for a spatial specification of the connecting factors depending on the legal area and its characteristics, see MünchKomm/Sonnenberger Einl Rn 383.

107 MünchKomm/Martiny Art 34 Rn 103 et seq; Reithmann/Martiny/Limmer *Internationales Vertragsrecht* Rn 405 et seq; Kreuzer *Schlechtriem/Leser* 89, 100 et seq; Radtke ZVerglRWiss 84 (1985) 325, 336; Mentzel *Sonderanknüpfung* 32.

108 See MünchKomm/Martiny Art 34 Rn 100, 105 et seq; Radtke ZVerglRWiss 84 (1985) 325, 336.

109 Kreuzer *Schlechtriem/Leser* 89, 101, 106; id *Ausländisches Wirtschaftsrecht* 64.

110 Kreuzer *Schlechtriem/Leser* 89, 103.

111 Wengler ZVerglRWiss 54 (1941) 168, 197; Lorenz RIW 1987, 569, 582; Mentzel *Sonderanknüpfung* 38; Radtke ZVerglRWiss 84 (1985) 325, 335.

control' of the content and purpose of the rule *as condition for the applicability*. In this study, this aspect will be called the condition of *equality of interests* or *shared values*.[112]

Different proposals have been made with regard to establishing the necessary 'degree' of equality of interests or shared values. Some authors wish to exclude from application only those rules which are directed against the forum state and those rules that have legal consequences that are not compatible with the forum.[113] Others consider whether the foreign internationally mandatory rule merits protection, for example, if the foreign state enacted the rule within the borders of its legislative competence and the content of the rule is appropriate for the forum.[114]

Many authors refer to German case law, which will be dealt with later in this chapter, and thus try to structure typical cases. For example, Großfeld and Rogers ask whether the mandatory rule expresses values that are *commonly shared* and that the receiving country is itself willing to protect (*shared values approach*). They refer to *typical international interests*.[115] Kreuzer maintains that the foreign provision must *promote the interests of the forum state*,[116] and provides different categories for this criterion. Promotion of the forum's interests or shared values are presumed if the foreign provision:

- *indirectly protects or promotes the interests of the forum*,[117] or
- protects *universally recognised legally protected interests* that are shared by the community of nations.[118]

Furthermore, foreign mandatory rules should be applied even though they do not protect universally recognised interests if:

---

112 MünchKomm/Martiny Art 34 Rn 121 et seq; Erne *Vertragsgültigkeit* 190 et seq; for some authors this is the main reason for the application, the precondition which enables a special connection Kreuzer *Ausländisches Wirtschaftsrecht* 92; MünchKomm/Sonnenberger Einl Rn 63; critically Mentzel *Sonderanknüpfung* 37.

113 Lorenz RIW 1987, 569, 582.

114 Erne *Vertragsgültigkeit* 191 et seq.

115 Großfeld/Rogers ICLQ 32 (1983) 931, 938, 939, 943.

116 Kreuzer *Ausländisches Wirtschaftsrecht* 90, 92 et seq; MünchKomm/Sonnenberger Einl Rn 61 et seq, 379; id *FS Rebmann* 819, 833.

117 Examples are the *US-embargo* cases of the Federal Supreme Court BGHZ 34, 169 et seq (*Borax*); BGH NJW 1962, 1436 (*Borsäure*) - see infra Chapter 5, II, 2, c, d.

118 Examples include the protection of cultural heritage BGHZ 59, 83, 85 et seq (*Nigerian Mask*), the protection of threatened animals and plants and the general protection of the public; RG JW 1927, 2288.

- the provision serves the fundamental co-ordination of national economic policies and/or the interest of the forum in the smooth functioning of international trade and the economic system,[119] or
- application would lead to a *mutual application* of German mandatory provisions in the foreign state.[120]

A necessary condition for the applicability of foreign mandatory rules is thus that the provision expresses values and interests that are somehow commonly shared by the forum and the foreign law. Otherwise, the provision is not applicable. As will be seen later, this corresponds with the German case law.[121] The Federal Supreme Court considered foreign mandatory rules as 'facts' within the notion of German *boni mores*. Accordingly, the court declared a contract infringing foreign rules to be illegal to the extent that the rules expressed values or served interests shared by Germany or the international community as a whole. Technically, however, the findings of illegality were based on German *boni mores* and not on a direct application of the foreign rule.[122]

j Legal consequence - Means and scope of application

The legal consequence of the *Special Connection Theory* is in general direct application of the foreign internationally mandatory rule to the contract.[123]

It should, however, be noted that according to some authors the legal consequence of a special connection may also be the consideration of the rule as 'fact' within the substantive law of the *lex causae*. These authors stress that there is little difference between applying the rule and considering the rule as fact, since in either case it is the foreign rule that is taken into account.[124] The

---

119 See also Schnyder *Wirtschaftskollisionsrecht* 185 et seq.

120 For all the categories, see Kreuzer *Ausländisches Wirtschaftsrecht* 93, 94; for the law of arbitration, see Voser 7 Am Rev Int'l Arb 319, Lexis-Nexis p 3 of 38; for criticism regarding this criterion, see MünchKomm/Martiny Art 34 Rn 99.

121 Chapter 5, II, 2.

122 Chapter 5, II, 2, d.

123 Wengler ZverglRWiss 54 (1941) 168, 211; Zweigert RabelsZ 14 (1942) 283, 295, 300; Schiffer *Normen* 195, 196; Erne *Vertragsgültigkeit* 197, 198.

124 See Kreuzer *Ausländisches Wirtschaftsrecht* 79, 81; Schurig *Lois* 55, 73, 74; Drobnig *FS Neumayer* 159, 174. The Swiss Federal Tribunal also stated that the distinction between application and consideration as fact is fallacious, see BG 18.9.1934 BGE 60 II 294, 311.

present author agrees with this view.[125] For example, if the rule itself provides for nullity, (provisional) invalidity or non-enforceability of the contract, the judge makes such an order and does not enforce the contract.[126] He then integrates the foreign internationally mandatory rule into the proper law of the contract.[127] The indirect consequences of the foreign rule, such as compensation for damages or remission of debt, depend on the *lex causae*.[128] If the rule, on the other hand, merely imposes a prohibition without itself providing for invalidity or other legal consequences, the consequences of an infringement, viz its private law effects on the contractual relationship, are founded upon the substantive law rules of the *lex causae*.[129]

If the direct application of the foreign mandatory provision and its legal consequences are not reconcilable with the proper law of the contract, the judge can alter or moderate the legal consequences in accordance to the legal system of the *lex causae*.[130] Furthermore, alteration and modification of the legal consequences of the foreign mandatory provision is possible if they conflict with the legal system of the forum.[131] This modification process is based on the (German) choice of law technique of *adaptation* or *adjustment* (*Anpassung* or *Angleichung*), which results when two conflicting legal systems are cumulatively applicable (*Normenhäufung*).[132]

---

125 This approach presupposes that, in contrast to the opinion of some academics and German courts, a recognition as fact within the substantive law does *not* provide relief from choice of law considerations.

126 Schäfer *FG Sandrock* 37, 46; Lorenz RIW 1987, 569, 580, 581; Drobnig *FS Neymayer* 159, 179; Radtke ZVerglRWiss 84 (1985) 325, 339; Staudinger/Magnus Art 34 Rn 145; but Kreuzer *Ausländisches Wirtschaftsrecht* 95 and Kropholler *IPR* § 52 XI 4 who wish to extract the legal consequences in principle from the lex causae only.

127 MünchKomm/Martiny Art 34 Rn 55, 60; Schiffer *Normen* 196; Zweigert RabelsZ 14 (1942) 283, 300.

128 Schiffer *Normen* 196; Zweigert RabelsZ 14 (1942) 283, 300; MünchKomm/Martiny Art 34 Rn 57, 60.

129 Drobnig *FS Neymayer* 159, 179; Schurig RabelsZ 54 (1990) 217, 240; MünchKomm/Martiny Art 34 Rn 60.

130 Schiffer *Normen* 196, 197; Erne *Vertragsgültigkeit* 198.

131 Lorenz RIW 1987, 569, 582, 583; for art 7 (1) RC, see infra Chapter 5, IV, 1, e.

132 See Schiffer *Normen* 196, 197; Erne *Vertragsgültigkeit* 198. For an explanation of the technique of adaptation which is in a way a problem of *qualification* in private international law and which is *res nova* in South African Law, see already Chapter 4, I, 1. Also see Bennett 105 III (1988) SALJ 444 et seq. However, in the case of a 'gap' following on situations where no internationally mandatory rule of a legal system claims application, the technique of adaptation is not necessary because a conflict in law does not exist. The consequence then is simply that no rule is applied.

k Subsidiary consideration as fact in the substantive law

There will be situations where the foreign provision cannot be applied or taken into account by means of a special connection, because it serves interests that are not commonly shared, or is directed against the interests of the forum state, or the connection is not close enough to justify a special connection. Nevertheless, the provision can require consideration on the level of substantive law. According to the advocates of the *Special Connection Theory*, a subsidiary consideration on this second level is still possible.[133] For example, where a foreign rule, which serves economic and political interests that are not shared by the forum state, sanctions a violation with heavy penalties, and performance would create undue hardship for the debtor, it might be necessary to consider the *factual effects of a foreign provision* as a reason for impossibility of performance. Non-consideration of the impact of mandatory provisions on the private relationship would create injustice for one or both of the contracting parties.[134]

On this 'second level', the analysis focuses upon the circumstances of the individual party who faces conflicting rules.[135] In contrast to the application of foreign mandatory rules by means of a 'special connection', where the forum uses its own values and standards to assess the foreign rule, the consideration of the factual effects of the foreign rule within the substantive law of the proper law should depend on the values and standards of the (foreign) proper law.[136]

4 '*Combination Theory*'

Some authors advocate a combination of the *Schuldstatutstheorie* and the *Special Connection Theory*.[137] In accordance with the *Schuldstatutstheorie* all rules of the proper law are applicable no matter whether they are of a private or

---

133 Großfeld/Rogers ICLQ 32 (1983) 931, 945; Siehr RabelsZ 52 (1988) 41, 94, 97; Erne *Vertragsgültigkeit* 209; Zweigert RabelsZ 14 (1942) 283, 302 et seq; Radtke ZVerglRWiss 84 (1985) 325, 340; Kropholler *IPR* § 52 XI 4 MünchKomm/Martiny Art 34 Rn 49; for a contrary opinion, see Schiffer *Normen* 197; Wengler ZVerglRWiss 54 (1941) 168, 202 et seq, 212.

134 Also see Kropholler *IPR* § 52 XI 4.

135 Großfeld/Rogers ICLQ 32 (1983) 931, 945

136 Siehr RabelsZ 52 (1988) 41, 93, 94, 98.

137 Siehr RabelsZ 52 (1988) 41, 73 et seq, 96 et seq, 103; Knüppel *Zwingendes Recht* 84 et seq, 212, 234; Becker *Sonderanknüpfung* 58, 74 et seq; similarly Lorenz RIW 1987, 569, 583; Vischer Rec des Cours 132 (1974 II) 1, 22 et seq; Erne *Vertragsgültigkeit* 188 et seq; Lando CMLR 24 (1987) 159, 213, 214; Lipstein *Conflict of Public Laws* 357, 365 et seq; see for references Schäfer *FG Sandrock* 37, 48; Kreuzer *Ausländisches Wirtschaftsrecht* 65 et seq; Radtke ZverglRWiss 84 (1985) 325, 349.

public law nature, whether the rule pursues private or public interests, or whether they are mandatory or facultative. The rules are applicable because the forum's conflict rules indicated to the legal system of which form part to govern the transaction. Mandatory provisions of a third country are not only considered as 'fact' within the material law of the *lex causae*, but are applied or given effect to by means of a 'special connection'.[138]

The advocates of this approach argue, that in respect of rules belonging to the *lex causae*, the principle of 'non-applicability of foreign public law' cannot be upheld, because the borders between private and public law are blurred and a clear distinction is hardly possible. Furthermore, the reason for referring to foreign law is to decide a factual situation in the same way as it would have been settled by the foreign court. Restricting reference to foreign private law would only distort the foreign law.[139]

With regard to third countries' mandatory rules, an application of these rules by means of a special connection is supported, because (1) foreign interests are filtered out of the case, (2) the judge assesses the foreign rule and considers an application in accordance with the forum's interests and political values, (3) application of a foreign rule does not depend on the assessment of the *lex causae*, which may differ from the *lex fori*, and (4) foreign rules are not 'facts' in the true sense that have to be taken into account simply because they exist. The substantive law approach leaves it up to the *lex causae* to decide whether effect is to be given to the foreign rule; a correction is possible only by means of the forum's *ordre public*. However, it is the *lex fori* that should ultimately decide whether foreign mandatory rules are to be taken into account. This principle cannot be ignored by considering the foreign rule as 'fact' within the substantive law of the *lex causae*.[140]

Many authors assume that the Rome Convention and the Swiss IPRG are based on this approach. This is because art 7 (1) of the Convention and art 19 of the Swiss IPRG refer only to internationally mandatory rules of a country other than the governing law, while those of the *lex causae* are not referred to and are thus held to be automatically applicable because they belong to the proper law.[141] In

---

138 Cf Radtke ZVerglRWiss 84 (1985) 325, 349; Mentzel *Sonderanknüpfung* 80, 81; Siehr RabelsZ 52 (1988) 41, 75 et seq, 96; Knüppel *Zwingendes Recht* 234, 235; Becker *Sonderanknüpfung* 56 et seq.

139 Siehr RabelsZ 52 (1988) 41, 75, 76; Knüppel *Zwingendes Recht* 20 et seq.

140 See Siehr RabelsZ 52 (1988) 41, 80. 81, 96.

141 MünchKomm/Martiny Art 34 Rn 40; Mentzel *Sonderanknüpfung* 80; Kreuzer *Schlecht riem/Leser* 89, 104; id *Ausländisches Wirtschaftsrecht* 69 N 237; Lehmann ZRP 1987, 319; Becker *Sonderanknüpfung* 58, 74 et seq; Schubert RIW 1987, 729, 736; see for

fact, art 7 (1) and (2) of the Convention and arts 18 and 19 of the Swiss IPRG refer to the rules of the *lex fori* and of a third country, and it would be absurd to conclude that internationally mandatory rules of the proper law are therefore inapplicable. However, it is debated in Switzerland and in Germany whether the legislature should regulate the matter and whether the loophole has to be closed by an analogous application of art 7 (1) of the Convention and art 19 of the Swiss IPRG to rules pursuing public interests of the *lex causae*.[142]

5 Consideration only on the level of substantive law

There are also a few authors who favour a consideration on the level of substantive law and omit any application on the level of conflict of laws ('*Substantive Law Approach*'). They contend that the only possible way of considering foreign internationally mandatory rules, those of the *lex causae* and those of a third country, is to subsume them under the substantive law of the *lex causae*. The reason for this approach is that the substantive law has better tools for dealing with the rules influencing a private relationship.[143] An application on a 'conflict of laws level' by means of a 'special connection process' would not consider all the possible actual effects of internationally mandatory rules on the private relationship, and would render applicable rules that do not have any effect on the contract.[144] Therefore, the consideration as fact within the substantive law is regarded as the better technical means of recognising foreign internationally mandatory rules.

This *Substantive Law Approach* is in principle the position of the German and Swiss courts. Mülbert attempts to give this approach a theoretical basis by means of the Datum theory.[145] The *Datum theory* was originally founded by Ehrenzweig,[146] and is supported in Germany mainly by Jayme.[147] Mülbert transfers this theory to the question of the application of foreign internationally

Switzerland Voser *Lois d'application immédiate* 73 et seq; Schnyder *Das neue IPRG* 29, 30; Honsell/Vogt/Schnyder/Mächler-Erne Art 13 Rn 23.

142 In Switzerland, art 13 of the Swiss IPRG contains a regulation regarding the scope of reference to the foreign law, the content of which is debated in Switzerland, see Voser *Lois d'application immédiate* 73 et seq; Honsell/Vogt/Schnyder/Mächler-Erne Art 13 Rn 21 et seq; and infra Chapter 5, IV, 4, b.

143 Anderegg *Eingriffsnormen* 199 et seq; Radtke ZVerglRWiss 84 (1985) 325, 355; see also Piehl RIW 1988, 843; Baum RabelsZ 53 (1989) 152 et seq.

144 Radtke ZverglRWiss 84 (1985) 325, 341, 355, 356.

145 Mülbert IPRax 1986, 140 et seq; Baum RabelsZ 53 (1989) 152, 160.

146 Ehrenzweig's analysis was not concerned with the question of applicability of mandatory rules, see Ungeheuer *Beachtung* 111 footnote 122; Becker *Sonderanknüpfung* 78; see the references of Siehr RabelsZ 52 (1988) 41, 80 footnote 206.

147 Jayme *GS Ehrenzweig* 35 et seq.

mandatory rules and thereby assumes that certain foreign rules are not rendered applicable by choice of law rules, but rather concretise the operative facts of the proper law's substantive rules as facts ('*local data*').[148]

In contrast to the *Special Connection Theory*, this approach does not lead to application of the foreign rule but only to its consideration as fact, since the foreign rule serves to realise the operative facts of the rules of the *lex causae* without having regard to their legal consequences.[149]

6 Summary

The different approaches to the application or consideration of foreign internationally mandatory rules by the court of the forum state can be summarised thus:

a Internationally mandatory rules of the foreign proper law

The *Schuldstatuts-theory* and the *Combination Theory* assume that the internationally mandatory rules of the proper law are in general rendered applicable by the ordinary conflict rules of the forum. They are, however, only applicable if they claim application to the situation and do not infringe the forum's *ordre public*.

The *theory of International Administrative Law* distinguishes between private and public law rules. While private law rules are rendered applicable by the ordinary conflict of law rules, public law rules are subject to international administrative law, which is based on the principle of territoriality. Thus, foreign public law rules are in principle only applicable within the territory of the enacting country. On the basis of a further subdivision, public law rules that pursue public interests are applicable (or at least considered) independently of their belonging to the proper law, provided that the enacting state has the *power to enforce* its rules or in cases of *equality of interests*.

The *Special Connection Theory* distinguishes between internationally mandatory rules serving the interests of the parties and those pursuing public interests. While the former are clearly subject to the proper law, the latter are connected separately and independently from the proper law of the contract. They are

[148] Mülbert IPRax 1986, 140, 141. But see Jayme *GS Ehrenzweig* 35, 43, 45 who stresses the differences between the datum theory and the question of the treatment of foreign internationally mandatory rules, and furthermore assesses the German case law considering foreign mandatory rules within the *boni mores* as '*moral data*'.

[149] Jayme *GS Ehrenzweig* 35, 39, 45; Mentzel *Sonderanknüpfung* 110.

rendered applicable by special conflict rules, the operative facts of which are not yet fully established. Generally, it is held that the following conditions must be fulfilled:

(1) there must be a close connection between the situation and the enacting country,
(2) the rule must claim application whatever the proper law of the contract, and
(3) the rule must express values that are commonly shared.

The same distinction between the interests pursued by the rule seems to be true for those authors who advocate a consideration of internationally mandatory rules on the level of substantive law only. With regard to rules belonging to the proper law, however, this approach does not express a clear point of view. Nevertheless, it seems reasonable to assume that, if the foreign rules serve private interests, they are applicable as part of the proper law, and if they serve public interests they may be taken into account as fact within the operative facts of the private substantive law rules of the proper law.

b Third country's internationally mandatory rules

Internationally mandatory rules of a third country are rendered applicable on a conflict of laws level by means of a special connection that is advocated by the *Special Connection Theory* and the *Combination Theory*, or in accordance with the *International Administrative Law Theory*. Otherwise, these rules can only be considered as facts within the substantive law of the *lex causae* in the areas of *boni mores*, frustration of the contract, or impossibility of performance. This solution is favoured by the *Schuldstatuts-theory (proper law doctrine)* and the *Substantive Law Approach*. Only where a special connection fails, does the *Special Connection Theory* take into account the actual effects of foreign rules within the substantive law governing the contract.

7 Critical analysis of the different approaches and final remarks

Before embarking on a critical analysis of the above approaches it has to be stressed that they usually have similar outcomes. It is the technical method and the foundation or reasoning that differ.[150] Furthermore, and this comment is relevant to the entire discussion about the application of third countries' internationally mandatory rules, not one academic author contends that foreign internationally mandatory rules, even if they emanate from a third country, should not somehow be considered or taken into account.[151] Under certain conditions foreign provisions are either held to be applicable on a conflict of laws level, or the rules or their factual effects are taken into account on the level of substantive law. Thus, it is clear that the dispute is concerned with the appropriate method and reasoning. The crucial question is not '*whether*' to consider foreign mandatory rules, but '*when*' (under what conditions) and '*how*'.

a Principle of unity of the conflict of laws relating to contracts versus the special connection

The *Schuldstatuts-theory* advocates that the contract should be governed by one law, including all rules, regardless of their nature. It is argued that the advantages of this approach are uniformity of the law applicable to the contract and protection of the justified expectations of the contracting parties.[152] Nevertheless, this approach is justifiably criticised by the advocates of the *Special Connection Theory* and the *Combination Theory*.

The criticism is mainly based on the aforementioned assumption that the ordinary conflict rules are designed to achieve a fair reconciliation of the (conflicting) interests of the contracting parties, but they do not contain appropriate criteria to determine the applicability of internationally mandatory rules pursuing public interests.[153] The connecting factors of the ordinary choice

---

150 Cf Radtke ZverglRWiss 84 (1985) 325, 357; the recommendation of the Max Planck Institute in RabelsZ 47 (1983) 669; MünchKomm/Martiny Art 34 Rn 33; critically, Mentzel *Sonderanknüpfung* 112 et seq.

151 MünchKomm/Martiny Art 34 Rn 33; Becker *Sonderanknüpfung* 77; Hentzen RIW 1988, 508, 509.

152 What is meant, is the expectation in the application of only one law, cf Mann *Effect* 31, 34; id FS Beitzke 607, 613, 623; see as well Schäfer *FG Sandrock* 37, 41; Radtke ZVerglRWiss 84 (1985) 325, 344; critically Schiffer *Normen* 91, 92; Erne *Vertragsgültigkeit* 142 et seq.

153 See Basedow RabelsZ 52 (1988) 8, 22; Schubert RIW 1987, 729, 732; Kreuzer *Ausländisches Wirtschaftsrecht* 81 et seq; MünchKomm/Martiny Art 34 Rn 34; for details, see Chapter 5, I, 3.

of law rules - in particular, the parties' choice of law, but also the objective connecting factors are not suitable for rendering applicable mandatory rules that pursue the economic and political interests of foreign states. All these rules are binding and do not permit any derogation, even in an international setting, since they must be applied by the courts of the enacting country regardless of the proper law of the contractual relationship. Therefore, it cannot be left to the parties to determine which country's internationally mandatory rules will apply.[154]

Furthermore, strict adherence to the principle of unity - all rules of the legal system designated by the connecting factors of the ordinary choice of law rules are applicable, while laws outside the *lex fori* and the *lex causae* do not apply - may lead to odd results.[155] For instance, this proposition would lead to application of an export prohibition of the seller's country (because it is the seller who must effect the characteristic performance), while an import ban of the buyer's country would be ignored.[156] That this result cannot be justified becomes obvious where the parties have chosen a neutral law, with which the situation has no spatial connection, as the proper law of their contract. It is inappropriate to apply internationally mandatory rules that pursue the public interests of a law that was chosen because it was *neutral*, while there might be another law that has a reasonable interest in the application of its mandatory rules because there is a close connection with the situation in question.[157]

It has also been convincingly argued that lip service alone is paid to the principle of 'uniformity of the law applicable to a contract' and protection of the expectations of the contracting parties. This is because third countries' internationally mandatory rules are, according to the *Schuldstatuts-theory*, given effect on the level of substantive law, despite their inapplicability on the level of conflict of laws.[158] Thus, in *fact* there is no uniformity of law nor are the potential expectations of the contracting parties protected. For the parties it is irrelevant *how* a third country's internationally mandatory rule renders the contract invalid or performance impossible - whether considering it on the level of conflict of laws or on the level of substantive law.

---

154 Hentzen RIW 1988, 508, 509; Kreuzer *Schlechtriem/Leser* 89, 107; Schäfer *FG Sandrock* 39, 43.

155 Vischer Rec des Cours 232 (1992 I) 13, 166; Remien RabelsZ 54 (1990) 431, 463; Schäfer *FG Sandrock* 39, 43.

156 See Vischer Rec des Cours 232 (1990 I) 13, 166; Schäfer *FG Sandrock* 39, 43.

157 Hentzen RIW 1988, 508, 509; von Bar *IPR Bd I* Rn 267; Remien RabelsZ 54 (1990) 431, 462; Schäfer *FG Sandrock* 39, 42.

158 Also see Schiffer *Normen* 91, 92; Erne *Vertragsgültigkeit* 142 et seq.

Moreover, is it not inconsistent to assume that ordinary conflict rules are acceptable to render foreign internationally mandatory rules applicable, but that they are unacceptable to exclude internationally mandatory rules of the forum?[159]

Finally, it should be noted that statutory exceptions to the unity principle do exist, and the scope of the proper law is not all-embracing. Some contractual issues - for example, capacity, formalities, mode of performance - are governed by separate laws (dépeçage). These issues are connected separately and lead to severable parts of the contract being governed by separate laws.[160] Articles 5 and 6 of the Rome Convention contain further statutory exceptions to this general principle. Thus, the special connection by special choice of law rules, separate from the ordinary conflict rules, is not excluded in principle, but is a well-known method for determining the appropriate legal system for certain legal issues.

b Does taking account of (third countries') internationally mandatory rules as 'facts' replace choice of law considerations?

Third countries' international mandatory rules may not be applicable, but their consequences and effects can be recognised as facts within the substantive law rules of the *lex causae*. The substantive law approach in general and the *Schuldstatuts-theory* supports this approach. This is certainly one possible method of considering the internationally mandatory rules of a third country, but for a number of reasons it is preferable to develop separate criteria on the level of conflict of laws that indicate under what conditions these rules are to be taken into account.

Firstly, foreign mandatory rules are not 'facts' in the *true sense*.[161] Only if the foreign state is able to enforce its prohibition and the performance becomes factually impossible, (for example, because of seizure attachment,) is it the factual effect of the foreign mandatory rule that is taken into account and not the rule itself.[162] It is debatable whether the mere existence of a prohibition suffices to render performance impossible (which then would be legal impossibility) or whether the state must have already enforced its prohibition.

---

159 Radtke ZVerglRWiss 84 (1985) 325, 339; Schubert RIW 1987, 729, 733; MünchKomm/ Martiny Art 34 Rn 34; Kropholler *IPR* § 52 IX 4.

160 See Lando CMLR 24 (1987) 159, 167 et seq; Siehr RabelsZ 52 (1988) 41, 69; Schiffer *Normen* 91 et seq; Becker *Sonderanküpfung* 57.

161 Siehr RabelsZ 52 (1988) 41, 80; Schurig RabelsZ 54 (1990) 217, 241 et seq.

162 Junker JZ 1991, 699, 702; Schäfer *FG Sandrock* 39, 51; Schurig RabelsZ 54 (1990) 217, 241, 242.

Some authors stress that, at least in the former situation, if not in general, it is not the actual effect (fact) that is taken into account in the strict sense, but rather the prohibition itself.

In general, it is questionable whether there is any difference between application of a rule and its consideration as fact.[163] Even recognition as fact demands an examination on different levels. The court will first have to answer the primary question of whether there is a foreign law that claims application to the transaction. Only if there is an affirmative answer, will the question arise whether the foreign rules may be taken into account as 'fact' so that performance is rendered impossible.[164]

The *Substantive Law Approach* and the *Schuldstatuts-theory*, referring to German and Swiss case law, submit that infringement of the foreign rule is the reason for immorality. Here one might argue that the foreign rule is not 'applied as a rule' in the strict sense, since the legal consequences are taken from the substantive law rules of the *lex causae*, which is the sanction of nullity imposed when the contract is contrary to *boni mores*. However, it is submitted that this assumption is incorrect, and that consideration of the foreign rule within the *lex causae* nevertheless constitutes a consideration as *rule* and not as *fact*, neither are the *actual effects* of the rule taken into account.

Although the notion of *boni mores* is determined by reference to the third country's law, the decision whether to give effect to the foreign rule is not a question of material law, but of conflict of laws.[165] As von Bar has pointed out, the recourse to substantive *boni mores* does not avoid choice of law considerations.[166] *Boni mores* are construed as a safeguard for the domestic code of practices and do not answer the question whether and under what conditions an infringement of foreign rules leads to immorality under the *lex causae*. Thus, the application of the *boni mores* rule in these cases is not based solely on the moral values of the *lex fori*, and often the contractual agreement does not violate the forum's *boni mores*. In fact, the agreement is held to be immoral because a foreign rule has been violated.[167] The private international

---

163 Schiffer *Normen* 94 et seq; Kreuzer *Ausländisches Wirtschaftsrecht* 79, 80; Schurig *Lois* 55, 73, 74; Lehmann ZRP 1987, 319, 320; Morscher *Rechtssetzungsakte* 64, 117 et seq.

164 Morscher *Rechtssetzungsakte* 64, 117 et seq; Schiffer *Normen* 94 et seq; for criticism, also see Schwander *Lois* 365; Schulte *Eingriffsnormen* 37.

165 Mentzel *Sonderanknüpfung* 106; Kreuzer *Ausländisches Wirtschaftsrecht* 86; Schiffer *Normen* 96.

166 Von Bar *IPR Bd I* Rn 265.

167 Also see Morscher *Rechtssetzungsakte* 67; von Bar *IPR Bd I* Rn 265; Kreuzer *Ausländisches Wirtschaftsrecht* 87.

law questions about whether and under what conditions foreign law is to be given effect to is thus transferred to the level of substantive law and dealt with under the '*fraudulent label*' of *boni mores*.[168]

c The ultimate control of the forum

In addition, the recognition of third countries' internationally mandatory rules as supposed 'facts' within the lex causae's substantive law depends on whether the substantive law offers means permitting a consideration of the effects of third countries' mandatory rules, such as impossibility of performance, frustration, or illegality. Whether the substantive law offers always a suitable relief/an appropriate means has been debated.[169]

The result of this approach is that, in cases where the proper law is a foreign law, the judge must interpret and extend foreign substantive rules in order to take the third country's mandatory rule into account.[170]

Lastly, it has often been stressed that the private international law of the forum decides whether foreign rules are to be applied. It then seems illogical, when taking into account third country's mandatory rules within the operative facts of the *lex causae's* substantive law rules, to hand this decision over to the proper law.[171] This runs counter to the general principle that the reason for taking account of foreign law is always to be found in the law of the forum state and not in the foreign *lex causae*.[172]

Thus, a 'special connection-process' for international mandatory rules by means of a *separate conflict rule* would be the systematically appropriate means of solving the problem, since it solves the question of application or recognition of internationally mandatory rules on a conflict of laws level, instead of blurring

168 Hentzen RIW 1988, 508, 509; Schwander *IPR* 542 et seq; MünchKomm/Martiny Art 34 Rn 35; similar von Bar *IPR* Bd I Rn 265; Lehmann *Zwingendes Recht* 200 et seq; Schubert RIW 1987, 729, 737; Mentzel *Sonderanknüpfung* 106 et seq; Schurig RabelsZ 54 (1990) 217, 242, 243 with further arguments; id *Lois* 55, 73; Junker JZ 1991, 699, 701.

169 For details, see Schwander *IPR AT* 250 et seq; see also Vischer Rec des Cours 232 (1992 I) 13, 168; Siehr RabelsZ 52 (1988) 41, 79.

170 Schwander *IPR AT* 250 et seq; Kreuzer *Ausländisches Wirtschaftsrecht* 86.

171 The only means of correcting unjustified results from forum's point of view, would be the *ordre public*; Siehr RabelsZ 52 (1988) 41, 80; see also Mentzel *Sonderanknüpfung* 113.

172 Kreuzer *Ausländisches Wirtschaftsrecht* 87; see also Junker JZ 1991, 699, 701.

primary choice of law issues with application of the *lex causae's* substantive law rules.[173]

d Principle of territoriality or non-applicability of foreign public law

The principle of 'non-applicability of foreign public law', on which the German and Swiss case law and *Kegel's* doctrine of *International Administrative* or *Public Law* are partly based, has been subjected to fundamental criticism and cannot be upheld.[174]

The criticism is based on different aspects. It is argued that, together with the difficulties of distinguishing private from public law rules (particularly because the boundaries are blurred and the notion of public law has a different meaning in common law), the principle of the non-applicability of foreign public law is not supported in its real form. Rather, it is subject to several exceptions (such as the exception that the principle does not apply to public law rules serving the protection of private interests).[175]

The fundamental objection, however, is that the principle of 'territoriality' on which this approach is based is of no use in determining whether foreign law should be applied by a judge.[176] The notion of the principle of territoriality is used in various senses, but none of them can provide any guidelines for determining when the forum should apply foreign law.[177] The inapplicability of certain foreign public law rules does not follow from the principle of territoriality; rather it is a decision of the forum's conflict of laws.[178]

It is more appropriate to talk about the principle of territoriality with regard to the enforcement of foreign public law rules that impose a positive duty on

---

173 Schiffer *Normen* 148, 156, 166; Schäfer *FG Sandrock* 39, 47; Hentzen RIW 1988, 508, 509; Schubert RIW 1987, 729, 745; Kreuzer *Ausländisches Wirtschaftsrecht* 79 et seq.

174 For details, see Mann Rec des Cours 132 (1971 I) 115, 182 et seq; Siehr RabelsZ 52 (1988) 41, 75 et seq; Vischer Rec des Cours 232 (1992 I) 13, 150 et seq; MünchKomm/Sonnenberger Einl Rn 374, 377; Schiffer *Normen* 79 et seq; Kropholler *IPR* § 22 II 2.

175 A further exception to this principle occurs where the foreign state is able to enforce its law and in cases of equality of interests, see supra section 2 and Chapter 5, II, 1, c.

176 Siehr RabelsZ 52 (1988) 41, 75 et seq; Lipstein *Conflict of Public Laws* 357, 358 et seq; Mann Rec des Cours 132 (1971 I) 115, 188; Erne *Vertragsgültigkeit* 82; Schiffer *Normen* 79, 80 with further references.

177 Erne *Vertragsgültigkeit* 81, 82; Schiffer *Normen* 79; MünchKomm/Sonnenberger Einl Rn 374.

178 Erne *Vertragsgültigkeit* 82, 83; Neuhaus *IPR* 179 et seq; Mann Rec des Cours 132 (1971 I) 115, 190.

government authorities in favour of the foreign State.[179] However, in *private* litigation the concern is *not* enforcement of foreign public laws, but instead whether a foreign law that represents the public interests of the foreign enacting state, and pursues these interests indirectly by intervening in the private contract, can be applied. The concern is thus not the enforcement or '*direct*' application of foreign public law in favour of the foreign state, but, rather the influence and consequences of public law on private law and private relationships, the '*reflex effects*' of public on private law.[180] A judge in the forum considers only the *private law effects* of the foreign public law, a process that has nothing in common with the direct application or enforcement of foreign law. If the principle of the non-applicability of foreign public laws is understood to exclude even the consideration of the *reflex effects* of public law rules on private law and relationships (which is the position in the German and Swiss case law and some academic writing), then it must clearly be rejected.[181]

This conclusion does not necessarily mean that the legal effects of the public law of the *lex causae* are always applicable, nor that they are exclusively applicable. Whether the forum applies or considers foreign public law rules as they affect the private relationship is still a decision of its own conflict of laws. As noted above, the applicability of these rules can be appropriately determined only by separate conflict rules. Vischer states that:

> The question, which state's public law and which of its regulations in particular are to be applied, is not prejudiced by the inclusion of foreign public law as such.... The *lex causae* ... includes neither all laws pursuing public interests of that state nor are public law rules of other states completely excluded....[182]

---

179 Schiffer *Normen* 79; MünchKomm/Sonnenberger Einl Rn 375; Vischer Rec des Cours 232 (1992 I) 13, 151; Mann Rec des Cours 132 (1974 I) 115, 184.

180 MünchKomm/Martiny Art 34 Rn 36; Schiffer *Normen* 76 et seq; Kropholler *IPR* § 22 II 2; Neymayer RabelsZ 25 (1960) 649, 651; Siehr RabelsZ 52 (1988) 41, 73; Knüppel *Zwingendes Recht* 25.

181 Schiffer *Normen* 77; Erne *Vertragsgültigkeit* 84; MünchKomm/Martiny Art 34 Rn 36; Vischer Rec des Cours 232 (1992 I) 13, 150 et seq. It has been assumed that the German case law is based on the error that application would mean enforcement, see Mann Rec des Cours 132 (1971 I) 109, 187; Schiffer *Normen* 75.

182 Vischer Rec des Cours 232 (1992 I) 13, 151.

e The advantage of the solution of the *Special Connection Theory*

The *Special Connection Theory* (*Sonderanknüpfungslehre*) is basically the opposite of the *Schuldstatuts-theory*. Therefore, some of the fundamental objections to the *Special Connection Theory* overlap with arguments in favour of a *Schuldstatuts-theory*, and vice versa: for example, the principle of unity of conflict of laws relating to contracts as opposed to dividing the proper law of the contract. These were discussed above. There are, however, further objections to the *Special Connection Theory*: While some of them are directed against the theory in general, others are interwoven with attacks on the statutory approaches of art 7 (1) of the Rome Convention and art 19 of the Swiss IPRG, because these provisions are based on similar considerations.[183]

Mann argues that there is no justification for a special connection since case law has developed clear criteria to deal with the problem - the consideration of third countries' mandatory rules within the substantive law of the *lex causae* - and the decisions of the courts were correct.[184] He maintains that there is no occasion for methodological and structural debates if the case law has developed acceptable solutions.

However, although Mann does not seem to approve of it, the discussion is not about the *outcome*, but rather about the principled reasoning and foundation for consideration of foreign internationally mandatory rules (the proper law's and a third country's). The crucial question is the appropriate means of determining the applicability or consideration of foreign mandatory rules.[185]

As already stated, a 'special connection process' conforms with the system of international private law, because it solves a question of that system - the applicability of foreign mandatory rules - on a conflict of laws level, by means of conflict rules. The *Schuldstatuts-theory* and the *Substantive Law approach* transfer this question to the level of substantive law and take account of a third country's mandatory rules as alleged 'facts', and not as rules, within the operative facts of substantive rules of the *lex causae*.[186]

---

183 For these articles, see Chapter 5, IV.

184 Mann *FS Beitzke* 607, 608, 614, 616. Sandrock/Steinschulte *Handbuch* Rn 196 argue along similar lines although they favour the principle of non-applicability of foreign public law. For this argument, also see Schiffer *Normen* 165 et seq.

185 Schiffer *Normen* 147, 166.

186 See supra section 3, b and g.

f Does the special connection imply a departure from the traditional allocation technique?

It has been said that the *Special Connection Theory* implies a methodological return to unilateralism, since the proposed conflict rules would not indicate a specific national legal system, but start from the foreign mandatory rule that claims application.[187] In theory, this would mean that the judge must examine every legal system in the world to establish whether it contains a mandatory provision claiming application.[188] But, as already emphasised,[189] this is *not* the starting point of most of the advocates of the *Special Connection Theory*, despite the fact that there are some authors who expressly favour a move towards unilateralism, and thus start with the question of which foreign law claims application.[190] No forum state is obliged to accept a foreign rule's claim of application. It is the autonomous decision of the *lex fori* whether and how it is to give effect to foreign rules.[191] Hence, the starting point should rather be discovering whether there is a country with which the situation has a close connection, or whether the forum has an interest in applying a foreign rule.[192]

The close connection is a connecting factor that is well known and broadly accepted in international private law.[193] In general, the plea of one contracting party will in any event indicate the legal system and its mandatory provision prohibiting a certain conduct or action, which might be taken into account by the forum.[194] A 'special connection' is examined *only* where the enacting legal system has a (close) connection with the situation, which implies that the claim of application is not the primary condition for a special connection, but only one of the conditions.[195] The self-limitation of foreign rules is regarded within the choice of law process as a kind of 'limitation-factor', since application of foreign mandatory rules that pursue public interests, and do not claim

[187] Schurig *Lois* 55, 66 et seq; id RabelsZ 54 (1990) 217, 236; Coester ZVerglRWIss 82 (1983) 1, 10, 29; Mentzel *Sonderanküpfung* 126.

[188] Schurig *Kollisionsnormen* 197, 323; Schubert RIW 1987, 729, 734, 741. Both favour a special treatment of internationally mandatory rules; von Bar *IPR Bd I* Rn 266.

[189] Supra section 3, b, g .

[190] For example, Vischer Rec des Cours 232 (1992 I) 13, 168.

[191] Also see Becker *Sonderanknüpfung* 56; Lorenz RIW 1987, 569, 578.

[192] See among others Mentzel *Sonderanknüpfung* 126; Sonnenberger *FS Rebmann* 819, 827, 833; Lorenz RIW 1987, 569, 578; Martiny IPRax 1987, 277, 279; MünchKomm/Martiny Art 34 Rn 99.

[193] Schiffer *Normen* 160 et seq; see art 4 (1) RC for the objective connection of contracts.

[194] Lehmann ZRP 1987, 319, 321; Schiffer *Normen* 161.

[195] Schiffer *Normen* 161; MünchKomm/Martiny Art 34 Rn 99; Schubert RIW 1987, 729, 734 et seq; already Zweigert RabelsZ 14 (1942) 283, 285 and Wengler ZverglRWiss 54 (1941) 168, 183; supra section 3, b, g.

application, cannot be justified.[196] Understood in this manner, a 'special connection' conforms with the principled and structured system of international private law.

Recognition of the foreign rule's self-limitation indicates an acceptance of *renvoi*, a matter that is normally excluded from the choice of law of contracts.[197] However, the supporters of all the theories apply or take into account foreign internationally mandatory rules only in so far as they claim application. This is even true of the advocates of the *Schuldstatuts-theory*, according to which internationally mandatory rules are applicable if they belong to the proper law as designated by the ordinary conflict rules, claim application, and do not infringe the forum's *ordre public*.[198]

Acceptance of *renvoi* does not create difficulties for the *Special Connection Theory*, since the application of internationally mandatory rules is based upon *separate conflict rules*, reference to which is dependent on the foreign law's claim of application.[199] In contrast, the *Schuldstatuts-theory* assumes that the reference to ordinary conflict rules covers internationally mandatory rules, which would normally mean that the attached conflict rule is to be disregarded. In order to recognise the self-limitation these authors have to argue that the territorial scope of the rule is part of its material content instead of an attached conflict rule.[200]

It is however acknowledged that a 'special connection process' differs from the orthodox choice of law process because it is supplemented by a more policy-orientated investigation. Such an investigation takes account of the purpose of the foreign rule, the interests of the involved states in an application of the foreign rule, and the result of its application.[201]

---

196 Schiffer *Normen* 160; Morscher *Rechtssetzungakte* 58, 59; MünchKomm/Martiny Art 34 Rn 99; Münch Komm/Sonnenberger Einl Rn 59 et seq. For similar proposals made by the critics of the 'putative' unilateral approach, see Schurig *Lois* 66 et seq; id RabelsZ 54 (1990) 217, 236; Schubert RIW 1987, 729, 735, 745.

197 Also see Radtke ZverglRWiss 84 (1985) 325, 343; Kreuzer *Ausländisches Wirtschaftsrecht* 90.

198 See Mann *FS Wahl* 139, 153, 160.

199 Schurig RabelsZ 54 (1990) 217, 238; also see Radtke ZverglRWiss 84 (1985) 325, 343 footnote 71; Kreuzer *Ausländisches Wirtschaftsrecht* 90, 91.

200 Critically Radtke ZverglRWiss 84 (1985) 325, 343 footnote 71; Schubert RIW 1987, 729, 732, 733.

201 Vischer Rec des Cours 232 (1992 I) 9, 169; Guedj *Am J Comp L* 39 (1991) 661 et seq.

g Other objections to a 'special connection process'

The other arguments refer to the conflict rules proposed for a 'special connection process'. Advocates of this theory have been criticised for being unable to develop clear criteria in terms of which foreign mandatory laws are applicable and capable of being connected separately. Nothing more than a *comprehensive* or *blanket clause* was formulated. In particular, Article 7 (1) of the Rome Convention, with its vague criteria and the broad discretion granted to the judge, would lead to uncertainty.[202] The objections to art 7 (1) of the Rome Convention will be discussed later.[203] Furthermore, all attempts to distinguish criteria for the comprehensive clauses, such as 'a close connection', failed.[204]

In the present author's opinion this criticism is not justified. Convincing attempts have been made to specify the criteria of a close connection with reference to different contracts and mandatory provisions.[205] Furthermore, the advocates of a special connection have developed useful criteria to assist judges in exercising their discretion, such as *equality of interests* and *shared values*.[206] Finally, it has to be noted that advocates of the *Special Connection Theory* have recently said that the problem cannot be solved by the development of a comprehensive clause, but rather by the creation of special conflict rules for certain areas of law where internationally mandatory rules are typically involved.[207]

It has further been argued that the *Special Connection Theory* is not useful because the diversity of opinions within it shows that the criteria of a conflict rule, pointing towards the applicable internationally mandatory rules, are not yet clarified.[208] However, it is doubtful whether this criticism is justified. As was shown above, all the different approaches use the same criteria to determine whether a foreign rule is applicable: the close connection as a spatial criterion and equality of interests as a kind of 'content-control' of the foreign rule. Nevertheless, it is conceded by the advocates of the *Special Connection Theory*

---

202 Schäfer *FG Sandrock* 39, 47, 48; Mann *FS Beitzke* 607, 613 et seq, 617; Sandrock Steinschulte *Handbuch* Rn 194; Coester ZverglRWis 82 (1983) 1, 29, 30; Heini ZSR 100 (1981) 65, 68 et seq.

203 See infra Chapter 5, IV, 1.

204 Heini BerGesVR 22 (1982) 37, 43; Mann *FS Beitzke* 607, 613.

205 MünchKomm/Martiny Art 34 Rn 100 et seq; see supra section 3, d, h.

206 See Kreuzer *Ausländisches Wirtschaftsrecht* 93 et seq and section 3, d, i.

207 Schubert RIW 1987, 729, 745; Sonnenberger *FS Rebmann* 819, 831 et seq, 834; Lorenz RIW 1987, 569, 581; Schurig RabelsZ 54 (1990) 217, 239.

208 Schäfer *FG Sandrock* 39, 47; Heini BerGesVR 22 (1982) 37, 38, 43; Lorenz RIW 1987, 569, 581.

that a central problem of this theory is specifying the criteria for a special connection.[209]

The *Special Connection Theory* has also been criticised for not being flexible enough to cope with the different effects of mandatory rules on private relationships, since the legal consequence of a special connection would clearly be the application of the foreign rule.[210] This argument is not necessarily correct with regard to the advocated 'special connection process' and is not true with regard to art 7 (1) of the Rome Convention and art 19 of the Swiss IPRG.[211] The judge has discretion to decide whether and how effect is to be given to a foreign rule, which can mean application or consideration as a rule or as a fact within the applicable substantive law. This flexibility is the very advantage of a comprehensive clause.[212]

The difficulty of determining whether a foreign rule claims application regardless of the proper law of the contract remains. It is not an easy task to determine the internationally mandatory character of a foreign rule, particularly where the rule does not contain an express term and its international scope has to be deduced from an interpretation of its purpose. All that can be submitted here is that in cases of doubt, where the scope of applicability cannot be clearly determined the foreign rule should not applied or considered.[213]

Furthermore, it should be noted that the *Special Connection Theory* cannot deal with all situations in which foreign rules claim application and affect private relationships. Therefore, in cases where a rule cannot be applied on a conflict of laws level, the factual effects of mandatory rules within the substantive rules of the *lex causae* have to be considered.[214] However, it can at least be stated that this *secondary* consideration on the level of substantive law can be reduced to the situation where the rule has an actual impact on the relationship, if the foreign state has enforced its rule already, or if the sanctions are so great that it would cause undue hardship to the debtor to perform in violation of the rule.

---

209 Becker *Sonderanknüpfung* 82; Lehmann *Zwingendes Recht* 321; Siehr RabelsZ 52 (1988) 41, 72.

210 Mülbert IPRax 1986, 140, 141; Schäfer *FG Sandrock* 39, 48; Radtke ZverglRWiss 84 (1985) 325, 353. The opposite view, that a consideration within the German *boni mores* would lead to a nullity sanction regardless of the foreign rule's legal consequences, is held by Kreuzer *Ausländisches Wirtschaftsrecht* 86.

211 Supra section 3, j and infra Chapter 5, IV, 1, e; Schurig RabelsZ 54 (1990) 217, 240.

212 Siehr RabelsZ 52 (1988) 41, 72, 73.

213 Lorenz RIW 1987, 569, 578, 579; Siehr RabelsZ 52 (1988) 41, 92, for criticism of the determination of the scope of a foreign rule, see Coester ZVerglRWiss 82 (1983) 1, 16.

214 Radtke ZVerglRWiss 84 (1985) 325, 355; Schäfer *FG Sandrock* 39, 53; Schubert RIW 1987, 729, 736.

h International comity, decisional harmony

The advantage of the *Special Connection Theory* is that it serves *decisional harmony*, because it does not exclude application of foreign internationally mandatory rules pursuing public interests, but has developed criteria and principles to give effect to these rules on a conflict of laws level.[215] *Secondary special conflict rules* refer to foreign internationally mandatory rules independently of the normal conflict rules, and therefore refer to rules from the *lex causae* and from a third legal system. The mutual assistance between states in pursuing their national interests is thus served, ie *comitas of nations*.[216] The *Special Connection Theory* is able to recognise, within the choice of law process, the realities of increasing state intervention in the economy.[217]

This reality is not ignored by advocates of the *Schuldstatuts-theory* either. These authors cannot avoid taking third countries' internationally mandatory rules into account within the substantive law rules of the *lex causae*, although they declare that these rules are inapplicable, because they are not referred to by a conflict rule.

The better solution, however, is to develop choice of law criteria, on a conflict of laws level, for the application of foreign internationally mandatory rules, instead of blurring choice of law considerations with the application of substantive law. The *Special Connection Theory* has convincingly shown that the ordinary conflict rules are not suitable for rendering internationally mandatory rules applicable. The normal conflict rules based on private interests do not recognise the public interests of the enacting state. Rules serving the economic and political interests of the state have to be connected separately on the basis of conflict rules that consider the conflicting interests of the foreign enacting state and the forum.[218]

---

[215] For this advantage see MünchKomm/Martiny Art 34 Rn 33; Schiffer *Normen* 148 et seq; Wengler ZverglRWiss 54 (1941) 168, 181; Max Planck Institut RabelsZ 47 (1983) 595, 668.

[216] Zweigert RabelsZ 14 (1942) 283, 291; MünchKomm/Martiny Art 34 Rn 33; Schiffer *Normen* 149 et seq; Wengler ZverglRWiss 54 (1941) 168, 181; Max Planck Institut RabelsZ 47 (1983) 595, 669; Erne *Vertragsgültigkeit* 184.

[217] MünchKomm/Martiny Art 34 Rn 33; Schäfer *FG Sandrock* 37, 47; Hentzen RIW 1988, 508 et seq.

[218] Schiffer *Normen* 151 et seq; Kreuzer *Ausländisches Wirtschaftsrecht* 83 et seq; Schubert RIW 1987, 729, 733; Vischer Rec des Cours 232 (1992 I) 13, 180 et seq; see supra Chapter 5, I, 3, a, e.

i *Combination Theory*

The *Combination Theory*, which applies all internationally mandatory rules of the *lex causae* because of their belonging to the proper law, and those of a third country by means of a 'special connection', can be criticised for the same reasons mentioned in respect of both the *Schuldstatuts*- and the *Special Connection theories*. Further objections to the combination of the theories include the following.

Because the theory uses two different choice of law rules for the same category (the internationally mandatory rule), and because the basic ideas underlying these rules are mutually exclusive, the theory is contradictory.[219] If one assumes that the ordinary choice of law rules for contract are suitable to solve the problem of internationally mandatory rules, then it is inconsistent to apply (under certain circumstances) a third country's mandatory rules by means of special conflict rules. The inconsistent result of this approach is that, on the one hand, internationally mandatory rules are applied on the basis of *special conflict rules* and, on the other hand, on the basis of the *normal conflict rules* as part of the proper law.[220]

However, in the opinion of the present author, and as stated before, the major objection is that the *Combination Theory* is based on an understanding that the scope of reference of the ordinary conflict rules also covers those rules that serve only the public interests of the foreign enacting state. As we have already seen, however, the normal conflict rules are not appropriate for rendering these rules applicable.

---

219 Radtke ZverglRWiss 84 (1985) 325, 332, 351; Schubert RIW 1987, 729, 736; Schäfer *FG Sandrock* 39, 48; for criticism, see Becker *Sonderanknüpfung* 56 et seq; Drobnig RabelsZ 52 (1988) 1, 5.

220 Radtke ZverglRWiss 84 (1985) 325, 351; Schubert RIW 1987, 729, 736. For criticism of this approach, see Becker *Sonderanknüpfung* 76 et seq, who assumes that the *lex causae* is in principle applicable, but that third countries' mandatory rules can be considered as facts of an issue.

II German and Swiss case law solutions

In this section, I will analyse German case law solutions to the question of foreign internationally mandatory rules. Unlike Germany, Switzerland has enacted a special provision dealing with foreign internationally mandatory rules - art 19 of the Swiss IPRG - and so the Swiss case law can be dealt with more briefly.[221] The two jurisdictions are grouped together because the courts' solutions are, at least theoretically, quite similar, and for the purposes of this study it is not necessary to examine both countries in detail.[222]

As will be seen below, German case law does not express one specific opinion on the academic approaches already described. Depending on the facts of the situation, the *ratio decidendi* of each decision varies from case to case, and it is difficult to identify an over-arching principle underlying all the cases.[223] Nonetheless, the starting point is the well-established principle in German private international law that the conflict rules refer to the foreign law, including its mandatory legislation, and that mandatory rules of the forum state or an otherwise applicable legal system are thus excluded.[224] With regard to the application of internationally mandatory rules, however, this principle is subject to a number of exceptions.

To begin with, the foreign law can be excluded if its application leads to a result that infringes the forum's *ordre public*. (This generally accepted negative function of the *ordre public* is not discussed.[225]) There are, however, further exceptions that are relevant to the application of mandatory rules of the proper law. The first is the non-applicability of foreign public law. Basically, the Federal Supreme Court distinguishes between (internationally mandatory) rules of *private law* and those of *public law*. Whereas the former rules are subject to private international law, the latter rules fall outside the scope of reference of the normal conflict rules. Irrespective of whether they stem from the proper law or a third legal system, public law rules are subject to a so-called *Public Conflict of Laws* that is based on the principle of *territoriality of public laws*.

---

221 It is dealt with art 19 later in Chapter 5, IV.

222 For an examination, see Erne *Vertragsgültigkeit* 12 et seq. However, this is restricted to the question whether third countries' internationally mandatory rules can be applied or taken into account so that the contract is null and void, see Erne ibid 1, 2.

223 See among all Reithmann/Martiny/Limmer *Internationales Vertragsrecht* Rn 461; Becker *Sonderanknüpfung* 86; Coester ZverglRWiss 82 (1983) 1, 30; Drobnig *FS Neumayer* 159, 160; Mentzel *Sonderanknüpfung* 89.

224 MünchKomm/Martiny Art 34 Rn 24 with further references; Reithmann/Martiny/Limmer *Internationales Vertragsrecht* Rn 452.

225 For this principle, see Firsching/von Hoffmann *IPR* 248 et seq; Raape/Sturm *IPR Bd I* 199 et seq.

The second exception to the general rule is that, under certain circumstances, German courts consider the internationally mandatory rules of third countries as facts within the substantive law rules of the proper law. This exception has been categorised as the '*substantive law approach*' of the German case law. The first exception - that public law rules are beyond the scope of reference of the normal conflict rules and are subject of *Public Conflict of Laws* - has been designated the '*conflict of law approach*', because the courts' arguments are situated on the level of conflict of laws.[226]

Drobnig explains that the German case law uses two different methodological rationales, independently of each other, for deciding whether to give effect to foreign internationally mandatory rules. On the level of conflict of laws, the application of such rules has often been rejected because of their public law character. However, third countries' internationally mandatory rules, in particular, have been taken into account as facts without any choice of law considerations on the level of substantive law.[227]

1 The general rule - Application of mandatory rules of the proper law of the contract

The general rule in conflict of laws in Germany is that, if the conflict rules of the forum refer to a foreign legal system as governing the transaction, the rules render applicable - within their scope - the foreign law, including its facultative and mandatory provisions, to the exclusion of the rules of the forum state and any other legal system.[228] The crucial question in Germany, however, is whether the choice of law rules, when indicating the applicable foreign law, refer to the foreign legal system as a whole, including its public law (more precisely, rules that serve public interests) or whether they refer only to private law (rules that serve private interests).[229]

---

226 For this description, see Busse ZverglRWiss 95 (1996) 387, 391, 394 et seq; Baum RabelsZ 53 (1989) 152, 155 et seq, Drobnig *FS Neumayer* 159, 160 et seq; Mentzel *Sonderanknüpfung* 94 et seq; for criticism, see Zimmer IPRax 1993, 65 et seq.

227 Drobnig *FS Neumayer* 159 et seq; Erne *Vertragsgültigkeit* 22 et seq; Baum RabelsZ 53 (1989) 152 et seq; Becker ZVerglRWiss 95 (1996) 386, 395 et seq; Mentzel *Sonderanknüpfung* 94, 97; the situation in Switzerland is very similar, see Erne *Vertragsgültigkeit* 12 et seq.

228 MünchKomm/Martiny Art 34 Rn 24; Lehmann *Zwingendes Recht* 22; Staudinger/Magnus Art 34 Rn 16. 19; Reithmann/Martiny/Limmer *Internationales Vertragsrecht* Rn 452.

229 Reithmann/Martiny/Limmer *Internationales Vertragsrecht* 452; Staudinger/Magnus Art 34 Rn 19, 21; Kropholler IPR § 52 IX 3; Schurig RabelsZ 54 (1990) 217, 244; this is equally true for Switzerland, see Voser *Lois d'application immédiate* 50 et seq.

a 'Proper law doctrine' of the Supreme Court of the German Reich

The Supreme Court of the German Reich assumed that the choice of law rules of international private law referred to the application of the proper law of the contract as a whole. Accordingly, internationally mandatory rules of the proper law were applied by the courts, no matter whether they had a private or public law character, or whether they served the interests of the contracting parties,[230] or public interests of the foreign state.[231] In accordance with this general rule, foreign export restrictions were held to be applicable as part of the proper law of the contract.[232] Similarly, under German law prior to art VIII (2) (b) of the Bretton Woods Agreement (IMF), the Supreme Court declared a contract governed by Russian law void, because it infringed Russian foreign exchange regulations.[233] In the same way, it applied foreign currency regulations of the proper law, despite their public law nature.[234] Notorious rulings include the so-called '*Goldklauselfälle*' in which the courts held that a United States enactment was applicable provided the proper law was that of the United States.[235]

However, although these rules were in principle held to be applicable, the German courts often refused to apply in particular public law rules, and

---

230 See Lehmann *Zwingendes Recht* 22 et seq. Provisions about the non-enforceability of gambling and wagering debts were applied by the RG if they formed part of the proper law of the contract and made the contract unenforceable, cf RG 10.5.1884 RGZ 12, 34 (the proper law was French and Art 1965 Code Civil was applied, which reads 'La loi n'accorde aucune action pour une dette du jeu ou pour le payement d'un pari'); RG 4.4.1929 IPRespr 1929 Nr 31 (the proper law was Swiss and the RG applied Art 513 (1) OR: 'Aus Spiel und Wette entsteht keine Forderung'); with regard to usury and immorality cf RG 26.5.1900, RGZ 46, 112.

231 Cf Lehmann *Zwingendes Recht* 22 et seq, 26 et seq; Kreuzer *Ausländisches Wirtschaftsrecht* 19.

232 RG 21.10. 1921 NiemeyersZ 1924, 452 et seq, The case concerned a sale of livestock. The court left it open whether the contract was governed by German or Dutch law, but stated that if the contract were governed by Dutch law the Dutch export restriction would have been applicable as part of the proper law. However, the foreign prohibition would violate the interests of German economy and would therefore infringe the German *ordre public.*

233 RG 1.7.1930 IPRespr 1930 Nr 15; for further references, see Kreuzer *Ausländisches Wirtschaftsrecht* 35 footnote 99; Becker *Sonderanknüpfung* 90.

234 See Kreuzer *Ausländisches Wirtschaftsrecht* 41; Lehmann *Zwingendes Recht* 35.

235 RG 28.5.1936 RabelsZ 1936, 385 et seq; JW 1936, 2085 et seq ; cf Lehmann *Zwingendes Recht* 33 with regard to the historical background and the 'Joint Resolution' of 5.3.1933, in which the legislature of the United States determined that all obligations expressed in US-Dollars were to be settled in the par value Dollar notes irrespective of agreed Gold clauses and irrespective of the *lex causae.*

corrected undesirable outcomes by an extensive application of the public policy exclusionary rule.[236] Another common method of avoiding the application of mandatory rules was to apply a different law as the proper law.[237]

b Principle of '*non-applicability of foreign public law*', '*International Administrative Law*' or '*Public Conflict of Laws*' of the Federal Supreme Court

In a leading case in 1959 the seventh Senate of the Federal Supreme Court abandoned the proper law approach of the Supreme Court of the German Reich and broke with the former case law.[238] The case concerned a foreign exchange control regulation and was based on German national law, since the Bretton Woods Agreement of 1/22 July 1944[239] was not applicable.

The facts of the decision were as follows. In 1948 the defendant borrowed the sum of RM 10.000. from Mrs W. Both parties to the loan agreement were resident in the Soviet Zone of Germany, the Democratic Republic (DDR) as it then was. A statute was enacted in 1950 stipulating that the assignment of debts in respect of debtors resident in the Federal Republic required the consent of the Ministry in the Soviet Zone, otherwise the cession was invalid according to the law of the Soviet Zone. In 1955 the defendant moved to the Federal Republic, and in 1957 Mrs W. assigned his debt to the plaintiff, who resided in the Federal Republic, without the consent of the Ministry. In his defence, the defendant relied on the statute of 1950 and argued that the cession was invalid.[240] The court, however, did not uphold his defence and the plaintiff succeeded.

The Federal Supreme Court investigated whether the assignment of the loan debt in 1957 was invalid because it violated the foreign exchange control regulation of the German Democratic Republic. In its reasoning the court left open the question of whether the proper law of the loan contract was that of the

---

236 Cf Kreuzer *Ausländisches Wirtschaftsrecht* 19; RG 21.10.1921 NiemeyersZ 1924, 452; RG 28.5.1936 RabelsZ 1936, 385, 388.

237 This happened in the so called '*Rubelfällen*' where German courts were faced with the economic consequences of the Russian Revolution between the two World Wars, Lehmann *Zwingendes Recht* 28 et seq; Becker *Sonderanknüpfung* 91; for example RG 3.10.1923 RGZ 108, 241.

238 BGH 17.12.1959 BGHZ 31, 367 et seq.

239 In legal force in Germany since 14.8.1952, BGBl. 1952 II, 728.

240 For a summary of the facts, see Mann Rec des Cours 132 (1971 I) 107, 161, 187 who criticises the rationale and conclusion of the judgment.

Federal Republic (FR) or that of the German Democratic Republic (GDR).[241] The court adopted the so-called principle of '*non-applicability of foreign public law*' (*Grundsatz der Nichtanwendung ausländischen öffentlichen Rechts)* from the law of expropriation, and applied it to the 'interzonal'[242] foreign exchange control law.

It was held that the applicability of the GDR's foreign exchange control regulation had to be determined *independently* of the proper law of the contract, because of the fundamental distinction between *private* and *Public Conflict of Laws*.[243] The former was said to rest 'upon the idea of recognition and application of foreign private law according to statutory or customary rules'. The latter emanated from the idea of *territoriality* of law: 'It is dominated by the concept that provisions of public law have in principle no effect beyond the frontiers of the legislating state', ie the principle of *non-applicability of foreign public law*.[244]

However, the court ruled that the *principle of non-applicability of foreign public law* was subject to exceptions. With reference to a decision by the Federal Tribunal of Switzerland,[245] it stated, very vaguely, that foreign restraints of competition of public law might nevertheless 'exclusively or at least primarily serve the protection or interests of individuals or the fair reconciliation between them', and that it is 'not unthinkable' that these rules might under certain circumstances have an influence (effect) on domestic private relationships.[246] However, this exception did not apply to foreign (restraints on disposition) rules of public law which served the implementation of the legislating state's economic or political purposes. These rules were subject to the *Public Conflict of Laws* and were thus in principle not applicable.[247]

---

241 The court of appeal held that the foreign law was not applicable because the proper law of the contract changed to the law of the Federal Republic by hypothetical intention of the parties, see 17.12.1959 BGHZ 31, 367, 369, 370.

242 Federal Republic and Democratic Republic of Germany, BGH 17.12.1959 BGHZ 31, 367, 371, 373, and later to international foreign exchange law BGH 19.4.1962 VII. ZS IPRespr 1962/63 Nr 163, cf Kreuzer *Ausländisches Wirtschaftsrecht* 37 for further references.

243 BGH 17.12.1959 BGHZ 31, 367, 370.

244 BGH ibid 371; cf Mann Rec des Cours 132 (1971 I) 107, 187.

245 BGE 80 II, 53, 61 et seq.

246 BGH ibid 371, the statement is extremely vague and difficult to translate, cf '...Es scheint auch nicht undenkbar, daß derartigem öffentlichen Recht ungeachtet seiner grundsätzlich territorial beschränkten Wirksamkeit unter bestimmten Voraussetzungen nicht jeder Einfluß auf inländische Privatrechtsverhältnisse abzusprechen ist....'

247 BGH 17.12.1959 BGHZ 31, 367, 371, 372.

The court noted that German courts apply and enforce such public laws only if and to the extent that the foreign state holds the *power to enforce their provisions*.[248] In the case of state interference in a debt, the foreign state has the power to enforce its law if the debtor resides within the enacting state.[249] With regard to the foreign exchange control regulation of the GDR, the court ruled that it served the welfare of the state, not the interests of the contracting parties, and was thus not applicable beyond the territorial borders of the GDR. In addition, the relevant authorities of the GDR did not have the power to enforce the legislation, because the debtor had assets in the Federal Republic.

Finally, the judgment referred to a further exception to the principle of *territoriality*: With regard to *International Conventions*, such as the Bretton Woods Agreement, art VIII (2) (b) IMF, foreign exchange restrictions should be recognised.[250] However, in the present case the IMF agreement was inapplicable because the foreign exchange regulation emanated from the GDR, which was not a member state of the Convention.[251]

These principles developed by the Seventh Senate in 1959 have been confirmed by the same senate in later judgments, with regard to Austrian exchange control regulations and Polish currency regulations,[252] and have been adopted by other senates of the Federal Supreme Court.[253] In most judgments, the court either left

---

248 The court's wording was that the foreign law 'is taken into consideration and enforced', BGH ibid 372, 373; see also BGH 28.1.1965 IzRspr 1964/65 Nr 68; BGH 16.4.1975 (I ZS) BGHZ 64, 183, 190.

249 BGH ibid 373.

250 BGH ibid 373.

251 Also see BGH 28.1.1965 IzRspr 1964/65 Nr 68. In BGH 19.4.1962 IPRespr 1962/63 Nr 163 an Austrian exchange control regulation was applied despite its public law character and the principle of territoriality of public law, because Austria was a member state of the Bretton Woods Agreement and the Austrian legislation was applied on basis of art VIII (2) (b) IMF.

252 BGH 19.4.1962 (VII ZS) IPRespr 1962/63 Nr 163; cf also BGH 18.2.1965 (VII ZS) BGHZ 43, 162, 165 et seq. The court held that a Polish currency regulation radically reducing the original amount of a loan, the proper law of which was Polish law, was not applicable. In place of the Polish regulation rules of German law were substituted. Alternatively, the court also upheld the territoriality of public law rules as well as the need to determine the law applicable to currency separately from the proper law of the contract. For the facts, see Mann Rec des Cours 132 (1971 I) 107, 193.

253 BGH 28.1.1965 (Ia ZS) IzRespr 1964/65 Nr 68 concerning the foreign exchange regulation as well as an expropriation provision of the GDR, which were held to be inapplicable; BGH 16.4.1975 (I ZS) BGHZ 64, 183, 189 ('*August Vierzehn*' or '*Solchenizyn*'). For the facts of this case see (2) (a); also see BGH 8.4.1976 (II ZS) VersR 1976, 678 (for a foreign import restriction); BGH 11.7.1985 (IX ZS) BGHZ 95, 256, 264, 265 (for foreign bankruptcy proceedings); BGH 17.11.1994 (III ZS) BGHZ 128, 41, 52

open the question of whether the foreign public law rule was part of the proper law, or was concerned with the application of a third country's public law rule to a German contract, a situation which is dealt with in the next section. Nearly all the cases where the principle of non-applicability of foreign public law rules was invoked by the courts resulted in such rules not being applied.[254]

c Exceptions to the 'principle of *non-applicability of foreign public law*'

The Federal Supreme Court mentioned on several occasions the exceptions to the principle of non-applicability of foreign public law. It asked whether the foreign regulation served to protect the interests of individuals or to reconcile those interests, or whether the foreign state had the power to implement its public law. The consequences of both exceptions are vague.

(1) The foreign public law rule serves predominantly private interests

Although the exception in favour of public law rules serving only or primarily private interests or the fair reconciliation of the contracting parties has been affirmed several times, it was applied only once in a judgment concerning the foreign adjudication of bankruptcy.[255]

As to the consequences of this exception, the Federal Supreme Court said in its leading case that it was 'not unthinkable' that these rules might affect 'domestic private relationships'. In later judgments the court stated that, at least with regard to those public law rules that do not serve private interests but serve economic and state-political interests of the foreign enacting country, the principle of territoriality, and, as its consequence, the principle of non-applicability of foreign public law applies.[256] Does this exception mean that these rules could be applied or considered only if they form part of the proper law, or could it lead to an application or consideration of a third country's

(foreign trade restriction based on a state monopoly); OLG Hamburg 6.5.1993 RIW 1994, 686, 687 (foreign import restrictions).

254 In BGH 19.4.1962 (VII ZS) IPRespr 1962/63 Nr 163 an Austrian foreign exchange control regulation was held to be applicable because of art VIII (2) (b) IMF, but the court made it clear that the foreign law would not otherwise have been applied.

255 11.7.1985 (IX ZS) BGHZ 95, 256, 264, 265 with regard to a Belgian bankruptcy proceeding and held that adjudication of bankruptcy in a foreign country includes the domestic assets, since the bankruptcy proceedings, despite their public law nature, serve the fair reconciliation of the interests of the contracting parties; see also Baum RabelsZ 53 (1989) 152, 158.

256 BGH 16.4.1975 BGHZ 64, 183, 189.

public law rule?[257] The scope of this exception is uncertain, particularly because, apart from in the bankruptcy case, the Federal Supreme Court never applied it.[258]

(2) The foreign state has the power to enforce its law

The second exception to the principle of non-applicability of foreign public law, that the foreign state is able to enforce its law, has also often been discussed.[259] It is debated by scholars whether this exception results in application of the foreign provision or in a consideration of the factual effects of the foreign provision within the substantive law of the governing legal system.[260]

The Federal Supreme Court applied this exception in only one case.[261] The facts were complicated and will not be repeated here. The crucial question was whether GDR foreign exchange regulations, as well as a rule of an expropriatory nature, applied to a contract. At the time of conclusion of the contract in 1955, both parties were residents of the GDR. In 1960, however, the plaintiff moved his habitual residence to the Federal Republic. Despite the fact that the court held that the contract was governed by the law of the GDR, it refused to apply both the foreign exchange regulation and the expropriatory rule, because these rules were subject to the *Public Conflict of Laws* and thus territorially limited in their scope to the GDR.[262]

The court examined the first exception to the principle of *territoriality* and the *non-applicability of foreign public law*, and held that both laws served the public interest and not the interests of the parties. With regard to the second exception it stated that:

> A German court considers and enforces only exceptionally the civil law consequences of a foreign exchange control regulation ... in the private relationship if and in so far the foreign state has the power to enforce its law.

---

257 For this assumption, see Busse ZverglRWiss 95 (1996) 387, 396; Baum RabelsZ 53 (1989) 152, 156.

258 See Drobnig *FS Neumayer* 159, 161, 167; Lehmann *Zwingendes Recht* 43, 45; Mentzel *Sonderanknüpfung* 97.

259 BGH 17.12.1959 BGHZ 31, 367, 372; BGH 28.1.1965 IzRespr 1964/65 Nr 68; BGH 16.4.1975 BGHZ 64, 183, 190.

260 For different interpretations, see Baum RabelsZ 53 (1989) 152, 156; Drobnig *FS Neumayer* 159, 161, 167; Busse ZVerglRWiss 95 (1996) 387, 397, 398.

261 BGH 28.1.1965 IzRespr 1964/65 Nr 68.

262 Ibid.

Concerning the foreign exchange control regulation, the court held that the foreign state did not have the power to enforce its law, since the debtor had assets in the territory of the Federal Republic and the plaintiff resided there. Concerning the foreign expropriation rule, the court held that the foreign state was able to enforce the law (and in fact, had already enforced it). Although the second exception was in principle applicable, the court nevertheless refused to apply the foreign regulation because it was held to be contrary to the German *ordre public*.

Finally, with regard to both provisions, the court held that despite their inapplicability because of the conflict of public laws and the violation of the German *ordre public*, the actual or de facto effects of the foreign provisions on the private relationship may be taken into account and may lead to impossibility of performance.[263]

Thus, it can be stated that the foreign public law rule is applied (as a result of conflict of laws considerations) if the foreign state has the power to enforce its law. In this case, the court refused to apply the foreign public law rule because of a violation of the German *ordre public*, despite the ability of the foreign country to enforce it. Nevertheless, it is still possible to take into account the de facto effects of the provision on the private relationship within the substantive law rules.[264]

d Swiss case law solutions

The principle of *non-applicability of foreign public law* was also used in Switzerland to prevent the application of foreign public law rules despite their belonging to the proper law. However, the early Swiss judgments were often based on a number of reasons. Sometimes non-application was based on an infringement of the Swiss *ordre public*,[265] on other occasions judgments referred to the principle of *non-application of foreign public laws*, based on the notion that choice of law rules refer only to foreign private law, not to public

---

263 For details of the facts and reasoning of this decision, see Drobnig *FS Neumayer* 159, 169; Busse ZVerglRWiss 96 (1995) 386, 398; Becker *Sonderanknüpfung* 92; Kreuzer *Ausländisches Wirtschaftsrecht* 38, 51.

264 For criticism of the application of the *ordre public* where the foreign state has the power to enforce its law and the double-examination of the provision on the level of conflict of laws and afterwards on the level of substantive law, see Drobnig *FS Neumayer* 159, 169 et seq.

265 BGE 60 II 294, 311 et seq (German exchange control regulations); BGE 62 II 108, 110; BGE 64 II 88, 96 et seq (gold clause prohibition); BGE 67 II 215; BGE 68 II 203, 210.

law. By relying on the *principle of territoriality* it was held that public law rules are only applicable within the borders of the enacting country.[266]

In the leading case of the Swiss Federal Tribunal in 1954,[267] the court deviated from the former case law in that it rejected a *strict* adherence to the principle of *non-application of foreign public laws*. However, it did not adopt the *proper law doctrine* according to which all mandatory rules of the proper law are in principle applicable, irrespective of their private or public law nature. Instead, the court differentiated between different kinds of public law rules and thus laid the foundations of German case law.[268]

Again, the facts of the case are complicated and shall not be repeated here.[269] The crucial question was whether Dutch emergency legislation, enacted after the Second World War, which rendered void any shares or securities acquired by looting during the German occupation, could be applied. The court held that the proper law of the transaction was Dutch and classified the Dutch legislation as public law. It referred to the principle of *non-applicability of foreign public law* but rejected the strict adherence to this principle, due to the principle of *unity of a legal system*. Instead it differentiated rules on the basis of their purpose. It stated that:

> As long as an encroachment upon private law or private relationships with public means intends to serve only or predominantly the protection of private interests (in contrast to direct interests of the state), there is no need for a Swiss judge to refuse to apply the foreign law for the sole reason of its public law nature.[270]

The Swiss court regarded the Dutch legislation as applicable despite its public law character, because its purpose was the protection of private property. The regulations were therefore held to be in the *interests of the individuals* and to *support the purpose of foreign private law*. Thus, the court distinguished between foreign public law serving *primarily 'selfish' interests of the foreign state* on the one hand, and foreign public law *protecting the interests of individuals* and *supplementing foreign private law* on the other.[271] Only the

---

266 BGE 39 II 640, 652; BGE 42 II 179, 183; BGE 61 II 242, 246 BGE 74 II 224, 229; BGE 76 II 33, 41 et seq; cf Sturm *FS Moser* 3, 14 et seq; Morscher *Rechtssetzungsakte* 48 et seq.

267 (BG 2.2.1954) BGE 80 II 53 et seq.

268 In BGHZ 31, 367 et seq.

269 For facts and reasoning Honsell/Vogt/Schnyder/Mächler-Erne Art 13 Rn 13; Voser *Lois d'application immédiate* 66; Vischer Rec des Cours 232 (1992) 21, 183.

270 BGE 80 II 53, 62.

271 See Voser *Lois d'application immédiate* 67 et seq; Morscher *Rechtssetzungsakte* 85, 86.

latter public law rules were held to be applicable, while the former are inapplicable on the basis of territoriality.[272]

The principles developed in this case have been affirmed several times in later decisions of the Swiss Federal Tribunal.[273] However, foreign public law rules were always applied if required by an international Convention or a special choice of law rule.[274]

e Concluding remarks

In conclusion, it can be stated:

(1) The Federal Supreme Court - by abandoning the *Schuldstatuts-theory*, which was at least formally supported by the Supreme Court of the German Reich - distinguished between internationally mandatory rules of a *private* and *public* law nature. The former are subject to private international law and are therefore applied if they form part of the proper law of the contract. The latter are subject to *Public Conflict of Laws*, based on the principle of *territoriality*, and are accordingly not applicable outside the territory of the legislating country.

(2) However, the principle of non-applicability is subject to exceptions. The first exception, which was developed by the Swiss Federal Tribunal in a leading case of 1954 and adopted by the Federal Supreme Court in 1959, emanates from a functional distinction between different kinds of public laws: viz. public law rules serving *private interests* and those that pursue the *public interests* of the foreign state. Only the latter are held to fall under the *principle of territoriality*, while the former, although of a public law nature, might well, under certain circumstances, 'have some effect on the private relationship' under certain circumstances, because they can be classified as an integral part of the system of private law.

    The content and the result of this exception is, however, uncertain. The decisions of the Federal Supreme Court lack clarity regarding the circumstances under which foreign public law serving private interests may be applied. Furthermore, it is by no means clear how the foreign rule is

---

272 BGE 80 II 53, 61 et seq.

273 Cf Sturm in *FS Moser* 3, 14 et seq; in particular BGE 95 II 109, 114; BGE 82 I 196, 197; BGE 83 II 312, 319; compare as well the relatively recent judgment of 26.11.1981 in BGE 107 II 489, 492

274 Cf only BGE 82 I 196, 197; BGE 95 II 109, 114, Honsell/Vogt/Schneider/Mächler-Erne Art 13 Rn 18.

given effect, viz. whether the court applies it in the direct sense or simply considers it as fact. German courts applied this exception only once in a case where an act of the state was in question, rather than a foreign rule, and this was in a bankruptcy case. In the leading Swiss case of 1954, however, this exception had already resulted in *application* of the foreign public law rule as part of the Dutch proper law.

Most academic authors refer to the distinction made by the Swiss Federal Tribunal and the German Supreme Court between different *kinds* of public law rules according to the interests pursued by the rule and this distinction is used to separate internationally mandatory rules from mandatory rules in a domestic sense.[275] It seems reasonable to agree with most of the German and Swiss commentators that foreign public law rules serving predominantly private interests are subject to private international law and are thus applied as part of the proper law.[276] Thus, the principle of non-applicability of foreign public laws is restricted to rules that pursue public interests of the foreign state.

(3) In a further step the Federal Supreme Court formulated a second exception to the general inapplicability of foreign public laws. This exception concerns, in particular, those rules that pursue public interests of the foreign state. The court held that according to the principles of *International Administrative Law* or *Public Conflict of Laws*, the latter rules are only applicable outside their territory to the extent that the foreign state has the *power to enforce* them. The scope of this exception is narrowly defined by the courts, and it has been applied in only one case where the foreign state

275 Foreign rules serving predominantly private interests are mandatory in a domestic sense and applied as part of the proper law. Rules pursuing public interests of the foreign state are internationally mandatory rules. See, for instance, Drobnig *FS Neumayer* 159, 161, 167; Voser *Lois d'application immédiate* 50 et seq, 66 et seq; Morscher *Rechtssetzungsakte* 87, 88; Vischer Rec des Cours 232 (1992 I) 13, 184; Schiffer *Normen* 30, 31, 74; Schubert RIW 1987, 729, 731; Radtke ZVerglRWiss 84 (1985) 325, 328.

276 See similar Lehmann *Zwingendes Recht* 43; Voser *Lois d'application immédiate* 58 et seq, 62 et seq, 66 et seq. But it has to be admitted that this conclusion is not cogent: The exception was mentioned in cases where the foreign mandatory provision emanated from the *lex causae* as well as in cases where it came from a 'third' country. Thus it might well be possible that these rules would be applied regardless of the proper law and thus connected separately (be subject to a 'special connection'). Cf Busse ZverglRWiss 96 (1995) 386, 400 also with regard to international mandatory rules of a private law; see also von Hoffmann RabelsZ 38 (1974) 397, 407, 418. However, in this regard case law gives no clear guidance, as it was more concerned with the question of whether foreign rules belonging to the *lex causae* were excluded from application because of their public law character.

had de facto already enforced the provision already.[277] Finally, there is the further possibility of taking into account only the actual effects of a foreign provision within the substantive law, despite its inapplicability on a conflict of laws level.[278]

2 Internationally mandatory rules of a third country

With regard to the internationally mandatory rules of third countries the Federal Supreme Court's above-mentioned structurally different solutions - the solution on a conflict of laws level and consideration as fact within the substantive law of the *lex causae* - become even more evident. In general, it can be stated that the '*conflict solution*', which is based on the so-called *Public Conflict of Laws*, had the result that the foreign rule which had been functionally classified as territorially limited public law, was never directly applied nor considered as fact within the substantive law of the *lex causae*.[279]

However, there are a number of cases where German courts considered the foreign legislation (irrespective of its public law character) within the German substantive law that constituted the governing law of the contract. This *Substantive Law Approach* (*materiellrechtlicher Ansatz*) originated in the Supreme Court of the German Reich and was adopted by the Federal Supreme Court. The infringement of the foreign rule was considered to the extent that the contract was deemed immoral, and the rule could thus render the contract invalid. Alternatively, the *actual effects* of the foreign rule on the private relationship were taken into account, and the rule could render performance impossible.

What is characteristic of these judgments is that the foreign provisions are considered on the level of substantive law without any conflict of laws consideration: The judgments do not refer to the so-called *Public Conflict of Laws*, or to the principles of *territoriality* and *non-applicability* of foreign public law.[280] In the Supreme Court of the German Reich the *inapplicability* of

---

277 See BGH 28.1.1965 IzRespr 1964/65 Nr 68; also see Drobnig *FS Neumayer* 159, 168.

278 Regardless of whether the foreign provision is inapplicable because it is of a public law character or because it violates the forum's *ordre public*, cf BGH 28.1.1965 IzRespr 1964/65 Nr 68; also see Drobnig *FS Neumayer* 159, 168; RG 28.6.1918 RGZ 93, 182, 183 about which see later; for the contrary opinion of Swiss courts, see BGE 60 II 294, 311 et seq; BGE 64 II 88, 100.

279 See only BGH 17.12.1959 BGHZ 31, 367 et seq; BGH 16.4.1975 BGHZ 64, 183 et seq.

280 All the decided cases concerned '*false third country*' cases: German law was held to govern the transaction and the issue was whether and how a foreign internationally mandatory provision could be applied. Cf MünchKomm/Martiny Art 34 Rn 49; Lehmann *Zwingendes Recht* 12, 45.

a third country's rule followed from the fact that the contract was governed exclusively and entirely by the *lex causae*.[281] However, the Federal Supreme Court rejected this theory in its leading case in 1959, and held that public law rules are subject to *Public Conflict of Laws,* which is independent from the proper law as indicated by the ordinary conflict rules of private international law.[282]

The differing solutions, the lack of uniform decisions, and the lack of methodologically sound explanations according to the general principles of conflict of laws have been the subject of criticism. It has therefore been argued that German case law has not been able to develop congruent and uniform criteria to deal with the problem of the application of foreign internationally mandatory rules.[283] However, in few judgments the Federal Supreme Court combined or at least referred to both solutions as follows: Third countries' internationally mandatory rules (of public law) have in principle not been applied on a conflict of laws level, but under certain circumstances have been taken into account as 'fact' within the substantive rules of the proper law.[284]

a Non-applicability of third countries' public law - *Public Conflict of Laws*

In some cases concerning the mandatory public law provisions of a third country, the Federal Supreme Court adopted the principle of *non-applicability of foreign public laws* and the distinction between different kinds of public laws.

For instance, in the notorious *Solzhenitsyn* case in 1975, the court was concerned with a Russian trade restriction. The plaintiff, a Swiss publisher, had purchased the copyright for the novel 'August 14' from the Russian author Solzhenitsyn in Switzerland. This publisher sued the defendant, who published the same book in Germany, for infringement of copyright. The defendant argued

---

281 Also see the above mentioned *Schuldstatuts-theory*.

282 As elaborated by Drobnig (id *FS Neumayer* 159, 160 et seq) the incompatible solutions emanate from the different senates of the Federal Supreme Court. The seventh senate submitted that foreign public law rules were inapplicable, while third countries' mandatory rules were - as will be seen - considered within the substantive law of the proper law several times by the eighth and the second senate. See BGH 21.12.1960 (VIII ZS) BGHZ 34, 169; BGH 24.5.1962 (II ZS) NJW 1962, 1436; BGH 22.6.1972 (II ZS) BGHZ 59, 82; BGH 29.9.1977 (III ZS) BGHZ 69, 295.

283 Reithmann/Martiny/Limmer *Internationales Vertragsrecht* 461; Mentzel *Sonderanknüpfung* 94; also see Schubert RIW 1987, 729, 737; Radtke ZVerglRWiss 84 (1985) 325, 341, 345 et seq; Kratz *Ausländische Eingriffsnormen* 80 - 84.

284 BGH 8.4.1976 VersR 1976, 678; also see BGH 17.11.1994 BGHZ 128, 41, 52, 53.

that the plaintiff could not acquire the copyright due to the Soviet state monopoly on foreign trade, but his defence was rejected by the court.

The court held that the foreign monopoly was of a public law nature and could thus have only *territorial effects*, *irrespective of the proper law of the contract*. The Federal Supreme Court referred to the 1959 case, and stated that at least those rules that do not *serve the protection and interests of individuals or their fair reconciliation*, but *pursue public interests of the foreign state*, are subject to the *principle of territoriality* and are thus in principle not to be applied or enforced outside their territory. The court went on to examine the second exception regarding the foreign authorities' power to enforce the relevant public law provision, but it ultimately rejected both exceptions.[285]

Thus it can be stated that the Federal Supreme Court confirmed the principle of *non-applicability of foreign public law* and the principle of *territoriality of public law rules* with regard to third countries' public law rules that do serve predominantly economic and political interests of the enacting state. Irrespective of the law governing the contract according to the rules of private international law, public law rules are subject to *Public Conflict of Laws* and, according to the principle of *territoriality,* are applicable only within the territory of the enacting state. Nevertheless, these rules can be considered if the foreign state has the power to enforce its law. These principles were again confirmed in a more recent judgment that concerned trade restrictions based on a state monopoly.[286]

b Public law rules serving private interests and internationally mandatory private law rules of a third country

The question of applicability of a third country's internationally mandatory rule of a public law nature serving private interests has not yet been decided.[287] In all decisions the German courts have interpreted the rules in question as pursuing the state's economic and political interests. The fact that the Federal Supreme Court mentioned this exception to the principle of *non-applicability of foreign public law,* even in a case of a third country's mandatory rule,[288] might indicate

[285] BGH 16.4.1975 (I ZS) BGHZ 64, 183, 189 (*August Vierzehn* or *Solschenizyn*); for the facts of this case, see Lehmann *Zwingendes Recht* 44 et seq.

[286] BGH 17.11.1994 BGHZ 128, 41, 52, 53; also see BGH 8.4.1976 VersR 1976, 678 (*obiter dicta*); OLG Hamburg 6.5. 1994 RIW 1994, 686, 687. Both decisions concerned third countries' import restrictions.

[287] Cf Lehmann *Zwingendes Recht* 45; Staudinger/Magnus Art 34 Rn 127.

[288] BGH 16.4.1975 BGHZ 64, 183, 189 with reference to BGHZ 31, 367, 371.

that the foreign rule would be applied or at least considered. Whether this is, in truth, the approach of the German courts is uncertain.[289]

The courts have never been faced with the question of whether a third country's internationally mandatory rules of a private law nature are also applicable.[290] This issue is disputed in academic writings.[291] Many authors favour an application of these rules only if they form part of the proper law of the contract and thus subject them to the ordinary conflict rules of private international law.[292]

c Consideration as factum within the substantive rules of the lex causae

Apart from the *conflict of law solution*, another solution has found authority in judgments of the Federal Supreme Court, which is based on the case law of the Supreme Court of the German Reich.[293] Third countries' internationally mandatory rules have been considered in the substantive rules of the *lex causae*, in particular German *boni mores* (§138 German Civil Code, BGB), provisions for impossibility of performance (initially § 306 BGB or subsequently § 275 BGB), or under the heading of frustration of contract because of unreasonableness of performance.[294]

d Infringement of foreign prohibition laws as a violation of German *boni mores*

The Supreme Court of the German Reich rendered contracts that infringed foreign mandatory rules void, under the plea of *contra boni mores* in the sense of § 138 BGB.[295] All judgments referred to the violation of *boni mores* and did

---

289 A '*special connection*' of foreign rules in the sense submitted by the *Special Connection Theory* was expressly rejected in the early German judgment, cf BGH 17.12.1959 BGHZ 31, 367, 373.

290 Lehmann *Zwingendes Recht* 46; Staudinger/Magnus Art 34 Rn 127.

291 See supra Chapter 3, II, 2 and Chapter 4, III, 2.

292 For instance, Drobnig *FS Neumayer* 159, 167; Kropholler *IPR* § 52 VIII 1; Anderegg *Ausländische Eingriffsnorm* 88; Sonnenberger *FS Rebmann* 819, 823; Staudinger/Magnus Art 34 Rn 127; for the contrary view: Busse ZVerglRWiss 96 (1995) 386, 400; von Hoffmann RabelsZ 38 (1974) 397, 407, 418.

293 See Drobnig *FS Neumayer* 159, 161; Lehmann *Zwingendes Recht* 46 et seq.

294 As already stated this solution has been particularly favoured by the eighth and second senates of the Federal Supreme Court: BGH 21.12.1960 (VIII ZS) BGHZ 34, 169 et seq; BGH 24.5.1962 (II ZS) NJW 1962, 1436; BGH 22.6.1972 (II ZS) BGHZ 59, 82; also see BGH 8.5.1985 (IVa ZS) BGHZ 94, 262, 268.

295 § 138 (1) reads 'Ein Rechtsgeschäft, das gegen die Guten Sitten verstößt, ist nichtig': 'A legal transaction (contract) that violates *boni mores* is void'.

not base the nullity sanction on the infringement of a statutory prohibition (§ 134 BGB),[296] because § 134 BGB is concerned only with domestic, not foreign, statutory prohibitions.[297] Only prohibitions that had been in force at the time of conclusion of the contract were considered by the courts as immoral violations of foreign law under § 138 BGB. Supervening illegality was dealt with under impossibility of performance or frustration.[298]

(1) Smuggling contracts and import restrictions

The first judgments of the Supreme Court of the German Reich that have dealt with the question of foreign internationally mandatory rules under German law as the *lex causae* concerned smuggling contracts.[299] Thus the court was concerned with contracts that directly involved the execution or promotion of smuggling in defiance of *foreign import duties*[300] or *import bans.*[301] For example, the Supreme Court held that a contract to smuggle textiles to Russia, which was governed by German law and infringed Russian custom laws, was invalid. The court rejected a nullity resulting from infringement of a statutory prohibition (illegality), since the infringement of the foreign law was not forbidden or penalised in Germany. Nevertheless, the court stated that smuggling was immoral and therefore a smuggling contract or a contract directed towards smuggling was invalid.[302]

The Supreme Court of the German Reich consistently ruled that smuggling contracts were immoral and thus invalid, if they were *directly* and *intentionally* directed towards customs fraud. The court was particularly concerned about cases involving the smuggling of alcohol into countries where the importing of alcohol was prohibited.[303] The immorality of these contracts, which violated foreign provisions, lay in the fact that smuggling leads to 'moral decadence and

---

296 § 134 reads 'Ein Rechtsgeschäft, das gegen ein gesetzliches Verbot verstößt, ist nichtig, wenn sich nicht aus dem Gesetz ein anderes ergibt': 'A legal transaction (contract) that infringes a legal prohibition is void, unless something else follows from the prohibition.'

297 See RG 5.11.1898 RGZ 42, 295, 297, 298 and RG 2.12.1903 RGZ 56, 179 et seq; RG 3.10.1923 RGZ 108, 241, 243; RG 17.6.1939 RGZ 161, 269, 299.

298 In RG 2.5.1923 RGZ 107, 174 et seq the court applied initial impossibility.

299 For many references, see Kreuzer *Ausländisches Wirtschaftsrecht* 13 et seq.

300 For instance RG 5.11.1898 RGZ 42, 295 et seq (Russian customs law).

301 RG 17.10.1930 JW 1931, 928; 26.10.1928 JW 1929, 244 (sales contract); RG 10.3.1927 JW 1927, 2287 (loan agreement to finance smuggling); RG 9.2. 1926 JW 1926, 2169 (shipping contract to support smuggling).

302 RG 5.11.1898 RGZ 42, 297, 298.

303 RG 26.10.1928 JW 1929, 244 (sales contract); RG 10.3.1927 JW 1927, 2287; RG 9.2. 1926 JW 1926, 2169, RG 2.12.1903 RGZ 56, 179; RG 30.9.1919 RGZ 96, 282. For references, see Kreuzer *Ausländisches Wirtschaftsrecht* 14 footnote 18, 19.

aberration that would jeopardise the general welfare'[304] or that smuggling would have a 'demoralising effect in the highest degree'.[305]

In 1927 the Supreme Court of the German Reich delivered a notorious decision on *foreign import restrictions.* The court had to deal with the validity of a contract governed by German law to export cocaine to India. The defendant did not have the required Indian import licence. The plaintiff knew this and at the request of the defendant gave a false description of the goods. The court considered the *policies pursued* by the foreign import restriction: If it was based on reasons of public health, then the contract would be *contra boni mores* and invalid. But, if the import restriction was based on trade policy, then, were it not for the false description of the goods, there could be no objection to the contract. However, if the parties intended to deceive customs authorities of the foreign state in order to evade customs duties, then the contract would be immoral on the ground of smuggling and therefore null and void.[306]

(2) The Federal Supreme Court

The Federal Supreme Court adopted the approach of the Supreme Court of the German Reich, and held that under certain circumstances contracts that infringed foreign prohibitions were immoral and thus invalid. Accordingly, the Federal Supreme Court ruled that § 134 BGB was inapplicable, since it was only concerned with German prohibitions, but applied the *boni mores* rule (§ 138 BGB).[307]

The subjective criterion of the conscious deception required for immoral contracts was slowly but surely detached from consideration of the foreign rule in the context of § 138 BGB, and the objective criterion of '*equality of interests*' was developed.[308] In time, the court developed principles specifying the circumstances in which such an *equality of interests* is assumed so that violation of a foreign prohibition leads to immorality under German *boni mores*.

---

304 RG 30.9.1919 RGZ 96, 282,283.

305 RG 5.11.1898 RGZ 42, 295, 297.

306 RG 24.6.1927 JW 1927, 2288, 2289; for the facts of this case: Kegel *Role of Public law* 29, 55; cf also RG 8.12.1927 JW 1927, 790 et seq; BGH 8.4.1976 VersR 1976, 678; OLG Hamburg 6.5.1993 RIW 1994, 686.

307 BGH 21.12.1960 BGHZ 34, 169, 176; BGH 22.6.1972 BGHZ 59, 82, 85; BGH 29.9.1977 BGHZ 69, 295, 296.

308 Cf Kreuzer *Ausländisches Wirtschaftsrecht* 22; Drobnig *FS Neumayer* 159.

(3) *Borax* and *Borsäure* case - the foreign prohibition also serves German interests

In the notorious *Borax*[309] case in 1960, the Federal Supreme Court was concerned with the validity of a contract between two German companies. The defendant had to deliver 100 tons of borax to the plaintiff. The borax was produced in Germany from the basic material Rasurit, which was imported from the United States. The USA granted export licences with the condition that the borax would not be transferred to socialist countries. The parties knew that the final destination of the Borax was Rostock in East Germany, and conspired to conceal this fact by selling the goods c.i.f. Copenhagen. However, the US law required every subsequent buyer in the line of trade to sign a statement of confession, which contained an obligation not to transfer the borax to socialist countries. When the buyer (plaintiff) refused to sign, the seller (defendant) declined to deliver the borax and was sued for damages for breach of contract.

The Federal Supreme Court rejected the claim, holding that the contract was immoral. The immorality was evident in the *intention of the parties* to deceive the United States Bureau of Foreign Commerce, in order to obtain the necessary consent, and in the *violation of German interests*, as the infringement of the foreign prohibition constituted a threat to the maintenance of peace and freedom. The Court stated that:

> The American export restrictions are enacted to prevent the increase of war potential of the Eastern countries by means of western economic assets and thus serve the protection to the maintenance of peace and freedom of the West. The measures are therefore not only in the American interest but also in the *interest of the entire free West and thus also in the interest of Germany*. The embargo regulation therefore serves vital interests of the general public ... and whoever frustrates the maintenance of these interests out of self-interest acts against public policy....'

Thus, consideration of the foreign prohibition within the German *boni mores* was based on the argument that the foreign prohibition served interests that were commonly shared by Germany and the entire free West.

Two years later the Federal Supreme Court confirmed this decision in a case concerning an insurance contract.[310] The court refused to enforce an insurance policy covering the transport of boric acid from the United States to Germany

[309] BGH 21.12.1960 BGHZ 34, 169 et seq; for a summary of the facts and the reasoning of the case, see Basedow GYBIntL 27 (1984) 109, 121 et seq.

[310] BGH 24.5.1962 NJW 1962, 1436 et seq (*Borsäure case*).

where a trans-shipment was planned for Poland. At that time the export of boric acid to socialist countries was prohibited under a United States law and the seller obtained an export licence by fraudulently stating that the goods were to remain in Germany. Nevertheless, the export licence was provisionally cancelled and the boric acid was seized in New York. A suit brought by a bank holding the bills of lading against the insurer was dismissed by the Federal Supreme Court. The court confirmed the previous *Borax* decision and held that insurance of carriage that was illegal under the law of the United States was immoral under § 138 BGB, and therefore void, since it was designed to shift the high risk of illegal conduct.[311]

(4) *Nigerian mask case* - the foreign provision serves interests shared in common by all civilised nations

In the *Nigerian Mask* case in 1972[312] the plaintiff had acquired an insurance policy covering the transport of art objects from Nigeria to Hamburg. This export was prohibited under Nigerian law. When six statues were lost during the sea passage the plaintiff sued the insurer for compensation. However, the court held that the export of the masks was immoral and could therefore not be insured. The court again stated that § 134 BGB was not applicable to foreign prohibitions, since a foreign law is not binding in Germany, but that a foreign prohibition can nevertheless be *indirectly* of relevance to the question of whether the insured contract is immoral in the sense of § 138 BGB.

The court recognised that the Nigerian export prohibition, in contrast to the US embargoes in the borax and boric acid cases, did not *indirectly protect German interests as well*. However, it held that it follows from a *basic persuasion of the international community,* as reflected in the 1970 Convention,[313] that every nation willing to protect its cultural heritage is entitled to foreign assistance. The Court stated that:

> The circumvention of such protective law has to be regarded as being reprehensible since it is against the *generally respected interests of all*

---

311 The court expressly referred to the borax case and added that in the meantime Germany had adopted the American embargo policy and had imposed its own prohibition (§134 BGB invalidity because of offence against the law); for a summary of the facts and reasoning of this case, see Basedow GYBIntL 27 (1984) 109, 126; Kegel *Role of Public Law* 29, 46.

312 BGH 22.6.1972 BGHZ 59, 82 et seq; NJW 1972, 1575 with note by Mann 2179.

313 Convention on the Means of Prohibiting and Preventing the Illicit Import, Export and Transfer of Ownership of Cultural Property, Paris 14.11.1970.

> *nations*, according to contemporary belief, to maintain cultural values in place...[314]

The Federal Supreme Court therefore considered the violation of the foreign import restriction within German *boni mores* because the foreign provision was held to be based on interests shared in common by all nations.

(5) Generally valid moral principles

In a judgment of the Federal Supreme Court in 1985,[315] the Court held that an offence against a foreign prohibition was immoral, because the violation of the foreign rule constituted an offence against *generally valid moral principles*. The court was concerned with the validity of an agency contract governed by German law, the main object of which was to bribe a Nigerian civil servant and to forward the money to him in violation of Nigerian law. The court held that:

> [A] request for, and acceptance of a bribe by foreign officials has to be disapproved of, inasmuch as they thereby offend the legal order of their native country. The offence against foreign prohibitions, which has to be recognised according to the legal and moral views that prevail in Germany, *at the same time constitutes an offence against generally valid moral principles...*

Foreign rules that prohibit and penalise corruption were held to fulfil these conditions.

(6) Inapplicability of German *boni mores*

In other judgments the Supreme Court of the German Reich and the Federal Supreme Court did not apply foreign internationally mandatory rules, and the infringement of the foreign provision was not held to be immoral and thus indirectly considered. Generally, the German courts did not give effect to a third country's provision if, from a German viewpoint, the provision was enacted for *improper reasons*, or *served interests not shared in common by German interests or by the interests of all civilised nations, but based on 'selfish' trade policies*, or was *directed against German interests*. The courts either ignored the foreign provision without investigating an invalidity on the ground of immorality, or expressly declared § 138 BGB inapplicable.

---

314 BGH 22.6.1972 BGHZ 59, 82, 85.

315 BGH 8.5.1985 BGHZ 94, 268, 271 et seq; but see a judgment of the RG 26.9.1919 JW 1920, 138, 139 where the court had indeed asked a Bulgarian seller to tip civil servants in order to make delivery possible during the First World War.

Those judgments already investigated, that subjected foreign rules of a public law nature to *Public Conflict of Laws* based on the principle of *territoriality,* may serve as examples of the former situation. In '*Solzhenitsyn*' the court rejected the application or recognition of a foreign law - a Russian trade monopoly - because of its territorially limited effect. The court did not even mention the possibility of the contract being contrary to German *boni mores*, although the German contract was according to the infringed legislation null and void.[316]

However, in other decisions the German courts did refer to § 138 BGB and held that it was inapplicable. The Supreme Court of the German Reich, for instance, did not apply the exchange control regulations of a third country or consider the violated rules indirectly within the German *boni mores* rule. This approach was substantiated by the argument that foreign exchange control regulations could not be justified by *legal-moral considerations shared in common by all civilised states; on the contrary, they were based on trade policies of the foreign state only, which were opposed to the German point of view.*[317]

Foreign trade restrictions were not given effect if enacted for *improper reasons or designed to curtail the competitive position of German companies or directed against German interests.*[318] Therefore, the Supreme Court of the German Reich upheld a contract to smuggle a cargo of linseed oil out of Sweden in violation of a Swedish trade embargo against Germany. The contract was held to be valid because 'export prohibitions of foreign states, caused by the war and directed against German interests will not be protected by German Courts'.[319]

---

316 BGH 16.4.1975 BGHZ 64, 183, et seq; but see BGH 17.11.1994 BGHZ 128, 41, 52, 53. The contract was governed by German law (Federal Republic), and was held to be valid and not violating *boni mores*, although it offended the export trade monopoly of the GDR.

317 RG 3.10.1923 RGZ 108, 241, 243 et seq (Russian exchange control regulation); for criticism of that argument, see Kreuzer *Ausländisches Wirtschaftsrecht* 35, 36. Foreign currency regulations were not applied or considered by the Supreme Court RG 27.4.1936 IPRespr 1935 - 1944 Nr 468. As was seen above the BGH applied the principle of *territoriality* to foreign exchange control regulations and currency regulations, and refused to give effect to these provisions.

318 See for this Basedow GYBIntL 27 (1984) 109, 121; BGH 21.12.1960 BGHZ 34, 169, 176 (*obiter dicta* with reference to the 'cocaine case' RG 24.6.1927 JW 1927, 2288).

319 RG 22.12.1916 Cruchot Vol 61 (1917) 460; in the same sense RG 15.2.1930 IPRespr Nr 13; RG 28.6.1918 RGZ 93, 182 et seq (the English Trading with the Enemy Act 1914 was refused application on this reasoning but within the dogmatic scope of the notion of *ordre public*).

Furthermore, in a case concerning an insurance contract for the transport of goods from Hamburg to Bolivia, the Federal Supreme Court indicated in an *obiter dictum* that the intended violation of Bolivian or Argentinean import restrictions and customs duties did not affect the validity of the insurance contract.[320] This was based on the following reasoning: Firstly, the intended violation of the foreign import restriction did not affect the insurance contract if the infringement was intended to take place after the transport. Secondly, the court referred to the *Borax* and *Nigerian Mask* cases and doubted whether 'the same principles apply to a violation of foreign import restrictions, since these are less important than export restrictions which were enacted for the protection of state security or the cultural heritage of a state'.

This judgment seems to deviate from the smuggling cases of the German Reich. However, the statement of the Federal Supreme Court was only *obiter* and, in addition, vague. Nevertheless, it is of some relevance for other reasons. It is one of the rare occasions when the Federal Supreme Court combined solutions which were usually applied independently: the principle of *non-applicability of foreign public law rules* and consideration on the level of substantive law. In considering whether the violation of the foreign import restriction could lead to immorality and violate German *boni mores*, the court stated that consideration of the violation of a foreign law within the notion of *boni mores* forms an exception to the principle that foreign public law rules do not have any effect outside the territory of the enacting country.[321]

Another famous judgment of the Federal Supreme Court in 1977 - the *Escape-agent* case[322] - clearly illustrates the principles developed by the case law. The facts of the case were as follows. The plaintiff, a Norwegian, helped the defendant, a citizen of the East Germany, to flee to West Germany in violation of East German penal law. Crossing the border from East to West Germany and assisting the defendant to flee East Germany could have rendered the Norwegian liable for prosecution. After the flight, the defendant agreed to pay the Norwegian a certain amount (DM 4.500, plus interest) for his assistance. The defendant refused to pay the entire debt, and the plaintiff sued for performance.

---

320 BGH 8.4.1976 VersR 1976, 678 et seq.

321 BGH 8.4.1976 VersR 1976, 678. Also see OLG Hamburg 6.5.1993 RIW 1994, 686, where the court did not take into account a foreign import restriction within the notion of German *boni mores* for the reason that it served economic political (trade political) interests, and referred to the public law nature of the rules and the principle of non-applicability of foreign public law.

322 BGH 29.9.1977 BGHZ 69, 295 et seq.

The court investigated whether the 'escape agent-agreement' was illegal or immoral. The Federal Supreme Court rejected illegality on the grounds of § 134 BGB and immorality on the grounds of § 138 BGB. An 'escape agent agreement' would not violate good morals, nor could the violation of the foreign penal law lead to immorality. The court stated that:

> [T]he violation of a foreign prohibition may lead to immorality and thus invalidity, if the infringed foreign prohibitions protect indirectly also German interests or the infringement is opposed to generally respected interests of all Nations.

The Court held that these conditions were not fulfilled.[323]

e Consideration within the operative facts of § 826 BGB

In the nineties the Federal Supreme Court considered foreign embargoes in the context of a tortious claim for damages (§ 826 BGB).[324] Because § 826 BGB is a tortious claim and not a contractual one, a detailed examination of these decisions is beyond the scope of this study. Nevertheless, the judgments are concerned with the effect given to third countries' internationally mandatory rules by the forum and they are dealt with in this context by the German academics.[325] In a judgment of 20 November 1990,[326] the Federal Supreme Court ruled that the violation of a foreign (Thai) import ban on products from South Africa could constitute immoral conduct and violate the notion of *boni mores*. The court thus considered the foreign import ban indirectly, within the tortious claim of § 826 BGB. In its reasoning the court referred to the *Borax* and *Borsäure* cases, but stressed that the violation of the foreign provision in itself did not suffice; the violation must result in the conscious endangerment of the pecuniary interests of an uninvolved third party.[327]

It is not clear whether the Federal Supreme Court transferred the principles developed with regard to the nullity sanction of immorality and consequently whether it is necessary that the foreign provision should either indirectly protect German interests as well, or should be based on interests commonly shared all

323 BGH ibid 298 et seq; see affirmative BGH 21.10.1980 NJW 1980, 1574, 1575.

324 § 826 BGB says 'Wer in einer gegen die guten Sitten verstoßenden Weise einem anderem vorsätzlich Schaden zufügt, ist dem anderen zum Ersatze des Schadens verplichtet': 'Who causes damage to another in a way offending intentionally against good morals, is obliged to compensate the damage of the other.'

325 See among others Reithmann/Martiny/Limmer *Internationales Vertragsrecht* Rn 466.

326 JZ 1991, 719 et seq; see also BGH 20.10.1992 NJW 1993, 194 et seq.

327 BGH 20.11.1990 JZ 1991,719, 721; BGH 20.10.1992 NJW 1993, 194 et seq.

civilised nations. Alternatively, the court would have meant that the foreign provision is considered only in so far as its actual effects on the private relationship are concerned, independently of its normative content and background.[328] The reference to the borax and boric acid cases and the immorality solution suggests the first assumption. The fact that at the time of the judgment the European Community joined the United Nations in its embargo against South Africa, which included the import of steel and iron from South Africa, could justify an equality of interest.[329] However, the Federal Supreme Court did not investigate the purpose of the foreign regulation or the need for an equality of interest; this could indicate the second assumption.[330]

f Impossibility of performance or frustration of contract

In other judgments the German courts took account of foreign internationally mandatory rules by considering the de facto or actual effects of the provisions on private relationships as a reason for impossibility of performance or frustration of contract. The foreign prohibition may result in the performance of the contract becoming factually impossible, for example, if the goods are seized in the seller's country or in a foreign country because of an export restriction. Performance may also cause undue hardship to the seller if, for instance, the violation of a restriction results in high penalties. Acceptance of performance can also be dangerous for the buyer, for example, if the import of the goods is prohibited and penalised with a prison or death sentence.

The actual effects on the private relationship cannot be ignored and the contractual obligations must be modified or cancelled. Only afterwards does the question arise as to which party should bear the consequences, viz. whether performance is to be excused or whether the duty-bearer is liable for compensation for non-performance based on fault or on guarantee.[331]

---

[328] See Junker JZ 1991, 699, 702 who sees the violation of *boni mores* not in the violation of the foreign embargo provisions as such, but in the use of a third person to violate these provisions. For the violation of *boni mores* in the sense of § 826 BGB it only matters that the foreign embargo can be enforced effectively, it is only a 'Datum'.

[329] Junker JZ 1991, 699, 701.

[330] For a discussion, see Junker JZ 1991, 699, 702; Reithmann/Martiny/Limmer *Internationales Vertragsrecht* Rn 466; von Hoffmann IPRax 1991, 345, 346.

[331] See also Basedow GYBIntL 27 (1984) 129, 130; Baum Rabelsz 52 (1989) 152, 158; Reithmann/Martiny/Limmer *Internationales Vertragsrecht* Rn 468; Schiffer *Normen* 87.

German scholars and courts accept that a foreign prohibition can lead to *physical* impossibility of performance, but not to *legal* impossibility.[332] If the impossibility of performance cannot be imputed to the debtor, the non-performance is excused, and the debtor is discharged from his obligation to deliver or to pay the damages caused by non-delivery. If the prohibition existed *ab initio* (at the time of conclusion of the contract) and the foreign sovereign was able to enforce its law, the contract can be declared invalid on grounds of initial factual impossibility.[333] But most cases involved foreign prohibitions that were enacted after the parties had concluded the contract and the courts considered the effects of the foreign prohibition as subsequent impossibility of performance.[334]

In 1918 the Supreme Court of the German Reich was concerned with the following case. An English company sold 'Quebracho extract' to a German buyer; then war was declared, and performance was prohibited under the British Trading with the Enemy Act.[335] Because of the Act the debtor refused to deliver the goods and the buyer sued for damages caused by non-delivery. The Supreme Court dismissed the buyer's claim on the grounds that the British prohibition made performance impossible.

At the first stage, the court held that the British prohibition was directed *against German interests* and infringed the German *ordre public* and consequently could not be applied. It went on to hold that application of the foreign prohibition was not the issue raised in the case, but that the *actual effects of the foreign provision* on the contractual obligation of the sued debtor had to be considered instead. The court said that it could not and must not ignore the existence of the English Act, because a violation of the Act was heavily

---

332 Reithmann/Martiny/Limmer *Internationales Vertragsrecht* Rn 467; Schiffer *Normen* 87; RG 13.11.1917 RGZ 91, 260, 262; RG 28.6.1918 RGZ 93, 182 et seq; RG 17.6.1939 RGZ 161, 296, 300.

333 See only recently BGH 17.11.1994 (III ZS) BGHZ 128, 41, 53; see also von Hoffmann IPRax 1981, 155, 156; MünchKomm/Martiny Art 34 Rn 53.

334 See eg the *'fish oil case'* RG 13.11.1917 RGZ 91, 260. For the facts and the reasoning of this case, see Vischer Rec des Cours 232 (1992 I) 13, 176 and Zimmer IPRax 1993, 65, 67; RG 17.10.1919 RG 97, 6, 9 et seq (Dutch export prohibition; the obligor was excused and thus not liable for damages); RG 17.6.1939 RGZ 161, 296, 300 et seq (foreign prohibiting law); RG 22.12.1916 Cruchot Vol 61, 460, 462 (unreasonable for the debtor to perform); BGH 30.11.1972 BGHZ 60, 14, 16 (proper law of the contract was German law, foreign prohibition on entry that was based on health political reasons made performance impossible); BGH 11.3.1982 BGHZ 83, 197 (but impossibility of performance was based on the political situation in the foreign country, not on an infringement of foreign law); for further references Anderegg *Ausländische Eingriffsnormen* 14 et seq.

335 RG 28.6.1918 RGZ 93, 182 et seq.

sanctioned. Accordingly, it was held that delivery by the English party was factually impossible.[336] In effect, the foreign prohibition was not applied, but considered as an impediment to performance, despite being contrary to German interests.[337]

In other cases the German courts considered the actual effects of a foreign prohibition by adapting the contract to the new situation on the basis of cessation of the contractual basis (*Wegfall der Geschäftsgrundlage*). This principle is comparable with the English law principle frustration of the contract. It is applicable if and to the extent that it would be unreasonable for the debtor to fulfil his obligation because of heavy sanctions and the possibility of the enacting state enforcing the prohibition.[338] In a judgment on the 8 February 1984,[339] the Federal Supreme Court was concerned with an Iranian Government ban on the import of alcohol to Iran. The ban on alcohol impeded the execution of a settlement between a German seller and an Iranian importer. Prior to the enactment of the ban, the parties had agreed to settle difficulties that had arisen under previous contracts: the German exporter was to pay damages, half of which would be due after the Iranian party had issued a letter of credit for further deliveries. The German party had further agreed to deliver beer at a preferential price for a certain period of time. After the enactment of the ban, the delivery of beer became impossible. The Iranian party claimed payment of the outstanding portion of the damages agreed upon in the settlement agreement.

The proper law of the transaction was held to be German law. The Federal Supreme Court held that, although the claim for damages had not become impossible, *the transaction had lost its fundamental contractual basis* and *had to be adapted to the new circumstances*. The court therefore held that both parties had to share the risk of the subsequent Iranian restriction. The German party had to pay half of the outstanding amount of the agreed damages and half of the hypothetical profit that the Iranian party would have made on further

---

336 RG 28.6.1918 RGZ 93, 182, 184.

337 For a discussion of this judgment, see Basedow GYBIntL 27 (1984) 129, 132, 134 who criticises the consideration of the foreign provision on grounds of the extraterritorial effect of the prohibition. The English company had contracted through its Argentine subsidiary and the goods were exported from the Argentine and thus situated outside the prohibiting state.

338 RG 22.12.1916 Cruchot Vol 61, 460, 462; BGH 8.2.1984 IPRax 1986, 154 et seq; Vischer Rec des Cours 232 (1992 I) 13, 176; Reithmann/Martiny/Limmer *Internationales Vertragsrecht* Rn 469.

339 IPRax 1986, 154; for a discussion of this case Mülbert IPRax 1986, 140 et seq and Baum RabelsZ 53 (1989) 152 et seq.

deliveries at the preferential rate.[340] It follows that account was taken of the actual effects of the foreign prohibition on the private relationship; the settlement agreement was adjusted to the altered circumstances on the basis of cessation of the contractual basis.

g Swiss case law

Using an approach similar to that of the German courts, the Swiss courts did not apply third countries' internationally mandatory rules on the basis of a *Special Connection Theory*.[341] They refused application of the rules either on the basis of their public law nature, or the *principle of territoriality*, or the *doctrine of Public Conflict of Laws*, or on the basis of Swiss *ordre public*.[342] However, as in Germany, there are some judgments where a third country's mandatory laws were considered as *fact* within the *substantive law of the lex causae*.[343] Furthermore, the Swiss courts were only concerned with a third country's internationally mandatory rules of public law that pursued state interests. They were never faced with the problem of public laws that served private interests.[344]

(1) Refusal of application of third countries' mandatory laws

The judgments that refused to give effect to a third country's public laws were all concerned with foreign exchange regulations that intervened in private contracts, for example, international loans,[345] endorsement contracts,[346] and the transfer of claims from loans.[347] Article VIII (2) (b) of the IMF was not applied by the Swiss courts since Switzerland is not a member of the International Monetary Fund.

---

340 For the facts and reasoning Vischer Rec des Cours 232 (1992 II) 13, 176.

341 A 'special connection' was expressly rejected in BGE 76 II 33 et seq; cf Schwander *IPR AT* 251.

342 Honsell/Vogt/Schnyder/Mächler-Erne Art 19 Rn 5; Erne *Vertragsgültigkeit* 12 et seq.

343 See Erne *Vertragsgültigkeit* 12.

344 Erne *Vertragsgültigkeit* 12, 119; see also Schnyder *Wirtschaftskollisionsrecht* Rn 27, 277 who stresses, in the context of a special connection of third countries' mandatory laws serving private interests, that a 'special connection' of those rules will be rare. The dispute whether those rules fall under the scope of art 19 IPRG is therefore of a rather theoretical nature, for the dispute, see Chapter 5, IV, 1, c.

345 BGE 68 II 203 et seq, for criticism of this ruling with regard to the ignorance of the court concerning the factual position of constraint Heini 100 ZSR (1981) 65, 73.

346 BGE 60 II 294 et seq.

347 BGE 95 II 109 et seq; see also BGE 62 II 108 et seq; Erne *Vertragsgültigkeit* 12.

The reasons for the decisions were often based on *ordre public* considerations, rather than on the general rule that a contract and its validity is governed exclusively by the proper law.[348] However, although the Federal Tribunal referred to the *ordre public* and vaguely remarked that the value judgment depends on the Swiss point of view. No attempt was made to define the content of this *ordre public* rule.[349]

It is interesting to note that, in contrast to Germany and England, Swiss courts were concerned with *real third country cases*.[350] Here, too, effect was not given to the third country's mandatory rule and the rulings were based on *ordre public* considerations. The Federal Tribunal had to deal with an international bond issue governed by the law of New York that infringed German foreign exchange control regulations, which claimed application to the situation in question.[351] According to the law of New York, the foreign exchange control regulations were inapplicable because they infringed the *ordre public* of the governing law. The Federal Tribunal asked whether non-recognition of the German regulations by the law of New York infringed the Swiss *ordre public*. It held that the Swiss *ordre public* was not violated, but that the principle *pacta sunt servanda* had to be protected.[352]

In other judgments the refusal to give effect to third countries' internationally mandatory provisions was based on the *principle of non-applicability of foreign public law* and/or the *principle of territoriality*.[353] Such a rationale is found in a ruling of the Federal Tribunal in 1969 regarding an assignment governed by Swiss law.[354] The question was whether effect should be given to a Hungarian foreign exchange control regulation. The court held:

---

[348] BGE 62 II 108; BGE 67 II 215; BGE 68 II 203; BGE 95 II 109, 114. For instance, in BGE 62 II 108, 110 the Swiss Federal Tribunal was concerned with an assignment of claims under a brokerage contract, the proper law of which was held to be Swiss law. The question was whether the assignment was void because it infringed German foreign exchange law. The Federal Tribunal held that 'the German foreign exchange control regulations regarding assignments are repugnant to the Swiss public order'. The court went on to hold that the foreign exchange control regulations would not have been applied even if the proper law had been German law.

[349] For criticism, see Erne *Vertragsgültigkeit* 14.

[350] BGE 67 II 215; BGE 68 II 203.

[351] BGE 68 II 203, 209 et seq; see also BGE 67 II 215, 221 et seq where a contract of guarantee was governed by the law of New York and a Hungarian foreign exchange control regulation was not applied on the basis of the *ordre public* of New York law.

[352] BGE 68 II 203, 210; for the facts and the reasoning Erne *Vertragsgültigkeit* 14.

[353] BGE 42 II 179; 44 II 163; 95 II 109, 114; 107 II 489, 492; cf Erne *Vertragsgültigkeit* 15.

[354] BGE 95 II 109, 114.

> According to a well established *principle of public international law* public law is applicable only within the territory of the enacting state, *principle of territoriality*. Therefore, [the Hungarian exchange control legislation] cannot be applied in Switzerland unless demanded by Swiss law, in particular if Switzerland is obliged by an international Convention or if the foreign public law supports the applicable private law by intervening into private law relationships in order to protect private interests.[355]

In a recent decision the Federal Tribunal applied or considered a third country's public law rule, a German subrogation law, to a Swiss contract on the basis of the principle of territoriality.[356] This is one of the rare examples where the invocation of the principle of territoriality resulted in an application of the foreign public law.

(2) Consideration as fact within the substantive law of the *lex causae*

A number of cases in Switzerland did not apply a third country's internationally mandatory rules, but considered the effect of those rules within the substantive law of the *lex causae*. In all the cases the proper law was Swiss law, and they were all concerned with smuggling in defiance of foreign import/export restrictions[357] or customs regulations.[358] The question before the courts was whether the contracts were valid according to the Swiss proper law. As in the German cases, the Swiss courts held that the contracts were not unlawful in the sense of art 20 (1) of the Code of Obligations (OR), since unlawfulness according to this provision can only be the violation of Swiss law.[359] The courts then asked whether the intended circumvention of a third country's mandatory laws would fall under the blanket clause of *boni mores* (art 20 (1) OR). Thus the crucial question was whether the violation of foreign law resulted in the immorality of the contract.[360]

A leading case of the Swiss Federal Tribunal in 1950[361] laid down the fundamental rules about when a third country's internationally mandatory rules can

---

355 BGE 95 II 109, 114.

356 BGE 107 II 489, 492.

357 BGE 80 II 45.

358 Commercial Court at Zurich 9.5.1968 SJZ 64 (1968) 354; see also BGE 76 II 33; 80 II 49; 81 II 227; BG SJZ 54 (1958) 218; SJZ 56 (1960) 43, for this ruling, see Erne *Vertragsgültigkeit* 12, 16 et seq.

359 BGE 76 II 33, 40; 80 II 49, 51; BG SJZ 54 (1958) 218, 219; SJZ 56 (1960) 43; Commercial Court at Zurich 9.5.1968 SJZ 64 (1968) 354.

360 BGE 76 II 33, 41; Commercial Court at Zurich 9.5.1968 SJZ 64 (1968) 354, 355; BGE 81 II 227, 232.

361 BGE 76 II 33.

be considered within the notion of Swiss *boni mores*. The case concerned a contract that guaranteed a foreign exchange contract, and the question was whether the violation of a third country's foreign exchange regulation could render the contract void. The court held that violation of foreign legislation can render a transaction immoral if and to the extent that the violation is immoral according to the Swiss viewpoint.

The court went on to distinguish different kinds of foreign rules according to their *object of legal protection*. Only those rules that, according to the general view, are of such importance that non-recognition of their violation affects the *Swiss ethical order* can be considered. The foreign rule infringed must serve the *protection of individual interests and the interests of the human community that are according to the general view of fundamental and lifesaving importance*. Alternatively, the foreign rule must protect *objects that are according to ethical opinion of higher importance than domestic party autonomy and the validity of the contract under the proper law*.

Foreign provisions concerning drug dealing or slave trading were regarded as fulfilling these conditions. Foreign exchange control laws and economic-political measures in general, however, do not fall under the same category, because they serve predominantly the *economic interests* of the foreign state.[362] The court therefore refused to give effect to the foreign exchange control regulation and held that the contract was valid according to its Swiss proper law.[363]

According to this leading case, therefore, the violated third country's internationally mandatory rule is deemed to fall within the notion of Swiss immorality if and to the extent that the *foreign rule protects fundamental values regarding the individual and the community*. Furthermore, violation of the foreign rule must lead to an *impairment of the foreign and domestic public*

362 BGE 76 II 33, 41. Also see the decision of the Federal Tribunal BGE 80 II 49 et seq. The violation of German foreign exchange control regulations was held to be not immoral because the violation would not infringe the public order; for vehement criticism, see Mann *FS Wahl* 139, 150; id Rec des Cours 132 (1971 I) 109, 195, 196.

363 BGE 76 II 33, 41. Based on this differentiation the Federal Tribunal in 1954, BGE 80 II 49, 51, refused to give effect to a German foreign exchange regulation which the parties intended to circumvent; the contract governed by Swiss law was held to be valid. The court held that this was not a contract for smuggling and that the violation in Germany of the German foreign exchange control law was not contrary to Swiss immorality, because exchange control laws were not 'laws affecting the ethical order' and could therefore be freely violated without offending Swiss conceptions of morality. For this decision, see Heini 100 ZSR (1981) 65, 81; for criticism Mann *FS Wahl* 139, 150; id *FS Beitzke* 607, 622; id Rec des Cours 132 (1971 I) 9, 195, 196.

order. Hence, a *correspondence* of the objects of legal protection is necessary.[364]

However, the Commercial Court at Zurich ruled that a Swiss contract for smuggling coffee into Italy, and thus infringing Italian customs regulations, was invalid on the grounds of immorality. The court held that the foreign customs regulations fulfilled the strict conditions of a rule being *worthy of protection* and that 'a smuggling action motivated by making profit for the disadvantage of a neighbouring country is rejected in this country by all decent and fair thinking people as injustice'.[365]

In other cases the question was whether violation of third countries' mandatory legislation could render performance impossible according to the Swiss proper law.[366] A Swiss Tribunal recognised an Austrian and German export restriction that had been enacted after the conclusion of the contract.[367] The court held that the contracts were governed by Swiss law, but that performance was impossible according to the same law because it would violate foreign export restrictions. Thus, impossibility was not restricted to factual impossibility, but was also taken into account where it caused undue hardship for the debtor who had to perform in violation of the foreign law, and could be exposed to heavy sanctions.[368]

In contrast to the German courts, however, the Swiss courts refused to take into account the actual effects of foreign internationally mandatory rules that were held to be contrary to the forum's *ordre public*. As a result of this rigid approach the debtor will not be released from fulfilling his obligation if performance violates a foreign legislation, the application of which would be contrary to the Swiss *ordre public*.[369]

---

364 Cf also Erne *Vertragsgültigkeit* 18.

365 Commercial Court at Zurich 9.5.1968 SJZ 64 (1968) 354; see also BGE 80 II 45, 48.

366 Cf for a discussion of these cases Schulte *Eingriffsnormen* 35 et seq; Morscher *Rechtssetzungsakte* 61 et seq.

367 BGE 42 II 379, 381 et seq; BGE 43 II 225, 230 et seq.

368 BGE 42 II 379, 381; BGE 45 II 42 et seq. However, this does not preclude the debtor from paying damages for non-performance in cases where he took the risk of non-performance on the basis of an opposed prohibition; see Morscher *Rechtssetzungsakte* 62, 63; BGE 72 I 278; BGE 111 II 354.

369 BGE 60 II 294, 311 et seq; BGE 64 II 88, 100. This contrasts with the German case law. The Supreme Court of the German Reich in RGZ 93, 184 expressly took into account on the level of substantive law the actual effects of foreign legislation that violated the German *ordre public*.

h Conclusion

With regard to third countries' internationally mandatory rules, German and Swiss courts used different solutions:

(1) Application of a third country's internationally mandatory rules was in general refused by reference to their public law nature on the basis of *Public Conflict of Laws* and the principle of *territoriality* of public law. In Switzerland the courts sometimes referred to the *ordre public* exclusionary rule. It is interesting to note, that the courts in both countries explained the inapplicability of a third country's rule by referring to their content. They did not refer to the fact that the rule formed part of a law other than the proper law or that the rule was not part of the proper law.[370]

(2) Application of the principle of *territoriality* of *Public Conflict of Laws* shows that Swiss and German courts treat foreign public law rules on the same footing, irrespective of whether the rule emanates from the proper law or a third country.

(3) In both countries the principle of *territoriality* has been restricted to those public law rules that served the public (viz. economic and political) interests of the enacting state. It is uncertain, however, whether the courts would apply public law rules serving private interests, as well as the internationally mandatory private law rules of a third country, because there have been no cases dealing with such rules.

(4) Third countries' internationally mandatory rules are applied if required by an international treaty, for example, art VIII (2) (b) IMF.[371]

(5) Under certain circumstances, courts have considered a third country's internationally mandatory rules as 'facts' within the substantive law of the *lex causae*. In Germany, apart from a few exceptional cases, this *Substantive Law Approach* has resulted in recognition of the foreign law. Swiss courts in contrast have been much more reluctant to take third countries' internationally mandatory rules into account.

(6) The German case law can be summarised as follows. Apart from the smuggling cases, which perhaps fall in a special category, third countries' internationally mandatory rules have been considered within the notion of

[370] See also Erne *Vertragsgültigkeit* 13. For the contrasting common law approach, cf Chapter 5, III.

[371] Switzerland, however, is not a member of the IMF.

German *boni mores* if they protected either *indirectly German interests* or *the generally respected interests* or *moral values of all nations*. However, provisions enacted for *improper reasons*, *directed against German interests* or based only on the *trade policies* of the foreign state (*interests not shared in common*) were not recognised within the notion of German *boni mores*. In time, the Federal Supreme Court deviated from the subjective criteria of the parties' intention to evade and violate the foreign law, and instead focused on the content and protected interests of the violated foreign law.[372]

(7) In Switzerland violation of a third country's internationally mandatory rules can be deemed immoral, if the foreign rule protected interests and policies of such importance that non-recognition of its violation would affect the *Swiss ethical order*. The foreign rule infringed must serve to *protect individual interests and the interests of humanity which are, according to general views, of fundamental importance*. Foreign laws serving predominantly the *economic interests* of the enacting state do not fall into this category.[373] Basing their decisions on these principles, the Swiss courts usually refused to consider third countries' internationally mandatory rules within the notion of Swiss *boni mores*.[374]

(8) In other cases German courts recognised the factual effects of the foreign legislation within the (domestic law) rules of impossibility of performance or frustration of contract. The factual effects of the foreign rule on the private relationship have been considered, even though the rule infringed the German *ordre public* or was directed against German interests. Swiss courts took a similar approach, but refused to consider the effect of foreign rules that were repugnant to the Swiss *ordre public*.

3 Critical remarks

The German (and Swiss) case law has been criticised for a number of reasons. In general it can be stated that, while the principled foundation and reasoning of the court's approach was constantly criticised, the final decisions were generally approved.[375] The objections therefore focus on the principles underlying the decisions of the courts: [376] the principle of *non-applicability of foreign public*

---

372 Cf also Zimmer IPRax 1993, 65, 67.

373 BGE 76 II 33, 41; BGE 80 II 49 et seq; see however the Commercial Court of Zurich 9.5.1968 SJZ 64 (1968) 354.

374 For criticism, see Erne *Vertragsgültigkeit* 20, 21.

375 See Baum RabelsZ 53 (1989) 152; Mülbert IPRax 1981, 140, 141.

376 For the academic approaches, see supra Chapter 5, I.

law and the consideration as 'fact' within the substantive rules of the proper law.

a Duality of solutions

The criticism that the courts[377] were unable to develop clear and consistent criteria to deal with the problem of the application of foreign internationally mandatory rules is of a very general nature.[378] In fact the German courts did not adopt a consistent approach or develop unified principles; they based their decisions on the facts of each case. The cases where the court refused to apply or consider a foreign rule on basis of the principle of *territoriality of foreign public law* did not in general mention the possible consideration of the rule within the substantive law of the proper law of the contract, and vice versa.[379]

However, the different approaches may nevertheless be synthesised as follows. The German case law never applied foreign internationally mandatory rules of public law that pursued the economic and political interests of the enacting country, but rather considered them as facts within the substantive law governing the contract.[380] Thus, despite their inapplicability, such rules may be recognised as fact within the substantive law.

The first mention of the divergence of approaches occurred in a judgment of the Federal Supreme Court in 1976: The Court indicated that the consideration of the foreign public law rule within the notion of *boni mores* was an exception to the general principle of *territoriality*.[381] In a judgment in 1994 the Federal Supreme Court stated that according to German case law foreign internationally mandatory rules pursuing economic and political interests of the enacting country can only be considered when the foreign state holds the power to enforce its law. Otherwise, it can only be considered as fact within the notion of *boni mores* or as impossibility of performance.[382] The court thus combined both solutions.

---

[377] This criticism was made in respect of the Federal Supreme Court in particular, but is equally true for Swiss decisions.

[378] Mentzel *Sonderanknüpfung* 94, 100; Reithmann/Martiny/Limmer *Internationales Vertragsrecht* Rn 461; Becker *Sonderanknüpfung* 86; Schubert RIW 1987, 729, 737; Soergel/von Hoffmann Art 34 Rn 79.

[379] Schubert RIW 1987, 729, 737; Mentzel *Sonderanknüpfung* 105; Drobnig *FS Neumayer* 159, 162, 174; Schurig *Lois* 55, 73, 74; Kreuzer *Ausländisches Wirtschaftsrecht* 79, 80.

[380] MünchKomm/Martiny Art 34 Rn 28, 49; Busse ZverglRWiss 95 (1996) 387, 394; Staudinger/Magnus Art 34 Rn 119; Mülbert IPRax 1941, 140; Soergel/von Hoffmann Art 34 Rn 79; critically Zimmer IPRax1993. 65 et seq.

[381] BGH 8.4.1976 VersR 1976, 678; see also OLG Hamburg 6.5.1993 RIW 1994, 686.

[382] BGH 17.11.1994 BGHZ 128, 41, 52, 53.

Still, many questions arise about the case law solutions, particularly because the criteria are vague and perhaps because cases in point are rare. For example, neither the Federal Supreme Court nor the Federal Tribunal has ever been confronted with a third country's internationally mandatory rules of a private law character or at least serving private interests, so that there is in fact no way of knowing what the approach of the courts might be. This does show, however, that the question is really of academic interest only.[383]

b *Public Conflict of Laws*; principle of *territoriality*

The system of *Public Conflict of Laws* and the principle of *territoriality of foreign public law*, on which the *non-applicability of foreign public law rules* is based has been the subject of fundamental criticism in Switzerland and Germany, and should not be maintained.[384]

As has already been explained in the discussion of the different academic approaches,[385] the formal distinction between private and public law has little merit in conflict of laws. Particularly in the modern welfare state, the distinction is blurred. The state may enact private law rules pursuing public interests and vice versa. Furthermore, the distinction between public and private law is a continental European peculiarity that does not have the same meaning in common law countries.[386] The fundamental objection to this approach is, however, that the *non-applicability of foreign public law* does not follow from the principle of *territoriality*. The principle is of no use in determining whether foreign law should be applied by the forum.[387]

---

383 For Switzerland, also see Schnyder *Wirtschaftskollisionsrecht* Rn 27, 277 who stresses in the context of a special connection of third countries' mandatory laws serving private interests that a special connection of those rules will be rare. The debate about whether these rules fall under the scope of art 19 Swiss IPRG is therefore of a rather theoretical nature.

384 See for criticism Mann Rec des Cours 132 (1971 I) 115, 182 et seq; Siehr RabelsZ 52 (1988) 41, 75 et seq; Vischer Rec des Cours 232 (1992 I) 13, 150 et seq; Schiffer *Normen* 79 et seq; MünchKomm/Sonnenberger Einl Rn 374, 377; Kropholler *IPR* § 22 II 2; Morscher *Rechtssetzungsakte* 48 et seq; Voser *Los d'application immédiate* 33 footnotes 21, 22; Erne *Vertragsgültigkeit* 82 et seq.

385 Supra Chapter 5, I, 7, d, see as well Chapter 3, II, 2, b.

386 MünchKomm/Sonnenberger Einl Rn 38; Siehr RabelsZ 52 (1988) 41, 75, 76, 91; Schubert RIW 1987, 729, 731; Busse ZverglRWiss 95 (1996) 387, 389, 390.

387 Siehr RabelsZ 52 (1988) 41, 75 et seq; Lipstein *Conflict of Public Laws* 357, 358 et seq; Mann Rec des Cours 132 (1971 I) 115, 188; MünchKomm/Sonnenberger Einl Rn 374; Erne *Vertragsgültigkeit* 82; Schiffer *Normen* 79, 80 with further references.

It has already been explained that the principle is reasonable with regard to the enforcement of foreign public law rules, which impose a positive duty on the governmental authorities in favour of the foreign state.[388] However, in private litigation the concern is not the enforcement of public law rules in favour of the foreign state, but rather the influence and consequences of public law on private law and private relationships: the '*reflex effects*' of public law on private law.[389]

The question is thus whether a foreign law that represents the public interests of the foreign enacting state, and pursues these interests indirectly by intervening in private contracts, can be applied. The forum considers only the effects of public enactments upon the private relationship. To the extent that the principle of non-applicability excludes even consideration of the reflex effects of public law rules on private relationships, as it has been understood by the German and Swiss courts and some writers, it must clearly be rejected.[390] Currently, the principle of *non-applicability of foreign public law* following on the principle of *territoriality* is almost never supported.[391]

This conclusion does not necessarily mean that the legal effects of the public law of the *lex causae* are always applicable, or the only applicable effects. The application or consideration of foreign public law rules (as well as private law rules) by the forum must still be determined by its conflict of laws.[392]

It was previously noted that the applicability of rules serving the economic and political interests of a foreign country should not be determined by the ordinary conflict rules. The latter are based on the private interests of the contracting parties and do not take into account the interests of the forum and foreign state.[393]

---

388 Schiffer *Normen* 79; MünchKomm/Sonnenberger Einl Rn 375; Vischer Rec des Cours 232 (1990 I) 13, 151; Mann Rec des Cours 132 (1974 I) 115, 184.

389 MünchKomm/Martiny Art 34 Rn 36; Schiffer *Normen* 76 et seq; Kropholler *IPR* § 22 II 2; Neymayer RabelsZ 25 (1960) 649, 651; Siehr RabelsZ 52 (1988) 41, 73; Knüppel *Zwingendes Recht* 25; Morscher *Rechtssetzungsakte* 49; Erne *Vertragsgültigkeit* 82 et seq; Schwander *Lois d'application immédiate* 73.

390 Schiffer *Normen* 77; Erne *Vertragsgültigkeit* 84; MünchKomm/Martiny Art 34 Rn 36; Vischer Rec des Cours 232 (1992 I) 13, 150 et seq. It has been assumed that the German case law is based on the misunderstanding that application would mean enforcement, cf Mann Rec des Cours 132 (1971 I) 115, 187; Schiffer *Normen* 75.

391 Apart from a few authors, such as Schäfer *FG Sandrock* 39, 48 et seq.

392 Erne *Vertragsgültigkeit* 82, 83; Neuhaus *IPR* 179; Mann Rec des Cours 132 (1971 I) 115, 190; Siehr RabelsZ 52 (1988) 41, 80, 81; Schäfer *FG Sandrock* 39, 48; Kreuzer *Ausländisches Wirtschaftsrecht* 77.

393 Vischer Rec des Cours 232 (1992 I) 13, 151, 180; Kreuzer *Ausländisches Wirtschaftsrecht* 81 et seq.

However, internationally mandatory rules are not in general inapplicable, although German and Swiss case law may give that impression because of the unfortunate principle of *territoriality*. They are subject to *separate conflict rules*, because they predominantly serve the economic and political interests of a state.[394] Nonetheless, third country's internationally mandatory rules serving public rather than the private interests were taken into account within the substantive law of the *lex causae*. It follows that special considerations are necessary to account for this type of rule.

c Different kinds of public law rules

The Federal Supreme Court and the Federal Tribunal distinguished between those public law rules serving predominantly private interests or the fair reconciliation between them, and those pursuing public interests of the foreign state.[395] Only the latter rules have been held to be subject to the principle of territoriality and therefore in principle inapplicable.

This distinction has been criticised for being impossible to apply.[396] However, apart from the starting point adopted by the courts - the subdivision of the foreign law only within the category of public law - which must be rejected for several reasons, the distinction developed by German and Swiss case law does have its merits.[397] It provides some guidance as to which foreign law falls under the scope of reference of the normal conflict rules and which deserves special consideration. Only those rules that are used by the foreign state to pursue its economic and political interests, and beyond the interests of the contracting parties and an attempt to effect a fair reconciliation between them, fall outside the scope of reference of the ordinary conflict rules. However, there remains a grey zone of rules that serve both private and public interests. In this regard no useful criteria have been found to identify these rules.[398]

---

394 Vischer Rec des Cours 232 (1992 I) 13, 180 et seq; Schurig RabelsZ 54 (1990) 217, 244; cf supra Chapter 5, I, 3.

395 BG 2.2.1954 BGE 80 II, 53, 61 et seq; BGH 17.12.1959 BGHZ 31, 367, 371; BGH 16.4.1975 BGHZ 64, 183, 190.

396 Busse ZverglRWiss 95 (1996) 387, 415; Mäsch *Rechtswahlfreiheit* 135 et seq; Schurig RabelsZ 54 (1990) 217, 227 et seq.

397 Vischer Rec des Cours 232 (1992 I) 13, 184 et seq; Voser *Lois d'application immédiate* 68; Morscher *Rechtssetzungsakte* 88; Schiffer *Normen* 30, 31.

398 See Vischer Rec des Cours 232 (1992 I) 13, 184 et seq; Voser *Lois d'application immédiate* 68; see the approaches of MünchKomm/Sonnenberger Einl Rn 32; Anderegg *Eingriffsnormen* 87 et seq; Schubert RIW 1987, 729, 731; Radtke ZVerglRWIss 84 (1985) 325, 328; BGH 17.11.1994 BGHZ 128, 41, 52; Schnyder *Wirtschaftskollisionsrecht* Rn 10, 13; see also supra Chapter 3, II, 2.

d Consideration as fact within the applicable substantive law

Advocates of the *Substantive Law Approach* have endorsed the consideration of foreign internationally mandatory rules within the substantive law rules of the governing law of the contract, and the *Schuldstatuts-theory* approves of this approach with regard to third countries' internationally mandatory rules. It has already been noted that consideration of a third country's mandatory rules within the substantive law of the *lex causae* is a possible solution, but that a solution on the level of conflict of laws is preferable. The many objections to the consideration within the substantive law have been discussed.[399]

In contrast to the academic approaches, court decisions lack even formal choice of law explanation, rather proceeding with an immediate examination of whether the violation of the foreign rule may lead to impossibility of performance, frustration of contract, or immorality.

(1) Are foreign rules facts? The need for choice of law considerations

As has been stated above, the argument that a violated foreign rule can be considered as supposed 'fact' within certain substantive rules of the proper law is unconvincing. It is a general accepted principle that foreign law cannot be applied or considered by the forum state unless a conflict rule, whether statutory or of a common law nature, so directs.[400] The conclusion drawn from this principle by the advocates of the *Schuldstatuts-theory* is that the conflict rules of the forum state refer to the proper law as a whole, to the exclusion of any other law. Therefore, it is held that third countries' internationally mandatory rules cannot be applied, but only considered as facts.[401]

However, it is doubtful whether there is any difference between the application of foreign law and its consideration as fact within the substantive law rules as far as choice of law considerations are concerned.[402] Foreign rules are not 'facts' in the true sense and to take the '*normative content*' of a rule into account means that it *is* applied in some sense, and deserves conflict of laws

---

399 See supra Chapter 5, I, 7, a, b, c.

400 Siehr RabelsZ 52 (1988) 41, 84; Schiffer *Normen* 98, 99; Junker JZ 1991, 699, 700; Kreuzer *Ausländisches Wirtschaftsrecht* 78; Schäfer *FG Sandrock* 39, 49.

401 See supra Chapter 5, I, 1.

402 Schiffer *Normen* 94 et seq; Schurig *Lois* 55, 73, 74; Kreuzer *Ausländisches Wirtschaftsrecht* 79, 80; Mentzel *Sonderanknüpfung* 105 et seq; von Bar *IPR Bd I* Rn 265; Lehmann ZRP 1987, 319, 320; Schubert RIW 1987, 729, 737; Schurig RabelsZ 54 (1990) 217, 241.

considerations.[403] The actual effects of a rule are only taken into account if the concern is truly the *de facto impact* of the foreign rule alone, and not its material or normative content.[404]

German courts have recognised the violation of foreign law as immoral and contrary to German *boni mores* if the foreign provision also indirectly serves German interests, or interests that are shared by all civilised nations, or are based on general moral values. This clearly shows that the rule *itself* is taken into account, not simply the *de facto* effects of the violated foreign rule, or the rule as a kind of 'fact'. The foreign rule has been the very basis of the court's decision.

The notion of *boni mores* usually protects an elementary domestic code of practices and does not indicate under what circumstances third countries' internationally mandatory rules, based on public interests, lead to immorality.[405] The application of the *boni mores* rule in the decisions that have been discussed is not based on German moral values, but rather on whether the interests of the forum state can be served by an application or consideration of the foreign law. The characterisation of the contract as immoral is connected with the content and purpose of the foreign rule. If the contract were completely legal under the foreign law, no question of immorality would arise.[406] In considering the material content and objective of the foreign rule or the interests pursued by the rule, German courts take account of the rule *itself*, not only its actual effects.

Consideration of the foreign rule within *boni mores* must first of all examine whether there is a foreign law that has been violated by the contracting parties. Thereafter, the judge must determine whether the foreign law protects interests shared in common by the forum state, and only then he can decide whether or not the violation of foreign law leads to immorality. Thus, before considering the infringement of the foreign rule within the notion of *boni mores*, the judge has to examine the primary question of when a foreign law *can* be considered within the notion of *boni mores*. He thereby looks at the existence, operative facts, and normative content of the rule.[407]

---

403 Schubert RIW 1987, 729, 737; Radtke ZverglRWiss 84 (1985) 325, 345 et seq; Schurig *Lois* 55, 73, 74; Kreuzer *Ausländisches Wirtschaftsrecht* 79, 80; Schiffer *Normen* 94. Likewise, the Swiss Federal Tribunal in BGE 60 II 294, 311 et seq stated that it is fallacious to distinguish between the application and the recognition of a foreign rule.

404 Schurig *Lois* 55, 73, 74; Schubert RIW 1987, 729, 737; critical Schiffer *Normen* 95, 96.

405 Kreuzer *Ausländisches Wirtschaftsrecht* 87; von Hoffmann *Contract Conflicts* 221, 230.

406 Mentzel *Sonderanknüpfung* 106; Morscher *Rechtssetzungsakte* 67; Vischer Rec des Cours 232 (1992 I) 13, 171.

407 For details, see Schiffer *Normen* 96 et seq; Lehmann *Zwingendes Recht* 200 et seq.

It is therefore argued that the choice of law question about whether and under what circumstances foreign law can be applied - or, more broadly, given effect to - is transferred to the level of substantive law and dealt with under the 'fraudulent label' of *boni mores*, or is blurred with or concealed behind application of substantive law.[408]

The consideration of the foreign rule as a reason for impossibility of performance or frustration of contract is not quite so obvious. According to Schiffer, this situation also implies a choice of law as to whether there is a foreign law to be taken into account, and whether the situation falls within the scope of the foreign rule. Only after the court has concluded that the transaction falls within the foreign law and that the foreign rule prohibits the conduct or action, can the judge determine whether that rule may be deemed to render performance impossible under the law of the *lex causae*.[409]

However, it is doubtful whether this is always the case. There are cases where only the actual effects of a foreign rule have in truth been taken into account, for example, where the foreign enacting state has already enforced its legislation by seizure attachment.[410] Difficulties arise in situations where the foreign state has not yet enforced its law, or the foreign law has not yet been violated because the debtor refuses performance. Is the mere existence of a foreign law, possibly with heavy sanctions for the violation thereof, enough to render performance impossible? The courts have ruled that it is.[411] But, is it in truth only the actual effect of a foreign rule that is being taken into account? It seems that in this case it is at least the 'normative content' of the rule that is being considered.[412]

Swiss courts have refused to take foreign rules into account and render performance impossible, because the foreign law was held to be contrary to the Swiss *ordre public*.[413] The Swiss Tribunal itself stated in this context that there is no difference between applying foreign legislation directly and applying it

---

408 See Hentzen RIW 1988, 508, 509; MünchKomm/Martiny Art 34 Rn 35; Schiffer *Normen* 96 et seq; Schubert RIW 1987, 729, 737; Lehmann *Zwingendes Recht* 200 et seq; Schurig RabelsZ 54 (1990) 217, 242; Morscher *Rechtssetzungsakte* 67; Junker JZ 1991, 699, 701; Drobnig *FS Neumayer* 159, 177; Reithmann/Martiny/Limmer *Internationales Vertragsrecht* Rn 463, 465.

409 Schiffer *Normen* 94 et seq.

410 Schurig RabelsZ 54 (1990) 217, 241, 242; id Lois 55, 73; for criticism, see Schubert RIW 1987, 729, 737; Zimmer IPRax 1993 65, 66 et seq.

411 28.6.1918 RGZ 93, 182 et seq.

412 Schurig RabelsZ 54 (1990) 217, 241, 242; id *Lois* 55, 73; Schubert RIW 1987, 729, 737.

413 BGE 60 II 294, 311 et seq.

indirectly by recognising its factual effects.[414] The approach of the Tribunal is to ask whether the content or the application of the foreign legislation would infringe the forum's *ordre public*, and thus determine whether its effects can be taken into account and thereby render performance impossible. This approach has been the subject of some scepticism, and it is argued that recognising the actual effects of the foreign legislation is independent from the *ordre public* of the forum. The reference to the *ordre public* exemption means that the Swiss court not only took into account the actual effects of the foreign rule within the substantive law rules, but also applied the foreign legislation on a conflict of laws level.[415]

In Germany, in contrast, the consequences of the existence of a foreign provision and foreign executed power have been considered on a *de facto* level as reason for impossibility, without any evaluation of the content of the foreign rule, which could even be directed against German interests.[416] According to German case law it is the physical pressure and constraints that can arise for the parties of a contract governed by a foreign law that are taken into account. The issue is whether the foreign law can be enforced.[417] Again, the question can be raised about when the pressure becomes a fact, or when the foreign rule is taken into account because it is held to be an undue hardship for a debtor to perform in violation of a foreign law. The latter can also result in a consideration of the foreign rule *itself*, and not its actual effects.

(2) The need for a conflict rule

The conclusion that can be drawn is that in cases where the foreign rule is considered as a rule and not only as 'true' fact, choice of law considerations are necessary to determine under what circumstances the foreign rule can be considered. According to the general principles of choice of law, this is a matter for the conflict rules of the forum state.

The need for a conflict rule cannot be avoided by the consideration of a foreign rule within the substantive law. In fact, a choice is made, albeit blurred and hidden within the substantive law. It is preferable to determine, on the level of the forum's conflict of laws, when it is justified to recognise third countries'

414 BGE 60 II 294, 311; BGE 64 II 88, 100.

415 Morscher *Rechtssetzungsakte* 64; Bär *Kartellrecht* 120; Schwander *Lois d'application immédiate* 365; Schubert RIW 1987, 729, 737.

416 Reithmann/Martiny/Limmer *Internationales Vertragsrecht* Rn 467; Baum RabelsZ 53 (1989) 152, 156; Drobnig *FS Neumayer* 159, 169; Basedow GYBIntL 27 (1984) 109, 132.

417 See RG 28.6.1918 RGZ 93, 182 et seq.

internationally mandatory rules, as well as those of the proper law.[418] It has been shown by advocates of the *Special Connection Theory* that the criteria that have been used by the courts can easily be transported to the level of conflict of laws in the form of a conflict rule.[419]

(3) The enlargement of substantive law rules

There are other objections to the consideration of the foreign law as 'facts/rules' within the substantive law of the proper law. For example, the substantive law rules, that are designed for domestic situations, need to be extended so that they can be applied to a violation of foreign law.[420]

In all decided cases where the foreign legislation was considered within the notion of *boni mores* or impossibility of performance, the contracts were governed by the law of the forum state. The courts have never been faced with a case where the proper law was a foreign law, and a protection-worthy or enforceable internationally mandatory rule of a third country claimed application. A judge can no doubt extend the law of his home country without any difficulty. But, if the governing law were a foreign law, he would be faced with the difficult task of extending the scope of foreign law, if it offered suitable relief.[421]

(4) The ultimate control of the forum state

Finally, it has been emphasised that, in cases where the foreign proper law can decide whether to recognise a third country's internationally mandatory rules, the decision about application of the rule is thus handed over to the foreign law. As has been noted, it is for the forum to decide when to recognise foreign law. Thus even those authors who support the substantive law solution of the case law submit that in cases where the foreign *lex causae* does not provide a means of applying the foreign legislation, the judge may have recourse to the forum's *ordre public* or to an '*ordre public universal*'.[422]

---

418 Also see Schiffer *Normen* 98 et seq; id ZverglRWiss 90 (1991) 390, 405; Kreuzer *Ausländisches Wirtschaftsrecht* 89 et seq; Staudinger/Magnus Art 34 Rn 139.

419 See Chapter 5, I, 3, f, g, h, i.

420 See Schwander *IPR AT* 250 et seq; Vischer Rec des Cours 232 (1992 I) 13, 177; Schurig RabelsZ 54 (1990) 217, 243; Drobnig *FS Neumayer* 159, 177.

421 For details, see Schwander *IPR AT* 250 et seq; Schurig RabelsZ 54 (1990) 217, 244; Sonnenberger *FS Rebmann* 819, 837; Hentzen RIW 1988, 508, 510.

422 Heini 100 ZSR (1981) 65, 73, 82. However, Heini does not clarify exactly what constitutes the *ordre public universal*.

e Conclusion

In the light of all these arguments, the German and Swiss courts' solution does not lead to legal certainty, nor does it conform to the fundamental principles of conflict of laws. The *non-application of foreign law* on the basis of the principle of *territoriality* must be rejected as erroneous. Consideration of foreign rules within the substantive law of the proper law is possible, but the judge must still primarily make a choice of law. This decision takes place at the level of substantive law, and is blurred and hidden within the substantive law.

The reasons for the courts' decisions change from case to case according to the particular situation. Because, the judgments use vague criteria and extend the substantive law rules, it is difficult, if not impossible, to predict the outcome of a case.[423] Finally, in cases where a foreign law governs the contract, the forum is faced with the difficult task of extending the scope of foreign domestic law, and the decision about whether a foreign rule is to be applied - a matter for the forum's conflict of laws approach - is handed over to the *lex causae*.

423 Also see Kreuzer *Ausländisches Wirtschaftsrecht* 87; Mentzel *Sonderanknüpfung* 106 et seq; Lehmann ZRP 1987, 319, 321.

III The English common law approach

English case law has developed relatively firm principles with regard to the application of foreign internationally mandatory rules of the proper law. According to English law the proper law of the contract governs most aspects of contract, whether this is the chosen law or the law, which is applicable in the absence of a choice (objectively determined law).[424] This was already the well-established basic rule under the common law before the Rome Convention: The material or essential validity of the contract, its interpretation, effect and discharge was determined by the proper law.[425]

However, with regard to the question of the application of internationally mandatory rules, exceptions have been made to the basic rule, and a contract that was valid according to the proper law was not enforced if it was unlawful according to another law.[426] Apart from the above mentioned application of the forum's internationally mandatory rules, the 'control of the proper law' has been limited by the occasional application or consideration of internationally mandatory rules of a third country. This aspect will be discussed later.

The crucial question in the following section is whether, according to the common law position, all mandatory rules of the proper law are applied for the sole reason that they belong to the proper law, or whether, as in Germany and Switzerland, some mandatory rules are not applied as a result of their public law nature or their material content, even though they do belong to the proper law of the contract.

1 The general rule: Application of mandatory rules of the *lex causae*

English courts have generally applied the mandatory provisions of the *lex causae* and do not enforce a contract that is void or illegal according to the applicable law.[427] English authors presume that the position under the Rome

---

424 Collier *Conflict of Laws* 185; Kaye *The New Private International Law* 15 et seq; Morse *Public Policy* England - 59.

425 Dicey & Morris *Conflict of Laws Vol II/12th ed* 1190, 1253, */13th ed* 1198, 1255; Carter BYBIL 57 (1986) 1, 7. The rule is subject to exceptions, such as capacity or formal validity, the proper law of which is indicated by special choice of law rules and does not correspond necessarily with the law governing the contract, cf Kaye *The New Private International Law* 18; Dicey & Morris *Conflict of Laws Vol II/12th ed* 1190, 1205.

426 See Dicey & Morris *Conflict of Laws Vol II/12th ed* 1190, 1241 et seq, */13th ed* 1198, 1244 et seq; Cheshire and North's *Private International Law/11th ed* 482 et seq, */13th ed* 600 et seq.

427 Cf Dicey & Morris *Conflict of Laws Vol II/13th ed* 1244, 1250, 1255; Cheshire & North's *Private International Law/12th ed* 518, */13th ed* 600; Collier *Conflict of Laws* 206; Jaffey ICLQ 23 (1974) 1, 3; Mann Rec des Cours 132 (1971 I) 109, 157; see also for judicial

Convention is the same: The essential validity of the contract is determined by the governing law (art 8 of the Rome Convention) so that mandatory provisions of the proper law are in principle applicable.[428]

To avoid confusion it is useful to mention at this point that the questions of *application of mandatory rules* and *illegality or material (or essential) validity* of a contract are closely connected. Therefore, in the past, and even now, the problem of mandatory rules has also been dealt with under the more general topic of illegality of contract.[429] The reason for the latter approach lies in the fact that mandatory rules are typically of a prohibitive nature and often contain the order that a contract is void or illegal. However, illegality logically presupposes the infringement of mandatory rules (statutory mandatory rules as well as mandatory common law rules).[430]

Application of the mandatory rules is based on the general principle that statutes forming part of the proper law of the contract will normally be applied (because they are rendered applicable by the ordinary choice of law rules), and/or on the basis of the principle that the essential validity depends on the governing law.[431]

a Private and public law

Although the distinction between public and private law is now known in England, it does not have the same effect on the question of applicability of foreign mandatory rules.[432] Unlike the continental European countries, England

---

authority *Royal Exchange Assurance Corp v Vega* [1902] 2 KB 384 (CA); *Vita Food Products Inc v Unus Shipping Co Ltd* [1939] AC 277 (PC), *Kahler v Midland Bank Ltd* [1950] AC 24, [1949] 2 All ER 621; *Libyan Arab Foreign Bank v Bankers Trust Co* [1989] 3 All ER 252; subject of course to the exclusion of foreign law on grounds of public policy and overriding statutes of the forum state.

428 Dicey & Morris *Conflict of Laws Vol I/12th /13th ed 21, 22* and *Vol II/12th ed* 1253, */13th ed* 1244, 1250; Cheshire & North's *Private International Law/12th ed* 518, */13th ed* 600.

429 Eg, Lando CMLR 24 (1987) 159, 205 'essential validity and *Lois de police*'; Hartley Rec des Cours 266 (1997) 341, 385 et seq 'illegality'; Cheshire & North's *Private International Law/12th ed* 518, */13th ed* 600; Carter BYBIL 57 (1986) 1, 28; Mann BYBIL 18 (1937) 97; clearly Collier *Conflict of Laws* 206, 207; Jaffey ICLQ 23 (1974) 1.

430 Jaffey ICLQ 23 (1974) 1.

431 'According to standard doctrine in the conflict of laws, a statute does not normally apply unless it forms part of the governing law of the contract', see Dicey & Morris *Conflict of Laws Vol I/12th ed* 21 with references in footnotes 1 – 5, */13th ed* 21 with references in footnotes 18 - 22 and *Vol II/12th ed* 1241, 1253, 1254, */13th ed* 1243, 1244, 1250; Forsyth *The role of public law* 94, 102 et seq.

432 See in this regard the complex article of Forsyth *The role of public law* 94 et seq, in which he defines rules of public law as 'rules which deal with the relationship between citizen and state, including ... revenue laws, penal laws, laws providing for confiscation

does not distinguish between the application of foreign public or private mandatory rules as such and there is no doctrine of *non-applicability of foreign public law*.[433] Nevertheless, in England the concept of public law surfaces in the context of exclusionary rules: *Foreign penal, revenue* or *other 'public laws'* will not be enforced by an English court. The content of this exclusionary rule and whether it in fact forms an exception to the general applicability of the rules of the *lex causae* will be investigated later.[434]

The general principle is that, when an English choice of law rule indicates a foreign legal system as the applicable law, this is usually understood as a reference to all the relevant rules of that legal system, including public law rules.[435] Therefore, English courts apply both foreign mandatory rules of a private law nature[436] and rules that may be considered as public law rules, or that are at least held to serve collective state interests rather than the fair reconciliation of the contracting parties. Examples of such public law rules are foreign currency or exchange control regulations, competition laws, and import and export restrictions. The courts therefore regard the contracts as illegal in terms of their proper law.[437]

One example of the English courts' general disregard of the private/public law distinction is *Re Helbert Wagg & Co Ltd's Claim.*[438] The question was whether a subsequent German moratorium law that provided that a foreign currency debt could be discharged by the payment of an appropriate sum of *Reichsmark* into a *Konversionskasse* was applicable to a loan agreement between an English and a

---

and expropriation of property, social security and national insurance laws, foreign exchange control regulations....' However in footnote 5 he remarks with reference to dicta in case law that 'confusion reigns in English law as to the content of public law'. Also see Lipstein *Conflict of Laws* 38 et seq; id *Öffentliches Recht* 39 et seq; id *Conflict of Public Laws* 357 et seq; Mann Rec des Cours (1971 I) 109 et seq; Hartley *Foreign Public Law* 13 et seq.

433 Mann Rec des Cours 132 (1971 I) 109, 184 with references; also see Lipstein *Conflict of Public Laws* 357, 358 et seq, 364; Forsyth *The role of public law* 94, 102.

434 See infra under section 1, b.

435 Forsyth *The role of public law* 94, 102; Lipstein *Conflict of Public Laws* 357, 364 et seq.

436 Cf the examples given by Dicey & Morris *Conflict of Laws Vol I/13th ed* 21 footnote 19 for statutes affecting wagering contracts.

437 Cf Forsyth *The role of public law* 94, 102 et seq; Mann Rec des Cours 132 (1971 I) 109, 184; Lipstein *Conflict of Public Laws* 357, 365; see *De Béeche v South American Stores Ltd* [1935] AC 148; *Re International Trustee for the Protection of Bondholders Act* [1937] 2 All ER 164; [1937] AC 500 (HL); *Re Banque des Merchands des Moscou (No 2)* [1954] 1 WLR 1108; *Re Helbert Wagg & Co Ltd* [1956] Ch 323; [1956] 1 All ER 129.

438 [1956] 2 WLR 183; [1956] Ch 323; [1956] 1 All ER 129; see for the facts Jaffey ICLQ 23 (1974) 1, 6.

German company. In terms of the loan agreement, the German company borrowed a sum of Pounds Sterling from the English company.

The court held that the German moratorium law was applicable on the grounds that the contract was governed by German law and consequently held that payment to the *Kasse* in accordance with the moratorium law had discharged the debt. Upjohn J stated that:

> [I]n general every civilised state must be recognised as having the power to legislate ... in respect of contracts governed by the law of that state [that enacted the legislation] and that such legislation must be recognised by other states as valid and effectual ... to modify or dissolve such contracts ....[439]

Another case often cited in this context is *R v International Trustee for the Protection of Bondholders Act.*[440] The proper law of the contract (a bond raised by the British government on the New York money market) was held by the House of Lords to be the law of the United States of America.[441] For that reason the majority of Judges of the House of Lords applied a Joint Resolution of Congress that was passed in July 1933 and had the force of law. This resolution rendered payment of a dollar debt in gold coin illegal and declared that all dollar obligations could be discharged only by payment of the dollar sum in any currency that was legal tender at that time (abrogation of gold clauses). The bondholders were therefore not entitled to payment in gold coin.[442]

The same result could have been reached by applying the *lex loci solutionis rule* (with which will be dealt with later). The contracting parties agreed that New York was the place of performance, and according to the *lex loci solutionis rule*

---

439 With regard to the German legislation he stated that a state has the right 'to protect its economy by measures of foreign exchange control and by altering the value of its currency.'

440 [1937] 2 All ER 164; [1937] AC 500 (HL); [1936] 3 All ER 407 (CA). For the facts of the case: Forsyth *The role of public law* 94, 103 and Jaffey ICLQ 23 (1974) 1, 5. But also see the case *New Brunswick Railway Co v British & French Trust Corporation Ltd* [1939] AC 1; [1938] 4 AllER 747 where the HL left the question of which country's law governs the bonds open, and held that the foreign (Canadian) gold clauses were inapplicable if the litigation took place in England. However, the bonds were already due three years before the Canadian mandatory provision entered into force.

441 In contrast to the Court of Appeal where it was held that the proper law was English law.

442 Lord Atkin stated 'that which comes first under consideration is what is the proper law of the contract; for if that is to be answered in one way no further issues remain.'

the mandatory provisions of the place of performance are applicable regardless of the proper law of the contract.[443]

In other cases the House of Lords upheld foreign exchange control regulations that prohibited the delivery of securities without the consent of the nominated foreign authority, because the regulations formed part of the proper law and the contracts were held to be invalid or discharged.[444]

For instance, in *Kahler v Midland Bank Ltd*[445] the House of Lords applied Czech foreign exchange control regulations on the grounds that the contract was governed by Czech law. It followed that the plaintiff could not have enforced delivery of the shares that were owed without the permission of the National Bank, and this permission had been refused. Consequently the plaintiff's action in detinue failed.[446] This judgment has been subject to fundamental criticism. It has been held that the court granted extraterritorial operation to the Czech exchange control regulations, because the Czech law could prevent the delivery of the shares from the debtor - an English bank - to the plaintiff, who was not even resident in Czechoslovakia.[447]

In *Zivnostenska Banka National Corporation v Frankmann*[448] the court was once again concerned with a contract governed by Czech law and a Czechoslovakian mandatory provision. Most of the judges applied the foreign mandatory legislation because it formed part of the proper law. *Lord Reid*,

---

443 See the dicta of Lord Wright in the Court of Appeal decision: the *lex loci solutionis rule* is 'too well established now to require any further discussion' [1936] 3 All ER 407, at 428. Also see Schulte *Anknüpfung von Eingriffsnormen* 93, who refers in his argument to the possibility of a '*special connection*'; however, the *lex loci solutionis rule* is far from clear. Although the rule is often designated as well-established principle in English law, the interpretation of the 'methodical content' of the principle differs amongst cases and academic writers. For further details, see infra under section 2, c, d.

444 *De Béeche v South American Stores Ltd* [1935] AC 148; *St. Pierre and Others v South American Stores (Gath and Chaves) Ltd and Chilean Stores (Gath and Chaves) Ltd* [1937] 3 All ER 349; *Kahler v Midland Bank Ltd* [1950] AC 24 (HL); [1949] 2 All ER 621; *Zivnostenska Banka National Corporation v Frankman* [1950] AC 57 (HL); *Re Banque des Merchands des Moscou (No 2)* [1954] 1 WLR 118.

445 [1950] AC 24 (HL); [1949] 2 All ER 621. Lord Radcliffe stated that the proper law of the contract not merely sustains, but because it sustains may also modify or dissolve the contractual bond (at page 641).

446 The facts of the case are complicated and shall not be repeated here. For details cf Forsyth *The role of public law* 94, 110 et seq and Morse *Public Policy* England - 130 et seq.

447 For criticism see Forsyth *The role of public law* 94, 110 et seq. For the sake of comparison, see that *Kahler v Midland Bank* was not followed by a South African decision *Standard Bank of South Africa v Ocean Commidities* 1983 (1) SA 276 (A).

448 [1950] AC 57 (HL); ([1949] 2 All ER 671.

however, referred to the *lex loci solutionis rule* and stated that it is settled law that 'whatever the proper law of the contract an English court will not require a party to do an act in performance of a contract which would be an offence under the law in force at the place where the act has to be done.'[449]

In *St Pierre and others v South American Stores (Gath and Chaves) Ltd and Chilean Stores (Gath and Chaves) Ltd*[450] the court was concerned with a contract governed by Chilean law, the performance of which was restricted by a Chilean mandatory exchange control regulation if the money was transferred to the United Kingdom. The reasoning of the judges in this case differed. While Lord Greer applied the foreign mandatory legislation because the proper law was Chilean, Lord Slesser applied the mandatory law because the order to transfer would take place in Chile and not anywhere else in the world.[451]

b Exceptions to the general rule; *non-enforcement of foreign penal, revenue and other public laws*

The exclusive and comprehensive application of the mandatory rules of the proper law and the principle that the essential validity depends on the governing law is subject to the ordinary rule that the application of the foreign rule must not violate the forum's public policy. English courts will not apply or give effect to a foreign mandatory provision (as well as foreign law in general) if it, or the result of its application, violates fundamental principles of public policy, despite the fact that the provision is applicable according to the English choice of law rules.[452] Therefore, the foreign proper law (including its internationally mandatory rules) may be disregarded on the basis of English public policy.[453] This effect of public policy corresponds with the so-called '*negative function*' of the continental European doctrine of *ordre public*.[454] This '*negative function*'

---

449 At page 78, (or at page 681).

450 [1937] 3 All ER 349.

451 Ibid 352 and 356.

452 Dicey & Morris *Conflict of Laws Vol I/13th ed* 81 et seq; id *Vol II/13th ed* 1276 et seq; Cheshire & North's *Private International Law/13th ed* 123 et seq, 584 et seq; Morse *Public Policy* England - 9 et seq, 59 et seq.

453 The application of the public policy rule may lead to the court regarding a contract that would be valid according to its governing law as void or unenforceable. On the other hand, it may well have the opposite effect that English courts enforce contracts that are illegal under their proper law and thus disregard the foreign mandatory legislation that invalidates the contract. On this aspect, see Dicey & Morris *Conflict of Laws Vol I /13th ed* 83; Morse *Public Policy* England - 63; Hartley Rec des Cours 266 (1997) 341, 351.

454 Morse *Public Policy* England - 63; Hartley Rec des Cours 266 (1997) 341, 351. The 'positive function' of public policy renders the law of the forum applicable despite the foreign proper law. In England the distinction between the negative and positive functions

of the *ordre public* or the so-called *public policy exclusionary rule* will not be considered further in this thesis.[455]

However, England adheres to the principle that *foreign revenue, penal and other public laws will not be enforced* either *directly* or *indirectly*.[456] This principle is well founded in many jurisdictions.[457] Its effect may be that mandatory rules of the proper law that have this character should not be applied, and this proposition will be investigated in the following paragraphs.

Although there is some academic debate concerning the *theoretical basis* of the principle,[458] the most suitable explanation is considered to be that given by Lord Keith in *Government of India v Taylor*.[459] The court held that the enforcement of a tax claim (as in *casu*) constitutes part of the sovereignty of the state that imposes those claims. '[A]n assertion of sovereign authority by one state within the territory of another, as distinct from a patrimonial claim by a foreign sovereign, is (treaty or Convention apart) contrary to all concepts of independent sovereignty'. The principle had already been referred to by Lord Watson in 1893, in the notorious case *Huntington v Attrill*,[460] where the court was dealing with foreign penal laws. The principle was held to designate 'that class of actions which, by the law of nations, are exclusively assigned to their domestic forum'. The court noted that:

---

of public policy or *ordre public* is often not mentioned. Cf Dicey & Morris *Conflict of Laws Vol I/13th ed* 81 et seq; see, however, Fletcher *Conflict of Laws* 172; Hartley Rec des Cours 266 (1997) 341, 350 et seq.

455 With regard to public policy and the conditions of its application, such as the *connection* with the forum or the violation of a *fundamental* principle of justice, see Dicey & Morris *Conflict of Laws Vol I/12th ed* 88 et seq, */13th ed* 81 et seq; id *Vol II/12th ed* 1277 et seq, */13th ed* 1276 et seq; Cheshire & North's *Private International Law/12th ed* 128 , 503 et seq, */13th ed* 123, 584 et seq; Morse *Public Policy* England - 9 et seq, 59 et seq. Another aspect of the English public policy rule will be dealt with in the context of third countries' internationally rules, see infra under 2, a.

456 Dicey & Morris *Conflict of Laws Vol I/13th ed* 89 Rule 3; Cheshire & North's *Private International Law*/13th ed 107 et seq; see also Mann Rec des Cours 132 (1971 I) 109, 166; Collier *Conflict of Laws* 359 et seq, Forsyth *The role of public law* 94, 112 et seq, all with a discussion of the principle and references to case law.

457 Eg in Germany, Switzerland and France, cf Basedow GYBIL 27 (1984) 109, 115 et seq. It is equally valid for South Africa, cf Forsyth *Private International Law* 104 et seq with references.

458 See Dicey & Morris *Conflict of Laws Vol I/12th ed* 97, 98, */13th ed* 89, 90; Mann Rec des Cours 132 (1971 I) 109, 166.

459 [1955] AC 491, at 511.

460 (1893) AC 150, at 156 (PC).

> [The principle has] its foundation in the well recognised principle that crimes, including in that term all breaches of public law punishable by pecuniary mulct or otherwise, at the instance of the state government or of someone representing the public are local in the sense that they are only cognisable and punishable in the country where they were committed. Accordingly, no proceeding, even in the shape of a civil suit, which has for its object the enforcement by the State, whether directly or indirectly, of punishment imposed for such breaches by the lex fori, ought to be admitted in the Courts of any other country.[461]

What type of foreign law is affected by this exclusionary rule? In general, English law has held that it decides whether the law of a foreign country falls within the categories of laws that will not be enforced by English courts.[462]

The non-enforcement of the categories of foreign *penal* and *revenue law* on the basis of this principle is clearly established. In *Huntington v Attrill*[463] the court was concerned with foreign penal law. It defined penal law as 'crimes, including in that term all breaches of public law punishable by pecuniary mulct or otherwise, at the instance of the state government or of someone representing the public'.[464] In *Government of India v Taylor*[465] the court held, with regard to revenue laws, that it would not uphold or enforce claims on behalf of a foreign state to recover taxes due under its law.[466] The category '*revenue law*' has never been defined, but certainly includes a rule requiring a non-contractual payment of money to a central or local government.[467]

---

461 The court, however, held that the principle was inapplicable, despite the penal nature of the New York statute, because the cause of action was exercising the rights of individual parties.

462 See *Huntington v Attrill* [1893] AC 150, at 156 (PC); Dicey & Morris *Conflict of Laws Vol I/12th ed* 98, */13th ed* 90. It has, however, been submitted by academic authors that the categorisation of laws using a pigeon hole technique is often problematic, as the determination and definition of what laws are of a penal, revenue or 'other public laws' nature is unclear. Cf Dicey & Morris *Conflict of Laws Vol I/13th ed* 92 (penal law), 93 (revenue law), 94 (other public laws) for definition and references to case law.

463 [1893] AC 150, at 156 (PC).

464 For a more detailed definition of *penal law*, see Dicey & Morris *Conflict of Laws Vol I/13th ed* 92 et seq.

465 [1955] AC 491; see Collier *Conflict of Laws* 367 for further references.

466 However, this rule was held to be subject to a contrary agreement or treaty, and the Court thus held that the state of Norway could seek the extradition of its nationals for tax-related offences.

467 Dicey & Morris *Conflict of Laws Vol /13th ed* 93; eg 'capital gains tax', cf *Government of India v Taylor* [1955] AC 491.

However, obscurity surrounds the existence and content of '*other public laws*' as a category of rules that the English courts will not enforce.[468] Dicey and Morris describe 'other public laws' as 'all those rules (other than penal and revenue laws), which are enforced as an assertion of the authority of central or local government.'[469] Examples are generally found in import and export restrictions, regulations banning trade with the enemy, price control and anti-trust laws.[470]

It is uncertain whether there is a residuary class of public laws that an English court will not enforce.[471] However, Dicey and Morris's three-fold classification of foreign penal, revenue and other public laws has been adopted by the courts.[472] The latter category was first adopted by Lord Denning in *Attorney-General of New Zealand v Ortiz*[473] where the court was concerned with ownership of a valuable Maori carving that had been unlawfully exported from New Zealand. The Attorney-General of New Zealand brought an action to restrain the sale in London and asked the court to order that it should be returned to New Zealand. The Court of Appeal rejected the claim, generally speaking because the violated New Zealand legislation was unenforceable. Lord Denning expressed the view that 'other public laws' were laws 'eiusdem generis with penal and revenue laws' and held that the violated law was unenforceable in England because of its public law nature.[474] In *US v Inkley*,[475] too, the Court of Appeal clearly accepted that foreign public law was an express category that the

---

468 Cf Collier [1989] CLJ 33 et seq; id *Conflict of Laws* 368 et seq; Morse *Public Policy* England - 13 et seq.

469 *Conflict of Laws Vol I/12th ed* 103, */13th ed* 94.

470 In principle it is held that 'other public laws' is apparently a wider concept that encompasses both revenue and penal laws, but includes other public laws as well, cf Dicey & Morris *Conflict of Laws Vol I/12th ed* 103, */13th ed* 95; Cheshire & North's *Private International Law/12th /13th ed* 114; this was approved in *US v Inkley* [1989] QB 255, 264 - 265 (CA). Collier *Conflict of Laws* 368, 369.

471 See Collier *Conflict of Laws* 368 et seq; Forsyth *The role of public law* 94, 117; Morse *Public Policy* England - 14 who rejects it as independent category. He holds that merely because a public law involves an act done in the exercise of sovereign authority does not itself indicate that such an act is unenforceable outside the territory of the foreign state.

472 See *Attorney-General of New Zealand v Ortiz* [1984] AC 1, 20 et seq; *Williams and Humbert v W & H Trade Marks (Jersey) Ltd* [1986] AC 386, 394 and 401; *Re State of Norway's Application* [1987] QB 433, 477 - 478 (CA). The rule was supported by the House of Lords in *Re State of Norway's Application (Nos 1 and 2)* [1990] 1 AC 723.

473 [1984] AC 1, 20 et seq.

474 However, Ackner LJ held that it was totally unrealistic to deny that the Act was penal. The decision was affirmed by the HL solely on the ground that the act was interpreted as not providing for automatic forfeiture. The Maori carving was not seized in New Zealand and, therefore, not forfeited to the Crown.

475 [1989] QB 255, 264 (CA).

court would not enforce.[476] Furthermore, the High Court of Australia and the Court of Appeal of New Zealand have confirmed the classification of public laws as a residuary category.[477] Still, the question whether all public law rules fall under the exclusionary rules, and thus the exact content of this category, remains uncertain.[478]

However, the crucial question that has to be asked in this study is whether the principle can *in fact* be an exception to the general rule that mandatory public law rules of the proper law will be upheld in the English forum. It is submitted that this is not the case and this argument will be borne out by the following considerations.

The crucial distinction that has to be drawn is that the principle relates only to *enforcement*; it does not prevent *application* or *recognition* of the same law. *Direct enforcement* occurs where a foreign country or its nominee seeks to obtain relief, property or monetary orders, on the basis of its public law.[479] *Indirect enforcement* means that a foreign state or its nominee pursues a remedy that is not founded on the public law in question, but which in substance is designed to give it extraterritorial effect.[480] Furthermore, indirect enforcement can occur where a private party raises a claim or defence based on the public law, to enforce the rights bestowed by the foreign country.[481]

In essence, the universal rule applies if the plaintiff or defendant is the foreign state, which claims its rights in any form, either directly or indirectly.[482] If the plaintiff or defendant is a *private person* who enforces his *own private right in his own interest*, the universal principle or rule has *no* application. This occurs

---

476 However, the court dismissed application of United States law primarily because it was a criminal or penal law.

477 *Attorney-General (UK) v Heinemann Publishers Australia Pty Ltd* (1988) 165 CLR 30, 42 - 43; *Attorney-General for the United Kingdom v Wellington Newspapers Ltd* [1988] 1 NZLR 129, 173 et seq; on which see Dicey & Morris *Conflict of Laws Vol I/12th ed* 105, 106, */13th ed* 97, 98; Collier *Conflict of Laws* 369.

478 Compare Dicey & Morris *Conflict of Laws Vol I/12th ed* 105, 106, */13th ed* 98 et seq.

479 Cf eg, *Williams & Humbert Ltd v W. & H. Trade Marks (Jersey)* Ltd [1986] AC 368, 437.

480 Cf *Peter Buchanan Ltd v McWey* [1955] AC 516 (Supreme Court of Ireland). In this case a foreign company in bankruptcy sought to recover assets from a director. The liquidator who was appointed by the court had, at the instance of the revenue agency of the foreign country, obtained the assets to satisfy the foreign country's claim for taxes due by the company and not to satisfy the creditors of the company.

481 Dicey & Morris *Conflict of Laws Vol I/12th ed* 99, */13th ed* 90, 91.

482 Mann Rec des Cours 132 (1971 I) 109, 177.

irrespective of whether the claim evolves as a consequence of a foreign state's public laws and the private person's application thereof in a cause of action.[483]

The proposition that the universal rule does not apply in private litigation is generally accepted[484] and is already supported by the seminal case of *Huntingdon v Attrill.*[485] Lord Watson held that 'contractual penalties or even statutory penalties imposed in favour of private parties are not exigible[486] by the state in the interest of the community - but by private persons in their own interest', and are hence exempt from the rule. Likewise, Lord Simonds stated in *Regazzoni v KC Sethia Ltd*[487] that '[i]t does not follow from the fact that ... the court will not enforce a revenue law at the suit of a foreign State, that ... it will enforce a contract which requires the doing of an act in a foreign country which violates the revenue law of that country ....'

Consequently, foreign public law rules will be applied in *private law relationships*. Therefore, in instances of foreign exchange control law, foreign tax laws and foreign export bans, such laws will not be directly enforced by the courts, but will be suitable as defences in contractual scenarios. In other words, the issue is not the enforcement of foreign legislation and claims that are based on the foreign legislation, but the *recognition* of foreign legislation in private litigation between private subjects. In cases where a private action to enforce a contract is resisted by relying upon foreign law, English courts will give effect to the foreign legislation, even though the foreign rule is of a penal, revenue or public law nature.[488]

Thus, although from the outset it appears that penal, revenue and public laws are exceptions to the general rule that mandatory rules of the proper law are upheld by the English courts, one can see that in instances of foreign legislation being utilised in private litigation between private persons such an exception does not stand.[489]

---

483 Mann Rec des Cours 132 (1971 I) 109, 180.

484 Dicey & Morris *Conflict of Laws Vol I/12th ed* 99, */13th ed* 91, 94; Cheshire & North *Private International Law/13th ed* 110, 114; Forsyth *The role of public law* 94, 112

485 [1893] AC 150, 156 (PC).

486 Or demanded.

487 [1958] AC 301, 322 (HL).

488 See *Huntington v Attrill* [1893] AC 150, at 156 (PC) (penal laws); *Ralli Brothers Ltd v Compania Sota Aznar* [1920] 2 KB 287 (HL) (revenue laws); *Foster v Driscoll* [1929] 1 KB 470 (CA) (penal laws); *De Beeche v South American Stores Ltd* [1935] AC 148; *Zivnostenska Banka v Frankmann* [1950] AC 57; *Re Helbert Wagg & Co Ltd's Claim* [1956] Ch 323; *Regazzoni v Sethia (KC) (1944) Ltd* [1958] AC 301 (HL) (penal laws); *Kahler v Midland Ltd* [1950] AC 24.

489 Lipstein *Conflict of Public Laws* 357, 365, 361; Hartley *Foreign Public Law* 13, 26.

c Concluding remarks

The above-mentioned principles and the relevant case law may be summarised as follows:

(1) Foreign (internationally) mandatory rules are applied to foreign contracts if they form part of the governing law of the contract. Therefore, contracts that are illegal under their proper law will not be enforced in English courts, even if they are valid according to English law. The reason for the applicability is the fact that they belong to the proper law.

(2) However, in many cases where the foreign internationally mandatory rule was applied, the proper law was also the *lex loci solutionis*.[490] Therefore, some judges reached the same result - that the foreign legislation was applicable - on the basis of the *lex loci solutionis* rule. When applying foreign mandatory provisions of the proper law to a contractual relationship between private parties, the courts do not distinguish between private and public law.

(3) The principle of *non-enforcement of foreign penal, revenue and other public laws* is not an exception to the general rule that the mandatory provisions of the proper law are applicable in private litigation. Thus, in applying all rules of the proper law, the common law position differs substantially from the solution of German and Swiss case law that rejects both the enforcement and application of foreign public law in private litigation.

2 Application of a third country's internationally mandatory rules

As stated above, the general rule is that the material validity of a contract is determined by the governing law, and the mandatory rules of the *lex causae* are in principle applicable.[491] It can therefore be stated that, thus far, unless an English choice of law rule directs otherwise, the foreign law is not applied by

---

490 For instance, *Re International Trustee for the Protection of Bondholders Act* [1936] 3 All ER 407, 428 (CA); [1937] AC 500 (HL); *St Pierre and Others v South American Stores (Gath and Chaves) Ltd and Chilean Stores (Gath and Chaves) Ltd* [1937] 3 All ER 349, 352, 356; clearly *Zivnostenska Banka National Corporation v Frankmann* [1949] 2 All ER 671, at 681.

491 See supra under section 1 and Dicey & Morris *Conflict of Laws Vol II/12th ed* 1241, */13th ed* 1244; Lipstein 26 ICLQ (1977) 884, 889, 897; id *Conflict of Public Laws* 357, 362; Mann Rec des Cours 132 (1971 I) 109, 153 et seq.

the English court even if that rule is mandatory in its nature.[492] Using this principle, the English courts upheld contracts that were legal according to the proper law and the *lex fori*, but illegal according to the *lex loci contractus*, the *law of the domicile*, *residence* or *nationality* of one of the parties[493]

Nevertheless, English case law has sometimes applied or at least considered foreign mandatory rules of a legal system other than the proper law of contract, and has refused to enforce a contract that infringed the foreign legislation. In this regard, two different 'techniques' can be distinguished.[494] The first rests on *comity* and English *public policy* considerations (see **(a)** below). The second reasoning is based on the principle that a contract, which is illegal under the *lex loci solutionis* should not be enforced by the English courts (see **(c)** below). The classification of these techniques is disputed in English academic writings (see **(b)** and **(d)** below).[495]

All the cases decided were *false third country cases*, because in all cases the contract was governed by English law.[496] Nevertheless, it is debated whether the approaches of the case law are suitable for addressing *real third country cases*.

a English public policy, 'international comity' solution

Prior to the incorporation of the Rome Convention, English courts, in limited circumstances, refused to enforce contracts that were illegal in terms of a foreign law although valid according to the proper law and the *lex fori*. The decisions were based on the principle that it would be contrary to *comity* and English *public policy* if English courts were to assist in the breach of the law of

---

492 With regard to foreign 'public laws', see Forsyth *The role of public law* 94, 110; see art(s) 3(3), 5(2), 6(1) and 7 Rome Convention and art VIII (2) (b) IMF-Agreement; Dicey & Morris *Conflict of Laws Vol II/12th ed* 1241, */13th ed* 1221, 1244; Mann Rec des Cours 132 (1971 I) 109, 157, 158; see, however, Lipstein *Conflict of Public Law* 357, 365 et seq and id *Conflict of laws and public law* 38, 49, who submits a special reference (connection) to third countries' public law rules.

493 *Kleinwort, Sons & Co v Ungarische Baumwolle Industrie AG* [1939] 2 KB 678 (CA) (defendants residence); similar *Metliss v National Bank of Greece and Athens S.A.* [1957] 2 All ER 1, 3, 11; *Toprak v Finagrain* [1979] 2 Lloyd's Rep 98; *Vita Food Products Inc v Unus Shipping Co* [1939] AC 277, 292, 296 (lex contractus); see also *British Nylon Spinners v ICI* [1955] Ch 37; *Rossano v Manufacturer's Life Insurance Co Ltd* [1963] 2 QB 352; see also infra section III, 2, f.

494 See also Morse *Public Policy* England - 69 et seq.

495 The question of whether the pre-existing common law rules are still valid under present law is dealt with later in Chapter 5, IV, 5.

496 In *Royal Boskalis Westminster NV v Mountain* [1999] QB 674 the court was concerned as a kind of interlocutory question with a real third country situation, cf infra III, 2, a, (3).

a foreign and friendly country.[497] This principle was regarded as 'well established', but it is nevertheless rather nebulous and vague with respect to its *juristic basis*. Dicey and Morris state that:

> According to one of the most important rules of English public policy a contract is void which is opposed to British interests of State and, in particular, which is apt to jeopardise the friendly relations between the British government and any other government with which this country is in peace.[498]

In accordance with this rule, the courts applied or at least considered the third country's law within the scope of English public policy. The relevant cases will be discussed before analysing the content and nature of this rule as a choice of law or domestic law rule.

(1) *Foster v Driscoll*

Foster v Driscoll[499] concerned a contract between a group of English people for the supply and sale of whisky that would be smuggled into the United States and ultimately sold and consumed there, thus violating the Prohibition Laws of the United States. The plan was to purchase whisky in Scotland that would clear British customs (in the usual manner) and would then be transferred to the smugglers' boat at some place outside the United Kingdom. This plan was never executed because the smugglers fell out with each other. The contract was governed by English law.

The question before the Court of Appeal was whether the contract was unenforceable under English law because it was illegal. The majority held that the contract could not be enforced.[500] Lawrence L.J. stated that:

---

497 *De Wutz v Hendriks* (1824) 2 Bing 314; *Foster v Driscoll* [1929] 1 KB 470 (CA); *Regazzoni v K C Sethia* [1958] AC 301 (HL).

498 Dicey & Morris *Conflict of Laws Vol II/12th /13th ed* 1280, 1281; cf also Cheshire & North's *Private International Law/13th ed* 127, 585; Morse *Public Policy* England - 68.

499 [1928] All ER Rep 130; [1929] 1 KB 470 (CA). For the facts and reasoning of the case, see Hartley Rec des Cours 266 (1997) 341, 389; Kaye *The New Private International Law* 19, 20. Also see *De Wutz v Hendriks* (1824) 2 Bing 314 where a contract to raise money to assist rebellion in Crete was not enforced.

500 *Scrutton LJ* dissented, holding that the contract was valid because the parties had a back-up plan to land the whisky lawfully in Canada or some other suitable place and sell it to some third party who would smuggle it into the United States. He thus held that the direct import into the United States was not proved, at page 138 et seq. The majority thought that the fact that the contracting parties had this possibility in mind was insignificant.

> On principle however I am clearly of opinion that *a partnership formed for the main purpose of deriving profit from the commission of a criminal offence in a foreign and friendly country is illegal*, even though the parties have not succeeded in carrying out their enterprise, and no such criminal offence has in fact been committed; and none the less so because the parties may have contemplated that if they could not successfully arrange to commit the offence themselves they would instigate or aid and abet some other person to commit it. *The ground upon which I rest my judgment that such a partnership is illegal is that its recognition by our Courts would furnish a just cause for complaint by the United States Government against our Government (of which the partners are subjects), and would be contrary our obligation of international comity as now understood and recognised, and therefore would offend against our notions of public morality.*[501]

The court therefore held that the contract was illegal according to public policy because the real object and intention of the parties was to break the law of a foreign country, despite the fact that there may have been alternative modes or places of performance under which the contract could have been performed legally. The violated foreign mandatory provisions were thus applied or taken into account on the grounds of English public policy and international comity regardless of the place of performance.

(2) *Regazzoni v K C Sethia*

In the leading case *Regazzoni v K.C. Sethia (1944) Ltd*[502] an English company agreed to sell jute bags to a Swiss buyer to be delivered to Genoa. The proper law of the contract was English law. On the face of it, the contract was not contrary to the law of any country. The contract itself contained no statement about the origin and the ultimate destination of the jute bags. However, both parties knew that the only country where the jute could be obtained was India, and the seller knew that the buyer intended to resell and deliver the goods to South Africa. They also knew that at that time India operated an embargo against South Africa and that it was a criminal offence to export jute from India that was destined for South Africa. The seller failed to deliver the goods and the buyer sued in England for breach of contract.

---

501 At page 143, see also Lord J Sankey at page 147.

502 [1958] AC 301 (HL); [1957] 3 WLR 752; [1957] 3 All ER 286. For the reasoning and the facts of the case, see Hartley Rec des Cours 266 (1997) 341, 390; id Foreign Public Law 13, 25.

The House of Lords refused to enforce the contract (or to award damages for its breach), because both parties knew and intended that its performance would violate Indian law. They ruled that it was contrary to English *public policy* to enforce a contract if the parties knew that the contract would require the performance of an act in a *foreign* and *friendly*[503] country that was illegal in terms of the law of that country. Viscount Simonds stated that '[j]ust as public policy avoids contracts which offend against our own law, so it will avoid at least some contracts which violate the laws of a foreign State, and it will do so because *public policy demands that deference to international comity*.'

The reason for the application of English *public policy* was therefore held to be *international comity*. The court thus stressed again the intention of the contracting parties to break the law of a foreign and friendly country and applied the same '*comity - public policy*' principle to the case where the parties intended to require another person to perform the illegal act.

(3) Other cases

This principle was confirmed several times in *obiter dicta* by English courts and is not only valid for import or export restriction - as was seen in the cases discussed above - but also applies if the foreign laws in question are exchange control regulations, revenue laws, or penal laws.[504] The Court of Appeal referred to the principle more recently in *Royal Boskalis Westminster NV v Mountain*[505] and held that it applied where one party (the Iraqi authorities) to an

---

503 A country that is not at war with the United Kingdom, at page 318 (Viscount Simonds).

504 As was seen supra the principle of non-enforcement of foreign revenue penal or other public laws does not stand in private litigation: *Regazzoni v Sethia*, supra, at page 322, 328; *Rossano Manufacturers' Life Insurance Ins Co* [1963] 2 QB 352, 376 et seq; *Re Emery's Investment Trusts* [1959] Ch 410 where the court struck down in pursuance of this principle a contract designed to defraud a foreign revenue authority; in *Ispahani v Bank Melli Iran* [1998] Lloyd's Rep. (Bank) 133 the Court of Appeal refused to enforce banking arrangements whose object was to transfer funds out of Bangladesh in contravention of that country's exchange control laws; in *Soleimany v Soleimany* [1999] QB 785 (CA) an Israeli arbitration award that was based on a contract governed by Jewish law to export carpets from Iran in violation of Iranian export control laws was not enforced.

505 [1999] QB 674 (CA); the court was concerned with an insurance contract governed by English law, however, as an 'interlocutory matter' had to deal with an agreement governed by the law of Iraq; the facts of the case were as follows: The plaintiff, five Dutch companies, owned and operated a dredging fleet, which was insured against war risks by the defendants. The insurance contract was governed by English law. The plaintiff concluded a dredging contract with the Iraqi authorities to undertake dredging work at an Iraqi port, which was governed by the law of Iraq and provided for arbitration in Paris. The dredging work was still being performed when Iraq invaded Kuwait in

agreement governed by the law of Iraq intended that it should be performed in the Netherlands in contravention of United Nation sanctions against Iraq being in legal force in the Netherlands. With reference to the *Foster v Driscoll* and *Regazzoni v KC Sethia* cases Stuart–Smith L.J. stated that '[i]n the application of this principle it is immaterial whether the contract is governed by English or foreign law.'[506]

(4) Inapplicability of English public policy despite the violation of foreign law

In some cases the principle of English public policy was referred to but was held to be inapplicable.[507] For example, this inapplicability was based on the fact that the contracting parties did not have the '*wicked intention*' to violate or assist in violating the law of a foreign country, and on the fact that a contract is not invalidated on grounds of public policy by the mere fact that a contract involves doing something that is prohibited under foreign law (unless the mandatory rule forms part of the proper law).[508]

The situation was different in the case of *Euro-Diam v Bathurst*[509] where the violation of foreign law was intended. An English diamond merchant (Euro-

---

August 1999. As consequence the United Nations imposed sanctions against Iraq that had legal force in the Netherlands. In order to secure the demobilisation of the fleet and the repatriation of their employees the plaintiffs signed a 'finalisation agreement' with the Iraqi authorities according to which the plaintiffs had to pay large sums and had to waive all further claims under the dredging contract. The plaintiffs sought to recover the loss arising from the waived claims under the insurance contract. The court held that due to the circumstance that the finalisation agreement would be unenforceable under English law, the waiver of claims would be ineffective as defence in an English court or tribunal at the behest of the Iraqi authorities on the ground of public policy and the plaintiffs claim under the dredging contract remained unaffected (French law was presumed to be the same). Accordingly the claim to recover loss under the insurance contract could not succeed.

506 At page 691, 692; cf also *Soleimany v Soleimany* [1999] QB 785, at page 794, 795.

507 *British Nylon Spinners Ltd v Imperial Chemical Industries Ltd* [1955] Ch 37; *Euro-Diam Ltd. v Brathurst* [1990] 1 QB 1 (CA); *Howard v Shirlstar Ltd* [1990] 1 WLR 1292 (CA).

508 Dicey & Morris *Conflict of Laws Vol II/13th ed* 1281; Morse *Public Policy* England 68, 70; *British Nylon Spinners Ltd v Imperial Chemical Industries Ltd* [1955] Ch 37, at page 52; see as well *Toprak v Finagrain* [1979] 2 Lloyd's Rep 98.

509 [1990] 1 QB 1; [1988] 2 WLR 517; [1988] 1 Lloyd's Rep 228 (CA); [1987] 2 All ER 113. For the facts of the case and the reasoning, see Hartley Rec des Cours 266 (1997) 341, 393 et seq; Forsyth CLJ 1987, 404 et seq; Kaye *The New Private International Law* 20. Also see *Mitsubishi Corporation v Alafonzos* [1988] 1 Lloyd's Rep 191 where the court was concerned with an English contract to deceive a third party. The contract was

Diam) sold a consignment of diamonds to a German buyer. At the latter's request the English company provided an invoice that understated the value of the diamonds. By providing such an invoice the company must have realised that the purpose thereof was to enable the buyer to defraud the German tax authorities. The diamonds were stolen when they were still Euro-Diam's responsibility, and Euro-Diam had insured them at their true value and paid the correct premium. The question before the court was whether the infringement of German tax law rendered the insurance contract illegal, since by providing the false invoice Euro-Diam was guilty of a criminal offence under German tax law. The Court of Appeal held that it did not render the insurance contract illegal. The Court argued that although the action of Euro-Diam's managing director in issuing the false invoice was reprehensible, it had no bearing on the loss of the diamonds; furthermore, it involved no defrauding of the insurers. It was thus held to be not contrary to public policy to enforce the insurance contract.

However, the reason why the infringement of the foreign tax legislation was not contrary to English public policy was not that the violated law was foreign, but that the *relationship between the criminal offence and the insurance contract was too remote*. The court expressly rejected the argument that English public policy is not concerned with a violation of foreign law.[510] Thus, if it had been the British tax authorities that had been deceived, the result would have been the same.

Hartley assumes that if the relationship between the insurance contract and the criminal offence had been more direct, the former would not have been enforced by the English court.[511] By example he refers to a scenario that has been decided by German courts.[512] A person exports works of art from a foreign country in violation of the law of that country. The person insures them against loss and they are in fact lost. In such a case, Hartley argues that the contract would not be enforced by the English courts and the exporter would not therefore be allowed to claim under the insurance contract (since otherwise the exporter would enjoy the fruits of his illegal activity).[513]

Lastly, it should be stressed that according to the general principle of public policy, a contract made for the purpose of violating the law of a foreign country

---

held to be unenforceable *on grounds of public policy although the deceiving transaction took place abroad*. For a discussion, see Morse *Public Policy* England - 67.

510 At page 40.

511 Hartley Rec des Cours 266 (1997) 341, 393.

512 See for the similar facts BGHZ 59, 82 et seq; cf on this case Chapter 5, II, 2, d, (4).

513 Hartley Rec des Cours 266 (1997) 341, 393.

will not be considered as contrary to English public policy if the foreign law itself is contrary to English public policy.[514]

It can therefore be stated that the violation of a foreign third country's law does *not* infringe English public policy if the violation of foreign law is *not the object of the contract*, or if the *relationship between the criminal offence and the contract is so remote* that even if the rules of the forum or the proper law had been violated the contract would still be valid. Furthermore, a contract that violates foreign law will not be considered contrary to English public policy if the foreign law itself is contrary to English public policy.

(5) Application of English public policy where foreign public policy is violated, not a foreign statute

In this context another English case, *Lemanda Trading Co v African Middle East Petroleum Co*,[515] will be considered. This case concerned a contract that contravened a foreign state's public policy. Two contracts were involved. The first was between Lemanda, a Bahamas company, and African Middle East Petroleum, a United Kingdom company. The latter company wished to secure the renewal of an oil-supply contract with a state-owned oil company in Qatar. In the second contract, a lobbying contract, it was agreed that the principal shareholder in Lemanda would use his influence to help African Middle East Petroleum obtain the oil-supply contract. It was agreed that if African Middle East Petroleum obtained the contract as a result of the shareholder's efforts, it would pay Lemanda a commission. After African Middle East Petroleum obtained the contract, it refused to pay the commission, and Lemanda sued in the United Kingdom.

The question before the court was whether the 'lobbying contract' was invalid and therefore unenforceable. The court held that the contract was governed by English law, and there was evidence that under the law of Qatar the lobbying contract was contrary to public policy, but not contrary to an actual rule of law. The court then investigated whether the contract was contrary to English public policy. Under English law, contracts to secure benefits from persons in public positions are contrary to English public policy, but do not constitute criminal offences and are not contrary to a positive rule of law.[516] But the crucial

---

514 'Such as laws concerning slavery or the like', see *Regazzoni v KC Sethia Ltd* [1958] 1 AC 301, 322, 328 et seq; Dicey & Morris *Conflict of Laws Vol II/13th ed* 1281.

515 [1988] 3 WLR 735; [1988] 1 All ER 513; [1988] QB 448; about which see Hartley Rec des Cours 266 (1997) 341, 394; Collier [1988] CLJ 169 et seq; Morse *Public Policy* England - 66 et seq.

516 Hartley Rec des Cours 266 (1997) 341, 394.

question was whether it is contrary to English public policy to agree to lobby a foreign government. The court stated that although the principles underlying public policy were essential principles of morality of general application, these principles were not so weighty that they prevented the enforcement of the contract *per se,* irrespective of the attitude and the law of the country of performance. Since under the law of Qatar the lobbying contract was contrary to public policy, the court refused to enforce the contract on the grounds of *international comity*, combined with English domestic *public policy*.[517]

Thus, if the contract does not infringe a rule of positive law, but is contrary to the *public policy* of a foreign and friendly country, and would offend the English public policy on general principles of morality, the contract might nonetheless *not be enforced on grounds of international comity and English public policy*.

(6) Summary

(1) The English case law discussed above shows that English courts will give effect to a third country's internationally mandatory rules within the notion of English public policy. The decisions were based on the well established rule of English public policy that 'a contract is void which is opposed to British interests of State and, in particular, which is apt to jeopardise the friendly relations between the British government and any other government with which this country is in peace.'[518]

(2) In all decided cases the *object* and *intention* of the parties to break the law of a foreign and friendly country were essential elements of the application of this public policy rule. In the absence of such 'wicked intention' the mere fact that the contract involves doing something which is prohibited under a third country's law will not invalidate the contract on the basis of public policy.[519] However, it is not a requirement that the parties themselves intend

517 For details see Collier [1988] CLJ 169, 170 et seq; Morse *Public Policy* England - 66, 67. The authors have different opinions regarding the question of whether the judgment was based on English public policy as a rule of substantive law or conflict of laws. Morse ibid 66, 67 speaks of *ordre public* international, whereas Collier ibid 171 stresses that it is a rule of English substantive law, but nevertheless applicable regardless of the proper law.

518 Dicey & Morris *Conflict of Laws Vol II/12th ed* 1281, */13th ed* 1280.

519 *British Nylon Spinners Ltd v Imperial Chemical Industries Ltd* [1955] Ch 37; *Toprak v Finagrain* [1979] 2 Lloyd's Rep 98; Morse *Public Policy* England - 68, 70; Dicey & Morris *Conflict of Laws Vol II/13th ed* 1281; in *Royal Boskalis Westminster NV v Mountain* [1999] QB 674, 691 the principle was applied where one party intended to break the law.

to perform the illegal act; requiring another person to perform the illegal act will suffice.[520]

(3) Furthermore, the application of the public policy principle is not restricted to situations where the illegal act is performed at the place of performance; it is valid in respect of *any legal system where the illegal act is intended to take place*.[521]

(4) However, the violated foreign legislation is not taken into account if the *relationship between the criminal offence and the contract is so remote* that even if the rules of the forum or the proper law had been violated, such violation would not affect the validity of the contract.[522]

(5) It appears to be necessary that the act envisaged must be *unlawful* according to the foreign law; if it merely contravenes foreign public policy, the contract will only be invalid if it is also contrary to English public policy.[523]

(6) A contract concluded with the intention of violating a foreign law will not be considered as contrary to English public policy if the foreign law itself is contrary to English public policy.

(7) The decisions rested on *English public policy* and *international comity*. A third country's mandatory legislation was thus applied within the notion of English public policy because English public policy 'demands that deference to international comity'.

b Academic discussion of the rule of public policy and critical remarks

Although the public policy rule on which the above judgments are based is said to be well established, the *juristic basis* of the rule is nevertheless uncertain.[524] Academic statements concerning the precise categorisation of the rule are cautious,[525] and it is uncertain whether the principle, developed under pre-existing law, is still applicable under the present English conflict of laws, which

520 *Regazzoni v KC Sethia Ltd* [1958] AC 301.

521 Lipstein *Conflict of Public Laws* 357, 368; Forsyth *The role of public law* 94, 105, 106.

522 See *Euro-Diam Ltd v Bathurst* [1987] 1 QB 1.

523 *Lemenda Trading Co Ltd v African Middle East Petroleum Co Ltd* [1988] 3 WLR 735.

524 Also see Kaye *The New Private International Law* 19, 240, 241.

525 Most authors assume that it is a rule of English domestic public policy, but nevertheless it is held to be applicable to contracts governed by a foreign law. See Dicey & Morris *Conflict of Laws Vol II/12th /13th ed* 1282; see, however, Hartley Rec des Cours 266 (1997) 341, 353, 354, 388, 403.

is now based on the Rome Convention.[526] The reason for the uncertainty in categorising this '*public policy-comity rule*' may either be that a clear division between domestic and international public policy is impossible,[527] or that the rule has been clearly established only in cases where the proper law of the contract was English.

(1) The scope of this rule of public policy

Most English academics assume 'beyond doubt', that if the contract had been governed by the law of a foreign country, in terms of which it was perfectly unobjectionable, the result would have been the same, since the decisions rested on *English public policy*.[528] Nevertheless, the precise scope of the public policy rule is unclear. Is it a rule of *English domestic public policy* or of *English international public policy*? And if it is a rule of *English international public policy*, is its function viewed positively or negatively? This classification is relevant to determining the legal basis for applying the rule to real third country cases.[529] It is beyond the scope of this dissertation to discuss the concept of public policy in English domestic and international law in great depth, so a few remarks shall suffice here.

(2) Public policy in English law

Public policy is a concept applicable to both English domestic law and international law. The concept, however, does not have quite the same meaning in the two contexts.[530] Nonetheless 'it is doubtful whether a formal distinction between those two concepts exists in English private international law. Rather it is more accurate to say that public policy in a private international law context is to be more narrowly circumscribed than it is in a context which is purely internal to the forum.'[531]

---

526 Eg Hartley Rec des Cours 266 (1997) 341, 403; Collier *Conflict of Laws* 211, 212, see on this problem detailed infra under Chapter 5, IV, 5, b.

527 Cf Morse *Public Policy* England – 19.

528 Morse *Public Policy* England - 68; Collier *Conflict of Laws* 211, 212, 373; id [1988] CLJ 169, 170, 171; Dicey & Morris *Conflict of Laws Vol II/12th /13th ed* 1282 'it is probable'; Hartley Rec des Cours 266 (1997) 341, 353, 354; Cheshire & North's *Private International Law/13th ed* 585 footnote 16; cf also the statement of Stuart-Smith LJ in *Royal Boskalis Westminster NV v Mountain* [1999] QB 674 (CA), at page 691, 692: 'In the application of this principle it is immaterial whether the contract is governed by English or foreign law'.

529 With regard to the relevance of the rule under present law, see Chapter 5, IV, 5, b.

530 Morse *Public Policy* England - 19; Hartley Rec des Cours 266 (1997) 341, 385 et seq.

531 Morse *Public Policy* England - 19.

In international law the concept of public policy is used in a narrower sense. Its normal effect is the exclusion of foreign law, otherwise applicable according to the choice of law rules, if that law is held to be contrary to English international public policy (*negative function*). Conversely, international public policy can render rules of the forum applicable that would be inapplicable according to the ordinary choice of law rules (*positive function*).[532] In the English decisions that were discussed above, public policy was used to give effect to a foreign rule. Therefore, under certain circumstances, English public policy requires application of foreign mandatory rules irrespective of the proper law of the contract.[533]

(3) The juristic basis of the public policy rule

Most authors assume that the public policy rule is one of *English domestic law* and not of *private international law*.[534] According to them the concern in the decided cases was with domestic law, not choice of law. The applicable law had already been chosen, and the crucial question was merely whether the infringement of foreign law was to be treated differently from an infringement of English law as the governing law and the *lex fori*.[535] However, despite the fact that in all decided cases the proper law was English law and the public policy rule is held to be a rule of English domestic law, these authors assume that the rule operates regardless of the governing law and is thus applicable to a foreign contract.[536] Many authors simply say that the rule is based on English public policy and is therefore applicable regardless of the proper law.[537]

---

532 See Hartley Rec des Cours 266 (1997) 341, 351 et seq.

533 Also Hartley Rec des Cours 266 (1997) 341, 353.

534 Dicey & Morris Conflict of Laws Vol II/*12th /13th ed* 1282; Mann (1937) 18 BYIL 97, 109. In *Ispahani v Bank Melli Iran* [1998] Lloyd's Rep. (Bank) 133 the Court of Appeal seems to favour this interpretation without expressing a final view on that point. But see Hartley who seems to advocate that it is a rule of international public policy as well as a rule of domestic public policy, id Rec des Cours 266 (1997) 341, 353, 354, 388, 403; Cheshire & North's *Private International Law/13th ed* 586 submits that it is rule of *private international law* rather than *English domestic law*.

535 See Hartley Rec des Cours 266 (1997) 341, 388; see, however, on page 403 where Hartley states that the decisions rested on international public policy.

536 Dicey & Morris *Conflict of Laws Vol II/12th /13th ed* 1282; Hartley Rec des Cours 266 (1997) 341, 353, 354; in *Royal Boskalis Westminster NV v Mountain* [1999] QB 674 (CA), at page 691, 692 the Court of Appeal was concerned with an insurance contract governed by English law, however, as interlocutory matter referred to this principle in connection with a contract governed by a foreign law.

537 Collier *Conflict of Laws* 211; id [1988] CLJ 169, 170; Morse *Public Policy* England - 68.

The effect of this rule, however, is the application or, more cautiously, the recognition of a third country's mandatory rules. Clearly, English public policy (whether a rule of domestic or international private law) has been *extended in scope* by the English courts in order to cover the intended violation of a third country's law.

Alternatively, it may be that English case law has developed a rule of public policy that determines the circumstances or criteria under which the violation of foreign law, other than the proper law, invalidates a contract. The present author submits that the *public policy-comity rule* of English case law is a rule of English private international law rather than of domestic law. The reason for this conclusion is that the justification for the application of public policy is found in the *international comity of nations*, and this is a criterion of private international law, not English domestic law.

(4) The public policy-comity rule as special conflict rule?

The English rule may also be interpreted as a *special conflict rule* indicating the circumstances in which third countries' internationally mandatory rules can be applied (despite being formally discussed under the notion of public policy).[538] This interpretation is based on the assumption that the English public policy rule has been extended in scope so that the violation of foreign law, rather than the result of the application of foreign law, can violate the English public policy. The true concern of the rule is not the protection of the fundamental values of English law, but the violation of third countries' law and the comity of nations.

The public policy rule indicates the circumstances in which an infringed foreign law can be applied or taken into account, but the conditions are vague.[539] The foreign legislation must emanate from a foreign and friendly country, and the contracting parties must intend to violate the foreign law. Furthermore, the violated foreign legislation is only considered on the basis of public policy in

---

538 See also Basedow GYBIL 27 (1984) 109, 120, 121. Lipstein *Conflict of Public Laws* 357, 365 and Cheshire & North's *Private International Law/13th ed* 586 seem to favour this interpretation. It is however acknowledged that there appears to be no other English author who advocates this point of view. In *Ispahani v Bank Melli Iran* [1998] Lloyd's Rep. (Bank) 133 the Court of Appeal favoured an interpretation as domestic rule, however, did not express a final view on that point.

539 Also see Kaye *The New Private International Law* 240 who states that it is not quite clear whether the breach of any criminal law is sufficient or whether the law in question must be especially imperative for the principle to be invoked. Furthermore, it is uncertain what is meant by a friendly foreign country.

situations where the prohibited act took place or was intended to take place in a foreign country.[540] This latter condition could constitute a type of *connecting factor* in the sense of a 'close connection'.

Finally, the *public policy-comity rule* is only invoked where application of the foreign legislation itself does not violate the forum's *ordre public*.[541] This recourse to the public policy exclusionary rule indicates that the process of taking account of the foreign law forms part of the choice of law process and is not simply a matter of the English substantive law. If recognition of the foreign law were solely a matter for English substantive public policy, the public policy exclusionary rule could not be invoked.

It is, however, submitted that such a conflict rule differs substantially from the ordinary choice of law rules, which are based on a more neutral allocation technique. The latter takes into account the interests of the contracting parties, rather than collective state interests. The *public policy-comity* rule, on the other hand, is concerned with an evaluation of policy considerations and state interests.[542] Therefore, it is understandable that English courts settled this question within the context of (international) public policy.

If the proper law of a contract is a foreign law, it becomes evident that the rule forms part of the choice of law process and is not purely domestic. The assumption that the public policy rule is applicable irrespective of the proper law can technically be founded either upon public policy in its positive sense (eg to render a fundamental rule of English law applicable), the internationally mandatory character of the rule of English law, or characterisation as a special conflict rule.

(5) The vagueness of the public policy rule

Similar to the German and Swiss case law, where consideration of a third country's rules was based upon the notion of domestic *boni mores*, the English *public policy-comity* rule is vague and uncertain in its scope and conditions.[543]

---

[540] Cf the dictum of Viscount Simonds in *Regazzoni v KC Sethia* [1958] AC 301, 318: 'it may well be that that different considerations will arise and a different conclusion will be reached if the law of the contract is English and the contract can be wholly performed in England or at least in some other country than that whose law makes the act illegal'.

[541] See *Regazzoni v KC Sethia* [1958] AC 301, 322, 325, 328 et seq; Dicey & Morris *Conflict of Laws Vol II/13th ed* 1281; Basedow GYBIL 27 (1984) 109, 121.

[542] Such as the interest of the foreign state in the application of its law and the interest of the forum state in the assistance of a friendly country.

[543] See Kaye *The New Private International Law* 240 et seq.

The German court practice is clearer as it developed a criterion that the *interests pursued by the rule must indirectly protect German interests or interests commonly shared by all nations*. German law thus provides an indication of the circumstances in which foreign law can be considered in terms of German *boni mores*.

The scope of application of the English rule is extremely vague, because only a few requirements are specified, for example, that the prohibition must emanate from a friendly country.[544] Nonetheless, the rule could have the advantage of determining questions about when foreign law is to be applied at a conflict of laws level.[545]

c The *lex loci solutionis* rule; *Ralli Bros v Compania Naviera Sota y Aznar*

A number of authorities have suggested that under English private international law prior to the Rome Convention, the English courts would not enforce a contract, if performance thereof were illegal under *the law of the place of performance*.[546] In Dicey & Morris it is stated that in the pre-existing common law there was a principle 'a contract whether lawful by its proper law or not is, in general, invalid in so far as the performance of it is unlawful by the law of the country where the contract is to be performed (*lex loci solutionis*)'.[547]

The leading case *Ralli Bros v Compania Naviera Sota y Aznar*[548] is often said to be authority for this principle, and it is argued that the Court of Appeal adopted the principle formulated by Dicey & Morris.[549] The principle has been confirmed in a number of cases, although mostly by way of *obiter dicta*.[550] Nevertheless, some writer doubt whether this broadly stated proposition can in fact

544 Or the 'wicked intention' of the contracting parties.

545 Of course, only to the extent that one assumes that it is a rule of English private international law and not of English domestic law.

546 Forsyth *The role of public law* 94, 104 et seq; Lipstein *Conflict of Public Laws* 357, 366.

547 As exception 1 to Rule 184, Dicey & Morris *Conflict of Laws Vol II/11th ed* 1218, see also Dicey & Morris *Conflict of Laws Vol II/12th ed* 1241, 1243 et seq, */13th ed* 1246 et seq.

548 [1920] 2 KB 287 (CA).

549 Dicey & Morris *Conflict of Laws Vol II/12th ed* 1243, */13th ed* 1246; Lipstein *Conflict of Public Laws* 357, 366; for criticism, see Collier CLJ [1988] 169, 171.

550 *Foster v Driscoll* [1929] 1 KB 470, 520; *Re v International Trustee for the Protection of Bondholders* [1937] AC 500, 519; *Kleinwort, Sons & Co v Ungarische Baumwolle Industrie AG* [1939] 2 KB 678 (CA); *Kahler v Midland Bank Ltd* [1950] AC 24, 48; *Zivnostensa Banka v Frankman* [1950] AC 57, 78; *Toprak v Finagrain* [1979] 2 Lloyd's Rep 98, 114; *United City Merchands (Investments) Ltd v Royal Bank of Canada* [1982] QB 208, 228 (reversed by the HL on other points); *Lybian Arab Foreign Bank v Bankers Trust Co* [1989] 3 All ER 252; *Euro-Diam Ltd v Bathurst* [1990] 1 QB 1, 15, 30.

represent the position under English private international law before the Rome Convention and whether the *Ralli* case is authority for it.[551]

The crucial question concerns the *juristic basis* of this principle, as well as its *scope* and *content*. Is it a *subsidiary rule of conflict of laws* to be used to determine whether the contract is unenforceable by virtue of illegality in terms of the *lex loci solutionis*, as the above mentioned formulation suggests? Is it an example of the *public policy exclusionary rule* as some recent judgments may indicate? Or is it a rule of the *English domestic law* of contract that applies when English law governs the contract and holds that a contract may be frustrated by (supervening) illegality according to the place of performance? Opinion amongst commentators differs.[552] The answer, however, affects the question of whether the principle survives the Rome Convention.[553]

In contrast to the cases previously discussed that concerned contracts that were illegal in terms of the foreign law when they were concluded (*ab initio*), *Ralli Brothers v Compania Naviera Sota y Aznar*[554] concerned a contract that was concluded legally, but *subsequently* became illegal as a result of a change of law in a foreign country. A Spanish ship owner contracted with an English charterer in London to carry jute from Calcutta, India, to Barcelona, Spain. In terms of the contract, half the freight was payable in England when the ship left India, and half was payable in Spain when it arrived. The contract was governed by English law and was lawful in terms of all the relevant legal systems when it was concluded.

The ship duly left India with its cargo and the English company paid half of the freight. Before the ship reached its destination, Spain enacted price control legislation that imposed a limit on the freight, and this legislation was in force when the second instalment became due. As payment was to be made in Spain, and the contractual amount was much more than the maximum permitted (50

[551] Cf Carter BYIL 57 (1986) 1, 29 et seq; already Mann BYBIL 18 (1937) 97 et seq; Forsyth *The role of public law* 94, 104 et seq; Collier CLJ [1988] 169, 171; id *Conflict of Laws* 212, 213; Cheshire & North's *Private International law/12th ed* 518, 519, */13th ed* 601, 602.

[552] Cf Kaye *The New Private International Law* 21; Lasok & Stone *Conflict of Laws* 373 footnote 26; Collier *Conflict of Laws* 212, 213; Lipstein *Conflict of Public Laws* 357, 366; id *Öffentliches Recht* 39, 47, 48; Mann BYBIL 18 (1937) 97; Cheshire & North's *Private International Law/12th ed* 518, 519, */13th ed* 601, 602; Carter BYBIL 57 (1986) 1, 28 et seq.

[553] At least according to English academic writers, Dicey & Morris *Conflict of Law Vol II/12th ed* 1245, */13th ed* 1248 et seq. This question is discussed in connection with art 7 (1) RC.

[554] [1920] 2 KB 287 (CA). For the facts and reasoning, see Collier *Conflict of Laws* 212; Carter BYBIL 57 (1986) 1, 30; Hartley Rec des Cours 266 (1997) 341, 391, 392. For a similar decision: *Kursell v Timber Operations & Contractors Ltd* [1927] 1 KB 298 (CA).

pounds sterling instead of the permitted maximum of 10 pounds sterling per ton), payment in full would have been illegal under Spanish law. Infringement of the legislation would result in the imposition of penalties. The English charterer would not pay any more than the maximum permitted by Spanish law. An action for the balance was brought by the Spanish company in England, and failed. The English Court of Appeal rejected the plaintiff's argument that because the proper law of the contract was English law, the Spanish legislation did not justify the English company's failure to pay the full amount.

However, the *ratio decidendi* of the case is unclear.[555] Some passages in the judgment suggest that the decision was based on a conflict rule that the *lex loci solutionis* governs illegality - at least illegality of the performance aspects of the contract - alongside the ordinary conflict rules that indicate the proper law of the contract. Other passages suggest that the decision was based on a rule of English domestic law, and not private international law, because the case concerned supervening illegality, which in terms of the internal rules of English law as the proper law would constitute an event that would frustrate the contract. The court thereby treated the Spanish legislation as a frustrating event, and relied on cases that concerned supervening illegality caused by British legislation.[556]

But besides these two interpretations, there is another possible reason why reference was made to Spanish law - *the lex loci solutionis* - in the matter of illegality. In a passage of Lord Scrutton's judgment, he examined the contract and held that there was an implied term in the contract that payment was due only to that extent that it was legal in terms of the law of the country where it was to take place. He stated that:

> I should prefer to state the ground of my decision more broadly and to rest it on the ground that where a contract requires an act to be performed in a foreign country, it is, in the absence of very special circumstances, an *implied term of the continuing validity of such a provision* that the act to be done in the foreign country shall not be illegal by the law of that state.[557]

It might then be said that it was not that the internal rules of the English proper law required supervening illegality under the Spanish *lex loci solutionis* to be taken into account as a frustrating event. *As a matter of contractual con-*

---

555 See the discussion of Kaye *The New Private International Law* 20 - 22; Dicey & Morris *Conflict of Laws Vol II/13th ed* 1246 et seq; Jaffey ICLQ 23(1974) 1, 25 et seq; Carter BYBIL 57 (1986) 1, 28 et seq.

556 Such as *Metropolitan Water Board v Dick, Kerr & Co* [1918] AC 119 (HL).

557 [1920] 2 KB 287, 304.

struction, the question was whether the parties could have *intended* that the contract would be unenforceable if illegal according to the *lex loci solutionis*, or even according to any other law.[558]

Since English law was the applicable law, the court was able to use all three reasonings, and was thus able to decide that the contract was frustrated because the Spanish legislation had the effect of preventing full performance.

d The juristic basis of the *lex loci solutionis* rule

As a result of the ambiguous reasoning of the judgement, a dispute arose in academic writings concerning the *juristic basis* of the rule expressed in the *Ralli Bros* case.

(1) Conflict of laws approach

Some authors assume that the rule constitutes a *choice of law rule*: A contract that is illegal in terms of the law of the place of performance cannot be enforced by an English court (regardless of whether it is lawful in terms of the governing law or not). The prohibitive law of the place of performance is thus referred to by a special subsidiary choice of law rule, in addition to the ordinary choice of law rules indicating which law governs the contract.[559] This is the suggestion of Lipstein, who stated with reference to the *Ralli Bros* case that:

> In the sphere of contracts a special conflict rule refers to the public law [mandatory law] of the place where a contract is to be performed in order to determine as an incidental datum whether the private law relationship is prohibited by an absolute rule of the latter.[560]

---

558 For this interpretation: Kaye *The New Private International Law* 22, 23. However, Lord Scrutton's reference to an *implied term* was made at a time when the English doctrine of frustration was based on the implied term theory. This suggests that he regarded the contract as having been discharged by a frustrating event (change of Spanish law) in accordance with English law. Cf Carter BYBIL 57 (1986) 1, 30.

559 Lipstein *Conflict of Public Laws* 357, 366, 367; id *Öffentliches Recht* 39, 47, 48; Kaye *The New Private International Law* 20, 21, 22, 69; cf the German author Schulte *Eingriffsnormen* 93 et seq; according to Cheshire & North's *Private International Law/13th ed* 601, 602 it is a rule of domestic law when the proper law or the place of performance is English law, but a rule of private international law when the place of performance is foreign and yet another foreign law governs the contract; despite the formulation of Rule 177 (in the 12th ed) Dicey & Morris suggests that the rule is a rule of domestic law, see id *Conflict of Laws Vol II/12th ed* 1243, 1247, cf also ibid/*13th ed* 1249.

560 Lipstein *Conflict of Public Laws* 357, 366, 367; id *Öffentliches Recht* 39, 47, 48; more careful id *Conflict of Laws* 38, 50, 51; id ICLQ 26 (1977) 884, 898, 899.

Kaye seems to favour 'the general proposition that the *lex loci solutionis* governs illegality - at least of performance aspects of contract - alongside the proper law.'[561]

This solution would mean that the (public) prohibitive law of the *lex loci solutionis* is applicable according to a *special subsidiary conflict rule* of English private international law.[562] If the contract is illegal according to the *lex loci solutionis*, the legal consequence of the *special conflict rule* is not necessarily that the contract will be regarded as illegal by the forum. The court may possibly refer to solutions offered by the *lex causae* with regard to the legal consequences of the illegality in the place of performance, or simply regard the contract as unenforceable.[563]

The advocates of this solution do not distinguish between initial or subsequent illegality.[564] Thus, although the court in *Ralli Bros* was concerned only with a Spanish prohibition enacted after the contract was concluded, the conflict rule would most probably also cover situations where the contract is *ab initio* illegal according to the *lex loci solutionis*.

The proper law of the contract in *Ralli Bros* was English law. However, the *lex loci solutionis rule* would equally be applicable to the situation where the forum is England, the contract is governed by a foreign proper law, and is illegal according to the mandatory legislation of a third country where performance must take place. This conclusion is based on the assumption that the rule is a special subsidiary choice of law rule of the forum that refers to the *lex loci solutionis*, irrespective of the proper law of the contract designated by the ordinary choice of law rules for contracts.

(2) Substantive law approach

However, the predominant view is that the rule of *Ralli Bros* is a rule of English domestic law regarding the doctrine of frustration of contract.[565] This

---

561 Kaye *The New Private International Law* 20, 22; 23. However, he assumes that the rule cannot apply under the Rome Convention and therefore prefers Lord Scrutton's solution for construing the contractual intentions of the parties.

562 That refers to the *lex loci solutionis* in order to determine the validity of the contract.

563 See the careful formulation of Lipstein *Conflict of Public Laws* 357, 366.

564 Cf Lipstein *Conflict of Public Laws* 357, 366; Kaye *The New Private International Law* 20, 22.

565 Mann BYBIL 18 (1937) 97, 107 - 113; id Rec des Cours 132 (1971 I) 109, 158; Collier *Conflict of Laws* 212, 213; id CLJ [1988] 169, 171; Hartley Rec des Cours 266 (1997) 341, 392; Forsyth *The role of public law* 94, 105; Jaffey ICLQ 23 (1974) 1, 29; Carter

proposition is based on the fact that in *Ralli Bros* the proper law of the contract was English and on the above-cited statement of Lord Scrutton. It is said that, if read in context, the principle in *Ralli Bros* was not a principle of conflict of laws, but simply an application of *internal English rules* dealing with the 'discharge or suspension of contractual obligations by supervening illegality.'[566] The illegality under the *lex loci solutionis* was thus taken into account as *factum* by the English court in determining whether performance had become impossible.[567]

The crucial question then was simply whether the English internal doctrine of frustration of contract applied to subsequent illegality under the *lex loci solutionis*. This question was answered in the affirmative. The advocates of this approach also suggest that under pre-Rome Convention English private international law, there was no general principle that a contract, whether lawful or not by its proper law, is unenforceable because of illegality under the *lex loci solutionis*. There is no direct authority for such a proposition, however, since the proper law in all the relevant cases was English law.[568]

This approach means that the principle is only applicable if the contract is governed by English law. If the contract is governed by another foreign law, the rule would not be applicable, and the proper law must determine whether illegality under the *lex loci solutionis* is to be taken into account. Thus, if the proper law of a contract is French law and performance is illegal by another foreign *lex loci solutionis*, it is a matter for French law to determine whether illegality of performance under the law of a third country is to be taken into account.[569] In other words, if French law does not regard the contract as illegal

---

BYBIL 57 (1986) 1, 28, 30 et seq. However, at page 32 Carter submits that one effect of illegality under the *lex loci solutionis* 'should be to inhibit the availability of a remedy such as specific performance'; Dicey & Morris *Conflict of Laws Vol II/13th ed* 1249. Cheshire & North's *Private International Law/13th ed* 601, 602 distinguishes: a rule of domestic law when the proper law or the place of performance is English law, but a rule of private international law when the place of performance is foreign and yet another foreign law governs the contract.

566 Dicey & Morris *Conflict of Laws Vol II/13th ed* 1248.

567 Dicey & Morris *Conflict of Laws Vol II/13th ed* 1248; Carter BYBIL 57 (1986) 1, 30; Collier *Conflict of Laws* 212.

568 Morse *Public Policy* England - 70; Carter BYBIL 57 (1986) 1, 30; Dicey & Morris *Conflict of Laws Vol II/12th ed* 1245, 1246, 1247, */13th ed* 1246, 1247, 1248.

569 Morse *Public Policy* England - 70; Dicey & Morris *Conflict of Laws Vol II/12th ed* 1247, */13th ed* 1248; Collier *Conflict of Laws* 212, 213; Carter BYBIL 57 (1986) 1, 30 et seq; Mann BYBIL 18 (1937) 97, 107 - 113; Jaffey ICLQ 23 (1974) 1, 29.

in terms of the *lex loci solutionis*, the contract will be enforced in England.[570] However, some authors doubt whether an English court would happily order a party to perform in a foreign country if performance there is illegal.[571]

Advocates of the English internal law character of the *lex loci solutionis rule* disagree with the legal approach to another situation, namely, where a contract was illegal *ab initio* according to a foreign law and the contracting parties did not intend to break the law of that country. How are contracts that are not against English public policy, but nevertheless involve an illegal act according to the law of place of performance, to be dealt with? Some authors restrict the *lex loci solutionis rule* to supervening illegality and suggest that in such a case the contract, governed by English law, will be enforced.[572] Others argue that the consequences of initial illegality according to the *lex loci solutionis* will be identical to those consequences that arise from initial illegality according to the English domestic law of a contract that is to be performed in England.[573]

(3) Dicta in English case law

The *lex loci solutionis rule* has been confirmed several times by the English courts.[574] However, in all cases where the principle was applied the proper law was held to be the law of England, and hence there is no direct authority on the point.[575] Furthermore, the *dicta* in the judgments are ambiguous and it is not

---

570 This is in fact the crucial difference between the 'conflict of law solution' and the 'domestic law approach'. Cf Collier *Conflict of Laws* 212, 213.

571 Morse *Public Policy* England - 70; Jaffey ICLQ 23 (1974) 1, 30. According to Mann BYBIL 18 (1937) 97, 113 the contract would not be enforced in such a case on the basis of English public policy.

572 Morse *Public Policy* England - 70. Also see *Toprak v Finagrain* [1979] 2 Lloyd's Rep 98 where the court enforced a contract although it violated Turkish mandatory law.

573 Dicey & Morris *Conflict of Laws Vol II/13th ed* 1247.

574 For instance, *Kleinwort Sons & Co v Ungarische Baumwolle* [1939] 3 All ER 38, at page 42 et seq where the court expressly referred to the rule in the *Ralli case*. Also see *R v International Trustee for the Protection of Bondholders Act* [1936] 3 All ER 407, 428 (CA), [1937] AC 500, 519 (CA); *Zivnostenska Banka National Corporation v Frankmann* [1949] 2 All ER 671, at page 681; *Kahler v Midland Bank Ltd* [1950] AC 24, 48; *Metliss v National Bank of Greece and Athens S.A.* [1957] 2 All ER 1, at page 3, 11; *Toprak v Finagrain* [1979] 2 Lloyd's Rep 98, 114; *United City Merchands (Investments) Ltd v Royal Bank of Canada* [1982] QB 208, 228 (reversed by the HL on other points); *Lemenda Trading Co Ltd v African Middle East Petrolium Co Ltd* [1988] 2 WLR 735; *Lybian Arab Foreign Bank v Bankers Trust Co* [1989] 3 All ER 252, 265, 266; *Euro-Diam Ltd v Bathurst* [1990] 1 QB 1, 15, 30.

575 Morse *Public Policy* England - 70; Dicey & Morris *Conflict of Laws Vol II/12th ed* 1245, */13th ed* 1248; Carter BYBIL 57 (1986) 1, 30 et seq.

always clear whether the courts understood the principle as applicable, regardless of the proper law, or whether it was applicable because English law governed the contract.[576]

For instance, in *Kahler v Midland Bank Ltd*,[577] Lord Reid, referring to *Ralli Bros*, stated that 'the law of England will not require an act to be done in performance of an English contract if such act ... would be unlawful by the law of the country in which the act has to be done....' However, in *Zivnostenska Banka v Frankman*,[578] the same judge regarded it as settled law that '...whatever be the proper law of the contract, an English court will not require a party to do an act in performance of a contract which would be an offence under the law in force at the place where the act is to be done....' The formulation of the former statement seems to support the view that the *lex loci solutionis principle* is a rule of English domestic law and therefore only applicable if the governing law of the contract is English law. But the latter statement clearly favours the view that the rule is applicable regardless of the proper law. This would support the suggestion that the principle is a rule of English private international law, not English domestic law.[579]

There are further ambiguous dicta which allow for interpretation either as rule of English domestic law[580] or as a rule of English private international law.[581]

---

576 Morse *Public Policy* England - 70; Dicey & Morris *Conflict of Laws Vol II/13th ed* 1248.

577 [1950] AC 24, 48 et seq, [1949] 2 All ER 621; for the case, see supra section III, 1.

578 [1950] AC 57, 78 et seq, [1949] 2 All ER 671, 681; for the case, see section III, 1.

579 The equivocality of the statements is stressed by Dicey & Morris *Conflict of Laws Vol II/13th ed* 1248. For criticism about the statement of *Lord Reid* in the *Zivnostenska* case, see Carter BYBIL 57 (1986) 1, 31. However, in both cases the court was concerned with contracts governed by Czech law (according to the predominant view of the judges) that violated Czech exchange control regulations. Thus the other judges deduced the applicability of the foreign legislation from their belonging to the proper law, whereas *Lord Reid* referred to the *lex loci solutionis rule* in order to justify the application of the Czech foreign exchange control law and the refusal to enforce the contract. Also see the differing reasoning of the judges in *St Pierre and others v South American Stores (Gath and Chaves) Ltd and Chilean Stores (Gath and Chaves) Ltd* [1937] 3 All ER 349. The court was concerned with a contract governed by Chilean law, the performance of which was restricted by a Chilean mandatory exchange control regulation if the money was transferred to the United Kingdom. While *Lord Greer* applied the foreign mandatory legislation on the basis that the proper law was Chilean, *Lord Slesser* applied the mandatory law because the order to transfer would take place in Chile and nowhere else, ibid. at page 352, 356.

580 In *De Béeche and Others v South American Stores (Gath and Chaves) Ltd and Others* [1934] All ER Rep 284; at page 288 Lord Sankeys stated that 'the law of this country will not compel the fulfilment of an obligation whose performance involves the doing in a foreign country of something which the supervening law of that country has rendered it

It has been stated that 'in the light of the authorities it is not possible to reach a definite conclusion on the effect of illegality by the place of performance'.[582] In fact, the dicta differ in their wording and in all cases where the rule was applied the proper law was English law. However, it is suggested by the present author that the English courts expressed - even though these statements were only *obiter dicta* - a strong view that the *lex loci solutionis rule* is applicable regardless of the proper law and that an English court will not enforce a contract that is valid according to its foreign proper law where its performance would be illegal in terms of the *lex loci solutionis*.[583]

e Concluding remarks

The following conclusions can be reached with regard to the *lex loci solutionis rule* in English law prior to the Rome Convention.

English authors unanimously hold that if England is the place of performance, and a contract is illegal under English law, English courts will refuse to enforce the contract, despite its validity in terms of its foreign proper law.[584] Furthermore, an English court will not enforce a contract governed by English law, if the performance of the contract is illegal under the law of the place of

illegal to do'. The court was examining the impact of a Chilean mandatory prohibition on an English contract and held that performance was 'impossible'. Read in this context, the *dictum* rather refers to the principle as rule of English domestic law.

581 The dictum of Lord Diplock in *Mackender v Feldia AG* [1967] 2 QB 590 may be interpreted as favouring an interpretation as a rule of English private international law: Furthermore, [save where the illegality stems from breach of a foreign revenue law], the English court will not enforce performance or give damages for non-performance of an act required to be done under a contract, whatever be the proper law of the contract, if the act would be illegal in the country in which it is required to be performed.

582 Morse *Public Policy* England - 70; Kaye *The New Private International Law* 21; in *Ispahani v Bank Melli Iran* [1998] Lloyd's Rep. Bank 133 the Court of Appeal favoured an interpretation as English domestic law rule, however, did not express a final view on that point.

583 Besides the already mentioned dicta, cf. eg *Toprak v Finagrain* [1979] 2 Lloyd's 98; *Lemenda Trading Co Ltd v African Middle East Petroleum Co Ltd* [1988] WLR 735; *Lybian Arab Foreign Bank v Bankers Trust Co* [1989] 3 All ER 252; *Euro Diam Ltd V Bathurst* [1990] 1 QB 1. It is perhaps justified to criticise the fact that the courts referred to *Ralli Bros* as supposed authority for the *lex loci solutionis* rule being applicable regardless of the proper law; cf Cheshire & North's *Private International/12th ed* 519, */13th ed* 602; Collier CLJ [1988] 169, 171.

584 This exception to the application of the proper law is based either on the internationally mandatory character of the rule or on English public policy, see Kaye *The New Private International Law* 20; Cheshire & North's *Private International Law/13th ed* 603; Morse *Public Policy* England - 70.

performance. This situation is exemplified by the *Ralli Bros* case. It is debated in English doctrine whether the principle in the *Ralli Bros* case is a rule of private international law or merely a rule of English domestic law that is applied because English law governs the contract. However, if the contract is governed by English law, both approaches will yield the same result: The contract will not be enforced.[585]

(1) The problematic situation

It is highly controversial what will happen if a contract that is governed by one foreign law, and is illegal to the law of another country where the contract is also to be performed. The debates concerning the *juristic basis* of the *lex loci solutionis* rule are of considerable interest in this situation.[586] If it were a *conflict rule*, then the contract would not be enforced because of the English rule of conflict of laws that a contract, whether lawful by its proper law or not, may not be enforced if its performance is unlawful under the *lex loci solutionis*. If the *lex loci solutionis* rule were a rule of English domestic law, however, then the rule would be inapplicable where the contract is governed by a foreign law. It would be for the governing law to determine whether and how the illegality under the *lex loci solutionis* is to be taken into account.

As was seen above, there is no direct authority on this point, since in all cases the proper law of the contract was English. Nevertheless, as was stated above, there are frequent *dicta* attributing decisive effect to illegality under the *lex loci solutionis*, regardless of the proper law. The present author is of the opinion that the courts thereby implicitly confirmed the existence of the *lex loci solutionis* as a rule of English conflict of laws.

(2) The necessity of choice of law considerations

A final remark needs to be made concerning interpretation of the rule expressed in *Ralli Bros*. The prevailing academic view is that the principle is merely an application of the English doctrine of frustration of contracts. However, even if the court in *Ralli Bros* referred to Spanish law merely as fact within the internal

---

585 Despite the fact that the *juristic basis* of the principle is uncertain, it can be stated that 'up to this point the consequences of illegality according to the *lex loci solutionis* is covered by authority', Dicey & Morris *Conflict of Laws Vol II/12th ed* 1244, 1245, */13th ed* 1247; see also Morse *Public Policy* England - 70.

586 The question of whether the *lex loci solutionis* principle survives the Rome Convention, so that it forms a principle of current private international law, is disputed by academics and will be discussed within the context of art 7 (1) RC, Chapter 5, IV, 5, b.

English proper law doctrine of frustration of contracts, the foreign rule, and not its factual effects, is nonetheless and necessarily considered.

There are clear parallels with the German and Swiss case law solutions. The critical remarks made in that regard are equally valid here.[587] English rulings cannot be reduced, however, to those situations where the foreign state has already enforced its prohibition, and thereby rendered performance impossible for the debtor, or alternatively to cases where violation of the foreign law is sanctioned with heavy penalties, so that it would mean an undue hardship for the debtor to perform. In such cases, it is of course the *effect* of the foreign rule that is taken into account as fact.

Rather, the case law indicates that an English court will not require a party to perform a contract if its performance would be an offence under the *lex loci solutionis*. In this situation it is clearly the foreign *rule* that is taken into account. Recognition thereof within the English doctrine of frustration of contracts requires a primary choice of law. The court must determine whether there is a foreign provision that prohibits performance, whether there is a kind of connection between the contract and the foreign provision (the place of performance is such a possible kind connection) and whether the contract or the performance of the contract falls within the scope of the foreign rule. Only when these questions have been answered in the affirmative, will the question arise whether the foreign prohibition can prevent enforcement of the contract on the basis of the English doctrine of frustration.

Thus, in most cases, the prior question is which law can be applied or taken into account within the internal rules of English law. This is a matter of private international law, not internal law. It may therefore be concluded that taking account of the *lex loci solutionis* on the illegality of performance, as an incidental question, is a reference to foreign law on the main issue of the validity and enforceability of a contract. The consideration of illegality in terms of the law of place of performance, within the internal English law, thus implicitly presupposes the existence of the *lex loci solutionis rule* as an English choice of law rule.[588]

---

587 See supra under Chapter 5, II, 3.

588 Cf Kaye *The New Private International Law* 22 and Jackson *Contract Conflicts* 59, 62.

f Illegality under legal systems other than the *lex loci solutionis*, in particular under the *lex loci contractus* and the law of the parties domicile or nationality

Under pre-existing English law the mandatory rules of third countries other than the *lex loci solutionis* were not taken into account on grounds other than *comity* and *public policy*.[589] In particular, mandatory provisions that were subsequently enacted, thus leading to supervening illegality, were disregarded by the English courts.

(1) *Kleinwort Sons & Co v Ungarische Baumwolle Industrie AG*

A notorious decision in this context is *Kleinwort Sons & Co v Ungarische Baumwolle Industrie AG*,[590] a case that concerned foreign exchange controls. The case exemplifies the attitude of English courts towards the application of foreign third countries' exchange control regulations in cases where the IMF Agreement with its special provision is not applicable. Furthermore, the case shows that a subsequently enacted foreign mandatory rule is only given effect under certain limited circumstances.

The facts of the case were as follows. A Hungarian company entered into a contract with an English bank in terms of which the Hungarian company was

---

[589] As was said above the recognition of foreign mandatory rules of a law other than the *lex loci solutionis* is possible on the grounds of comity and public policy. See *Regazzoni v Sethia*, where the mandatory rule stemmed from the country from which the goods were exported and not the country of destination or final performance. The rule was nevertheless given effect because international comity so demanded, and the court refused to enforce the contract on grounds of public policy. Also see *Foster v Driscoll* where the place of performance was unclear. For the general statement, see Kaye *The New Private International Law* 23; Mann Rec des Cours 132 (1971 I) 109, 157 et seq; Forsyth *The role of public law* 94, 107 et seq; for criticism, Lipstein *Öffentliches Recht* 39, 48, 49; id *Conflict of Public Laws* 357, 367 et seq.

[590] [1939] 2 KB 678; [1939] 3 All ER 38 (CA). For the facts and the reasoning, see Hartley Rec des Cours 266 (1997) 341, 421 et seq; Jaffey ICLQ 23 (1974) 1, 25. Also see *British Nylon Spinners v ICI* [1955] Ch 37; [1953] Ch. 19 where the Court of Appeal restrained ICI from committing any such breach of contract and thus extended American anti-trust law into Britain. Also see *Toprak v Finagrain* [1979] 2 Lloyd's Rep 98 et seq, (CA) where the Court of Appeal was concerned with a contract between a Swiss seller and a Turkish buyer who intended to import the goods to Turkey. The Turkish party refused to pay on the grounds that the Turkish authorities refused to consent to the import of the goods and held that the contract was invalid according to Turkish law. The Court of Appeal, however, held that the contract - governed by English law by the choice of the parties - was valid, and disregarded the initial Turkish import restriction because the place of performance was not Turkey for the Turkish buyer (at page 114).

obliged to pay a sum of money in British currency in England. At the time the contract was concluded, it was lawful under all relevant legal systems. Before payment became due, however, Hungary introduced exchange control legislation that made it illegal for the Hungarian party to fulfil its payment. The company therefore defaulted, and the English bank sued in England.

Because the proper law of the contract was English, the court refused to allow the Hungarian party to rely on the defence that payment was prohibited by the Hungarian legislation.[591] The court referred to the principle in *Ralli Bros*[592] - that a contract which is illegal under the *lex loci solutionis* will not be enforced by English courts - and said that, if the place of payment had been Hungary, the position would have been different. Since the place of payment was England, however, this principle could have no application, and so the court refused to apply the Hungarian legislation.

Thus, it is clear that English courts will allow foreign exchange controls that do not form part of the proper law to be pleaded as a defence only *if payment is to take place in the foreign country*. If the contract, when it was concluded, had been illegal under the law of the place of payment (initial illegality), the *public policy-comity* rule in *Regazzoni v KC Sethia*[593] would possibly apply. If the exchange control regulations were imposed subsequently, it would fall under the rule in *Ralli Bros*.[594] However, apart from the *public policy-comity* rule, which is not restricted to the *lex loci solutionis*, illegality in terms of the law of a place, other than that of the place of performance, is not taken into account. The court disregarded the fact that the *debtor was situated* in Hungary, and did not consider the question of *where the contract was concluded*.[595]

Similarly, in *Libyan Arab Foreign Bank v Bankers Trust Co*,[596] the court refused to apply United States sanctions that were intended to block accounts held by Libya in London branches of the United States banks, because the deposits were governed by English law and did not require performance in the United States. The London branch could thus not refuse to return the deposits

---

591 The court's argument is in fact quite incredible, if one compares the reasoning in *Ralli Bros*, where the court rejected the argument that the foreign law was inapplicable because English law was the proper law. In both judgments, however, the true reason for application or non-application of the foreign legislation is to be found in the connection with the foreign country: the place of performance rule.

592 [1920] 2 KB 287 (CA).

593 [1958] AC 301.

594 [1920] 2 KB 287. For this interpretation, see Hartley Rec des Cours 266 (1997) 341, 422.

595 Also see *Toprak v Finagrain* [1979] 2 Lloyd's Rep 98.

596 [1989] QB 728.

on the strength of the United States legislation, despite the fact that it was a branch of a United States bank.

(2) The *lex loci contractus*

It is a well established rule in English conflict of laws that illegality in terms of the place of contracting is disregarded, and that a contract that is valid under its proper law is enforceable.[597] Thus, in the early case *Re Missouri Steamship Company*,[598] the court disregarded illegality under the *lex loci contractus*.

Vita Food Products Inc v Unus Shipping Co Ltd[599] also dealt with this question. The case concerned the liability of the respondent, a company from Nova Scotia, under certain bills of lading issued in Newfoundland. The bills of lading contained an express choice of English law. The crucial question was determining which law governed the respondent's liability for damage of the cargo. Under the law of the place of contracting, the law of Newfoundland, the bills of lading were null and void because they were not issued in accordance with the law of Newfoundland (Carriage of Goods by Sea Act 1932). Under the English proper law the bills of lading were held to be valid and liability was thus to be determined by the exemption clauses contained in the bills. The court disregarded the mandatory rules of the law of Newfoundland as *lex loci contractus* because the proper law of the contract was English law, and the bills of lading were valid according to English law.[600]

---

597 For this rule, see Forsyth *The role of public law* 94, 107; Kaye *The New Private International Law* 23; Carter BYBIL 57 (1986) 1, 29.

598 (1889) 42 Ch D 321; but Lord Halsbury stated *obiter*: 'Where a contract is void [under the *lex loci contractus*] on the grounds of immorality or is contrary to such positive law as would prohibit the making of such contract at all, then the contract would be void all over the world, and no civilised country would be called on to enforce it' (at page 336).

599 [1939] AC 277 (PC). Also see *Coast Lines Ltd v Hudig & Veder Cartering NV* [1972] 1 All ER 451, where the Court of Appeal refused to take into account mandatory Dutch legislation in respect of an English contract (a charter party), despite the fact that the contract was concluded in the Netherlands and the bills of lading were to be issued in Holland. For the facts of the case and the reasoning, see Jaffey ICLQ 23 (1974) 1, 27.

600 At that time the Hague-Visby Rules as part of English law were held to be self-limiting and in the Vita Foods case they were not held to be applicable. But see *The Hollandia* [1983] 1 AC 565, 576; Dicey & Morris *Conflict of Laws Vol II/13th ed* 1245. There is only one case indicating that a contract would be regarded as invalid if it was invalid in the place where the contract was concluded, whether lawful by its proper law or not - *The Torni* [1932] P 78 (CA). Also see *Re Missouri Steamship Co* (1889) 42 Ch. D 321, 336; but this view was disapproved of by the Privy Council in the *Vita Food* decision and much criticised. For references, see Dicey & Morris *Conflict of Laws Vol II/13th ed* 1245; Mann 18 (1937) BYBIL 97, 103 - 107

(3) *Rossano v Manufacturers' Life Insurance Co*

Another well known example in English case law is *Rossano v Manufacturers' Life Insurance Co*,[601] where the court was concerned with subsequent Egyptian legislation. Rossano, an Egyptian national, resident in Egypt, acquired life insurance policies from the defendant, a Canadian company with its head office in Toronto. The contract was concluded through the company's Cairo branch. At the time the parties concluded the contract, the agreement was lawful according to all relevant legal systems. However, many years later - but before the payment of the policies was due - Egypt enacted legislation according to which the payment of the policies without the consent of the Egyptian exchange control authorities was illegal. Rossano, then living in Italy, sued the Canadian company in London. The latter pleaded in defence that payment of the policies without the consent of the Egyptian exchange control authorities was illegal. The court, however, held that the contract was governed by the law of Ontario, and was legal according to that law. The court thus rejected the defence and recognised the creditor's right to claim the money outside Egypt.[602]

The English court thus disregarded the subsequent Egyptian legislation on the basis that the contract was governed by the law of Ontario, despite the fact that the contract was *concluded in Egypt* between the company's Cairo branch and Rossano, an *Egyptian national* and at that time *resident in Egypt*.

3 Concluding critical remarks

English courts have developed a relatively firm position with regard to the question of the application of foreign internationally mandatory rules of the *lex causae*. Such rules are applied, if they belong to the foreign proper law as indicated by the ordinary conflict rules of contracts, whether subjectively or objectively. The foreign law is applied subject to the forum's public policy, and the principle of non-enforcement of foreign revenue, penal or other public laws does not apply to private litigation.

Third countries' internationally mandatory rules are in principle neither applied nor considered as fact, subject, however, to two exceptions: the *public policy-comity* rule and illegality in terms of the *lex loci solutionis*. A contract that has the direct purpose of violating the law of a foreign and friendly country will usually be illegal under English law and not enforced. The illegality is based on

---

601 [1962] 2 All ER 214 (QB); [1963] 2 QB 352.

602 A garnishee order by the Egyptian Government in respect of tax due did not afford the debtor a defence, as this would have amounted to an indirect enforcement of the revenue law of a foreign state.

public policy because English public policy demands such deference to international comity. This rule is *not* restricted to the *lex loci solutionis*.

Furthermore, an English court will not enforce a contract (regardless of the proper law of the contract) if performance is illegal under the law of the *place of performance*. English courts however, disregard illegality in terms of the lex loci contractus, the law of the domicile, habitual residence, place of business, or nationality of the contracting parties. In these situations, internationally mandatory rules are not given effect.[603]

Although the English position seems to be relatively settled with regard to third countries' internationally mandatory rules, the legal situation is nevertheless rather vague and uncertain. In all cases where third countries' internationally mandatory rules were recognised, the proper law of the contract was English law. The courts never applied a foreign internationally mandatory rule to a contract governed by another foreign law.[604] The statements of the English courts are ambiguous and the commentators have difficulties with classifying the *juristic basis* of the principles as *conflict of law* solutions or solutions *of domestic law*.

The *juristic basis* of both principles has been discussed above. It was seen that both principles - the *public policy-comity* rule and the *lex loci solutionis* rule - result in the application or consideration of third countries' laws. However, it is not entirely clear whether these rules are principles of conflict of laws (perhaps even special conflict rules) or, alternatively, principles of English substantive law. The present author favours the interpretation that the principles are rules or, at least, principles of private international law rather than domestic law.[605] At the very least, the domestic rules and principles have to be broadened in scope so as to cover the violation of foreign law as well.

a The need for choice of law considerations

The cognizance of foreign rules as *facts* within the substantive law of the English proper law also involves a choice of law, in order to answer the question which foreign law is to be taken account of within the substantive law rules.[606] A judge will first have to decide whether there is a foreign rule

603 For criticism, see Lipstein *Öffentliches Recht* 39, 48, 49; id *Conflict of Public Laws* 357, 367, 368; also see Jaffey ICLQ 23 (1974) 1 et seq.

604 But see the situation in *Royal Boskalis Westminster NV v Mountain* [1999] QB 674.

605 See supra section III, 2, b and d, e.

606 Chapter 5, I, 7; II, 3, d; also see Kaye *The New Private International Law* 22; Jackson *Contract Conflicts* 59, 62.

claiming application, and whether the contract falls within the scope of the provision. Only afterwards can he decide whether the foreign rule renders performance impossible or invalidates the contract according to the proper law. In the view of the present author, therefore, there is not much difference between direct application of the third country's rule and recognition thereof within the substantive law rules of the proper law.

If the foreign prohibition itself does not determine the private law consequences of, for instance, the sanction of nullity, recourse must be made to the proper law rules to find how they regulate the effect of violating a prohibition (originally of the *lex causae*). It is submitted that, even if the rule is interpreted as a rule of private international law, the judge should not be bound to apply the foreign law directly, but should be granted discretion to modify the legal consequences in order to reach a fair result. Thus if the foreign rule sanctions a violation with nullity, the judge might as well alter the consequences in accordance with the proper law.[607]

A different point of view may be required if the foreign rule has either affected the legal relationship already, or if the violation is sanctioned with such heavy penalties that it would constitute an undue hardship for the debtor to perform in violation of the foreign law. In such cases, the foreign legislation affects the parties like a 'stroke of fate'. To consider the effects of these rules on the contract may mean taking the effects into account as facts, without any choice of law considerations.

b Internationally mandatory rules stemming from a law other than the *lex loci solutionis*

With regard to the consideration of third countries' internationally mandatory rules, the English decisions have been criticised. They take account only of illegality under the law of the place of performance, whereas illegality in terms of other laws, such as the law of the defendant's residence or the *lex sitae* of assets, is disregarded.[608] It has been argued that 'though real and effective in most cases, the place of performance is sometimes chosen artificially and other states may be closely affected by the execution of the obligation.'[609]

It does not follow from this statement that the illegality in terms of the law of the debtor's residence or the *lex sitae* is always to be taken into account - as

607 Also see Kreuzer *Ausländisches Wirtschaftsrecht* 79 et seq; Schwander *IPR AT* 254.

608 Lipstein *Conflict of Public Laws* 357, 367 et seq; for criticism, see Jaffey ICLQ 23 (1974) 1, 24 et seq.

609 Lipstein *Conflict of Public Laws* 357, 367.

seems to be the case with regard to the *lex loci solutionis rule*. Rather, *de lege ferenda*, choice of law criteria should be developed to take third countries' internationally mandatory rules into account. These criteria should not be restricted locally to the *lex loci solutionis*. Objective criteria can be developed, for example, a close connection between the contract and the enacting country with regard to the type of contract and the type of performance. Thus, it may mean an undue hardship for the debtor to perform in violation of the law of his habitual residence and to bear the consequences of a violation, especially when all his assets are situated there.[610] In Germany, the law of the habitual residence of the debtor when all his assets are situated there is a special exception to the principle of the non-applicability of foreign public law.[611]

The other situation in which English courts can consider a third country's internationally mandatory rules is in terms of the rule that it is against public policy to enforce a contract intended to break the law of a friendly country. Because the rule can embrace the law of any country which is friendly with the United Kingdom and which the parties intended to circumvent, it has been said to concede an excessively wide scope to foreign internationally mandatory rules.[612] However, in most cases where the rule was applied, there was a connection between the contract and the country that enacted the violated rule.[613] The public policy rule is also subject to other restrictions, such as the contracting parties having a 'wicked intention' and the relationship between the contract and violation of foreign law not being too remote.[614]

Despite the vagueness of its criteria, the *public policy-comity* rule enables the court to take into account third countries' internationally mandatory rules at a conflict of laws level. As a result, the forum can take account of the interests of the foreign state and its own interests in assisting the foreign state. Although the reason for applying the public policy rule is said to be international comity,

---

610 Lipstein *Conflict of Public Laws* 357, 367; but: *Kleinwort Sons & Co v Ungarische Baumwolle Industrie AG* [1939] 2 KB 678; *British Nylon Spinners v ICI* [1955] Ch 37; *Toprak v Finagrain* [1979] 2 Lloyd's Rep 98 et seq; *Rossano v Manufacturers' Life Insurance Co* [1963] 2 QB 352.

611 BGHZ 31, 367, 371.

612 Lipstein *Conflict of Public Laws* 357, 368.

613 *Regazzoni v KC Sethia* [1958] AC 301; see, however, *Foster v Driscoll* [1929] 1 KB 470 where it was held to be irrelevant that the parties had a back up plan to sell the whisky legally in Canada, from where a third party would smuggle it into the United States.

614 *British Nylon Spinners Ltd v Imperial Chemical Industries Ltd* [1955] Ch 37; cf also *Toprak v Finagrain* [1979] 2 Lloyd's Rep 98; Morse *Public Policy* England - 68, 70; Dicey & Morris *Conflict of Laws Vol II/12th ed* 1282, /*13th ed* 1281; *Euro-Diam Ltd v Bathurst* [1990] 1 QB 1.

other criteria are at play. In this regard it seems preferable to develop more objective criteria than, for example, the wicked intention of the contracting parties, and to make the choice of law process more transparent.[615]

c Internationally mandatory rules of the proper law

Much has been said in the previous chapters about the application of internationally mandatory rules as part of the proper law. It is questionable, however, whether all internationally mandatory rules of the proper law should be applied for the sole reason that they belong to the proper law.[616] *Kahler v Midland Bank*[617] is an example. The case has been criticised for giving extraterritorial effect to foreign public law. The plaintiff's action for delivery of shares failed because it was held that Czechoslovakian foreign exchange control affected the deposit, although the contract concerned a deposit of shares with a London bank, the shares were situated in London, and their redelivery was sought in London.[618]

Forsyth has suggested that the question of possession of the shares, like title, should have rather depended on the *lex rei sitae*.[619] Furthermore, Forsyth states that 'if incidentally, some question of contractual rights arises, that question should be resolved as an incidental question, and normally this would mean the application of either the *lex fori* or the *lex situs*, in this case both English'.[620] In other words, Forsyth appears to favour a 'special connection'. In any event the proper law should not have been applied to the question of possession which would normally be subject to the *lex situs*.

Apart from this example, the present author is of the view that the ordinary conflict rules are not suitable for rendering foreign internationally mandatory rules applicable that are based on public state interests, ie interests beyond the private interests of the contracting parties. The ordinary conflict rules, such as the choice of law or the objective allocation rules, are based on private interests

---

615 With regard to the content of the criterion 'friendly country', and what kind of rules are considered, see Kaye *The New Private International Law* 240 et seq; Jackson *Contract Conflicts* 59, 70.

616 See Chapter 5, I, 7, a, b, d. For a rare criticism of the application of all rules of the proper law amongst English authors, see Jaffey ICLQ 23 (1974) 1, 24 et seq.

617 [1950] AC 24. For the facts of the case, see Forsyth *The role of public law* 94, 110 et seq.

618 For detailed criticism, see Forsyth *The role of public law* 94, 110 et seq.

619 Forsyth *The role of public law* 94, 110 et seq.

620 Forsyth *The role of public law* 111.

and do not take into account the state's economic and political interests.[621] Therefore, internationally mandatory rules of the proper law should not be applied simply because they form part of a certain legal system, as indicated by the ordinary conflict rules.

As was explained above, strict adherence to the principle of uniformity of the law applicable to a contract may lead to odd results.[622] Internationally mandatory rules require special considerations. They should only be applied if, according to the principles of a separate conflict process, it is reasonable to give effect to them. In fact, these rules should be treated on the same basis as a third country's internationally mandatory rules. *De lege ferenda,* the choice of law considerations which should indicate the applicable mandatory rules that pursue collective state interests could be developed alongside the *Special Connection Theory*.[623] It may even be possible to extend the English *public policy-comity* rule, which consists of similar policy considerations and also requires a local connection between the transaction and the country that enacted the rule in question, to all internationally mandatory rules, whether they are part of the proper law or a third legal system. Alternatively, recourse might be made to art 7 (1) of Rome Convention, which is discussed later.[624]

Further objections have been raised to the general application of internationally mandatory rules of the proper law.[625] One example is the problem of acceptance of *renvoi*. As was explained earlier, internationally mandatory rules contain an express or implied unilateral conflict rule, alongside their material content, indicating their scope of application. This general characteristic is true of those rules belonging to the *lex fori*, and also of foreign rules. According to the general rule in private international law the initial reference of the forum's conflict rules to foreign law is final.[626] The question which has to be asked in this context is whether an English court should, in accordance with the general rule in the private international law of contracts, apply the internationally mandatory rules as part of the proper law and disregard spatial restrictions. The foreign rule will then be applied even if it does not claim application. The only situation where it could not be applied is when the 'self limitation' of the rule does not follow from the attached conflict rule alone, but from its material

---

621 See supra Chapter 5, I, 3 and 7; also see Vischer Rec des Cours 232 (1992 I) 13, 178 et seq.
622 For details, see supra Chapter 5, I, 7, a.
623 See supra Chapter 5, I, 3.
624 See Chapter 5, IV, 1.
625 For these arguments, see supra Chapter 5, I, 7, a, f.
626 See on this Lipstein ICLQ 26 (1977) 884, 892.

content, viz. the situation in question does not fall under the scope of this provision.

It has, however, been submitted that these rules should only be held applicable if they claim application, despite their belonging to the proper law.[627] In cases where the territorial scope is determined by an unilateral conflict rule and does not follow from the material content of the rule itself, recognising the spatial restriction of the foreign rule results in an acceptance of *renvoi* - a matter which is normally excluded from the ordinary choice of law process in contracts.[628]

In fact, the objections to *renvoi* are not relevant to internationally mandatory rules. These rules generally intend to pursue collective state interests and intervene in the private relationship by prohibiting certain conduct or requiring certain actions. The consequence of recognising the spatial restriction of these rules is simply that the rule is not applied as part of the proper law and the contract is not affected by it. However, the proper law still governs the contract and the problem of 'cumulation' or 'gap', or the application of a third legal system as governing law, which can arise from the acceptance of *renvoi*, are not present. Therefore it is reasonable to recognise the spatial restriction of internationally mandatory rules even if they belong to the proper law. It is therefore also preferable to subject internationally mandatory rules to a separate choice of law process. This process renders internationally mandatory rules applicable only to the extent that they claim application, and thereby accepts *renvoi*. No exception needs to be made during the ordinary conflict process, and choice of law considerations take into account the particular interests on which these rules are based.

---

627 For a discussion, see Lipstein ICLQ 26 (1977) 884, 892, 893; also see id *Conflict of Laws* 38, 48; also see supra Chapter 5, I, 1, 7, f.

628 Also see Lipstein ICLQ 26 (1977) 884, 892 et seq.

IV Foreign internationally mandatory rules under the Rome Convention and the Swiss IPRG - approaches of the legislature

In this chapter legislative attempts (by the countries under investigation) to create conflict rules regarding the application or consideration of foreign internationally mandatory rules will be examined. The discussion will therefore focus on the solution adopted by the Rome Convention since it was drafted by leading legal specialists of many countries and reflects modern approaches. The new Swiss IPRG also deserves attention, because it is a rare occasion where a national legislature developed its own choice of law rules on the issue. The Swiss approach, however, is heavily influenced by the Rome Convention. Therefore, both solutions will be presented, compared and analysed in the following section.[629]

(**1**) Firstly, art 7 (1) of the Convention and the corresponding Swiss provision, art 19, that indicate under what circumstances a third country's mandatory rule can be given effect, will be presented. (**2**) The academic debates and criticism will then be discussed, in particular, criticism of the Convention's art 7 (1), which was so strong that (**3**) the United Kingdom and Germany entered a reservation in respect thereof. In contrast, Switzerland enacted art 19 despite the strong criticism. (**4**) Then, the position of the Rome Convention and the Swiss solution with regard to the application of internationally mandatory rules of the proper law will be presented. (**5**) It will be interesting to note the impact of the Convention and, in particular, the non-incorporation of art 7 (1), on the current law of England and Germany. With regard to Switzerland, the question has to be posed whether any change has occurred as a result of the enactment of the new statutory conflict rules. (**6**) The concluding remarks will focus on the question whether the reservation to the Convention's art 7 (1) was justified.

---

629 There are further examples of special conflict rules taking cognisance of foreign mandatory laws. A well-known example is art VIII (2) (b) of the IMF Agreement 1945, which indicates the applicability of foreign exchange control regulations irrespective of the law governing the contract. This provision forms part of the law of many countries, including England, Germany and South Africa. See on this provision and its peculiarities Collier *Conflict of Laws* 370; Hartley Rec des Cours 266 (1997) 341, 423; MünchKomm/Martiny Art 34 Anh II Rn 1 et seq; also Spiro CILSA (1984) 197, 209; Forsyth *Private International Law* 301. Other examples are art 16 of The Hague Convention on the Law Applicable to Agency 1978, cf Spiro CILSA (1984) 197, 209; Erne *Vertragsgültigkeit* 159, 173; Schiffer *Normen* 142 all with further references, or art 137 of the Swiss IPRG which indicates the application of domestic or foreign anti-trust law, cf Chapter 4, III, 1, b.

1 Article 7 (1) of the Rome Convention, article 19 of the Swiss IPRG

Article 7 (1) and the corresponding Swiss provision, article 19, concern internationally mandatory rules of a country other than the proper law and the forum.[630] Article 7 (1) reads as follows:

> When applying under this Convention the law of a country, effect may be given to the mandatory rules of the law of another country with which the situation has a close connection, if and in so far as, under the law of the latter country, those rules must be applied whatever the law applicable to the contract. In considering whether to give effect to these mandatory rules, regard shall be had to their nature and purpose and to the consequences of their application or non-application.[631]

Article 7 (1) thus enables the court to give effect to a third country's mandatory rules, if the situation has a *close connection* with the third country and the rule *claims application* according to the third country's, regardless of the proper law of the contract. The judge has the *discretion* to decide whether to give effect to the mandatory rule. In deciding to give effect to the rule, the court must consider the *nature and purpose* of the rule and the *consequences* of their *application or non-application*.

Article 19 of the Swiss IPRG reads as follows:

> (1) A provision of a law, other than the one designated by this statute that is meant to be applied mandatorily, may be taken into account if and in so far as interests of a party that are according to the Swiss legal viewpoint legitimate and clearly overriding so require and the situation is closely connected to that law.

---

630 Art 7 (2) RC and art 18 Swiss IPRG refer to internationally mandatory rules of the forum state, see supra under Chapter 4, II.

631 The German version of Art 7 (1): Bei Anwendung des Rechts eines bestimmten Staates aufgrund dieses Übereinkommens kann den zwingenden Bestimmungen des Rechts eines anderen Staates, mit dem der Sachverhalt eine enge Verbindung aufweist, Wirkung verliehen werden, soweit diese Bestimmungen nach dem Recht des letztgenannten Staates ohne Rücksicht darauf anzuwenden sind, welchem Recht der Vertrag unterliegt. Bei der Entscheidung, ob diesen zwingenden Bestimmungen Wirkung zu verleihen ist, sind ihre Natur und ihr Gegenstand sowie die Folgen zu berücksichtigen, die sich aus ihrer Anwendung oder ihrer Nichtanwendung ergeben würden.

(2) Whether such a provision should be taken into account depends on its policy and the consequences for a judgment that is fair according to the Swiss concept of law.[632]

Thus, like the Convention's art 7 (1), art 19 allows Swiss courts to consider the mandatory provisions of a third legal system if the provision in question *claims application* according to the foreign legal system, the *legitimate* and *overriding interests of a party so require*, and the situation has a *close connection* with the foreign legal system. Again, the judge is granted a broad *discretion* in deciding whether to consider the foreign rule. The decision should depend on the *policy* of the foreign rule and the *consequences for a fair judgment according to Swiss law*.

The two articles are very similar, but there are nevertheless differences. Both concern only internationally mandatory rules and both use the very broad criterion of a close connection between the situation and the enacting country as the connecting factor.[633] Both rules are designed to refer to all kinds of internationally mandatory rule and all types of contracts and are thus general clauses.[634] In contrast to the Rome Convention, however, the Swiss statute introduced a further controversial condition: Foreign mandatory rules will only be considered if, according to the Swiss legal viewpoint, the legitimate and overriding interests of a contracting party so require.[635]

The wording of the provisions stipulate the following conditions for the application of third countries' mandatory rules.

---

632 (1) Anstelle des Rechts, das durch dieses Gesetz bezeichnet wird, kann die Bestimmung eines anderen Rechts, die zwingend angewandt sein will, berücksichtigt werden, wenn nach schweizerischer Rechtsauffassung schützenswerte und offensichtlich überwiegende Interessen einer Partei es gebieten und der Sachverhalt mit diesem Recht einen engen Zusammenhalt aufweist. (2) Ob eine solche Bestimmung zu berücksichtigen ist, beurteilt sich nach ihrem Zweck und den daraus sich ergebenden Folgen für eine nach schweizerischer Rechtsauffassung sachgerechte Entscheidung.

633 Philip *Recent Provisions* 241, 248, 249; Vischer Rec des Cours 232 (1992) 21, 172, 173.

634 Lehmann *Zwingendes Recht* 197. In contrast to art 7 (1), art 19 is not limited to the international law of contracts but is concerned with all fields of international law, Ungeheuer *Beachtung* 152.

635 Von Overbeck IPRax (1988) 329, 333; Vischer Rec des Cours 232 (1992) 21, 174; Ungeheuer *Beachtung* 152.

a The law of another country

Articles 7 (1) and 19 envisage recognition of mandatory rules emanating from *a law other than the proper law* of the contract and the *lex fori*.[636] Whereas this prerequisite is broadly accepted and unquestioned in the United Kingdom, it is disputed in Germany. Many authors favour an analogy or direct application to internationally mandatory rules of the *lex causae*.[637] According to them, internationally mandatory rules fall out of the scope of reference of the normal conflict rules and can only be applied if a *special conflict rule* renders them applicable. However, the approach of the Rome Convention appears to be that art 7 (1) refers to a third country's *ius cogens* only and not to those rules forming part of the proper law.[638]

Swiss authors have a similar argument regarding art 19.[639] Some adhere to the wording and insist that the rule must form part of a legal system other than the proper law.[640] In particular, those authors who favour a *special connection* of internationally mandatory rules argue that this criterion unnecessarily limits the scope of art 19 to third countries' rules.[641] It is argued that the internationally mandatory rules of the proper law serving predominantly collective state interests should be treated in the same way as third countries' rules. Therefore, art 19 should at least be applied analogously to indicate under what circumstances internationally mandatory rules are applicable.[642]

---

636 Morse YB Eur L 2 (1982) 107, 145; Jackson *Contract Conflicts* 59, 73; Droste *Begriff* 101, 116 et seq.

637 See Radtke ZverglRWiss 84 (1985) 325, 350; Kreuzer *Ausländisches Wirtschaftsrecht* 97 et seq; Martiny IPRax 1987, 277, 278; Schubert RIW 1987, 729, 736; Knüppel *Zwingendes Recht* 84, 85; Becker *Sonderanknüpfung* 58; Kleinschmidt *Anwendbarkeit* 283 et seq; Droste *Begriff* 116 et seq.

638 Martiny IPRax 1987, 277, 278; Schurig RabelsZ 54 (1990) 217, 246; Kreuzer *Ausländisches Wirtschaftsrecht* 69 et seq; Jackson *Contract Conflicts* 59, 64, 73.

639 See Morscher *Rechtssetzungsakte* 101 et seq.

640 Cf Schnyder *Wirtschaftskollisionsrecht* Rn 304; Schwander *IPR AT* 248, 249.

641 For details, see Voser *Lois d'application immédiate* 73, 79 et seq; see also Philip *Recent Provisions* 241, 247 et seq; Vischer Rabelsz 53 (1989) 438, 440, 445 et seq. Morscher *Rechtssetzungsakte* 101 et seq argues that, in so far as a foreign public law rule falls outside the scope of reference to a foreign legal system, it does not form part of the proper law and is thus another law according to art 19 IPRG.

642 Morscher *Rechtssetzungsakte* 101 et seq; Voser *Lois d'application immédiate* 73, 79 et seq.

b With which the situation has a close connection

The foreign mandatory rule can only be given effect if and to the extent that the situation has a *close connection* with the third country. In providing for a close connection between the situation and the third country, the wording of art 7 (1) and art 19 has been criticised for using vague and imprecise criteria.[643]

In general, it can be stated that a vague connection does not suffice; there must be a *substantial* or *genuine connection* with the other country and the situation.[644] Furthermore, the *Report* makes it clear that the contract *as a whole* must have a connection with the other law; a connection between only the issue in dispute and the law of the other country is not sufficient.[645] Examples provided of such genuine connections are where the contract is to be performed in that other country (*lex loci solutionis*) or where one party resides there or has his main place of business there.[646]

Academic authors who support recognition of third countries' law under certain circumstances have suggested that *special conflict rules* for certain kinds of contracts should be developed, rather than using a broad general clause. Specified criteria, depending on the type of contract, can thus be used, and the close connection criteria will therefore differ depending on the type of contract and the rules in question.[647]

c Internationally mandatory rule

A third country's mandatory rules are given effect only to the extent that, in terms of the law of the third country, they 'must be applied whatever the law applicable to the contract'. The rule must therefore be *internationally mandatory*. Article 19 is less explicit in requiring that the foreign provision

---

643 Morse YB Eur L 2 (1982) 107, 145; Schurig *Lois* 55, 75; Coing WM 1981, 810, 813; Coester ZverglRWiss 82 (1983) 1, 19 et seq. See, however, Vischer Rec des Cours 232 (1992) 21, 173 who notes slight differences concerning the *close connection*. It is true that the German version in translation reads '*close cohesion*' instead of '*close connection*'. However, there is no difference in meaning.

644 Giuliano/Lagarde Report in *Contract Conflicts* 381; Jackson *Contract Conflicts* 59, 73;

645 Giuliano/Lagarde Report in *Contract Conflicts* 381; for justified criticism, see Kaye *The New Private International Law* 254 et seq.

646 Giuliano/Lagarde Report in *Contract Conflicts* 381.

647 MünchKomm/Martiny Art 34 Rn 48, 100 et seq; Kropholler *IPR* § 52 IX 3; Schiffer *Normen* 175 et seq; Mentzel *Sonderanknüpfung* 231 et seq; Reithmann/Martiny/Limmer *Internationales Vertragsrecht* 455 et seq; contra with regard to the criterion of a close connection Lehmann *Zwingendes Recht* 223 who proposes the finding of a uniform criterion.

demands mandatory application to the situation. However, it is nevertheless interpreted as referring only to *internationally mandatory rules*.[648]

The internationally mandatory character of a foreign rule follows either from its wording, if an express term regulates its territorial scope, or from interpretation of the rule. At this point all the previously discussed difficulties arise: determining the international scope of a rule; finding a uniform definition for internationally mandatory rules; and finding criteria to distinguish them from mandatory rules in a domestic sense.[649]

With regard to foreign rules the court is also faced with the difficult task of eventually being required to interpret the law of another country in order to determine whether mandatory rules are international or domestic.[650] In cases of doubt, it has been submitted that the foreign rule should be interpreted as domestic mandatory.[651]

Nevertheless, this issue deserves a few further remarks, because some authors tend to include within the category of internationally mandatory rules those rules that are based on *socio-political considerations*, viz. rules that protect the weaker contracting party, even though the rules are simultaneously held to fall within the scope of reference of the ordinary conflict rules to the proper law.[652] This 'additional' or 'cumulative' application of third countries' protective rules is justified because of their '*double-functionality*'. They serve the fair reconciliation of the parties' interests, but also pursue the socio-political goals of the whole community.[653]

There is therefore an *inequality* in the treatment of internationally mandatory rules. Those serving predominantly state interests are excluded from the scope of reference to the *lex causae* and are connected separately in accordance with art 7 (1) and art 19. However, public law rules serving private interests are applied on the basis of the *ordinary conflict rules* as well as on the basis of a separate process of *special connection*.[654]

---

648 All commentators emphasise that the provision has to be internationally mandatory, see amongst others Schwander *IPR AT* 252. However, the wording is slightly different from that of art 7 (1) Rome Convention.

649 Supra Chapter 3, II.

650 Kaye *The New Private International Law* 253.

651 Lorenz RIW 1987, 569, 579, 581, 582.

652 Vischer RabelsZ 53 (1989) 438, 449; Schnyder *Wirtschaftskollisionsrecht* Rn 29, 77; Honsell/Vogt/Schnyder/Mächler-Erne Art 9 Rn 24.

653 For the reasoning, see Voser *Lois d'application immédiate* 59 footnotes 42, 60.

654 For this phenomenon and criticism, see Voser *Los d'application immédiate* 59, 60.

This result has been justly criticised, and the Swiss author, Voser, submits that it can be avoided. One can treat internationally mandatory rules of the proper law that mainly serve the interests of the parties on the same footing as rules serving state interests, and thus exclude them from the scope of reference of the ordinary conflict rules. Alternatively, one can restrict the *special connection* of third countries' internationally mandatory rules to those rules serving the foreign state's economic and political interests. Voser prefers the second possibility and submits that the scope of art 19 of the IPRG should be restricted to internationally mandatory rules that serve public state interests, while mandatory laws serving private interests should be applied only if they form part of the applicable law.[655]

In principle the present author supports Voser's view. However, some flexibility with regard to the definition of internationally mandatory rules may be preferable. Certain rules, although they also serve private interests, might necessarily be excluded from the scope of reference, yet others of a law other than the proper law may reasonably require application. For instance, public labour law serves public as well as private interests, and a clear demarcation is not possible. Nevertheless, these rules deserve special consideration and can be subject to a *special connection*, and might also be excluded from the scope of reference to the proper law.[656]

d Article 19: Legitimate and overriding interests of a party

In contrast to art 7 (1) of the Rome Convention, art 19 stipulates that the *legitimate* and *overriding interests of a party require* the consideration of the foreign mandatory law.[657] This condition has been the subject of controversy, because the wording of the French text differs from that of the German and Italian versions. Unlike the latter, the French text does not contain the specification that the relevant interests must be those 'of a party'.[658]

Some authors assume that the French text, as the original, should be decisive, thus arguing that the restrictive focus on the interests of a party is too narrow.[659]

---

[655] Voser *Lois d'application immédiate* 60 et seq.

[656] Voser *Lois d'application immédiate* 61 needs to make exceptions from her general rule in this regard.

[657] About this condition, see Morscher *Rechtssetzungsakte* 104 et seq; Sturm *FS Moser* 3, 17; Vischer RabelsZ 53 (1989) 438, 452 et seq.

[658] Schwander *IPR AT* 253. For the debates in the commission, see von Overbeck IPRax (1988) 329, 334.

[659] Vischer Rec des Cours 232 (1992) 21, 174; von Overbeck IPRax (1988) 329, 334; Schwander *IPR AT* 253.

Therefore, the governmental interests of the enacting country in the application of the foreign mandatory rule are also legitimate.[660] Others, however, adhere to the wording and assume that the interests of the parties are relevant, and that the interests of both contracting parties have to be taken into consideration.[661] By referring to the interests of 'a party' the legislature did not intend to restrict the legitimate and overriding interests to one party alone, but intended to emphasise that the foreign mandatory rule should not be applied against the interests of the parties.[662]

In most cases the different interpretation does not affect the outcome of the decision whether to consider a foreign rule, since one party to the contract usually has an interest in application or recognition of the foreign rule. An example of this is when performance is prohibited by the foreign law, and the debtor wants to be excused.[663]

Nevertheless, it is doubtful whether the latter interpretation is reasonable. Firstly, the different wording is the result of a mistake made during the drafting of the legislation. The French, not the German or Italian texts, was the 'original'.[664] Secondly, there are cases when it is not in the interests of the parties that a foreign rule is given effect, but according to Swiss law the foreign state has a legitimate interest in the application of its mandatory rule.[665] This is in principle acknowledged by the authors who support the German wording. However, since recognition of the foreign mandatory rule cannot - according to their point of view - be based upon art 19, they have to rely on the *ordre public*.[666] This runs counter to the aim of narrowing the scope of application of the *ordre public*, and circumvents the conditions for a consideration of third countries' mandatory laws stipulated in art 19.[667]

---

660 Schwander *IPR AT* 253 argues that sometimes the parties intended to circumvent the foreign mandatory rule. In this case the foreign rule should be applied against the interests of the parties if according to Swiss law it is legitimate and worthy of protection.

661 See Honsell/Vogt/Schnyder/Mächler-Erne Art 19 Rn 21; Morscher *Rechtssetzungsakte* 104; Ungeheuer *Beachtung* 151.

662 Ungeheuer *Beachtung* 151; Morscher *Rechtsetzungsakte* 104 et seq.

663 Von Overbeck IPRax (1988) 329, 334; Morscher *Rechtssetzungakte* 109.

664 Von Overbeck IPRax (1988) 329, 334; Vischer RabelsZ 53 (1989) 438, 453.

665 See von Overbeck IPRax (1988) 329, 334; Schwander *IPR AT* 253.

666 Morscher *Rechtssetzungakte* 109 et seq; Vischer RabelsZ 53 (1989) 438, 453.

667 Cf the complicated reasoning of Morscher *Rechtssetzungakte* 110 et seq.

e Discretion of the court

According to art 7 (1) a court 'may give effect' to the foreign mandatory rules. Article 19 similarly states that a foreign provision 'may be taken into account'. Therefore, the court is not obliged to give effect to the foreign law, but is granted a *wide discretion* to decide whether and how the foreign rule is to be given effect.[668]

(1) Evaluation of the nature and purpose and regard to consequences

Article 7 (1) provides that, when debating whether to give effect to the foreign rule the court shall have regard to the *nature* and the *purpose* of the rule and the *consequences* of its application or non-application, while article 19 (2) provides that the decision 'depends on its *policy* (purpose) and the *consequences* with regard to a *fair result according to the Swiss concept of law*'.[669]

These requirements are intended to assist judges in the exercise of their discretion. With regard to the relevance of the *nature and purpose of the foreign rule,* the *Report* states that 'the application of a mandatory rule must be justified by its nature and purpose'.[670] With regard to the *consequences of application and non-application*, the *Report* stresses the judge's power of discretion, particularly where mandatory rules of different countries conflict, and where a choice must be made between them.[671]

Similarly, when deciding whether to take into account foreign mandatory rules, a Swiss court has to determine the policy of the foreign rule and the consequence of its application. *The policy and, in particular, the result of its application must conform with Swiss concepts*. This results in a *comparison of the interests of the enacting state with those of the forum*.[672] It is assumed that at

---

668 Ungeheuer *Beachtung* 151, 152; Vischer Rec des Cours 232 (1992) 13, 173, 174; Morscher *Rechtssetzungsakte* 116 et seq.

669 With regard to the discretion see Vischer RabelsZ 53 (1989) 438, 454; Schwander *IPR AT* 254; Morscher *Rechtssetzungsakte* 124 et seq.

670 It is further stated that one delegation suggested that this question should be defined by saying that the nature and purpose of the foreign rule should be established by internationally recognised criteria. For example, similar laws exist in other countries, or they are based on generally recognised interests. This suggestion was not disapproved of but was nevertheless rejected because these international criteria did not exist and would create difficulties for courts. See *Giuliano/Lagarde* Report in *Contract Conflicts* 381.

671 *Giuliano/Lagarde* Report in *Contract Conflicts* 381.

672 Ungeheuer *Beachtung* 151, 152; Schwander *IPR AT* 253, 254 *value-judgment*; Schnyder *Das neue IPR-G* 33. This has often been compared with the American solution of *policy weighing*, see Vischer RabelsZ 53 (1989) 438, 450, 451.

least in the case of *interest-conformity* the foreign rule will be considered, as submitted by the former case law.[673]

The whole process of evaluating the *content* and *purpose* or *policy* of the foreign rule, as well as the *consequences* of its application or non-application, has often been compared with the American '*governmental interest analysis*'.[674] However, authors differ as to whether this comparison should be rejected or accepted, and they also differ with regard to the content of the interest analysis. Some authors understand this process as meaning that a 'state may have such an interest in the contractual situation ... that it has some justification for directing that its laws are to apply irrespective of the "proper" law'.[675] Others criticise the process because it means that 'in effect the court is being required to balance the interests of the States whose laws are potentially involved, but is given little guidance on how the interests are to be balanced'.[676]

The view of the present author is that there are certainly similarities with the 'governmental interest analysis' doctrine,[677] but there is nevertheless no fundamental departure from *prior* European conflict of laws. As the Report states, 'Article 7 merely embodies principles which already exist in the laws of the Member States of the Community'.[678] It has also been stressed that art 7 (1) (and likewise, art 19) is based on the German *Special Connection Theory* or on the French doctrine of *lois d'application immédiate*.[679] It is submitted that the evaluation of the nature and purpose of the foreign rule also refers to the court practice of the member states, perhaps particularly the German practice, or the Dutch *Alnati case*, to which express reference is made.[680]

As discussed above, these practices have developed criteria for taking into account third countries' internationally mandatory rules based on a valuation of their content, such as whether the rule *protects interests shared in common by*

---

673 Ungeheuer *Beachtung* 151, 152; Morscher *Rechtssetzungsakte* 108, 124 et seq; for details, see supra Chapter 5, II, 2, c, d and Erne *Vertragsgültigkeit* 12 et seq.

674 Morse YB Eur L 2 (1982) 107, 146; Williams ICLQ 35 (1986) 1, 22; similarly, Forsyth *The role of public law* 94, 107: Art 7 RC 'implies an abandonment of the traditional jurisdiction selecting method of resolving conflict problems and the adoption instead of policy based ("nature and purpose") result selecting ("consequences") techniques that have more in common with the other side of the Atlantic than the other side of the Channel'.

675 Williams ICLQ 35 (1986) 1, 22.

676 See for instance Morse YB Eur L 2 (1982) 107, 146.

677 Guedj Am J Comp L 39 (1991) 661 et seq; Vischer Rec des Cours 232 (1991 I) 9, 169.

678 Giuliano/Lagarde Report in *Contract Conflicts* 380.

679 Coing WM 1981, 810, 811; Dicey & Morris *Conflict of Laws Vol II/12th ed* 1242, */13th ed* 1245; Droste *Begriff* 104.

680 *Giuliano/Lagarde* Report in *Contract Conflicts* 380.

all nations or *shared in common by the forum state*.[681] The English *lex loci solutionis* rule and the *public policy comity* rule can also be regarded as principles in English private international law which are 'tailor-made' for the situation envisaged in art 7 (1). Both rules are based on considerations of policy and governmental interests, rather than on the traditional rigid and neutral allocation technique.

Furthermore, it has been stressed that the evaluation of the content of a foreign rule is not unfamiliar to European conflict of laws, because courts have often, within the *ordre public*, evaluated foreign rules and their content in relation to the forum law.[682] What is meant by this 'nature and purpose' criterion in art 7 (1) is a kind of '*content control*'.[683] Here it is also necessary to develop criteria and to establish through case law various guides that justify the rule's application or cognizance.[684]

(2) To give effect/to take into account

In deciding *how* to take the foreign legislation into account, the judge is neither bound to apply the foreign rule with its legal consequences directly, nor is he restricted to recognising the foreign law as fact within the domestic law of the *lex causae*.[685] Despite the broad wording, some authors either interpret art 7 (1) as leading to an application of the legal consequences of third countries' internationally mandatory rules or they insist on an application of the foreign rule nevertheless.[686]

The present author's view is that this interpretation is incorrect. The formulation 'effect may be given' can mean all kind of recognition. The judge is not obliged to apply the legal consequences of the foreign rule, but may simply take its purpose into account.[687] As has been stated, internationally mandatory rules often contain a mere prohibition, without regulating the legal consequences of a

---

681 Ungeheuer *Beachtung* 95; Kreuzer *Ausländisches Wirtschaftsrecht* 92; Hentzen RIW 1988, 808, 810; Lipstein *Conflict of Public Laws* 357, 368.

682 Erne *Vertragsgültigkeit* 197; also see Lehmann *Zwingendes Recht* 226 et seq.

683 Lehmann *Zwingendes Recht* 226 et seq; Mentzel *Sonderanknüpfung* 122; Erne *Vertragsgültigkeit* 197.

684 Also see Lehmann *Zwingendes Recht* 226 et seq; see for instance Kreuzer *Ausländisches Wirtschaftsrecht* 92; also see Lasok & Stone *Conflict of Laws* 379, 380.

685 Schiffer *Normen* 195 et seq; Erne *Vertragsgültigkeit* 197 et seq; Radtke ZVerglRWiss 84 (1985) 325, 339, 340; Coing WM 1981, 810, 811.

686 Schiffer *Normen* 196; Lehmann *Zwingendes Recht* 229; Erne *Vertragsgültigkeit* 198; for further references, see Radtke ZverglRWiss 84 (1985) 325, 339, 340.

687 MünchKomm/Martiny Art 34 Rn 55; Radtke ZVerglRWiss 84 (1985) 325, 339, 340; Coing WM 1981, 810, 811; contra Erne *Vertragsgültigkeit* 198.

violation on the private contract. In this case, recourse must be had to the substantive law rules that regulate the consequences on the private contract.

In cases where internationally mandatory rules of different legal systems conflict, or in cases where the internationally mandatory rules of a third legal system conflict with the proper law, the words 'effect may be given' grant the judge the discretion to *modify the regulation* in order to reach a *fair result* in accordance with the *proper law* and the *lex fori*. This process corresponds with the German private international law technique of *adaptation* that has been developed to resolve problems that have resulted from the choice of law process, notably, 'cumulation' or 'gap'.[688] Thus, a judge can and should develop case law rules that will take account of the peculiarities of international transactions.[689] The *Report* suggests in this regard that 'the words "effect may be given" impose on the court the extremely difficult task of combining the mandatory provisions with the law normally applicable to the contract in the particular situation in question'.[690] The Swiss academic Vischer has stated that:

> [The court must] investigate whether the contract can be enforced despite the prohibition, which consequences the non-application of the rule will have for the parties, whether the prohibition was predictable; but in particular it is of relevance whether the sanction of the foreign rule is held to be reasonable by the judge, because he affirms the purpose and aim of the rule.[691]

Article 7 of the Rome Convention and art 19 of the Swiss IPRG can therefore be called 'an attempt to combine rigid conflict rules with a flexible, result-selecting process, with the respective provisions being not [always] directly applied but rather simply taken into account'.[692]

---

688 Lehmann *Zwingendes Recht* 229; Kreuzer *Ausländisches Wirtschaftsrecht* 95; Schiffer *Normen* 195, 196; on the technique of adaptation in general, see Lipstein Rec des Cours 135 (1972 I) 99, 209; Forsyth *Private International Law* 69 et seq; Bennett (1988) 105 SALJ 444 et seq and supra Chapter 4, I, 1 and Chapter 5, I, 3, j.

689 Cf Schwander *IPR AT* 254, 255; Vischer RabelsZ 53 (1989) 438, 454; contra Erne *Vertragsgültigkeit* 198.

690 *Giuliano/Lagarde* Report in *Contract Conflicts* 381, 382.

691 Vischer RabelsZ 53 (1989) 438, 454.

692 Vischer RabelsZ 53 (1989) 438, 460.

2 Academic debates and criticism

Article 7 (1) was subjected to criticism from its first draft in 1972 to the final version, and it became the most controversial aspect of the Convention.[693] The criticism included general objections to the principle of giving effect to third countries' laws, as well as the concrete formulation of the conflict rule, which is regarded as having failed.[694] In view of the fact that art 19 is very similar to art 7 (1) it is not surprising that identical disputes arose in Switzerland. Thus the arguments in favour of and against art 7 (1) are equally valid for art 19.[695]

The idea underlying the two provisions was criticised on the ground that, by giving effect to third countries' internationally mandatory rules in particular, they will create *uncertainty*.[696] Art 7 (1) is said to be a *recipe for confusion* since courts may have to consider multiple sets of (conflicting) mandatory rules.[697] Moreover, it requires the courts to perform a task for which they are ill equipped.[698] Because proof of a whole range of potentially applicable mandatory rules might be required, the article could increase the *expense of litigation* and *delay litigation*[699] and lead to an *outrageous additional charge* to

693 Lehmann *Zwingendes Recht* 4, 171; North JBS (1980) 382, 387; Ungeheuer *Beachtung* 93; Williams ICLQ 35 (1986) 1, 23.

694 For a detailed discussion of the criticism, see Lehmann *Zwingendes Recht* 171 et seq; for an overview Erne *Vertragsgültigkeit* 162 et seq; see Droste *Begriff* 104 et seq for references; for criticism with regard to the Draft 1972, see Mann *Effect* 31 et seq; id *FS Beitzke* 607, 616 et seq; Collins ICLQ 25 (1976) 35, 49 et seq; with regard to 7 (1) Rome Convention Coester ZVerglRWiss 82 (1983) 1, 17 - 30; Kegel *FS Seidl-Hohenveldern* 243, 278; id *Schlechtriem/Leser* 111; Schurig *Lois* 55, 75; Sandrock RIW 1986, 841, 853; Hentzen RIW 1988, 508 et seq; Coing WM 1981, 810, 812; North JBL (1980) 382, 387; id *Contract Conflicts* 3, 19 et seq; Morse YB Eur L 2 (1982) 107, 145 et seq; further references: Lehmann *Zwingendes Recht* 180 et seq; Droste *Begriff* 105 footnote 103.

695 For the dispute during the legislation, see Erne *Vertragsgültigkeit* 166 et seq; Schwander *IPR AT* 252; also see Lehmann *Zwingendes Recht* 194.

696 See North JBL (1980) 382, 387; North *Contract Conflicts* 19, 20; Collins ICLQ 25 (1976) 35, 50; Coester ZverglRWiss 82 (1983) 1, 25; Coing WM 1981, 810, 813; Mentzel *Sonderanknüpfung* 129; with regard to art 19, see Mann *FS Beitzke* 607, 621; Sturm *FS Moser* 3, 21; Heini ZSR 100 (1981) 65, 75; id BDG VöR 22 (1981) 37, 43.

697 Kaye *The New Private International Law* 249; North *Contract Conflicts* 19, 20; also see Collins ICLQ 25 (1976) 35, 51; Morse YB Eur L 2 (1982) 107, 146; Coester ZverglRWiss 82 (1983) 1, 27, 28.

698 Morse YB Eur L 2 (1982) 107, 146.

699 In England it is feared that the provision might discourage potential arbitration in the United Kingdom, cf Morse YB Eur L 2 (1982) 107, 147; North *Contract Conflicts* 19, 20.

the courts. Moreover, the provision leads in certain respects to the '*acknowledgement of a foreign ordre public*', which is thus far unknown.[700]

Further objections were that art 7 (1) will lead to a *scission* of the contract and will jeopardise the *principle of uniformity of the law applicable to the contract.*[701] It unduly restricts *party autonomy*,[702] and could open the door to the *dirigisme of foreign states*,[703] which is without counterpart in pre-existing legislation or case law.[704]

Besides these general reservations about the concept of art 7 (1), the overall character of the article, the use of *vague criteria*, and the granting of a *broad discretion* to judges have led to criticism, even from authors who in principle favour a *special connection* of third countries' internationally mandatory rules.[705] In particular, the *uncertainty* following from the *vagueness* of the terms, such as '*situation*' and '*close connection*'. The provision gives no guidance in the exercise of discretion and is even designated as non-rule that transfers the decision to the judge.[706] In short, the parties to a contract cannot determine the law applicable to their transaction, because they cannot foresee how a court will decide to exercise its discretion.[707]

---

700 See the arguments of the Upper House of Parliament ('Bundesrat') which were adopted by the Federal Government and the legal committee of the Lower House of Parliament ('Bundestag') BT-Drucks. 10/504, 100, 106; cf for a discussion of these arguments Kreuzer IPRax 1984, 293; Lehmann ZRP 1987, 319 et seq; Lehmann *Zwingendes Recht* 205 et seq; Sonnenberger *FS Rebmann* 825, 826.

701 Mann *Effects* 31, 34, 36.

702 Sandrock/Steinschulte *Handbuch* Rn A 196; Coester ZverglRWiss 82 (1983) 1, 27; with regard to art 19, see Heini *FS Moser* 67, 73, 74; id ZSR 100 (1981) 65, 77; id BDG VöR 22 (1981) 37, 43.

703 Sandrock/Steinschulte *Handbuch* Rn A 196; Mann *Effect* 31, 36; for a detailed discussion of further arguments see Lehmann *Zwingendes Recht* 170 et seq; Lehmann ZRP 1987, 319, 321; Kratz *Eingriffsnorm* 96 et seq, Radtke ZverglRWiss 84 (1985) 325, 350; for the above mentioned arguments against art 19, see Heini *FS Moser* 67, 73, 74; id ZSR 100 (1981) 65, 77; id BDG VöR 22 (1981) 37, 43.

704 Sandrock/Steinschulte *Handbuch* Rn A 196; Coing WM 1981, 810, 812, 813; Morse YB Eur L 2 (1982) 107, 147 footnote 188; Mann *FS Beitzke* 607, 620; id *Effects* 31.

705 Sonnenberger *FS Rebmann* 819, 826; MünchKomm/Sonnenberger Einl Rn 60; Schurig *Lois* 55, 75; id RabelsZ 54 (1990) 217, 235; Lorenz RIW 1987, 569, 572, 580, 584.

706 Coing WM 1981, 810, 813; Coester ZverglRWiss 82 (1983) 1, 21, 29.

707 Coing WM 1981, 810, 813; Mentzel *Sonderanknüpfung* 129; Fletscher *Conflict of Laws* 170.

Nevertheless, there have been also more positive statements in favour of art 7 (1) (and the Swiss art 19) that particularly welcome the intention of the 'innovative provision'.[708] The provision has the beneficial effect of achieving *uniformity of results*, irrespective of the forum seized of the dispute, and it fulfils the need for mutual consideration of states' interests, ie *comity*.[709] It was also argued that the parties to a contract would not be exposed to contradictory rules.[710] Finally, it has been observed that art 7 (1) is not a fundamental change, but rather a codification of former court decisions and academic approaches.[711]

In principle the authors who favour art 7 (1) Rome Convention do because it serves as a good basis for further developments.[712] Earlier *legal praxis* could be criticised as *uncertain* because it used comprehensive clauses of substantive law of the *lex causae* to consider foreign internationally mandatory rules as supposed facts and thus manoeuvred issues of conflict of laws into the substantive law. Thus, the enactment of art 7 (1) served to find a uniform solution. The renunciation of such a provision would run counter to the aim of certainty in international law.[713]

---

708 Cf with regard to the Draft 1972: Drobnig *Comments* 82 et seq; Lipstein *Comments* 155, 159; Lando RabelsZ 38 (1974) 6, 33; with regard to 7 (1) RC Stellungnahme des MPI RabelsZ 47 (1983) 595, 668 et seq; Kreuzer IPRax 1984, 293 et seq; id *Ausländisches Wirtschaftsrecht* 97 et seq; Lehmann ZRP 1987, 319 et seq; id *Zwingendes Recht* 181, 205 et seq; Martiny IPRax 1987, 277 et seq; Lando CMLR 24 (1987) 159, 213; Williams ICLQ 35 (1986) 1, 30; Carter BYBIL 57 (1986) 1, 20; Basedow GYBIL 27 (1984) 109, 140, 141; Kaye *The New Private International Law* 257; Jackson *Contract Conflicts* 59, 72 et seq; Lasok & Stone *Conflict of Laws* 378 et seq; with regard to art 19: Neuhaus RabelsZ 43 (1979) 277, 287 et seq; Schwander *IPR AT* 250; generally positive with regard to a 'special connection': Schwander *Lois* 316 et seq; Bär *Kartellrecht* 192 et seq, 214 et seq, 225 et seq; Voser *Lois d'application immédiate* 50 et seq, 69 et seq

709 Lehmann ZRP 1987, 319, 321; Drobnig *Comments* 82, 83; Lando CMLR 24 (1987) 159, 213.

710 Drobnig *Comments* 82, 83.

711 Carter BYBIL 57 (1986) 1, 20; Jackson *Contract Conflicts* 59, 62; Basedow GYBIL 27 (1984) 109, 140, 141; Kreuzer *Ausländisches Wirtschaftsrecht* 98, 99; MünchKomm/Martiny Art 34 Rn 45; von Bar *IPR Bd I* Rn 267; see the *Giuliano/Lagarde* Report in *Contract Conflicts* 380.

712 Lehmann ZRP 1987, 319, 321; Kreuzer IPRax 1984, 293, 295; cf the approach of Münch Komm/Martiny Art 34 Rn 48,103; also see Lasok & Stone *Conflict of Laws* 378 et seq.

713 Von Bar *IPR Bd I* Rn 265, 266; Kreuzer IPRax 1984, 293, 295; Lehmann ZRP 1987, 319, 320, 321; Schurig RabelsZ 54 (1990) 217, 242; Mentzel *Sonderanknüpfung* 131, 141; also see Jackson *Contract Conflicts* 59, 74, 75; Kaye *The New Private International Law* 257; for art 19, see Keller/Siehr *IPR* 277, 550, 551; also see Ungeheuer *Beachtung* 148; also see Siehr *FS Keller* 485, 507, 508.

To the claim that art 7 (1) constitutes an additional burden on the courts, it is argued that arts 5 and 6 of the Convention have the same effect. Moreover, the problem is less serious than asserted, as there will usually be only a few foreign mandatory provisions under consideration and these will appear from the party's pleadings.[714]

With regard to the argument that art 7 (1) will lead to recognition of a foreign *ordre public*, the solution adopted by former case law similarly led to such a recognition.[715]

3 Reservations to article 7 (1)

The anxieties about art 7 (1) resulted in a right of reservation being given under the Convention, so that a Member State would not be required to apply it (art 22 (1) (a) of the Convention). The United Kingdom made this reservation when it signed the Convention.[716] Germany did not exercise the right on signing the Convention, and the draft of the new EGBGB therefore contained an incorporation of art 7 (1) in art 34 (1).[717] This provision, however, was not retained in the final draft of the EGBGB due to the doubts of the Upper House of Parliament ('Bundesrat')[718] and the extensive criticism by German commentators. In addition, Germany made a reservation with regard to art 7 (1) pursuant to art 22 (1) (a) of the Convention.[719]

The question that must be posed is whether the fact that art 7 (1) is not in legal force in the United Kingdom and Germany has any impact on their laws. Do the former case law solutions survive the Convention? How can the legislative gap be closed?

---

714 Lehmann ZRP 1987, 319, 321; Jackson *Contract Conflicts* 59, 75.

715 Lehmann ZRP 1987, 319, 321; Kreuzer IPRax 1984, 293, 295. It was further stated that the decision whether effect is to be given to foreign legislation in international contracts is a question of conflict of laws and must be made by the forum, not left to the foreign *lex causae*. Cf Schwander *IPR AT* 251, 252; id *Lois* 362, 372; Bär *Kartellrecht* 157.

716 North *Contract Conflicts* 1, 20; Morse YB Eur L 2 (1982) 107, 147.

717 BT-Drucks 10/504, 20.10.1983, 34.

718 The Federal Government and the legal committee of the Lower House of Parliament ('Bundestag') endorsed this point of view, cf. BT-Drucks. 10/504, 100, 106; cf Sonnenberger *FS Rebmann* 825, 826; Kreuzer IPRax 1984, 293.

719 For criticism, see Kreuzer IPRax 1984, 293, 294; Lehmann ZRP 1987, 319 et seq.

4 Internationally mandatory rules of the proper law

According to the Rome Convention and the Swiss IPRG are internationally mandatory rules of the proper law automatically applicable?

a The Rome Convention

The Rome Convention does not regulate *expressis verbis* the applicability of internationally mandatory rules of the proper law. The Convention's art 7 (1) and (2) refers only to rules of the forum state and those of a third country. The predominant point of view assumes, therefore, that according to the Convention the internationally mandatory rules of the proper law are applied as part of the law applicable to the transaction.[720]

Only a few authors think differently. The German academic Kegel, for instance, assumes that *public law rules* fall outside the scope of reference of the normal conflict rules, and outside the scope of private international law in general. He holds that, if the drafters of the Convention intended to include public enactment within the scope of reference, they should have stipulated this statutorily.[721] However, most authors think that this opinion is erroneous. They say that, if the drafters intended to *exclude* public law rules they would have regulated this expressly.[722] Particularly in respect of art 7 (1) and (2) that refers to the forum's and a third country's internationally mandatory rules, it cannot be assumed that the drafters did not intend to regulate application of the rules emanating from the proper law.[723]

In England the applicability of internationally mandatory rules of the proper law is so generally accepted as correct that the issue is often not even mentioned in the context of internationally mandatory rules.[724]

---

720 Kreuzer *Ausländisches Wirtschaftsrecht* 69, 70; Siehr RabelsZ 52 (1988) 41, 71, 73; Schubert RIW 1987, 729, 736; Lehmann ZRP 1987, 319; Martiny IPRax 1987, 277, 278; Radtke ZverglRWiss 84 (1985) 325, 350; Knüppel *Zwingendes Recht* 84, 85; Becker *Sonderanknüpfung* 58; Dicey & Morris *Conflict of Laws Vol II* 1241; Lasok & Stone *Conflict of Laws* 372; Lando CMLR 24 (1987) 159, 213;

721 Kegel *Schlechtriem/Leser* 111; Droste *Begriff* 117 et seq, 122, 123; Philip *Contract Conflicts* 81, 85.

722 See Jackson *Contract Conflicts* 59, 64; Kreuzer *Ausländisches Wirtschaftsrecht* 73.

723 Kreuzer *Ausländisches Wirtschaftsrecht* 73; id *Schlechtriem/Leser* 105; Schubert RIW 1987, 729, 736.

724 Or the following type of statement is made: Mandatory rules of the law which governs the contract under the Convention of course apply by virtue of the general principle of the conflict of laws that a statute forming part of the governing law of the contract will normally be applied: by ... art(s) 8 and 10 Rome Convention questions relating to such

The Rome Convention thus results in what was above called the *Combination Theory*: The application of internationally mandatory rules forming part of the proper law on the basis of the normal conflict rules indicating the governing legal system, and recognition of third countries' internationally mandatory rules on the basis of a special connection process in accordance with art 7 (1).[725]

Despite the Convention, it is debated in Germany whether the scope of reference of the normal conflict rules to a foreign legal system is all-embracing, or whether rules that pursue predominantly the foreign state's interests are excluded from the scope of reference.[726] The crucial question is whether Germany is bound by the Convention to apply internationally mandatory rules of the proper law as part of the proper law. This question will be discussed in the forthcoming section that examines the impact of the Rome Convention on the present legal situation in Germany and England.

b Article 13 of the Swiss IPRG

Article 13 of the new Swiss IPRG contains a rule that determines the scope of the reference to the foreign applicable law:

> Die Verweisung dieses Gesetzes auf ein ausländisches Recht umfaßt alle Bestimmungen, die nach diesem Recht auf den Sachverhalt anwendbar sind. Die Anwendbarkeit einer Bestimmung des ausländischen Rechts ist nicht allein dadurch ausgeschlossen, dass ihr ein öffentlich-rechtlicher Charakter zugeschrieben wird.[727]

The second sentence of this article provides that reference to a foreign law includes public law rules. The Swiss legislature thus enacted a rule addressing an area that had formerly been controversial. As was seen above,[728] it was uncertain whether the scope of reference of the conflict rules included foreign

---

matters as validity of the contract or its performance can be affected by mandatory rules of the governing law. Cf Dicey & Morris *Conflict of Laws Vol II/12th ed* 1241, */13th ed* 1244; Hartley ELR 4 (1979) 236, 240; Lasok & Stone *Conflict of Laws* 372.

725 Schubert RIW 1987, 729, 736; Kreuzer *Ausländisches Wirtschaftsrecht* 69 et seq; id *Schlechtriem/Leser* 89, 105; MünchKomm/Martiny Art 34 Rn 40; Radtke ZVerglRWiss 84 (1985) 325, 350.

726 See only Droste *Begriff* 116 et seq; MünchKomm/Martiny Art 34 Rn 40 et seq.

727 The scope of reference to a foreign law includes all rules that are applicable to the situation according to the designated law. The application of a foreign rule is *not excluded by the mere fact* that it is supposed to be of a *public law-character*.

728 Chapter 5, I.

public law rules or rules predominantly serving the economic and political interests of the foreign state.[729]

The intention of the legislature was obviously to reject the *strict* non-application of foreign public law rules on the basis of the *principle of territoriality*, as was submitted by early Swiss case law and by some academic authors.[730] This doctrine is therefore clearly superseded.[731]

However, despite the second sentence of art 13 the question of whether the scope of reference includes all rules of public law is still controversial.[732] By using the expression 'nicht allein dadurch ausgeschlossen' ('not excluded by the mere fact'), the wording of the statute is vague and lends itself to a variety of interpretations.[733] The former arguments about this issue are therefore still upheld by academics. Thus, the crucial questions are how this sentence is to be interpreted and whether there has been any change to the earlier situation.

5 Impact on the law in Germany, England and Switzerland

The issue addressed in this section is the impact of the reservation to the Convention's art 7 (1) on the present legal situation in England and Germany. Another question that must be posed is whether Members of the Rome Convention are obliged to apply internationally mandatory rules of the proper law for the sole reason that they form part of the proper law.

a Germany

(1) Closing the loophole

How is the loophole resulting from the reservation to art 7 (1) to be closed? According to the prevailing opinion, in exercising its power of reservation in

---

729 See Voser *Lois d'application immédiate* 50 et seq; Keller/Siehr *IPR* 488 et seq.

730 Morscher R*echtssetzungakte* 86; for Swiss case law, see Chapter 5 II, 1, d.

731 Morscher *Rechtssetzungsakte* 86.

732 Cf Vischer Rec des Cours 232 (1992) 21, 178 et seq; id RabelsZ 53 (1989) 438, 441 et seq; Voser *Lois d'application immédiate* 50 et seq, 76 et seq; Honsell/Schnyder/Vogt/ Mächler-Erne Art 13 Rn 15 et seq; Schwander *IPR AT* 248; Morscher *Rechtssetzungsakte* 85 et seq; Ungeheuer *Beachtung* 146.

733 Honsell/Vogt/Schnyder/Mächler-Erne Art 13 Rn 17; Vischer RabelsZ 53 (1989) 438, 441.

respect of art 7 (1), the German legislature did not express a fundamental refusal to apply a third country's mandatory rules.[734]

It has been argued that the objections were directed against the actual formulation of the conflict rule and not against a special connection at all. The problem remained unregulated and closing the *conscious loophole* was left to academics and the courts. Therefore the long-standing controversy about whether and how third countries' internationally mandatory rules can be given effect is still relevant.[735]

German academic approaches have shown that the predominant point of view favours a recognition of third countries' internationally mandatory rules on the basis of a special connection. However, this recognition should not be based on a broad general clause covering all kind of contracts, rules and possible situations, but on *special conflict rules* that have to be *de lege ferenda* developed for each particular field of law, with due regard to the type of contract and the nature of internationally mandatory rules typically intervening in this type of contract.[736]

German case law seems to adhere to both of its former solutions. In a judgment in 1994,[737] the Federal Supreme Court was concerned with the question of whether a contract governed by the law of the Federal Republic of Germany was illegal because the contracting parties, one of whom was resident in the GDR at the time of contracting, concluded the contract without the permission of the relevant authority of the GDR. Contracts that were concluded in violation of the state monopoly of the GDR were null and void.

The court stated that according to established principles of German case law foreign internationally mandatory rules pursuing economic and political interests of the foreign state can only be recognised if that state has the power to enforce its law. Otherwise, the foreign legislation can only be considered as fact

734 Martiny IPRax 1987, 277, 279; Sonnenberger *FS Rebmann* 825, 826; Soergel/von Hoffmann Art 34 Rn 2; Schurig RabelsZ 54 (1990) 217, 235; Hentzen RIW 1988, 508, 509; Sandrock RIW 1986, 841, 852; Lorenz RIW 1987, 569, 581; Droste *Begriff* 109; Schiffer *Normen* 210.

735 Sonnenberger *FS Rebmann* 825, 826; Soergel/von Hoffmann Art 34 Rn 2; Schurig RabelsZ 54 (1990) 217, 235; Hentzen RIW 1988, 508, 509; Lorenz RIW 1987, 569, 581; Sandrock RIW 1986, 841, 852; Remien RabelsZ 54 (1990) 431, 462. Contra: Piehl RIW 1988, 841 et seq.

736 See supra Chapter 5, I, 3.

737 BGH 17.11.1994 BGHZ 128, 41 et seq.

within the substantive law rules of the German *lex causae*. In this case the court rejected both the application of the foreign rule and its cognisance as fact.[738]

(2) Scope of reference of the normal conflict rules

With regard to the question of whether internationally mandatory rules of the proper law are applicable for the sole reason that they form part of that law, the Rome Convention could not end the long-standing debate about the scope of reference of the normal conflict rules. As was stated above, the predominant opinion assumes that the creators of the Convention presumed that public law rules serving the state's interests are also referred to by the normal conflict rules and are thus applicable.[739]

Nevertheless, the question of whether the scope of reference of the conflict rules also refers to internationally mandatory rules pursuing economic and state political interests of the foreign country is still avidly discussed. Only a few authors feel bound by the legislative intention of the Rome Convention.[740] Most presuppose an *unconscious* loophole that again has to be closed by literature and case law.

The general objection to the application of internationally mandatory rules of the proper law is that the normal conflict rules of the Convention such as arts 3 and 4 are based on private interests and do not take public interests into account. Internationally mandatory rules pursuing economic and state political interests are therefore not rendered applicable by the normal conflict rules, but their application has to be determined by special conflict rules independently of the proper law. It has been suggested that either art 7 (1) Rome Convention or the principles developed for third country's mandatory rules should be applied by analogy.[741]

---

738 BGH 17.11.1994 BGHZ 128, 41, 52, 53.

739 See Radtke ZverglRWiss 84 (1985) 325, 350; Kreuzer *Ausländisches Wirtschaftsrecht* 72; MünchKomm/Martiny Art 34 Rn 40; Martiny IPRax 1987, 277, 278; Schubert RIW 1987, 729, 736; Knüppel *Zwingendes Recht* 84, 85; Becker *Sonderanknüpfung* 58; Kleinschmidt *Anwendbarkeit* 284 et seq; Kegel *Schlechtriem/Leser* 111; Droste *Begriff* 117 et seq, 122, 123.

740 For instance Becker *Sonderanknüpfung* 58, 74 et seq.

741 MünchKomm/Martiny Art 34 Rn 41; Schurig RabelsZ 54 (1990) 217, 244 et seq; Kleinschmidt *Anwendbarkeit* 288 et seq; Kreuzer *Ausländisches Wirtschaftsrecht* 97; Kropholler *IPR* § 52 IX 3; Droste *Begriff* 116 et seq, 123, 124; Schubert RIW 1987, 729, 745.

b England

In contrast to Germany, the application of internationally mandatory rules of the proper law is broadly accepted in England, as it was prior to the Rome Convention.[742] With regard to the question of whether third countries' internationally mandatory rules can be considered, a dispute arose as to whether the former case law solutions survive the Rome Convention.

(1) Does the *public policy-comity* rule survive the Rome Convention?

Most English authors think that the cases in which foreign law was taken into account on the basis of English public policy and comity exemplify the situation envisaged in art 7 (1).[743] They also consider that the *public policy-comity* principle is subsumed under art 7 (1), not only in cases where the proper law is English, but also in *real* third country cases, where the proper law is that of a foreign country.[744] However, since England entered a reservation to the article, it cannot be used as basis for the continued application of the English *public policy-comity* principle.

Which provision of the Rome Convention, then, can be used to accommodate the principle? Academic views differ. Most authors assume that the English *public policy-comity* rule can be covered by art 16 of the Convention.[745] However, this article performs in essence the 'negative function' of *ordre public*, as it is concerned with the refusal to apply an objectionable foreign law. It does not have a 'positive function', in terms of which a third country's rule should be applied.[746]

---

742 See supra Chapter 5, III, 1.

743 Hartley Rec des Cours 266 (1997) 341, 403; Cheshire & North's *Private International law/12th ed* 504, */13th ed* 584, 586; but cf Morse YB Eur L 2 (1982) 107, 147 footnote 188.

744 Collier *Conflict of Laws* 211; also see Hartley Rec des Cours 266 (1997) 341, 403.

745 Collier *Conflict of Laws* 211, 212; Lasok & Stone *Conflict of Laws* 372, 373; Cheshire & North's *Private International Law/12th ed* 504, */13th ed* 585, 586, 600.

746 Cf Hartley Rec des Cours 266 (1997) 341, 403; this fact is acknowledged by Cheshire & North *Private International Law/12th ed* 504, */13th ed* 585, 600. Collier rejects the argument that in this situation the effect of the public policy application is to include foreign rules (positive function) rather than to exclude them (negative function). He submits that in the situation where the contract is governed by a foreign law and the mandatory rule of a third country is applied on the basis of public policy considerations (and for that reason the contract is not enforced by the English court) public policy is being used to *exclude* the rule of the foreign proper law that makes the contract valid. The law of the third country is treated as fact that produces a situation where it would be contrary to public policy to apply the rule of the proper law. Cf Collier *Conflict of Laws* 211, 212. This interpretation may be possible, however, it is submitted that the English cases refer to the principle in

The *public policy-comity* principle, as expressed in cases like *Regazzoni v KC Sethia*, indicates the circumstances in which a foreign law, that would otherwise be inapplicable, is applied or considered by an English court. Thus, the English principle has a positive function, which is not contemplated by art 16. It is therefore doubtful whether the English principle could be applied under art 16 in cases where the proper law is not English law.[747]

Hartley prefers art 7 (2) of the Convention as a legal basis. This article authorises the court to apply internationally mandatory rules of the forum. His opinion is that the principle expressed in cases like *Regazzoni v KC Sethia* is one of English domestic law that is internationally mandatory and therefore applicable according to art 7 (2), regardless of the proper law of the contract.[748]

This argument seems irrefutable if Hartley's assumption is correct that the principle expressed in cases like *Regazzoni v KC Sethia* is *domestic law*. However, if the principle were an internationally mandatory rule of England, alongside its material content, it would contain a unilateral conflict rule indicating the circumstances in which it applies. The rule expressed in *Regazzoni v KC Sethia* would then form an internationally mandatory rule on the legal basis of which foreign internationally mandatory rules of a friendly country are considered under certain circumstances.

In the view of the present author, the whole of this debate is misguided. There is no reason why the previous common law solution should not continue to exist under the Rome Convention. Although art 7 (1) was said to be tailor-made for

---

another sense: The reason for the application of the public policy principle is found in comity. It is, thus, not a question of whether the proper law is contrary to public policy and therefore inapplicable, but rather a question of under what circumstances English public policy demands the application of a third country's law. The issue is a positive and not a negative one. Furthermore, Collier's argument omits the fact that the decision about whether the foreign mandatory provision creates a factual situation that would render the application of the proper law as being against public policy is already a conflict of law decision. The first step of the examination is whether or not to recognise a foreign third country's rule. This decision is the primary question that has to be answered. Only afterwards the impact on the applicable proper law can be pertinent. For criticism, see Kaye *The New Private International Law* 76 and supra Chapter 5, III, 2, b.

747 The present author's view is that the application of the English rule can also not be based upon art 16 in situations where the contract is governed by English law.

748 Hartley Rec des Cours 266 (1997) 341, 403; in *Ispahani v Bank Melli Iran* [1998] Lloyd's Rep (Bank) 133 (CA) Robert Walker LJ stated 'These principles are, it seems, part of English law of contract (as opposed to part of English law of conflict) and as such are unaffected by the Rome Convention. But it is unnecessary to express any final view on that point.'

these situations, it was not enacted by the British legislature. The legislature purposely did not regulate this matter with the result that there is a *conscious loophole* in the current conflict of laws of contracts, as in Germany. The English courts may now close the gap by using common law rules derived from former cases. This solution seems preferable to adapting the *public policy-comity* principle to a conventional provision that was not designed to cover the situation.

(2) Does the *lex loci solutionis* rule survive the Rome Convention?

According to English academics, the question whether the *lex loci solutionis principle* survives the Rome Convention is dependent on the role or nature of the principle under pre-existing law, viz. its *juristic basis*.

If it is regarded merely as a rule of English internal law, thus providing indirect recourse to the *lex loci solutionis* via the internal rules of English law (or the internal rules of another proper law if it exists) regulating frustration or impossibility of performance, then the principle is held to allow for the operation of the *lex loci solutionis* within the regime of the Rome Convention. According to some authors, this is because the *lex loci solutionis* is merely taken into account by English domestic law as the governing law *after* the choice of law process has been followed.[749]

If the proper law of the contract is English law, some authors reach this result by virtue of arts 8 and 10 (1) (b) and (d) of the Rome Convention.[750] When the proper law of the contract is the law of a foreign country and the contract is to be performed there, then the effect of arts 8 and 10 is that the rules rendering performance illegal are applicable on the basis of their belonging to the proper law. Conversely, when the contract is governed by a foreign law and illegal according to the English place of performance, it is held that the English forum

---

749 Dicey & Morris *Conflict of Laws Vol II/12th ed* 1245, */13th ed* 1248, 1249; Kaye *The New Private International Law* 21; Collier *Conflict of Law* 213; in Cheshire & North's *Private International Law/13th ed* 601, 602, 603 it is distinguished: a rule of domestic law when the proper law is English, but a rule of private international law when the place of performance is foreign and yet another foreign law governs the contract; in *Ispahani v Bank Melli Iran* [1998] Lloyd's Rep (Bank) 133 the CA favoured an interpretation as domestic law principle without expressing a final view on that point.

750 Cheshire & North's *Private International Law/12th ed* 519, */13th ed* 601; Kaye *The New Private International Law* 21; Collier *Conflict of Laws* 213.

will refuse to enforce the contract on the basis of art 7 (2) of the Convention, or on the basis of public policy.[751]

However, if the contract is governed by a foreign law and valid according to that law, but is illegal according to the law of yet another foreign country where performance is to take place, the finding of an appropriate rule becomes difficult. Some authors assume that art 7 (1) of the Convention would have governed that situation and rendered the mandatory rules of the *lex loci solutionis* applicable. However, because art 7 (1) is excluded from United Kingdom law, it is argued that English courts do not have the discretion to apply such foreign law.[752] Others assume that art 10 (2) would be the appropriate rule to render the *lex loci solutionis* applicable. It has, however, been vigorously argued that the 'manner of performance' is a fairly narrow category and it would not be possible to regard it as an issue covering cases where performance as a whole is illegal.[753]

Others rely on art 7 (2) of the Rome Convention in referring to illegality under a foreign *lex loci solutionis*. The *lex loci solutionis rule* is then held to be mandatory notwithstanding a foreign applicable law.[754] However, it has been argued that if the place of performance is outside England, the *lex loci solutionis principle* cannot itself be regarded as a mandatory rule of English law.[755]

It has even been suggested that art 16 of the Convention should be applied to regulate illegality of the place of performance.[756] But it is not likely that a contract governed by foreign law that becomes illegal by the law of the place of performance would be regarded as contrary to public policy. And it is not likely that a foreign contract that is *ab initio* illegal according to the foreign law would

---

751 Cheshire & North *Private International Law/12th ed* 520, */13th ed* 603; Dicey & Morris *Conflict of Laws Vol II/12th ed* 1246, */13th ed* 1249.

752 Cheshire & North *Private International Law/12th ed* 520, */13th ed* 602, 603; Dicey & Morris *Conflict of Laws Vol II/12th ed* 1246, */13th ed* 1248, 1249.

753 Cheshire & North's *Private International Law/12th ed* 520, */13th ed* 602; Kaye *The New Private International Law* 21.

754 See Kaye *The New Private International Law* 21, 69.

755 Dicey & Morris *Conflict of Laws Vol II/12th ed* 1246, */13th ed* 1249.

756 Lasok & Stone *Conflict of Laws* 373. Also see the tendency in English case law to describe the *lex loci solutionis* rule as being rooted in the notion of public policy *Toprak v Finagrain* [1979] 2 Lloyd's Rep 98, 107; *Euro-Diam Ltd v Bathurtst* [1987] 1 Lloyd's Rep 178, 187, [1987] 2 All ER 113, 120; Cheshire & North's *Private International Law/12th ed* 520, */13th ed* 602, 603 with further references on this point.

be held to violate English public policy if the parties contracted in ignorance of the prohibition.[757]

If the *lex loci solutionis principle* forms a *choice of law rule* of English private international law, English writers argue that it would not be possible under the Convention's regime to take cognisance of illegality under the *lex loci solutionis*, since art 7 (1) is not in legal force in the United Kingdom.[758]

According to the present authors view it can be referred to what was stated above regarding the survival of the *public policy-comity* rule under the regime of the Rome Convention that is equally valid for the *lex loci solutionis* rule. If the *lex loci solutionis* rule really is a principle of private international law, and thus implicitly contains a choice of law rule as has been submitted, the exclusion of art 7 (1) from English law may mean that the legislature did not intend to regulate this matter. Then English courts should close a *conscious loophole* by developing principles and choice of law rules so as to determine when effect can be given to third countries' internationally mandatory rules. The *lex loci solutionis* principle could constitute such a conflict rule.

c Switzerland

Unlike the United Kingdom and Germany, Switzerland has enacted a choice of law rule with regard to the applicability of third countries' mandatory provisions: art 19 of the Swiss IPRG. Furthermore, the new Swiss IPRG contains in the second sentence of art 13 a regulation of the scope of reference to foreign law. However, what is the impact of these provisions on the current Swiss legal situation and has there been any change?

(1) Article 19: A special connection of third countries' internationally mandatory rules

In view of the long-standing academic debates concerning the question of whether and how third countries' internationally mandatory rules can be given effect, it is not surprising that art 19 was fiercely debated amongst scholars.[759] Nevertheless the Swiss legislature decided to enact a conflict rule that enables a

[757] The position is different where the parties intended to break the law of a foreign and friendly country, see Dicey & Morris *Conflict of Laws Vol II/12th ed* 1246, */13th ed* 1249 and Cheshire & North's *Private International Law/12th ed* 520, */13th ed* 602, 603.

[758] Kaye *The New Private International Law* 22; Dicey & Morris *Conflict of Laws Vol II/13th ed* 1248; Cheshire & North's *Private International Law /13th ed* 602, 603.

[759] For the academic discussion, see Chapter 5, I.

Swiss court to give effect, on a discretionary basis. to third countries' internationally mandatory rules at the level of conflict of laws.

The authors who favoured the *Schuldstatuts-theory* criticise art 19.[760] According to this theory, the governing law is applicable comprehensively and exclusively, and mandatory rules of a third country are not applied at the conflict of laws level, but are taken into account as supposed facts in the substantive rules of the *lex causae*. This doctrine, however, can be regarded as superseded by the enactment of art 19.[761] Even before the new Swiss IPRG entered into force the general legal trend was in favour of a *special connection* of foreign internationally mandatory rules.[762] Those who supported this approach welcomed the enactment of art 19.[763]

The enactment of art 19 is generally interpreted as meaning a change of former Swiss case law.[764] As was seen above, Swiss courts in principle did not apply third countries' internationally mandatory rules on the basis of a *special connection*.[765] In contrast, internationally mandatory rules were refused application by reference to their *public law* nature, the principle of *territoriality* or the Swiss *ordre public*.[766] Moreover, Swiss courts seldom considered third countries' mandatory laws within the substantive law of the *lex causae*.[767]

Article 19 makes it possible for a judge to recognise foreign legislation at the level of conflict of laws. In addition, judges are free as to how to give effect to the foreign legislation and are not bound by the solutions offered by the

---

760 Mann *FS Beitzke* 607, 623; Heini 100 ZSR (1981) 65, 75; id BerDVöR 1982, 37 et seq.

761 Voser *Lois d'application immédiate* 73.

762 For this development, see Voser *Lois d'application immédiate* 50 et seq, 55; *Vischer* and *Schnyder*. Both were originally advocates of the '*proper law doctrine*', the changed their minds and now favour a '*special connection*' of foreign internationally mandatory provisions, see Vischer Rec des Cours 232 (1992) 21, 178 et seq; id RabelsZ 53 (1989) 438 et seq; Schnyder *Wirtschaftskollisionsrecht* Rn 34 et seq, 301; see also Morscher *Rechtssetzungsakte* 55 et seq, 85 - 89, 101 et seq; Voser *Lois d'application immédiate* 50 et seq, 57. Other authors favouring a special connection are Bär *Kartellrecht* 271 et seq; Schwander *Lois* 322 et seq.

763 Schwander *IPR AT* 249 et seq; Erne *Vertragsgültigkeit* 199 et seq; Vischer Rec des Cours 232 (1992) 21, 165 et seq; id RabelsZ 53 (1989) 438; 448 et seq; Siehr *FS Keller* 485, 507, 508; Schnyder *Wirtschaftskollisionsrecht* 243 et seq; Honsell/Vogt/Schnyder/ Mächler-Erne Art 19 Rn 10 et seq with further references.

764 See Schwander *IPR AT* 251, 252; Honsell/Vogt/Schnyder/Mächler-Erne Art 19 Rn 5, 12.

765 Swiss courts expressly rejected a special connection BGE 76 II 33 et seq; see Schwander *IPR AT* 251 for further references.

766 Honsell/Vogt/Schnyder/Mächler-Erne Art 19 Rn 5; Erne *Vertragsgültigkeit* 12 et seq.

767 See Erne *Vertragsgültigkeit* 12.

substantive law of the *lex causae*. Lastly, it should be mentioned that the effect of art 19 will probably be a more frequent recognition of foreign internationally mandatory legislation. Switzerland, in contrast to Germany and England, used to be much more reluctant to take such legislation into account.

(2) Influence of art 13 sentence 2 of the Swiss IPRG

As was noted in the discussion of Swiss case law prior to the IPRG, the courts distinguished between foreign public law rules of the *lex causae* that served *primarily collective interests of the foreign state*, on the one hand, and foreign public law that *protected the interests of individuals* and *supplemented foreign private law*, on the other. Application was allowed only for the latter, while the former were not applied on the basis of the *principle of territoriality*.[768] The Swiss courts had thus already deviated from early case law and had abandoned the strict *non-application of foreign public laws*.[769]

Thus, the strict principle of *non-applicability of foreign public law* was already no longer supported by the former case law. Does the distinction between different *kinds* of public law rules of the Swiss courts, however, survive the new Swiss IPRG? The question of the application of foreign public internationally mandatory rules of the *lex causae* has not been decided by the courts since the IPRG came into legal force. However, some judgments have been concerned with this problem and certain tendencies have become apparent: The Federal Tribunal has decided in unreported cases that foreign public law rules are applicable in so far as they *serve private law interests*.[770] It can therefore be assumed that the former legal practice concerning public law rules serving the *interests of individuals* will be upheld.[771]

With regard to foreign public laws of the *lex causae* that serve mainly the *collective interests of the state*, there is only an *obiter dictum* from the Federal Tribunal.[772] The case concerned a loan agreement governed by Chilean law, and the question was whether a Cuban foreign exchange restriction was applicable to the contract. The court rejected application of the foreign exchange restriction, and held *obiter* that if Cuban law had been the proper law the foreign exchange restriction would not have been applied either. The Court acknowledged that the IPRG is less averse to application of foreign public law

768 Chapter 5, II, 1, d; BGE 80 II 53, 61; 83 II 312, 319; 95 II 109, 114; 107 II 489, 492.
769 See Chapter 5, II, 1, d.
770 Decisions of the Federal Tribunal of 3.12.1991 and 23.4.1992. For these cases, see Honsel/Vogt/Schnyder/Mächler-Erne Art 13 Rn 18.
771 Also see Honsel/Vogt/Schnyder/Mächler-Erne Art 13 Rn 18.
772 BGE 118 II 348 et seq.

than the former jurisdiction, but public law rules can nevertheless not be recognised (in private litigation) if and to the extent that they serve to enforce claims of a foreign states' power.[773]

Thus, it seems reasonable to conclude that the Swiss case law will most probably adhere to its former solutions. According to this assumption, sentence two of art 13, which states that the public law character of a foreign rule does not *per se* preclude its application, must *be interpreted* so that public law rules serving the interests of the contracting parties are rendered applicable by the normal conflict rules, whereas internationally mandatory rules of public law pursuing mainly interests of the foreign state are not applied via the ordinary choice of law rules.[774] But this is only an assumption; it has not yet been established by case law.

Swiss academic literature is still debating the long-standing issue about the scope of the reference to a foreign legal system. The second sentence of article 13 did not end the controversy since its wording is too broad to be definite and thus leaves room for interpretation. Therefore, the 'old' arguments are still relevant under current law. In general one can see that the authors who favoured a certain approach uphold their arguments despite the new regulation in art 13.[775]

Swiss academics who previously favoured the *Schuldstatuts-theory*[776] feel affirmed by the legislature's introduction of the second sentence of art 13 into the IPRG. They submit that under current law the reference to the foreign legal system includes all public law rules.[777] Some authors in Switzerland favour the

---

773 BGE 118 II 348, 353. However it should be noted that the reasoning of the court is also based on the *ordre public* reservation, see Honsel/Vogt/Schnyder/Mächler-Erne Art 13 Rn 22 et seq.

774 For a similar interpretation of the case law, see Voser *Lois d'application immédiate* 66 et seq N 74, 55 et seq; but see also the interpretation of Honsell/Vogt/Schnyder/Mächler-Erne Art 13 Rn 22 et seq.

775 However the principle of *non-applicability of foreign public law* cannot be sustained under art 13, which is regretted by Sturm *FS Moser* 3, 14 et seq.

776 Heini 100 ZSR (1981) 65 et seq; cf for references Vischer RabelsZ 53 (1989) 438, 447 footnote 29. See on this approach Chapter 5, I, 1.

777 See also Sturm in *FS Moser* 3, 15, 16. Sturm himself favours the solution of the Swiss case law and proposes that at least public law rules that serve economic interests of the foreign should not be applied because of the *principle of territoriality*;. However, since the introduction of art 13 IPRG he regrets that the Swiss judge is obliged to apply foreign public law.

Combination Theory.[778] These authors feel bound by the legislature's decision to enact art 13. The advocates of this approach interpret the second sentence of art 13 to mean that the scope of reference to foreign law includes all rules, both private and public.[779] The only possible means of avoiding the application of the foreign rule is the forum's *ordre public.*[780]

However, other academics favour a *special connection* process for foreign internationally mandatory rules, particularly public law rules. These authors argue that the choice of law rules for contracts designate the law which regulates the conflicting private interests between the parties, but they do not take into account the proper scope of the state enactment, which intervenes in the private relationship in the public interest.[781] As was seen above,[782] according to these authors only public law rules that serve predominantly the interests of private parties are included in the reference to the foreign law and therefore applicable if they belong to the proper law.[783] Whereas public law rules that have no direct relation to private law are beyond the scope of reference to the foreign legal system. They are subject to a different conflict of law process, which is independent from whether the foreign rule belongs to the proper law or to a third legal system.[784]

As a result of this approach, the second sentence of art 13 must be interpreted so that the scope of reference to the foreign law does not include public law rules

778 For a detailed discussion of this theory, see supra Chapter 5, I, 4; Erne *Vertragsgültigkeit* 201 et seq, 209; Schwander *IPR AT* 248; Schnyder *Wirtschaftskollisionsrecht* Rn 303; id *Das neue IPRG* 29, 30, 35; Siehr RabelsZ 52 (1988) 41, 73 et seq; 93 et seq; Honsell/Vogt/Schnyder/Mächler-Erne Art 13 Rn 23, 24. According to the latter author the scope of reference to the proper law should also include public law rules subject to the forum's *ordre public*. But the same author submits that in considering whether the foreign rule violates the public policy, the judge should use the conditions of art 19 IPRG by analogy.

779 Schnyder *Das neue IPR-G* 29, 30, 35; Schnyder *Wirtschaftskollisionsrecht* Rn 304; Schwander *IPR AT* 248, 249; Honsell/Vogt/Schnyder/Mächler-Erne Art 13 Rn 23.

780 However, this is the fundamental difference from the *Schuldstatuts-theory*, the application of third countries' internationally mandatory rules on the basis of a *special connection* is not excluded. Third countries' mandatory provisions are applicable if and in so far the conditions of art 19 IPRG are fulfilled. Cf the detailed discussion of this inter pretation of art 13 s 2 and art 19 IPRG, Voser *Lois d'application immédiate* 73, 83 et seq.

781 Vischer Rec des Cours 232 (1992) 21, 179; id. RabelsZ 53 (1989) 438, 441, Voser *Lois d'application immédiate* 51 et seq, 69 et seq; Morscher *Rechtssetzungsakte* 88.

782 Supra Chapter 5, I, 3.

783 Vischer Rec des Cours 232 (1992) 21, 179, 180 et seq; id RabelsZ 53 (1989) 438, 440 et seq, 443, 445; Morscher *Rechtssetzungsakte* 88; Voser *Lois d'application immédiate* 53; Bär *Kartellrecht* 310, 311.

784 Vischer Rec des Cours 232 (1992) 21, 181; id RabelsZ 53 (1989) 438, 445; Morscher *Rechtssetzungsakte* 88, 89; see Chapter 5, I, 3.

that serve mainly state interests.[785] It is therefore held that art 19 of the IPRG should apply (at least by analogy) to these public law rules of the proper law.[786] These rules are thus only applied or considered if the conditions stipulated in art 19 are fulfilled, despite their belonging to the proper law.

In conclusion it can be stated that, although Switzerland has enacted a statute concerning the scope of reference to foreign law, the question of the application of foreign internationally mandatory rules of the *lex causae* remains open. It is unanimously held that the doctrine of *non-applicability of foreign public law* cannot be sustained under the current law. But, apart from this, opinions differ concerning the scope of reference, and case law is not yet fully established. However, it is likely that the Swiss courts will adhere to their former distinction between different kinds of public law and consequently apply those rules that serve private interests. It is uncertain whether the courts will refuse to give effect to public law rules serving collective state interests on the basis of the unfortunate principle of *territoriality* or by means of an extensive application of the *ordre public*, or whether they will give effect to those rules if the conditions of art 19 are fulfilled.

6 Concluding critical remarks: Was the reservation in respect of Article 7 (1) of the Rome Convention justified?

In conclusion, it can be stated that the approach of the Rome Convention is that internationally mandatory rules of the proper law are applicable because they belong to the law governing the contract. At any rate, in the absence of an express regulation, this seems to be the position of the Convention. With regard to third countries' internationally mandatory rules, the Convention has drafted a *conflict rule* that enables the court of the forum to give effect to third countries' internationally mandatory rules, if the situation is closely connected with the enacting country, and if the recognition of the foreign rule is reasonable with regard to its content, purpose, and consequences of its application. Article 7 (1) of the Convention is a *general clause* covering all types of contracts and therefore uses vague and broad criteria, and grants extensive discretion to the courts.

---

785 The legislature is said to have intended to leave a *conscious loophole*. Vischer RabelsZ 53 (1989) 438, 440 et seq; id Rec des Cours 232 (1992) 21, 181, 182; Keller/Siehr *IPR* 491; Voser *Lois d'application immédiate* 58 et seq, 64, 73 et seq, 78 et seq.

786 Vischer Rec des Cours 232 (1992) 21, 181, 182; id RabelsZ 53 (1989) 438, 440, 445; Morscher *Rechtssetzungsakte* 101 et seq; Bär *Extraterritoriale Wirkung* 3, 16 footnote 9; Voser *Lois d'application immédiate* 72, 83, 84 for a detailed discussion about whether art 19 IPRG should be applied by analogy or directly.

This section will investigate whether, in view of case law solutions and the various academic approaches, the reservation to art 7 (1) was justified.[787]

a Unity of the law applicable to contracts and the confidence of the parties in the application of only one legal system

It has been argued that art 7 (1) leads to *scission* of contract and jeopardises the principle of *unity of the law applicable to a contract*.[788] The arguments that have been raised against the so-called principle of unity of the law applicable to a contract have already been discussed, and what was stated there is equally true in the context of art 7 (1).[789]

The principle of unity has never been all-embracing, however, and exceptions have always been made to the application of the proper law and particular issues have been connected separately on the basis of *special choice of law rules*.[790] In particular, arts 5 and 6 of the Convention eventually lead to a scission of the law applicable to the contract and to a special connection.[791]

But what is even more striking is the fact that the critics of the scission effect reject a '*special connection*' of a third country's internationally mandatory rules by referring to the principle that only one law should govern the transaction, but do also take these rules into account as supposedly facts.[792] Does this method not lead also to a recognition of another law and thus to a scission effect?[793]

The analysis of the German, Swiss and English case law solutions has shown that courts do not only take into account the actual effects of the foreign rule, but also consider the rule itself or at least its normative content. The courts have thus broadened the substantive law rules in order to cover violation of foreign law instead of domestic law.[794] This process is based on several steps. The primary question that has to be answered is whether there is a mandatory rule in

---

787 Clearly, one can and should regard the following discussion as equally true for art 19. The reason for focussing on art 7 (1) lies in the fact that it is not in legal force in England and Germany, while Switzerland has enacted art 19.

788 Mann *Effects* 31, 34.

789 See supra Chapter 5, I, 7, a, b.

790 Lando CMLR 24 (1987) 159, 167; Siehr RabelsZ 52 (1988) 41, 69; Schiffer *Normen* 91 et seq; Becker *Sonderanknüpfung* 57; see supra Chapter 5, I, 7, a.

791 For a detailed representation of these articles, see supra Chapter 2.

792 See supra Chapter 5, I, 1 and 7, b.

793 As was seen above in Chapter 5, I, 7, b the recognition as fact requires *choice of law considerations* as well; cf Schurig RabelsZ 54 (1990) 217, 243; MünchKomm/Martiny Art 34 Rn 35.

794 See MünchKomm/Martiny Art 34 Rn 35; Lehmann *Zwingendes Recht* 200 et seq.

a foreign country that has been violated by the contracting parties. Then the court examines whether the situation falls under the scope of the provision. Only afterwards can the court decide whether or not it will take the foreign rule into account within the substantive law, so that its violation may lead to immorality or impossibility of performance. Choice of law considerations are thus blurred with the application of substantive law.[795]

Thus, only *lip service* is paid to the principle of unity of the law applicable to the contract. This principle is not really upheld in considering a third country's rules as supposed facts within substantive rules. So what then is the merit of this principle?

It has also been stated that the *vagueness* of art 7 (1) and the *broad discretion* conferred upon the judge will make it impossible for the parties to determine the law applicable to their transaction. The parties will not be able to foresee the way in which a court will decide to exercise its discretion and give effect to mandatory rules of another law.[796] This is perhaps true, but in the course of time, courts will develop criteria. Certainty in law will thus be served and parties will be able to predict which foreign laws might be given effect regardless of the proper law.

Furthermore, under the current law, the situation is equally unpredictable for the parties.[797] Courts have blurred choice of law considerations with application of the substantive law. They have not relied on firm principles but on general clauses that are not only extremely vague, but also broadened in scope to cover the foreign law. Parties do not know whether or not courts will take third countries' law into account, nor do they know what the legal basis for the decision will be. In contrast, art 7 (1) would enable courts to develop firm criteria at the level of choice of laws.[798]

b Party autonomy is unduly restricted

It has also been held that art 7 (1) will unduly restrict party autonomy.[799] Firstly, art 7 (1) does not restrict party autonomy, but rather the scope of the proper law,

[795] See Chapter 5, II, 3, c, III, 3; subject to the case where truly only the factual effects of the foreign rule on the private relationship are taken into account without considering the rule itself; see also MünchKomm/Martiny Art 34 Rn 35; von Bar *IPR Bd. I* Rn 265.

[796] Coing WM 1981, 810, 813; Mentzel *Sonderanknüpfung* 129; Fletcher *Conflict of Laws* 170.

[797] Also see Schiffer *Normen* 92; Erne *Vertragsgültigkeit* 142 et seq.

[798] Kreuzer IPRax 1984, 293, 295.

[799] Sandrock/Steinschulte *Handbuch* A Rn 196; Coester ZverglRWiss 82 (1983) 1, 27.

no matter whether chosen by the parties or determined objectively. Secondly, this argument cannot be sustained because it makes no difference to the contracting parties whether their choice is limited by an application of third countries' internationally mandatory rules by means of a special connection or by recognition of the rules as 'facts' within the substantive law of the *lex causae*. In either case, their choice will not be fully upheld.

The present author maintains that strict adherence to the principle that only the chosen law is the governing law is in itself somewhat contradictory. Parties who have chosen a foreign law in the belief that only that law governs their transaction and who have made their choice in order to circumvent foreign laws, simply act in accordance with this doctrine. Why then should the foreign law suddenly be considered as 'fact', possibly rendering their contract invalid or unenforceable?[800]

c Uncertainty in law

It has also been argued that art 7 (1) will create *uncertainty* in choice of law of contracts.[801] Of course, the vagueness of the criteria and the broad discretion do create some uncertainty in law. It is therefore preferable to develop *special conflict rules* for certain fields of law taking cognisance of the particularities of the legal field and the involved interest, rather than using a *general clause* covering all types of contracts and all situations that may arise, as well as all fields of laws where internationally mandatory rules typically intervene in private relationships.[802]

The vague criteria definitely need to be concretised, and principles must be developed that will guide the courts in their deliberations as to when it is reasonable for the forum to give effect to a third country's rules.[803] Courts can thus have recourse to former case law solutions and can utilise these principles within the provisions of art 7 (1), since it is based on former court decisions and academic approaches.[804]

---

800 Also see MünchKomm/Martiny Art 34 Rn 35.

801 North JBL (1980) 382, 387; id *Contract Conflicts* 19, 20; Morse YB Eur L 2 (1982) 107, 146, 147; Collins ICLQ 25 (1976) 35, 50; Coing WM 1981, 810, 813.

802 Vischer RabelsZ 53 (1989) 438, 455; see also Philip *Recent Provisions* 241, 249; Erne *Vertragsgüligkeit* 153 et seq.

803 Also see Schiffer *Normen* 164; Lehmann *Zwingendes Recht* 206 et seq.

804 See *Giuliano/Lagarde* Report in North *Contract Conflicts* 380.

It has, however, been convincingly argued that the former legal situation was even more uncertain.[805] Courts simply broadened substantive law rules, parti cularly comprehensive clauses such as public policy and immorality, to cover violations of foreign mandatory rules. Choice of law considerations were thereby hidden behind application of substantive law rules. The principles that the courts thus developed, such as the English public policy doctrine, are far from being firm and clear.[806] Compared with the *public policy-comity* rule, art 7 (1) provides for firm criteria and certainty in law. The criterion of a close connection is better than formulating none at all, which is the case with English public policy. In fact, in all the English cases, the courts clearly took account of a connection between the situation and a foreign rule, but the connection was not seen as a condition for applying English public policy.

Similar considerations are valid for German and Swiss case law, although in addition, the German courts used a variety of solutions. Thus there was no way of knowing what the court's decision would be: whether it would refuse application of foreign law on the basis of the principle of non-applicability, or whether it would consider the foreign law as fact within the substantive law.

Furthermore, it is uncertain how courts will decide real third country cases because the juristic basis of the 'established principles' is uncertain. If it were only substantive law rules that were broadened to cover the foreign law then it would be for the proper law to decide whether or not third countries' rules can be considered. This clearly does not lead to certainty in law. Finally, the forum would hand over the ultimate decision about application of the foreign law, a result that is obviously contrary to fundamental principles of conflict of laws.

Thus, in view of the law that was previously applied, it seems contradictory to argue that art 7 (1) of the Convention leads to uncertainty.[807]

d Move towards Unilateralism

Does art 7 (1)[808] imply a departure from the traditional multilateral allocation technique and a move towards a unilateral approach similar to the statutist

[805] Von Bar *IPR Bd I* Rn 265, 266; Kreuzer IPRax 1984, 293, 295; Lehmann ZRP 1987, 319, 320, 321; also see Jackson *Contract Conflicts* 59, 74; Kaye *The New Private International Law* 257.

[806] For criticism regarding the uncertainty of the public policy rule, Kaye *The New Private International Law* 19 et seq, 240 et seq.

[807] Also see Kaye *The New Private International Law* 257; Jackson *Contract Conflicts* 59, 74; Kreuzer IPRax 1984, 293, 295.

theory? It is argued that the foreign law is applied because it claims application, and only afterwards do close connection and other criteria serve as limitations on exorbitant claims of application.[809] This argument, which was also raised against the *Special Connection Theory* in general, has already been discussed.[810] The same considerations are valid with regard to art 7 (1): If there is any move towards *unilateralism*, it is incomplete.[811]

It is certainly true that art 7 (1) differs from ordinary conflict rules in that the issue (operative fact or *Anknüpfungsgegenstand*) is not a legal relationship or question that is connected to a certain legal system, but certain foreign mandatory laws. Firstly, it has been convincingly argued that there is no difference between the connection of a legal question, a factual situation, or rules of law to a certain legal system.[812]

Secondly, the present author's view is that this assumption is based on a misinterpretation of art 7 (1) and the condition that the foreign rule 'claims application whatever the proper law'.[813] Article 7 (1) differs substantially from art 7 (2), which really does imply a move towards *unilateralism* because the forum's internationally mandatory rules are applied if they claim application. Foreign internationally mandatory rules are applied only if the conditions of art 7 (1) are fulfilled. The foreign law's claim of application is a condition, but it is only one amongst others.[814] The assumption that one has to start with the claim to apply does not follow from the wording of art 7 (1). According to the article, the *primary connecting factor* is a *close connection* between the situation and the country that enacted the particular rule. The claim to apply serves rather as a

---

808 This objection was also made in respect of the Swiss art 19, compare Vischer RabelsZ 53 (1989) 438, 450; id Rec des Cours 232 (1992) 21, 168; Siehr RabelsZ 52 (1988) 41, 71.

809 Coester ZverglRWiss 82 (1983) 1, 5, 8 et seq, 29; Schubert RIW 1987, 729, 734 et seq; Schurig *Lois* 55, 66 et seq; Heini ZSR 100 (1981) 65, 68; Siehr RabelsZ 52 (1988) 41, 71.

810 See supra Chapter 5, I, 3, d, g, 7, f.

811 Cf Ungeheuer *Beachtung* 14, 150. Schwander *IPR AT* 246, 252 refers to a unilateral concept with regard to the internationally mandatory rules of the forum, but emphasises that those rules of a foreign legal system are to be treated differently.

812 Schurig *Kollisionsnorm* 89 et seq. Id *Lois* 55, 70 who argues that it would not make a difference whether one connects a legal question, a legal situation or rules of law in order to determine the applicable law; Schubert RIW 1987, 729 et seq. For criticism on this point of view: Mentzel *Sonderanknüpfung* 56 et seq.

813 Also see Schiffer *Normen* 159 et seq; Ungeheuer *Beachtung* 150.

814 Some authors view the close connection as limitation on unreasonable claims of foreign rules: Vischer RabelsZ 53 (1989) 438, 451; id Rec des Cours 232 (1992) 21, 169; Philip *Recent Provisions* 241, 249. Most authors, however, assume that the claim to apply serves as a kind of limitation, because if the rule does not claim application it is not justified to apply it, Schurig *Lois* 55, 66, 70; id *Kollisionsnorm* 89 - 94.

kind of limitation: A court may not apply a third country's law that intervenes in the private relationship in the public interest of the foreign state if the law does not claim application. Furthermore, the judge is granted broad discretion as to whether and how he will give effect to the foreign rule.

Therefore, the foreign internationally mandatory rule is not applied because it claims application, but because the forum has decided to take a third country's internationally mandatory rules into account, under certain circumstances, such as those stipulated in art 7 (1).[815] It is still an autonomous decision of the forum state whether the foreign rule is to be given effect or not. The matter is thus not a move towards *unilateralism*, nor does it involve a search of all the world's legal systems for rules that claim application to the situation.

In view of these arguments, this objection cannot be upheld. The forum's decision to take foreign internationally mandatory rules into account is an autonomous one, and art 7 (1) conforms with this interpretation. [816] There are, nevertheless, obvious differences from the orthodox conflict rules, because art 7 (1) in effect leads to acceptance of *renvoi*.[817] Moreover, the vague criteria and the broad discretion granted to the judge differ from other conflict rules. This means a departure from the traditional 'rigid' and 'blind' allocation technique towards a more flexible and result-orientated process.

e International comity and decisional harmony

Art 7 (1) Rome Convention has the merit of serving *decisional harmony* and the mutual assistance between states in the furtherance of their interests. States seek not only to apply their own internationally mandatory rules but also to take into account the justified interests of foreign states.[818]

---

815 See Schiffer *Normen* 159; MünchKomm/Martiny Art 34 Rn 99; Ungeheuer *Beachtung* 97, 150; Keller/Siehr *IPR* 549; despite his interpretation as 'turn to an unilateral approach', cf Vischer RabelsZ 53 (1989) 438, 451; id Rec des Cours 232 (1992) 21, 169.

816 It is anyway only a matter of wording to create a multilateral choice of law rule designating the internationally mandatory rules applicable to a contract. For instance: 'The contract may be governed by internationally mandatory rules of the legal systems with which the situation is closely connected', also see Ungeheuer *Beachtung* 150; Schurig *Lois* 55, 69, 71, 75.

817 With regard to the discussion concerning *renvoi*, see supra Chapter 5, I, 7, f and III, 3, c.

818 Schiffer *Normen* 148; Coing WM 1981, 810, 813.

f The structurally preferable solution

In an attack on the first draft of art 7, Mann challenged the supporters of the article and the *Special Connection Theory* to prove the need for changing the existing case law.[819] As many authors have said, however, art 7 (1) is not a radical departure from former case law. The issue is in fact the method of reasoning. Case law has already taken into account the effects of third countries' internationally mandatory rules within the substantive law. The question is therefore not *whether* third countries' rules can be given effect, but *how*, or *on what basis*.[820] Article 7 (1) will enable courts to take third countries' internationally mandatory rules into account in a systematic manner, which is to be preferred. Courts can refer to situations that have been established in former case law in order to concretise the broad and general clause of art 7 (1).[821] In fact, art 7 (1) has been characterised as 'a restatement of the pre-existing case law'.[822]

Furthermore, art 7 (1) offers the better solution with regard to real third country cases where the proper law is foreign. The substantive law approach depends on whether the substantive law of the *lex causae* offers relief and sanctions, which permit a consideration of the effects of third countries' mandatory rules, such as impossibility of performance, frustration, or illegality. It has been questioned whether this is always the case.[823] The consequence of this approach is that the judge will have to interpret and extend the foreign rule in the light of the foreign legal system.[824]

According to the general principles of the conflict of laws it is a decision of the forum's private international law whether foreign rules are to be given effect. Recognition of a third country's mandatory rules within the operative facts of substantive law rules would mean that this decision is ultimately handed over to the proper law. The only means to correct unjustified results from the point of

---

819 'Show me the case you would like to meet. Show me the case which should be decided differently from the present practice', cf Mann *Effect* 31, 35; also see id *FS Beitzke* 607, 613.

820 See MünchKomm/Martiny Art 34 Rn 33; Schiffer *Normen* 147; Martiny IPRax 1987, 277, 279, 28. Kreuzer IPRax 1984, 293, 295 speaks of 'accuracy or truth of reasoning' (*Begründungswahrheit*). He means that choice of law considerations are made at the level of conflict of laws instead of broadening substantive rules and thus blurring choice of law considerations with the application of substantive law.

821 See Kreuzer *Ausländisches Wirtschaftsrecht* 140; id IPRax 1984, 293, 295.

822 Basedow GYBIL 27 (1984) 109, 140, 141 with regard to foreign export controls.

823 For details, see Schwander *IPR* 542 et seq; Vischer Rec des Cours 232 (1992 I) 13, 168; Siehr RabelsZ 52 (1988) 41, 79.

824 Schwander *IPR* 542 et seq; Kreuzer *Ausländisches Wirtschaftsrecht* 86..

view of the forum would be the *ordre public*.[825] Article 7 (1) thus constitutes the superior method of solving real third country cases, since it solves a problem of international private law at a conflict of law level.[826]

g Conclusion

In view of the former legal situation, it is regrettable that both the United Kingdom and Germany entered a reservation with regard to art 7 (1) of the Rome Convention.

825 Siehr RabelsZ 52 (1988) 41, 80; see also Mentzel *Sonderanknüpfung* 113.

826 Schiffer *Normen* 148, 156, 166; Schäfer *FG Sandrock* 39, 47; Hentzen RIW 1988, 508, 509; Schubert RIW 1987, 729, 745; von Bar *IPR Bd I* Rn 265 et seq.

Chapter 6
Proposal for the application of internationally mandatory rules with a view to South African private international law of contracts

In this chapter a proposal for regulating the application of internationally mandatory rules in the South African private international law of contracts will be submitted. The submitted approach, however, may be equally suitable to other countries the private international law of which is based on the traditional allocation technique. For the purpose of developing a proposal the previous discussion and analysis of the court decisions and the various academic approaches in the countries under investigation will be helpful. Before beginning, however, the current South African common law and academic statements regarding application of internationally mandatory rules stemming from the *lex fori*, the *lex causae* and a third legal system will be examined.

I Legal situation in South African private international law

In South Africa discussion of the problem of applying internationally mandatory rules commenced recently.[1] At least with regard to its theoretical foundations, the whole issue is to a large extent still unexplored in South Africa. Decided cases on the issue are also rare.[2]

1 Application of the internationally mandatory rules of the *lex fori*

The South African approach to the application of internationally mandatory rules of South African law as *lex fori* seems clear. Those rules that can be classified as *lois d'application immédiate* and that accordingly claim application to a transaction, even though South African law is not the *lex causae* of the transaction, are in principle applicable. The internationally mandatory rules of the forum may thus render a contract illegal or unenforceable, even if it is valid and legal in terms of its proper law. This approach is supported by

---

1 See on this Forsyth *Private International Law* 298 et seq; Edwards *Conflict of Laws* para 469; Spiro XVII CILSA (1984) 197 et seq; Viejobueno XXVI CILSA (1993) 172 et seq; Kahn 20 (1990) BML 35 et seq; Neels 1991 TSAR 694 et seq; see Van Rooyen *Die Kontrak* 40 et seq, 145 et seq, 162 et seq; 232; Booysen *International Transactions* 77.

2 But see *Cargo Motor Corporation Ltd v Tofalos Transport Ltd* 1972 (1) SA 186 (W); *Standard Bank of SA Ltd & another v Ocean Commodities & others* 1980 (2) SA 175 (T); *Murata Machinery Ltd v Capelon Yarns (Pty) Ltd* 1986 (4) SA 671 (C); *Herbst v Surti* 1991 (2) SA 75 (Z); *Henry v Branfield* 1996 (1) SA 244 (D).

academic writers[3] and the South African courts, albeit by way of *obiter dicta*.[4] According to one author, application of the forum's rules is based on *public policy*,[5] while other authors refer to these rules as *directly applicable statutes*.[6]

Clearly not all *ius cogens* rules of the forum can be classified as internationally mandatory, and South African courts have often enforced contracts that contravened South African *ius cogens* on the basis that they were valid according to the governing law.[7] According to Forsyth, a rule of the *lex fori* must be carefully interpreted to ensure that it was intended to override the choice of law process and to render illegal a contract that is valid under its proper law.[8]

An example of a South African statute that is directly applicable on the basis of its express terms can be found in the South African Merchant Shipping Act 57 of 1951. Section 306 of this Act provides that Chapter VII, concerning salvage and incidental matters, 'shall be applied in all cases determined in any court in the Republic, in whatever waters the salvage services in question were rendered'. Another example is s 1 (1) (a) of the Carriage of Goods by Sea Act 1

3 Forsyth *Private International Law* 13, 299; Edwards *Conflict of Laws* para 469; Spiro XVII CILSA (1984) 197, 201 et seq.

4 See, however, the somewhat vague *dictum* in *Murata Machinery Ltd v Capelon Yarns (Pty) Ltd* 1986 (4) SA 671 (C), 673 I - J. Edwards *Conflict of Laws* para 469 footnote 2 also cites *Commissioner of Inland Revenue v Estate Greenacre* 1936 NPD 225, 229 as *dicta*-support for this position. There is another example which is not an *obiter dictum*, but the case concerned the enforcement of a foreign judgment instead of a contract: *Taylor v Hollard* 1886 (2) SAR 78. The SA court refused to recognise and enforce an English judgment because the underlying agreement exceeded the capital sum of the money advanced and was thus contrary to SA usury law. For the facts of the case, see Spiro XVII CILSA (1984) 197, 201.

5 Spiro XVII CILSA (1984) 197, 201 et seq.

6 Forsyth *Private International Law* 299; Edwards *Conflict of Laws* para 469.

7 See *Berman v Winrow* 1943 TPD 213 which concerned the prohibition of a *pactum successorium* in South Africa. The court held that the contract was valid and enforceable, despite the SA prohibition, because it was legal according to the proper law. In *Bishop & others v Conrath & another* 1947 (2) SA 800 T at 803, a contract for the purchase of lottery tickets was upheld and regarded as enforceable in South Africa notwithstanding a local prohibition of lotteries in SA because it was legal under the governing law. The court held that the contract was not repugnant to public policy. For the facts of these cases, see Spiro XVII CILSA (1984) 197, 201, 202; Kahn (1991) 20 BML 147, 149. Also see, however, *Timms v Nicol* 1968 (1) SA 299 (R) where a wagering agreement which was valid in Zambia was held to be unenforceable because of the public policy exclusion.

8 Forsyth *Private International Law* 299.

of 1986, which provides that the Hague Rules apply to carriage of goods by sea where the port of shipment is a port in the Republic.[9]

Other statutes, however, have to be interpreted, as they do not expressly stipulate their scope of application. This interpretation is required whether the statutes implicitly claim application to a contract even though it is governed by a foreign legal system, or whether the statute is subject to the ordinary conflict rules and applies only if the *lex causae* is South African law. Forsyth notes that despite the fact that both the Basic Conditions of Employment Act 75 of 1997 and the Credit Agreements Act 75 of 1980 do not contain any term determining their scope of applicability, they are doubtless directly applicable.[10] Thus by implication the employer cannot avoid application of the Basic Conditions of Employment Act and his obligation thereunder to the employee, 'simply by ensuring that the law governing their contract was not South African'.[11] Forsyth presumes that the Credit Agreement Act would almost certainly apply where the contract was concluded in South Africa concerning a *res* situated locally. However, he questions whether the Act would apply if the contract were concluded in South Africa, but one party was resident in Namibia and the *res* was situated there.[12]

2 Application of (internationally) mandatory rules of the *lex causae*

It can be stated that, in principle, according to South African private international law, the mandatory provisions of a foreign *lex causae* will be applied by a South African court, and a contract that is illegal under the proper law will not be enforced, regardless of its validity under the *lex fori*.[13]

With regard to cases where the proper law was determined by a choice of law of the contracting parties, South African courts have never decided the question of whether the parties can avoid the mandatory rules of the otherwise applicable law and can render applicable those of the chosen law. However, this position is supported by academic writings and by *obiter dicta* in South African decisions.[14] In addition, including in an expressly chosen proper law a full

9 The Act is also self-limited as it does not apply to the carriage of goods from a port outside the Republic, see Forsyth *Private International Law* 12.

10 Forsyth *Private International Law* 13 footnote 62.

11 Forsyth *Private International Law* 13. Another Act that may well be internationally mandatory is the Labour Relations Act 66 of 1995.

12 Forsyth *Private International Law* 13, 14.

13 Forsyth *Private International Law* 299; Spiro XVII CILSA (1984) 197, 200; Edwards *Conflict of Laws* para 469 and footnote 1; Kahn 20 BML (1990) 147, 150.

14 See supra Chapter 2, VI, 1.

reference to foreign law, and not only its facultative norms, has considerable merit (such as legal certainty in law)[15] and has been accepted world wide.[16] It is therefore submitted that this concept at least should be retained with regard to *domestic* mandatory rules.[17]

The general statement that the mandatory provisions of the proper law are in principle applicable, and that a contract that is illegal under its governing law will not enforced by a South African court, is supported by South African case law. However, this support is based on a reference to English law and expressed in the form of *obiter dicta*.[18] Although there is no express *ratio* in binding precedent, the principle is nevertheless held to be universally acceptable by South African academics.[19]

This proposition seems to be equally true of internationally mandatory rules or public law rules of the proper law. Although the public/private law dichotomy is a significant feature of South African law, it has not yet been applied in the context of private international law, with the possible exception of the *non-enforcement of foreign revenue and penal law*.[20] However, as was discussed above, this principle does not prevent a court from taking cognizance of a foreign revenue or penal law in the context of private litigation.[21] Apart from this principle, there is no doctrine of *non-applicability of foreign public law*, as has been proposed in Germany and Switzerland.[22]

---

15 This seems now broadly accepted amongst academics in South Africa, cf supra Chapter 2, IV, 1.

16 For details, see Forsyth *Private International Law* 278 et seq; also see Lando CMLR 24 (1987) 159, 169 et seq; id Rec des Cours 189 (1984 VI) 119, 237, 255 et seq.

17 I adhere to the view that internationally mandatory rules serving predominantly public interests of the state should be subject of a separate choice of law process, no matter whether they stem from the proper law or a third country. The parties' choice is not an appropriate connecting factor (or choice of law rule) to render these kind of rules applicable. Cf infra section II, 1, b and 2, c.

18 *Cargo Motor Corporation Ltd v Tofalos Transport Ltd* 1972 (1) SA 186 (W) at 195 F - 196 A; *Ocean Commodities Inc v Standard Bank of SA Ltd* 1978 (2) SA 367 (W) 372 H - 374 A, F - H; *Herbst v Surti* 1991 (2) SA 75 (Z) at 78 G.

19 Forsyth *Private International Law* 299 footnote 155; Spiro XVII CILSA (1984) 197, 200; Edwards Conflict of Laws para 469; Van Rooyen *Die Kontrak* 162 et seq.

20 For the principle in South African law, see Forsyth *Private International Law* 104 et seq; for case law, cf *Commissioner of Taxes, Federation of Rhodesia v Mc Farland* 1965 (1) SA 470 (W) (foreign revenue law); for the principle, see the Roman-Dutch authority Voet *Commentarius* 38.17 App 29.

21 See Chapter 5, III, 1, b; cf also Forsyth *Private International Law* 106, 107 for the recognition of these laws in private litigation.

22 For the doctrine, see supra Chapter 5, II, 1, b. For the South African position one might refer to the case *Cargo Motor Corporation Ltd v Tofalos Transport Ltd* 1972 (1) SA 186

As in all the countries under investigation, in South Africa, the forum's public policy constitutes an exception to the general rule that the mandatory rules of the proper law must be applied. Mandatory rules that violate the forum's *ordre public* are therefore not applied.[23]

3 Internationally mandatory rules of a third legal system

The approach of South African private international law to the application of internationally mandatory rules of yet another legal system, which is neither the forum nor the proper law, is uncertain. There are different approaches to this issue, which are reflected in the writings of the major commentators.

a Public policy of the forum state

Most academic authors, relying on English law, seem to favour an approach based on *public policy*.[24] However, it is submitted that some South African authors do not distinguish between the two solutions developed by English courts; they combine the rules, thus creating a new, more restrictive approach to public policy.

As was shown above, there are two principles in English law that allow for consideration of third countries' internationally mandatory rules. These are the *lex loci solutionis* rule and the *public policy* rule that a contract is void if it is opposed to British state interests, particularly if it is likely to jeopardise relations with a friendly nation.[25] South African authors refer to the English case law in stating that it is against public policy to enforce a contract (regardless of its proper law) that requires the performance of an act that is illegal under the law of the place of performance.[26] This is unfortunate: The

---

(W) at 195 F - 196 A. Here the court considered the applicability of a foreign exchange control regulation to a South African contract and refused to apply the rule because it did not belong to the proper law of the contract. The public law nature of the regulation was not even mentioned.

23 See Spiro XVII CILSA (1984) 197, 201; *Berman v Winrow* 1943 TPD 213; *Bishop & others v Conrath & another* 1947 (2) SA 800 (T) (*obiter dicta*, since in both cases the public policy rule was not applied). See *Timms v Nicol* 1968 (1) SA 299 (R) where a wagering agreement that was valid in Zambia was held to be unenforceable because of public policy exclusion. Also see Kahn ASSAL (1991) 583 et seq for the policy aspects in *Herbst v Surti* 1991 (2) SA 75 (Z).

24 For instance, Forsyth *Private International Law* 299 et seq; Spiro XVII CILSA (1984) 197, 207, 208; Viejobueno XXVI (1993) 172, 207.

25 See supra Chapter 5, III, 2, a and c.

26 Forsyth *Private International Law* 299, 301, 302.

public policy-comity rule is not and should not be restricted to the *lex loci solutionis*.

According to Forsyth, the mandatory rules of third legal systems are in principle inapplicable, even if their application would render the contract illegal. A contract that is valid under its proper law and the *lex fori* is thus held to be enforceable despite its illegality under the *lex loci contractus*. However, Forsyth also argues that *public policy* can lead to the application of a third country's mandatory legislation if the inapplicability of these rules leads to 'a result offensive to deeply held local principles'.[27]

Forsyth examines whether it is contrary to *public policy* to enforce a contract that is illegal under the law of the *place of performance*. According to him, 'this is an issue that is largely *res nova* in South African courts'.[28] In the course of his examination he discusses the solution of art 7 (1) of the Rome Convention, according to which the mandatory rules of a third legal system may be applicable if the rule claims application and there is a close connection between the legal system and the contract. Forsyth is clearly not in favour of the introduction of this principle. He claims that 'introduction of such a principle - to be applied on a discretionary basis by the court - threatens to undermine that very certainty which is so vital in international commercial contracts and which is one of the major beneficial results of adopting party autonomy'.[29]

Moreover, he believes that it is a fundamental principle of South African law that foreign law is applied locally only when so ordered by the local sovereign. In other words, the legislature enacts choice of law rules to enable or order foreign law to be applied in certain instances. Forsyth is therefore extremely critical of application of foreign law by means of a nebulous '*nature and purpose*' approach, which in his opinion is reflected in art 7 (1) of the Rome Convention.[30] However, he accepts that the legislature may enact rules that

---

27 Forsyth *Private International Law* 299.

28 Ibid 301; sceptically Kahn ASSAL (1991) 584 and Edwards *Conflict of Laws* para 469.

29 Ibid 301.

30 Ibid. It was shown above that art 7 (1) is not based solely on a *nature and purpose-approach*, but also consists of traditional elements of a choice of law rule, such as the use of a connecting factor: *close connection*. It is also debatable whether art 7 constitutes a move away from the general rule that a foreign law is applied only if the local sovereign so orders. The present author's view is that the foreign internationally mandatory rule is not applied because it claims application, but because art 7 (1) (on a discretionary basis) so directs if certain conditions are fulfilled, and it is the local sovereign that either incorporates art 7 (1) or enacts a similar provision.

provide for the application of the mandatory rules of a third legal system *in particular instances*.[31]

Turning back to his initial question of whether it is contrary to public policy to enforce a contract, the performance of which is illegal under the *lex loci solutionis*, he refers to decided English cases. He concludes that there is a principle in English law that it is contrary to public policy to enforce contracts, whatever their proper law, that require the performance of acts that are illegal under the *lex loci solutionis*.[32] Forsyth submits that, in applying Roman-Dutch law, South African courts 'should not enforce contracts - irrespective of their proper law - that require the performance of acts contrary to the *lex loci solutionis*.'[33] Generally, Forsyth maintains that the question of lawfulness (or lack thereof) is the prerogative of the sovereign state of the place of performance, and that it 'is contrary to local public policy to allow the local courts to be used in support of illegal acts there'.[34] The reason for applying this rule is based on 'comity and common sense rather than rigid logic'.[35]

According to Spiro, 'it is for the (internal) *ordre public* of (South Africa as) the *lex fori* to decide whether or not to implement or else to consider imperative provisions of other legal systems which have or have not been chosen by the parties to govern their contract'.[36] This statement would indicate that the public policy of the forum state must determine whether or not third countries' internationally mandatory rules will be taken into account. However, Spiro proceeds to state that, in the absence of any adverse *ordre public* of the *lex fori*, the proper law governs, and therefore it is the *ordre public* of the governing law that determines whether the mandatory rules of the third country will be

31 It would thus be possible to apply third countries' mandatory legislation where a statutory special conflict rule provides for such application. Forsyth refers to art VIII (2) (b) of the IMF Agreement, ibid 301. The requirement of a statutory choice of law rule is remarkable, since South African private international law is based to a large extent on Roman-Dutch common law rules established by case law, see Forsyth *Private International Law* 274. Therefore, the present author submits that a statutory choice of law rule is not in any event necessary. South African courts may develop common law choice of law rules in this field as they did in others.

32 In contrast to the proposition that it is for the *lex causae* to determine under what circumstances the law of the place of performance is to be taken into account. He refers to cases like *Regazzoni v KC Sethia* (1944) Ltd [1958] AC 301; *Libyan Arab Bank v Bankers Trust Co* [1988] 3 WLR 314; Forsyth *Private International Law* 302.

33 Forsyth *Private International Law* 302.

34 Ibid.

35 Ibid 302, 303.

36 Spiro XVII CILSA (1984,) 197, 207.

applied.[37] Spiro's submission is thus not quite clear: Is it the *ordre public* of the forum or of the *lex causae* that must determine whether to apply or consider a third country's mandatory legislation?[38]

Viejobueno simply reformulates Spiro's view[39], but she does add that there must be a connection between the third legal system and the contract. It is thus for the *public policy* of the forum state to decide whether effect is to be given to a third country's internationally mandatory rules.

b Reasonable claim of application

Van Rooyen on the other hand, in an extensive analysis states that in South Africa the law governing a contract is applied subject to (public policy and) the (imperative) rules of a third country which reasonably claim application.[40] Thus, the mandatory rules of a third legal system might be applicable and influence the validity of a contract if their claim of application is reasonable.[41] Therefore, the legal systems of the *lex fori*, the *lex loci contractus*, the *lex loci solutionis*, and yet another legal system could all qualify as the law of a third country and be applied under certain circumstances.[42]

Edwards follows Van Rooyen's approach.[43] He rejects the *lex loci solutionis rule*, arguing that it is for the proper law of a contract, not the *lex fori*, to decide whether and how illegality at the place of performance is to be taken into account. Nevertheless, he favours the general position that the mandatory rules of a third country with which the contract is connected may be applicable and possibly even displace the proper law.[44] For example, application of a third

---

37 Spiro XVII CILSA (1984) 197, 208.

38 It seems as if Spiro supports a cumulative application of the *ordre public* of the forum as well as of the *lex causae*. In the first instance the *ordre public* of the proper law is decisive, and the *ordre public* of the forum state is the *ultima ratio*. In addition, it is not clear whether he refers to the internal or international *ordre public* of the *lex causae*. Bearing in mind the principle of exclusion of *renvoi,* he is most probably referring to the internal *ordre public* of the *lex causae*.

39 Viejobueno XXVI CILSA (1993) 172, 207.

40 Van Rooyen *Die Kontrak* 164 - 165. In general, as the present author interprets Van Rooyen, he takes a modern approach as it is expressed in art 7 (1) RC. His approach may serve as a useful solution for South African private international law.

41 Van Rooyen *Die Kontrak* 164 et seq.

42 Critically Spiro XVII CILSA (1984) 197, 206 et seq; Forsyth *Private International Law* 281, 300.

43 Edwards *Conflict of Laws* para 469.

44 He refers to *Ocean Commodities Inc v Standard Bank of SA Ltd* 1978 (2) SA 367 (W) 375 F - H with regard to the IMF Agreement.

country's mandatory (economic) legislation is reasonable if the authorities of the enacting country have the power to enforce it.[45]

c South African cases on this issue

Although there are few decided cases on this issue, there are at least some *dicta*, albeit often *obiter*, that indicate how South African courts tend to deal with internationally mandatory rules from a third legal system.

Bishop & Others v Conrath & Another[46] concerned a wagering contract that was illegal in terms of the law of the place where it was concluded (the Transvaal),[47] because of a prohibition on lotteries and the sale or disposal of lottery tickets. The contract, however, was valid and legal under its proper law (Rhodesian law). The court held that the prohibition did not have extraterritorial effect, and the contract was enforced by the South African court.

This *dictum* has been interpreted as support for the proposition that illegality under the *lex loci contractus* is irrelevant.[48] It is questionable, however, whether one should go so far. Although the court referred to the *lex loci contractus*, it cannot be overlooked that the *lex loci contractus* was also the *lex fori*, and that the Transvaal statute was a statutory prohibition of the forum state. The court reached its conclusion by interpreting the statute, and held that in the absence of a clear contrary intention, a statute does not have extraterritorial effect if it applies to acts committed beyond the limits of the legislature's jurisdiction.[49]

Cargo Motor Corporation Ltd v Tofalos Transport Ltd [50] provides *obiter* support for the application or at least recognition of mandatory rules of the *lex loci solutionis*. In this case Margo J referred to English law[51] and held that 'the Courts of that country will not enforce a contract if the *locus solutionis* is in a foreign country, and if that contract or its performance would be illegal under the laws of that foreign country'.[52] The court went on to note that in English law illegality under a third legal system other than the *lex loci solutionis* is not taken

45 Edwards *Conflict of Laws* para 469.
46 1947 (2) SA 800 (T).
47 Which was also the *lex fori*, see Spiro XVII CILSA (1984) 197, 203.
48 For instance, Viejobueno XXVI CILSA 1993, 172, 207.
49 At 803.
50 1972 (1) SA 186 (W) at 195.
51 Quoting *Ralli Brothers v Compania Naviera Sota Y Aznar* [1920] 2 KB 287; *Foster v Driscoll* [1929] 1 KB 470; *De Béeche v South American Stores (Garth & Caves) Ltd* [1935] AC 148; *Regazzoni v KC Sethia (1944) Ltd* [1958] AC 301.
52 At 195 A, B.

into account, and stated that 'this proposition, as a matter of principle and of common sense should be equally valid in the system of private international law applied by our courts, where direct judicial authority on unenforceability does not seem to be plentiful'.[53]

Using the English rule, the court therefore ruled that by applying the *lex loci solutionis* (which coincided with the *lex loci contractus* and the proper law), the contract was not invalidated because it infringed an exchange control regulation of a third country, other than the *lex loci solutionis*. The court held that the contract was enforceable in South Africa as the place of performance, regardless of the foreign exchange control regulations of a third state, which one contracting party claimed had to be applied as he was a *national* and *carried on business* in that country.[54]

Obiter support for the recognition of illegality under the *lex loci solutionis* is also found in the case *Herbst v Surti*[55] where Adam J referred to *dicta* in English cases that support the *lex loci solutionis rule.*[56]

It can thus be stated that these cases support the view that illegality under the *lex loci solutionis* is taken into account, regardless of the proper law of the contract. Furthermore, a contract that requires the performance of acts that are illegal under the law of the place of performance will not be enforced by South African courts. It also seems reasonable to conclude from the case law that illegality under yet another foreign law is not taken into account, and that the mandatory rules of the *lex loci contractus*, or the *habitual residence*, or *place of business*, or *nationality* of one of the parties, are therefore inapplicable.

4 Conclusion

The position of internationally mandatory rules in South African law in respect of international contracts is uncertain, since there have been few decided cases. Nevertheless, the current position may be recapitulated as follows.

Firstly, the proper law will be applied by the courts and hence a contract that is illegal under its proper law will be unenforceable. It seems that no distinction is made between public and private law rules. Secondly, the imperative provisions of the South African forum that claim application to the transaction, either expressly or by statutory interpretation, irrespective of the proper law, are

---

53 At 196 E.

54 For an interpretation of the case, see Viejobueno XXVI CILSA (1993) 172, 207.

55 1991 (2) SA 75 (Z) at 78 F - I.

56 See for obiter support also *Henry v Branfield* 1996 (1) SA 244 (D).

applicable and may render a foreign contract illegal or unenforceable despite its legality under the proper law. Thirdly, the application or recognition of internationally mandatory rules of a third legal system is - apart from few obiter dicta – still to a large extent an issue *res nova* before the courts, the discussion amongst academic writers has started recently.

Most authors rely on English case law and in particular on illegality under the *lex loci solutionis*. Some authors submit that the internal *ordre public* of the forum state must decide whether and how third countries' mandatory rules are to be taken into account.[57] Others seem to rely on the international *ordre public* of South African private international law, since the invocation of public policy is based on *comity and common sense*.[58] Others take a more progressive view and argue that third countries' mandatory rules should be applied or considered if they reasonably claim application and if there is a close connection between the legal system and the transaction.[59]

However, apart from some very vague statements, for example, that the public policy of the forum state must determine whether foreign *ius cogens* is to be applied or considered, no real suggestions have been made by academic writers indicating when foreign rules should be given effect,[60] and the South African courts have yet to deal with the issue.

II Proposed Approach

In this section, a solution will be proposed on a general basis for the application or consideration of internationally mandatory rules in private international law of contracts. These suggestions may serve to guide the South African courts in combining internationally mandatory rules with the ordinary choice of law process.[61] Furthermore, this proposal may serve as a contribution to a discussion

57 Spiro XVII CILSA (1984) 197, 207, 208; Viejobueno XXVI CILSA (1993) 172, 207.

58 Forsyth *Private International Law* 302, 303.

59 See Van Rooyen *Die Kontrak* 164 et seq; Edwards *Conflict of Laws* para 469.

60 However, for a possibly useful approach, see Van Rooyen *Die Kontrak*.

61 The SA parliament is currently busy with a full programme that involves issues as fundamental as the introduction of an inquisitorial procedure in criminal proceedings and a new law of succession. In these circumstances the private international law of contracts will probably not be considered a priority. In any event, it would not be advisable to legislate on the applicability of (foreign) internationally mandatory rules. First, the SA private international law of contracts needs to develop principled rules in the course of time. Secondly, the issues are complex, and as has been shown in this study, application of internationally mandatory rules is an area that is still unsettled and contested in the countries under investigation.

amongst South African scholars. The proposal may be equally suitable to other countries in case their private international law is based on the traditional allocation technique.

1 The common denominator

The previous discussion and comparative analysis of the different case law solutions, the various academic approaches, and the relatively recent legislative solutions adopted by the Rome Convention and the Swiss IPRG will be taken into account and serve as a cornerstone. As was seen during the course of this study, the approaches differ substantially, and the legal situation in the various countries is far from clear. However, the analysis of the different approaches has also identified similarities. These similarities may serve as a *lowest common denominator*, which will form the basis of and justification for a proposal.

a Internationally mandatory rules of the forum

Internationally mandatory rules of the forum state always prevail over the choice of law process. This proposition is apparently true for all the countries under investigation.[62] The reason for application of these rules by the court of the forum is simply that the court is bound by its sovereign. Aside from constitutional issues of human rights, the legislature of the forum state is always free to create rules that override the choice of law process. There is nothing remarkable about this.[63]

There are differences, however, with regard to the juristic basis of this principle. A duality of method existed or exists in all the countries under investigation. On the one hand, the application of the mandatory laws of the forum state regardless of the foreign proper law, was based on the forum's *ordre public*,[64] or alternatively, on the nature of the mandatory rule itself (overriding the choice of law process).[65] A statute has an implied or express unilateral choice of law rule attached to it, indicating its territorial scope of application. The major problem faced by the court is to identify internationally mandatory rules and to distinguish them from those mandatory rules that are subject to the normal conflict rules, particularly where the territorial scope of the rule has to be determined by interpretation of a statute.[66]

---

62 See Chapter 4.

63 Forsyth *Private International Law* 299 footnote 156; Schurig *Lois* 55, 59 et seq.

64 Chapter 4, I, 1.

65 Chapter 4, I, 2 and II.

66 See Chapter 3, II and Chapter 4, II, 2, for examples III.

b Internationally mandatory rules of the proper law

Academic and judicial approaches differ with regard to the application of internationally mandatory rules of the proper law. In England mandatory rules of the proper law are generally applied because they belong to the law governing the contract, as indicated by the ordinary conflict rule.[67] In private litigation no distinction is made between public and private law rules, or rules serving private interests and those pursuing predominantly public interests of the foreign state.[68] These rules are applicable subject only to the English public policy exclusionary rule.

In Germany and Switzerland, however, the approach is different and is extensively debated amongst scholars.[69] According to the German and Swiss courts, private and public law rules serving predominantly the private interests of the contracting parties or the fair reconciliation between them, are applicable if they emanate from the proper law. However, public law rules that pursue mainly the interests of the foreign state are in principle not applied. This *non-application of foreign public laws* is based on the '*Public Conflict of Laws*' or '*International Administrative Law*', which are founded on the principle of *territoriality* of public laws.[70] However, foreign public law rules can be considered if the foreign state is in a position to enforce its law. Alternatively, the foreign rule can be given effect within the substantive law of the *lex causae*.[71]

Most academics reject such a restrictive approach. Generally speaking, they either favour a comprehensive application of the proper law as it is in force in the foreign country (*Schuldstatuts-theory* and *Combination Theory*),[72] or propose a special connection of internationally mandatory rules (*Special Connection Theory*).[73] The former solution leads to application of the internationally mandatory rules of the proper law. These authors nonetheless submit that cognisance must be taken of the self-limitation of the foreign rule. Thus, if the foreign rule does not claim application, it is not applied.[74] According to the latter solution, the foreign rule is not rendered automatically applicable by the

---

67 Chapter 5, III, 1.
68 Chapter 5, III, 1, a, b.
69 Chapter 5, I.
70 Chapter 5, II, 1, b, d.
71 Chapter 5, II, 1, c; d.
72 See Chapter 5, I, 1, 4.
73 Chapter 5, I, 3.
74 As was seen above, this at least sometimes leads to the result that *renvoi* is accepted, Chapter 5, I, 7, f, III, 3, c.

ordinary conflict rules, but is subject to special conflict rules that indicate its application. The internationally mandatory rules of the proper law are thus treated on the same basis as the rules of any other foreign legal system, the so-called 'third country's' internationally mandatory rules.

Thus the crucial question is whether these rules should be applied as part of the proper law, or whether they are subject to a special connection and are only applicable if the conditions of a special choice of law process (or a special conflict rule) are fulfilled. However, according to all the approaches, the self-limitation is respected despite the general principle in private international law of contracts of exclusion of *renvoi*. Accordingly, the proper law's internationally mandatory rules are not applied if they do not claim application to the situation in question.

c Internationally mandatory rules of a third country

The application of a third country's internationally mandatory rules is the main issue in dispute. Combining these rules with the ordinary choice of law process is extremely controversial and so far legal scholars have been unable to agree on one solution.[75]

Article 7 (1) of the Rome Convention enables the court of the forum to give effect to third countries' internationally mandatory rules on a discretionary basis. However, Germany and England entered a reservation to this article, with the result that it is not in legal force in either country.[76] Switzerland, on the other hand, has enacted art 19 of the IPRG which enables Swiss courts to consider third countries' internationally mandatory rules, if the foreign rule is internationally mandatory; the situation is closely connected with the enacting country; and the legitimate and overriding interest of a party requires the consideration of the foreign rule according to a Swiss viewpoint. Furthermore, the court has to consider the purpose of the foreign rule and the consequences of its application for a judgment that is fair according to the Swiss law.[77]

The German courts pay little attention to academic approaches and decide cases in a more pragmatic manner.[78] They have therefore relied on the principle of *territoriality of foreign public law* or the forum's *ordre public* to avoid application of a third country's internationally mandatory rules. In other cases, however, the courts recognised foreign internationally mandatory rules within

---

75 Chapter 5, I.
76 Chapter 5, IV, 1, 3.
77 Chapter 5, IV,1.
78 Chapter 5, II, 2.

the substantive law of the *lex causae* (which corresponded with the *lex fori* in all decided cases).[79] The violation of foreign law could lead to immorality under German law and thus render the contract null and void, or the foreign rule could lead to impossibility of performance or frustration of contract. The courts thus extended the scope of the substantive law rules in order to cover the violation of foreign law as well. German courts have considered foreign internationally mandatory rules within the notion of *boni mores* if the foreign rule also indirectly served German interests, or interests shared in common by all civilised nations, or pursued general valid moral values.[80]

German academics in general have rejected the principle of *territoriality* as basis for refusal to apply foreign public law.[81] It is much debated whether and how third countries' internationally mandatory rules can be applied or considered. Even so, no one supports the idea that third countries' internationally mandatory rules should not be given effect at all. The dispute focuses rather on the *method* that should be used to apply or consider these rules.[82]

According to the *Schuldstatuts-theory*, third countries' mandatory rules are in principle inapplicable, because they do not form part of the proper law as indicated by the normal choice of law rules. The advocates of this approach argue that there is no conflict rule that could render these rules applicable, apart from such exception as art VIII (2) (b) of the IMF Agreement. Despite their inapplicability, however, these rules are taken into account as supposed 'facts' within the substantive law of the *lex causae*.[83]

The *Special Connection* and *Combination Theories* favour recognition of a third country's internationally mandatory rules on the basis of choice of law criteria by means of a *special connection*.[84] Although there are many disagreements amongst the advocates of a *Special Connection Theory* about the special conflict rule,[85] the different views in essence have four propositions in common: (1) a sufficiently *close connection* between the situation and the enacting country; (2) the rule in question must be *internationally mandatory*; (3) the conditions in terms of which the rule applies must be fulfilled; and (4) the

---

79 Chapter 5, II, 2.
80 Chapter 5, II, 2, c, d.
81 See however Chapter 5, I, 2.
82 See Chapter 5, I, 7.
83 Chapter 5, I, 1.
84 Chapter 5, I, 3, 4.
85 Chapter 5, I, 3, b, c.

content of the provision and its legal consequences must be *compatible* with the legal system of the forum.[86]

English courts have in general rejected application or recognition of a third country's internationally mandatory rules because they do not form part of the proper law. There are, however, two exceptions.[87] Firstly, third countries' mandatory rules have been taken into account by reference to the *English public policy* rule that a contract opposed to British interests of state is void, particularly if it is likely to jeopardise friendly relations with another. The basis of this public policy rule is *international comity*.[88] The second exception is the rule that a contract (whether lawful by its proper law or not) will not be enforced if its performance is illegal under the *lex loci solutionis*.[89] As was noted, however, the juristic basis of these principles - whether they are principles of choice of law or English substantive law - is uncertain.[90]

2 The structurally preferable solution: A *special connection* of internationally mandatory rules

It is submitted that internationally mandatory rules should be applied or given effect on the basis of a *special connection*. A *special connection* constitutes the *systematically* preferable solution and can serve as a general concept for integrating these rules into the ordinary choice of law process. This solution does not replace the ordinary choice of law rules, nor is it intended to depart from the traditional allocation technique by substituting a policy-orientated selection process. On the contrary, a *special connection* of internationally mandatory rules *supplements* the ordinary choice of law process.

This solution indicates under what circumstances internationally mandatory rules are applicable to the contract, *alongside* the traditional process for determining the law governing the contract. Internationally mandatory rules are thus connected separately by means of different choice of law rules that apply alongside the traditional conflict rules. These separate choice of law rules take into account the peculiarities of internationally mandatory rules, the interests of the states involved, and the interests of the contracting parties in the application or non-application of the relevant rules. Admittedly, they are very much based on policy considerations, with a focus on the content and purpose of the rule in

86 Chapter 5, I, 3, f.
87 Chapter 5, III, 2.
88 Chapter 5, III, 2, a.
89 Chapter 5, III, 2, c.
90 Chapter 5, III, 2, c, d, 3.

question and the consequence of its application. One may therefore speak of a 'duality of methodology'.[91]

In the present author's opinion, however, this statement is inaccurate if it is based on the understanding that a special connection process depends *solely* on an interpretation of the nature and purpose of the rule in question. To the contrary, I argue that, although this choice of law process is more result- and policy-orientated, it still conforms to the traditional allocation technique. Internationally mandatory rules of the *lex fori* are applied because they have an attached conflict rule indicating their territorial scope, while foreign internationally mandatory rules are applied because special conflict rules of the forum so provide.

Therefore, it is preferable to refer to this separate connection of internationally mandatory rules as a necessary further development in adapting to legal changes, because private international law can and should develop further.[92] States are increasingly tending to enact mandatory laws that protect the weaker contracting party or regulate the economy - these are examples of such changes in law. The traditional choice of law process has to be further developed in order to accommodate these changes in law.[93]

The examination and critical analysis of the different case law solutions and academic approaches has shown that the *special connection* of internationally mandatory rules is, as a system, better than the principle of *territoriality* of public law rules. With regard to foreign rules, it is also preferable to the principle of *non-applicability of foreign public laws*,[94] the *Schuldstatuts* theory, the *Combination Theory*, the *Substantive Law Approach*,[95] and the approaches in England.[96]

The most important arguments in favour of a *special connection* follow.[97]

---

91 Cf the articles of Drobnig, Basedow and Siehr in RabelsZ 52 (1988) 1 et seq.

92 See Schurig *Lois* 55, 61 et seq, 69 et seq; RabelsZ 54 (1990) 217, 229 et seq; Voser *Lois d'application immédiate* 193 et seq.

93 For a discussion of this development, see the introductory remarks in Chapter 1; for the need to accommodate the choice of law process, also see supra Chapter 5, I, 3, a, e.

94 Chapter 5, II, 3.

95 Chapter 5, I, 7.

96 Chapter 5, III, 3.

97 The arguments will be discussed in the context of the submitted solutions for (**a**) the internationally mandatory rules of the *lex fori*, (**b**) the rules of a third country and (**c**) the rules of the *lex causae*. Cf the discussion and analysis in Chapter 4, I, 3; Chapter 5, I, 7; II 3; III, 2, b, e, 3; IV, 6.

a Internationally mandatory rules of the *lex fori*

With regard to the internationally mandatory rules of the forum it is submitted that courts should apply these rules, regardless of a foreign proper law, on the basis of a *special connection* rather than by referring to the forum's *ordre public.*[98]

(1) Special connection of internationally mandatory rules

A *special connection* is based on the understanding that internationally mandatory rules are not subject to the ordinary conflict rules of the forum. They contain next to their substantive content, a special (unilateral) conflict rule (express or implied) indicating their territorial scope. In other words, these rules must be accompanied by a unilateral conflict rule and they are applicable on the basis of their own express or implied claim to apply.

A *special connection* offers a solution that is consistent with existing choice of law techniques and means that the courts need not resort to the *ordre public.* The *ordre public* should not be used. Firstly, a *special connection* is systematically preferable, since the application of directly applicable statutes on the basis of their own terms as special conflict rules forms part of the choice of law process. The reliance upon public policy, on the other hand, indicates that the choice of law process has already been completed, and its outcome will be corrected by the exclusion of foreign law or by the application of the forum's fundamental *lois d'application immédiate.*[99]

Secondly, it is submitted that the *ordre public* should be restricted to its *negative function*: the exclusion of the foreign proper law if its application leads to a result manifestly incompatible with the forum's *ordre public.* This negative function may possibly result in an application of mandatory rules of the forum instead of the foreign proper law, but this is not how application of the *ordre public* is intended. Particularly in England no clear distinction has been made between application of the forum's mandatory rules and the public policy refusal to apply foreign law. In continental European countries, it has convincingly been argued that the gap that results from the refusal to apply foreign law should be closed by an interpretation and application of the foreign law, rather than application of the forum's rules.

---

98 Chapter 4, I, 1, 2, 3.

99 For this distinction, also see Forsyth *Private International Law* 102 footnote 63.

If the forum applies its own internationally mandatory rules because they are held to be manifestations of the *ordre public*, the latter requires a '*positive function*'. This runs counter to the aim of a restrictive application of the *ordre public* and is based on an understanding of the *ordre public* that is nowadays not accepted by most scholars.[100] Furthermore, internationally mandatory rules do not necessarily express such fundamental ethical values and policies that they can be characterised as 'crystallised rules' of public policy. Most of them are in fact based on economic or political policies, rather than on fundamental morality.

It should be repeated that application of the forum's law despite the existence of a foreign proper law must be an exception. The generally well-established rule in private international law is that reference to a foreign legal system, either by the choice of the parties or by the ordinary objective conflict rules, includes the mandatory rules of the foreign law. Consequently, the mandatory rules of the forum, as well as the rules of the potentially otherwise applicable law, are in principle replaced by those of the proper law, and thus rendered inapplicable. Furthermore, an extensive application of the forum's internationally mandatory rules despite a foreign proper law runs counter to the aim of *uniformity of result* or *decisional harmony*.[101] Courts and academics should therefore exercise restraint in interpreting mandatory rules as internationally mandatory.

(2) Identification of internationally mandatory rules

Identifying these rules and distinguishing them from other mandatory laws that should be subject to the choice of law process remains a problem. The view of the present author is that a general all-embracing characterisation is not possible. All attempts to find a uniform definition have in some way failed.[102] De Boer says that:

> So far, no criterion has been found by which the ambit of priority rules can be delimited from those of other mandatory rules. So there is virtually no way of knowing when the court will shift from allocation to policy-determination and *vice versa*.[103]

100 For details, see Chapter 4, I, 3.

101 The crucial point is that while the South African forum may grant South African rules an overriding effect in respect of a foreign law governing the contract, the same effect might not be granted to the South African provisions by a foreign court as forum.

102 See supra Chapter 3, II.

103 De Boer RabelsZ 54 (1990) 24, 61.

It is submitted, however, that this statement is too pessimistic, and that basic principles and useful criteria have been established.

If a statute stipulates its scope in an express term there is no great difficulty. The rule must be applied according to its own terms. If the rule or act does not contain an express term as to its scope of application, the judge faces the difficult task of interpreting it to determine whether it was intended to override the normal choice of law process. This policy-orientated interpretation of a statute necessarily creates some uncertainty. Although there are no absolute rules about the conditions for classifying a rule as internationally mandatory, there are guidelines.[104]

Most authors assume that, if a rule does not expressly stipulate its territorial scope, it can be classified as internationally mandatory provided it pursues the economic and political interests of the state and has no direct relation to private law. A rule is mandatory only in a domestic setting if it predominantly serves the interests of the contracting parties.[105] Rules with a 'double function' - that serve private and public interests - are problematic.[106] Here it is particularly difficult to find a criterion to distinguish domestic from internationally mandatory rules. It is submitted that those rules serving mainly the fair reconciliation of conflicting interests of the contracting parties qualify as domestic only.

This assumption should also prevail for those rules intending to protect the weaker contracting party. English authors are too ready to characterise protective laws as internationally mandatory for the sole reason that they intend to protect the weaker party. A protective rule should be classified as internationally mandatory only as an exception, if the rule in question pursues the public interests of the community, rather than private interests.[107] It is submitted, for example, that, under the appropriate circumstances, the South African Basic Conditions of Employment Act 75 of 1997 can reasonably be characterised as internationally mandatory, while South African courts should

---

104 This question also depends on the type of mandatory rule, the policy pursued by the particular rule, and the facts of the individual case. See also the approach of Schurig *Lois* 55, 64 et seq: It must be determined whether the intention of the rule is that a foreign legal system should govern the issue if the conditions of the rule are not fulfilled. If so, the rule is an internationally mandatory one. If the rule intends that other provisions of the same legal system should regulate the matter if the conditions of the provision are not fulfilled, it is simply mandatory.

105 For details, see Chapter 3, II.

106 Chapter 3, II and Chapter 4, III, 2.

107 For example, public labour law. For details, see Gamillscheg ZfA 14 (1983) 307 et seq.

be reluctant to classify the Credit Agreements Act 75 of 1980 as internationally mandatory.[108]

In cases of doubt, where the intention of the legislature or the policy of the rule does not clearly indicate its scope of application, it is submitted that the rule should *not* be classified as internationally mandatory.[109]

b Internationally mandatory rules of a third country

The situation is different with regard to foreign internationally mandatory rules. Judges are not bound to apply foreign legislation unless a statutory or common law conflict rule so directs. In respect of third countries' internationally mandatory rules this is due to the general proposition of conflict of laws that, unless the forum's choice of law rules so direct, foreign law is not applicable.

Statutory conflict rules indicating the application or consideration of third countries' internationally mandatory rules are rare. A well known example is art VIII (2) (b) of the IMF Agreement for foreign exchange control regulations. Article 7 (1) of the Rome Convention and art 19 of the Swiss IPRG are examples of a more general nature, since they cover all types of contracts and internationally mandatory rules. Similar rules can be found in art 16 of the Convention on the Law Applicable to Agency of 1978[110] and art 16 (2) of the Trust Convention of 1985.[111] Apart from these statutory conflict rules, nearly all approaches nevertheless take third countries' internationally mandatory rules into account under certain circumstances, either as supposed facts within the substantive law, or by means of special conflict rules.

The crucial question is when and on what legal basis application of a third country's internationally mandatory rule is justified. As was seen, *de lege lata*, no *special conflict rule* exists in the South African conflict of law of contracts. The courts tend to follow English precedents.[112] It is submitted, however, that South African courts should now, *de lege ferenda*, develop *special conflict rules* or at least choice of law principles to take third countries' rules into account. In order to find conditions and criteria, they may nevertheless refer to the well-established principles of English and German case law.

---

108 See Forsyth *Private International Law* 13, 14 referring to the Basic Conditions Employment Act 3 of 1986.

109 Also see Lorenz RIW 1987, 569, 578, 581, 582.

110 Act, Doc La Haye 13 Sess 1976 I 42; RabelsZ 43 (1979) 176.

111 Act, Doc La Haye 15 Sess 1984 I 25 - 39; RabelsZ 50 (1986) 698; see Siehr RabelsZ 52 (1988) 41, 70; Erne *Vertragsgültigkeit* 173; Schiffer *Normen* 142.

112 See Chapter 6, I, 3.

At the same time, South African courts should avoid repeating mistakes of the German and English courts, and should clarify from the outset that the process of giving effect to third countries' laws is a process of conflict of laws.

(1) The structurally preferable solution

The application or consideration of a third country's internationally mandatory rules on the juristic basis of a *special connection* is preferable to referring to the forum's *ordre public*, or to extending substantive law rules of the proper law so that they can cover the violation of foreign law.[113] It is not intended to repeat what was explained above, and a few remarks will suffice.

International contracts are usually connected with two or more legal systems, that may have a reasonable interest in the application of their mandatory provisions. The interest might be even greater than that of the law chosen by the parties or determined objectively by the forum's conflict rules. This is the case, for example, if the chosen law is a neutral legal system with which the contract or the contracting parties have no objective connection, apart from the choice.

Nowadays, private law is not only based on private interests, but is increasingly influenced by the interests of the state and the community: the so-called 'double functionality' of the law of contracts.

State intervention in the domestic legal sphere for purposes of redressing social and economic imbalances by rules that inhibit the freedom of contract cannot be ignored in private international law. The logical consequence is a need to accommodate provisions of mandatory rules of law that would not be applicable according to the traditional conflict approach and to adjust the ordinary choice of law process.

In effect, all the approaches - whether *Special Connection*, the *Combination Theory*, the *Substantive Law Approach* of German case law, the *Schuldstatuts-theory*, or the English *public policy-comity* or the *lex loci solutionis* rule - take third countries' internationally mandatory rules into account. The *Special Connection Theory*, however, seems to be the most methodologically sound solution. Although it is argued that this theory would run counter to the principle of *unity of the law applicable to a contract*, this principle is of no use with regard to internationally mandatory rules.[114]

---

[113] For details about the following arguments, see Chapter 5, I, 7, II, 3, III, 3, IV, 6.

[114] Chapter 5, I, 7, a.

Authors who support treating foreign mandatory rules as facts within the substantive law of the *lex causae* assume an incorrect starting point. According to them, the recognition as supposed facts would not require a choice of law. It is left to the governing law to decide whether third countries' internationally mandatory rules can be considered. However, foreign rules are not facts in the true sense and often it is the rule itself or its normative content that is given effect.[115] In truth, the choice of law question about whether the rule is applicable is combined with application of substantive law rules and thereby hidden behind the substantive law. The substantive law, however, is not intended to decide choice of law questions.

Finally, it should be kept in mind that, according to general principles in choice of law, the question of whether and how foreign law is to be given effect is a matter of the conflict of laws of the forum state.[116] The consideration of a third country's rules within a foreign *lex causae* would mean that this decision is in effect handed over to the foreign proper law.[117] The *Special Connection Theory*, however, leaves this decision in the hands of the forum state.[118]

A few additional remarks about the English *public policy-comity rule* and the *lex loci solutionis rule* seem in order, since it is likely that South African courts will tend to adopt these solutions. The *public policy-comity* rule is obviously vague, but several issues remain unnecessarily uncertain: What *types* of rules are referred to? Is reference being made to *any* prohibition, or is it necessary that the foreign rule claims application to the situation in question? Does the *public policy-comity* rule require a connection between the situation and the foreign enacting country? Is a friendly country really any country with which the United Kingdom is not at war? Must the public policy rule be restricted to cases of conspiracy and thus not apply in cases where the parties did not intend to break the foreign law?

A final point of criticism is that - except the *public policy-comity* rule - only illegality under the *lex loci solutionis* is taken into account. Illegality under other laws - the law of the habitual residence, place of business or the *lex sitae* of the goods - is ignored. Yet these latter laws might have an even closer connection with the contract.[119]

---

115 See the discussion in Chapter 5, I, 7, b, c, e, f; II, 3, d; III, 2, b, d, 3, a.

116 This is equally true for SA, cf Forsyth *Private International Law* 58.

117 Chapter 5, I, 7, c.

118 Furthermore, choice of law considerations will take place at the level of conflict of laws and will not be confused with the application of a (possibly) foreign substantive law.

119 For details, see Chapter 5, III, 3, b.

Apart from the fact that the juristic basis of the common law principles is uncertain, a *special connection* is the preferable means of taking third countries' rules into account and offers a systematically superior basis for the courts' findings. The results reached by the courts in their application of the *public policy-comity* rule or the *lex loci solutionis* rule could equally be reached by means of a *special connection*. Furthermore, courts would be able to take into account the peculiarities of each individual case, since a *special connection* is not restricted to, for example, cases of conspiracy of the parties or the place of performance. The necessary conditions for a *special connection* are a close connection, the foreign rule's claim to apply, and further conditions regarding the policy of the foreign rule and the consequences of its application.

(2) A special connection in conformity with conflict of laws

A *special connection* conforms to principles of conflict of laws and leads to results that correspond in most cases with the outcome of the decided case law. It thus changes the method rather than the outcome. In order to avoid the reproach that a *special connection* would imply a methodological move towards *unilateralism*, it must be stated that this is only partly true, since the *unilateral* approach starts from the foreign mandatory rule's claim to apply.

Most authors that advocate a *special connection* of foreign internationally mandatory rules assume that the foreign rule is applied not because it claims application, but because such application is required by the choice of law rules (whether common or statutory law rules) of the forum state.[120] The connecting factor for indicating the application of the foreign rule is, very broadly, a close connection, a factor that is well known and widely accepted in private international law. There is thus no need to scrutinise every legal system for internationally mandatory rules claiming application to the situation. All that is required is determining whether the forum state has an interest in considering a violated foreign rule of a closely connected country.

It is, however, acknowledged that this approach departs from the traditional choice of law technique in so far as the latter is held to be 'neutral', indicating the applicable legal system without regard to the content of the foreign rules and with the exclusion of *renvoi*. A *special connection* of foreign internationally mandatory rules is necessarily more policy- and result-orientated since it controls the content of the foreign rule and the results of its application

[120] Chapter 5, I, 7, c, f.

on the contract, and requires that the rules serve interests that are somehow shared with the forum state.[121]

Furthermore, it must be reiterated that the consideration of third countries' internationally mandatory rules serves the goal of decisional harmony, regardless of where the matter is heard.[122] And lastly, the comity of nations is served.[123]

(3) General guidelines for special conflict rules

It is submitted that the following conditions may serve as *general guidelines* for a *special connection* of foreign internationally mandatory rules. It must be reiterated that the tendency has been to move away from a general conflict rule that covers all types of contracts and internationally mandatory rules. This type of rule is necessarily vague. Instead the recent trend is to develop special conflict rules for certain areas of law, where state interests are typically involved and are pursued by means of internationally mandatory rules intervening in private relationships, for example, anti-trust law, import and export restrictions, and foreign exchange controls.[124]

The present author adheres to this view. Special rules for certain types of internationally mandatory rules allow for consideration of the peculiarities of the legal field and for the development of firm criteria indicating under what circumstances these rules can be reasonably applied. For example, export and import restrictions require different considerations in respect of a close connection and the interests of the forum than in the area of anti-trust law. The former restrictions require the goods either to come from the enacting country or be delivered there, and, if the foreign prohibition serves interests that are directed against the forum state or are not shared in common by the states, the forum will not give effect to the prohibition, despite a local contact. In the area

---

121 However, court decisions where third countries' internationally mandatory rules were taken into account were clearly policy-orientated, for example, the consideration of foreign rules within the English *public policy-comity* rule or the notion of German *boni mores*. Furthermore, policy considerations and a control of the content and effect of foreign rules have taken place ever since within the notion of the forum's *ordre public*.

122 This is a goal that SA private international law also desires, cf Forsyth *Private International Law* 60, 61.

123 See supra Chapter 5, I, 7, h. The principle has considerable value in SA private international law, see Forsyth *Private International Law* on pages 36 et seq. For a discussion of the meaning of comity as used by the Roman-Dutch authorities, see Huber *De conflictu legum*; Voet *De Statutis*, Voet *Commentarius*. Also cf Forsyth ibid on pages 58, 59 for his personal conclusion on the way forward for modern Roman-Dutch law.

124 See Chapter 5, I, 3, c, d.

of anti-trust law, on the other hand, the so-called 'effect principle' is usually appropriate to determine whether a foreign rule reasonably claims application, viz. the agreement that is prohibited by a certain anti-trust rule of a foreign country must have an effect on the market of that particular country.

Nevertheless, in the present stage of development, a general clause might be useful in commencing the process of developing refined rules for particular fields of law.[125] The process of refining and concretising criteria for the application of foreign rules may in the course of time also lead to the development of multilateral conflict rules, that are not restricted to indicating the applicability of foreign countries' rules, but may also refer to the forum's internationally mandatory rules in this field. A good example is the Swiss art 137 that indicates under what circumstances the foreign and the forum's anti-trust law is applicable on the basis of the 'effects principle'.

However, in the absence of specific conflict rules, it is necessary first to establish *general principles*. The following are submitted as general guidelines for a consideration of foreign (third) countries' internationally mandatory rules.

i. Mandatory rules of a foreign country that solely or predominantly pursue the economic and political interests of the foreign enacting state, and not the interests of the contracting parties in settling disputes, or the fair reconciliation between them, can be given effect if the contract has a *close connection* with the enacting country and, according to the law of the foreign country, the rule claims application, regardless of the proper law of the contract (*internationally mandatory rules*). The close connection should be *specified* with reference to the *legal relationship* and the *rule in question.* (For example, in the field of anti-trust law, the crucial question should be whether the agreement affects the market of the country that enacted the internationally mandatory anti-trust regulation, while in the field of export restrictions, the question whether the goods have been exported from the enacting country should be decisive.)

[125] It is submitted that it is in any event not necessary for the legislature to enact conflict rules that provide for the application of foreign internationally mandatory rules. Because SA private international law is to a large extent based on common law, there is no reason why courts should not develop common law choice of law rules in this field.

ii. In order to reach a *fair result* in the individual case, the judge should be granted a broad discretion in deciding whether and how the foreign internationally mandatory rule is to be recognised. The consideration of the following four aspects enables the court to take into account not only the interests of the forum and the foreign enacting state, but also the interests of the contracting parties.

(a) In considering whether and how to give effect to the foreign rule, regard should be had to its *nature* and *purpose*, with reference to whether it serves *interests shared in common with the forum state*, or is in other respects reasonable from the forum's point of view. *Categories* can thus be developed to indicate under what circumstances it is reasonable to give effect to the foreign rule, such as:

- does the foreign rule indirectly protect interests of the forum state?
- does it protect universally recognised interests?
- does it protect generally required moral values?
- does it promote comity and harmonise international relations?
- does it simply serve to co-ordinate the national economy?

(b) Furthermore, the court should have regard to the *consequences of applying* the foreign rule, ie its effect on the contract private relationship. At this stage the court should consider the *interests of the contracting parties* with a view to promoting a fair reconciliation of their interests.

(c) In addition, the court should be free to decide *how* effect is given to the foreign rule. Strict adherence to application of the foreign rule might sometimes not be justified. The court could also take the foreign rule into account as a reason for nullity of the contract under the *lex causae* rules, for impossibility of performance or frustration of the contract. Alternatively, it might be necessary to alter the legal consequences of the foreign rule if its application would lead to unjust results for the contracting parties. Thus, it might be better to assume frustration of contract than to nullify the contract as demanded by the third country's rule.[126]

---

[126] This process of modifying the application of laws and their consequences with a view to a fair outcome can also be characterised as adaptation (in a broader sense). For adaptation, see the text following this footnote.

(d) In general, the relationship between the proper law and the application of third countries' internationally mandatory rules should be solved by the private international law technique of *adaptation*.[127] The doctrine involves the alteration or modification of either the conflict rules or the relevant conflicting substantive laws.[128] Thus, if the proper law conflicts with the third country's rule, the judge may alter or adapt the substantive law rules of either, in order to avoid contradictions and to reach a fair result in accordance with the forum's viewpoint.[129] Alternatively, it may even be reasonable to shift or alter the scope of application of the relevant conflict rules or to create a new conflict rule for the situation in question.[130]

---

127 See supra Chapter 4, I, 1, Chapter 5, I, 3, j, IV, 1, d, (2); for authors referring to the technique of adaptation in this particular context, see Lorenz RIW 1987, Lehmann *Zwingendes Recht* 229; Kreuzer *Ausländisches Wirtschaftsrecht* 95; Schiffer *Normen* 195 et seq; Erne *Vertragsgültigkeit* 198.

128 On the technique of adaptation in Germany and Switzerland, see Kegel *IPR* 7th ed § 8; Firsching/von Hoffmann *IPR* 213 et seq; Neuhaus *Grundbegriffe* 354 et seq; Keller/Siehr *IPR* 450 et seq. The technique is granted much less theoretical attention in England, which is regrettable because the problems there are the same as elsewhere, in that norms of different legal systems may conflict due to the choice of law process (viz. 'cumulation' or 'gap'). English authors refer to these situations in the context of 'Characterization' (or 'Classification') and take a much more pragmatic view. Compare Dicey & Morris *Conflict of Laws Vol I/12th ed* 34, 38 et seq, */13th ed* 33 et seq; Cheshire & North's *Private International law/12th ed* 43 et seq, */13th ed* 35 et seq. Although the doctrine of *adaptation* is *res nova* for SA private international law, authors are much more aware of the problem and profound in their analysis and theoretical foundation, see Bennett 105 III (1988) SALJ 444 et seq; Forsyth *Private International Law* 69 et seq. In the present study, the problem of adaptation does not arise in the context of characterization, but as a result of the special connection of internationally mandatory rules, because different (and possibly even the same) aspects of a case are governed by different legal systems. It has been recognised in SA law that cumulation and gap may arise in contexts other than characterization, cf Bennett ibid and Forsyth ibid 69 footnote 35. Also compare Lipstein Rec des Cours 135 (1972 II) 99, 209 for the principle of adaptation in situations where the choice of law leads to the application of different laws to different aspects of the case; also compare Lipstein *Characterization* ss 15, 16, 17, 48 et seq.

129 *Materiellrechtliche Lösung* (substantive law solution). In effect the judge is permitted to modify substantive law and thus create new rules so that the contradictions are avoided. Which rules he alters depends again on a value decision of the judge. The crucial point is which law can modified without violating the legal system, see Kegel *IPR* § 8 III, 1, 3.

130 *International privatrechtliche Lösung* (conflict of law solution). The alteration of conflict rules or the creation of new principles can lead to the result that the whole legal transaction is held to be governed by only one legal system. Which legal system shall govern is a value-decision of the judge, see Kegel *IPR* § 8 III, 1, 2; Firsching/von Hoffmann *IPR* 215. Although authors like Firsching/von Hoffmann prefer this latter 'conflict solution', the present author prefers the 'substantive law solution', because the

iii. The following principles should prevail in the rare case of conflicting internationally mandatory rules from different legal systems. (This situation is hypothetical, since such cases have not yet occured.)[131] Firstly, the judge should examine whether these rules really do conflict, or whether it might be reasonable to apply both rules, despite their differing content and legal consequences. Thus different considerations might be necessary for different obligations, such as payment or delivery, and if these obligations have been discharged or have to be performed in different countries, it might well be reasonable to consider the rules of different countries for each obligation.

If the internationally mandatory rules of the forum do indeed conflict with those of a foreign country in so far as they concern the same obligation or conduct, the rules of the forum state should prevail. This simply follows from the fact that the forum is bound by its sovereign. If there is a conflict between foreign internationally mandatory rules, this conflict should be solved as follows. The judge should first determine whether it is possible to combine the content of both rules. If this is not possible, he should then determine with which country the contract has the closer connection. If an equally close connection exists, the judge should establish which rule serves interests more favourably, from the forum's point of view.

(4) Subsidiary consideration of the factual effects on the private relationship

According to these principles, it may not be reasonable to give effect to the foreign rule. It might nevertheless be reasonable to take the *actual effects* of the foreign rule into account within the applicable substantive law if the existence of the foreign rule renders performance *de facto* impossible. In this case it is not the foreign rule or its legal content that is taken into account, but only its *effect* on the private relationship.

This will be the case where the foreign state has enacted a rule that has already been enforced, for example, confiscation of the goods that renders performance de facto impossible. Alternatively, performance may be sanctioned by heavy penalties so that it would constitute an undue hardship for the debtor to perform. Under these circumstances the debtor should be relieved of his obligations, in the interests of justice. Here we are dealing with a 'factual

conflict solution does not avoid the fact that the parties are sometimes faced with contradictory laws, which may *de facto* effect their legal transaction. Also compare Lipstein Rec des Cours 135 (1972 II) 99, 209.

131 This can also be classified as a situation covered by the doctrine of adaptation.

circumstance abroad' that can be taken into account by the substantive law rules applicable to the contract. However, the question of which contracting party has to carry the risk of (non-) performance is a separate issue.

c Internationally mandatory rules of the proper law

The crucial question about internationally mandatory rules of the proper law is whether they should be applicable for the sole reason that they form part of the proper law, or whether they should also be subject to a *special connection*. It is submitted that internationally mandatory rules that serve only the economic and political interests of the foreign state should not be applied as part of the proper law, but should instead be connected separately on the basis of special choice of law considerations. They are thus treated in the same way as the mandatory rules of a third legal system. This is based on the presumption that the ordinary choice of law rules in contract designate the law that will regulate the interests of the contracting parties, but these rules do not take into account all state enactments that intervene in private relationships, namely those that serve mainly state interests.[132]

Neither the parties' choice of law nor the objective allocation technique are suitable connecting factors to take into account state interests. The choice of a neutral law - a law with which the contract has no further connection, apart from the fact that the parties chose it - is an example. There is no justification for applying the export restrictions of this country, or any other rule pursuing state interests, for the sole reason that the rules belong to the chosen neutral law. Instead, the legislation of a country with which the contract has a close connection, according to special considerations of the nature of the rule and the type of contract, should be applied.[133]

A distinction must be drawn between those rules that have no direct relationship to private law and that are intended to further the state's economic or political interests (*macro function*), and those rules that serve the interests of private parties.[134] While the latter rules are included in the reference to the foreign law

---

132 See Chapter 5, I, 3, a, f, 7, a; Vischer Rec des Cours 232 (1992) 21, 179; id RabelsZ 53 (1989) 438, 441, Voser *Lois d'application immédiate* 51 et seq, 69 et seq; Morscher *Rechtssetzungsakte* 88; Kreuzer *Ausländisches Wirtschaftsrecht* 82 et seq.

133 Similar considerations are valid with regard to the objective allocation, cf Chapter 5, I, 3, e, 7, a.

134 For the 'double functionality' of the law of contracts, regulating the interests of the private parties, as well as being the object and instrument of governmentally guided economy in the modern welfare state, see Kreuzer *Ausländisches Wirtschaftsrecht* 82 et seq; id *Schlechtriem/Leser* 89, 106; for details, see Chapter 5, I, 3, e.

and are therefore applicable if they belong to the proper law, the former rules fall outside the foreign legal system's scope of the reference.[135] Those rules that serve the interests of the state, not the fair reconciliation of the interests of the contracting parties, deserve special conflict considerations. These are in principle independent of the question whether the foreign rule belongs to the proper law as designated by the ordinary conflict rules, or to a third legal system with which the situation has a close connection.

Often, the result of a *special connection* and an application of internationally mandatory rules as part of the proper law will be the same. This is because parties frequently choose a law with which the contract is most closely connected as the legal system to govern their transaction. Furthermore, internationally mandatory rules of the proper law are, according to all approaches, applied only if they claim application. Thus, despite the general principle of private international law in contract that *renvoi* is disregarded, the self-limitation of these rules is respected. The *special connection* is nevertheless the better solution,[136] since the special reference to the foreign law is *ab initio* subject to the proviso that the foreign rule claims application.[137] If an internationally mandatory rule does not claim application, the rule is not given effect.[138] If the rules of different legal systems conflict with each other, the principles mentioned above should be applied.[139]

---

135 Chapter 5, I, 3, e, 7.

136 The authors who advocate that internationally mandatory rules of the proper law apply because they belong to the proper law either have to interpret the territorial scope of the rules as part of its material content instead as an attached unilateral conflict rule or they need to make exceptions from the general principle that *renvoi* is disregarded, see supra under Chapter 5, I, 1, 7, f, III, 3, c.

137 Thus neither comity of nations nor decisional harmony is endangered. Regardless of where litigation takes place, the forum would not apply its internationally mandatory rule to the transaction, nor should this be done by another forum applying the foreign law despite the law's self-limitation. There is no justification for comity in situations where the foreign state's rule does not claim application.

138 In the field of economic legislation the problems that result from the acceptance of *renvoi*, particularly the 'negative conflict' that no law is applicable, do not arise. Cf Lipstein ICLQ 26 (1977) 884, 892 et seq.

139 Chapter 6, II, 2, b.

Bibliography

Anderegg, Kirsten, Ausländische Eingriffsnormen im internationalen Vertragsrecht, Dissertation, Tübingen 1989, (cited: Ausländische Eingriffsnormen).

id, Anwendung ausländischer Eingriffsnormen, in: RabelsZ 52 (1988) 260 - 270.

Anton, A.E./Beaumont, P.R., Private International Law, A treatise from the standpoint of Scots law, 2nd ed, Edinburgh 1990, (cited: Anton Private International Law).

Banakas, Efstathios K., United Kingdom Law in the 1980's, Comparative and Common Law Studies for the XIIth International Congress of Comparative Law, Volume 8, London 1988 (cited: see the authors).

Bar, Christian, von, Internationales Privatrecht, Band I, Allgemeine Lehren, München 1987, Band II, Besonderer Teil, München 1991 (cited: IPR Bd I / Bd II).

Bär, Rolf, Kartellrecht und internationales Privatrecht: Die kollisionsrechtliche Behandlung wirtschaftsrechtlicher Eingriffe (dargestellt am Beispiel des Gesetzes gegen Wettbewerbsbeschränkungen), Dissertation, Bern 1965 (cited: Kartellrecht).

id, Extraterritoriale Wirkung von Gesetzen, in: Die Schweizerische Rechtsordnung in ihren internationalen Bezügen, Festgabe zum Schweizerischen Juristentag 1988, Jenny-Kälin (ed), Bern 1988, 3 - 26 (cited: Extraterritoriale Wirkung).

Basedow, Jürgen, Das amerikanische Pipeline Embargo vor Gericht, Anmerkung zu Rechtbank Den Haag (Präsident) 17.9.1982, in: RabelsZ 47 (1983) 141 - 172.

id, Private Law Effects of Foreign Export Controls -An International Case Report-, in: 27 GYBIL (1984) 109 - 141.

id, Wirtschaftskollisionsrecht, Theoretischer Versuch über die ordnungspolitischen Normen des Forumstaates, in: RabelsZ 52 (1988) 8 - 40.

id, Entwicklungen des Internationalen Kartellrechts, in: NJW 1989, 627 - 638.

Basle Symposium, Basle Symposium on the Rôle of Public Law in Private International Law, Klein, Frédéric Edouard (ed), Bâle et Francfort-sur-le-Main 1991 (cited: see the authors).

Baum, Harald, Faktische und potentielle Eingriffsnormen, Der iranische Bierlieferungsfall, in: RabelsZ 53 (1989) 152 - 164.

Becker, Christoph, Theorie und Praxis der Sonderanknüpfung im Internationalen Privatrecht, Dissertation, Stuttgart 1991 (cited: Theorie).

Becker, Michael, Zwingendes Eingriffsrecht in der Urteilsanerkennung, in: RabelsZ 60 (1996) 691 - 737.

Beitzke, Konrad, Bemerkungen zur Kollisionsrechtsvergleichung in der Praxis, in: RabelsZ 48 (1984), 623 - 647 (643 f.).

Bennett, Tom W., Cumulation and Gap: Are they systematic defects in the Conflict of Laws? in: 105 III (1988) SALJ 444 - 456.

Birk, Rolf, Die Bedeutung der Parteiautonomie im Internationalen Arbeitsrecht, in: RdA 1989, 201 - 207.

Blessing, Marc, Impact of the extraterritorial Application of Mandatory Rules of Law on International Contracts, Basel, FfM 1999.

Boer, Th. M., De, The EEC Contracts Convention and the Dutch Courts, in: RabelsZ 54 (1990) 24 - 62.

Booysen, Hercules, International Transactions and the International Law Merchant, Pretoria 1995 (cited: International Transactions).

Busse, Daniel, Die Berücksichtigung ausländischer Eingriffsnormen durch die deutsche Rechtsprechung, in: ZvglRWiss 95 (1996) 386 - 418.

Carter, P. B., Contracts in English Private International Law, in: 57 BYBIL (1986) 1 - 32.

Cavers, David, A Critique of the Choice of Law Problem, in: Harv L Rev 47 (1933 - 1934) 173 - 208.

id, The Choice of Law Process, Ann Arbour 1965.

Cheshire & North's, Private International Law, North, P.M. & Fawcett, J.J. (eds), 13th ed, London 1999, 12th ed, London 1992, 11th ed, London 1987, (cited: Private International Law/11th, 12th or 13th ed).

Cockrell, Alfred J., Can you paradigm? - Another perspective on the public law/private law divide, in: 1993 Acta Juridica 227 et seq.

Coester, Michael, Die Berücksichtigung fremden zwingenden Rechts neben dem Vertragsstatut, in: ZVerglRWiss 82 (1983) 1 - 30.

Coester-Waltjen, Dagmar, Der Eskimo-Mantel aus Spanien - Ist der Kollisionsrechtliche Verbraucherschutz zu kurz gestrickt? in: Festschrift für Werner Lorenz, Tübingen 1991, 297 - 319 (cited: FS Lorenz)

Coing, Helmut, Zur Anwendung zwingender ausländischer Verträge: Art. 7 des Übereinkommens über das auf vertragliche Schuldverhältnisse anwendbare Recht, in: WM 1981, 810 - 813.

Collier, J. G., Conflicts of Laws, 2nd ed, Cambridge 1994.

id, Contract to promote corruption in Qatar, Non-enforcement in England, in: 47 CLJ [1988] 169 - 171.

id, Conflict of Laws and Enforcement of Foreign Public Laws Antipodean Attitudes, in: 48 CLJ [1989] 33 - 36.

Collins, Lawrence, Contractual Obligations - The EEC Preliminary Draft Convention on Private International Law, in: 25 ICLQ (1976) 35 - 57.

id, Practical Implications in England of the E.E.C. Convention on the Law Applicable to Contractual Obligations, in: Contract Conflicts, North (ed), London 1982, 205 - 216, (cited: Contract Conflicts).

Currie, Brainerd, Selected Essays on the Conflict of Laws, Duke U P, Durham N C 1963, (cited: Selected Essays).

Czernich, Dietmar/Heiss, Helmut, EVÜ - Das Europäische Schuldvertragsübereinkommen, Kommentar, Czernich/Heiss (eds), Wien 1999 (cited: Czernich/Heiss EVÜ).

Diamond, Aubrey, Harmonisation of Private International Law Relating to Contractual Obligations, in: Rec des Cours 199 (1986-IV) 233 - 308.

Dicey & Morris, On the Conflict of Laws, Collins et al (eds), Volume 1, 13th ed, London 2000, Volume 2, 13th ed, London 2000, Volume 1, 12th ed, London 1993, Volume 2, 12th ed, London 1993, Volume 2, 11th ed, London 1987 (cited: Dicey & Morris Conflict of Laws Vol I, II/11th, 12th or 13th ed).

Drobnig, Ulrich, Comments on Art. 7 Drafts Convention, in: Lando/v. Hoffmann/Siehr, European Private International Law of Obligations, Tübingen 1975, 82 - 86 (cited: Comments).

id, Die Beachtung von ausländischen Eingriffsgesetzen, eine Interessenanalyse, in: Festschrift für Karl Neumayer, Baden Baden 1985, 159 - 179 (cited: FS Neumayer).

id, Das Profil des Wirtschaftskollisionsrecht, in: RabelsZ 52 (1988) 1 - 7.

Droste, Thomas, Der Begriff der "zwingenden Bestimmungen" in den Art. 27 ff. EGBGB, Dissertation, Freiburg 1992 (cited: Begriff).

Edwards, A. B., Conflict of Laws, in: The Law of South Africa, Volume II, Joubert, W A (ed), Durban 1993 (cited: Conflict of Laws).

id, Some Reflections on the Reception of the "Proper Law" Doctrine into South African Law, in: Huldigingsbundel Paul Van Warmelo, Pretoria 1984, 38 - 67 (cited: 'Proper Law' Doctrine).

Erauw, Johan A., International Advancement of Consumer Interests through Conflicts Rules, in: Sarcevic International Contracts and Conflicts of Laws (1990) 71 - 85 (cited: International Contracts).

Erne, Monica, Vertragsgültigkeit und drittstaatliche Eingriffsnormen, Dissertation, Zürich 1985 (cited: Vertragsgültigkeit).

Fawcett, J. J., Evasion of Law and Mandatory Rules in Private International Law, in: 49 CLJ [1990] 44 - 62.

Firsching, Karl/Hoffmann, Bernd, von, Einführung in das Internationale Privatrecht, 5th ed, München 1997 (cited: IPR).

Flessner, Axel, Interessenjurisprudenz im internationalen Privatrecht, Dissertation Tübingen 1990 (cited: Interessenjurisprudenz).

Fletcher, Ian F., Conflict of Laws and European Community Law, Amsterdam, NY, Oxford 1982 (cited: Conflict of Laws).

Forsyth, C. F., Private International Law, 3rd ed, Ndabeni, Cape 1996.

id, When can a Foreign Illegality taint an English contract? in: 46 CLJ [1987] 404 - 406.

id, The role of public law in the English conflict of laws, in: United Kingdom law in the 1980's, Volume 8, E.K. Banakas (ed), 1988, 94 - 119 (cited: Role of Public Law).

Francescakis, Phocion, La théorie du renvoi et les conflits de systèmes en droit international privé, Paris 1958 (cited: La théorie du renvoi).

id, Lois d'application immédiate et règles de conflit, in: Rev dir int priv proc 3 (1967) 691 - 698.

Gamillscheg, Franz, Ein Gesetz über das internationale Arbeitsrecht, in: ZfA 14 (1983) 307 - 373.

Giuliano, Mario/Lagarde, Paul, Report on the Convention of the Law Applicable to Contractual Obligations, reprinted, in: North Contract Conflicts Appendix B, 355 - 401 (cited: Report).

Grossfeld, Bernhard/Rogers, Paul, A Shared Values Approach to Jurisdictional Conflicts in International Economic Law, in: 32 ICLQ (1983) 930 - 947.

Guedj, Thomas G., The Theory of the Lois de Police, A Functional Trend in Continental Private International Law - A Comparative Analysis with Modern American Theories, in: Am J Comp L 39 (1991) 661 - 697.

Hartley, Trevor C., Beyond the Proper Law, Mandatory Rules under the Drafts Convention on the Law Applicable to Contractual Obligations, in: 4 ELR (1979) 236 - 243.

id, Consumer Protection Provisions in the E..C. Convention, in: Contract Conflicts, North (ed), London 1982, 111 - 141 (cited: Contract Conflicts).

id, Foreign Public Law and Private International Law: English Report, in: Basle Symposium on the Rôle of Public Law in Private International Law, Klein (ed), Bâle et Francfort-sur-le-Main 1991, 13 - 28 (cited: Foreign Public Law).

id, Mandatory Rules in International Contracts: The Common Law Approach, in: Rec des Cours 226 (1997) 341 - 425.

Heini, Anton, Die Rechtswahl im Vertragsrecht und das neue IPR-Gesetz, in: Festschrift für Rudolf Moser, Beiträge zum neuen IPR des Sachen, Schuld und Gesellschaftsrechts, Zürich 1987, 67 - 78 (cited: FS Moser).

id, Ausländische Staatsinteressen und internationales Privatrecht, in: ZSR 100 (1981) 65 - 83.

id, Die Anwendung wirtschaftlicher Zwangsmaßnahmen im Internationalen Privatrecht, in: BerDGesVölkR 22 (1982) 37 - 55.

Hentzen, Matthias, Zur Anwendung fremden Eingriffsrechts seit der IPR Reform, in: RIW 1988, 508 - 511.

Hoffmann, Bernd, von, Über den Schutz der schwächeren Vertragspartei bei internationalen Schuldverträgen, in: RabelsZ 38 (1974), 396 - 420.

id, Assessment of the E.E.C. Convention from a German point of view, in: Contract Conflicts, North (ed), London 1982, 221 - 233 (cited: Contract Conflicts).

id, Inländische Sachnormen mit zwingendem internationalen Anwendungsbereich, in: IPRax 1989, 261 - 271.

id, Consumer Contracts and the 1980 Rome EC Convention on the Law applicable to Contractual Obligations, in: J Cons P 15 (1992) 365 - 380.

Honsell, Heinrich/ Vogt, Nedim Peter/ Schnyder, Anton K., Kommentar zum schweizerischen Privatrecht, Stand: 30.6.1995, Basel, FfM 1996, authors: Art(s) 13 - 19: Mächler-Erne, Monica, Art(s) 120, 121: Brunner, Alexander, (cited: Honsell/Vogt/Schnyder/author).

Huber, Ulrich, De Conflictu Legum in: Prealectiones Juris Civiles, Francher 1687, translated by DJ Llewelfryn Davies 18 (1937) BYBIL 64, (cited: De Conflitu Legum).

Jackson, David, Mandatory Rules and Rules of "ordre public", in: Contract Conflicts, North (ed), London 1982, 59 - 80 (cited: Contract Conflicts).

Jaffey, Anthony J.E., Essential Validity of Contracts in the English Conflict of Laws, in: 23 ICLQ (1974) 1 - 31.

id, The English Proper Law doctrine and the EEC. Convention, in: 33 ICLQ (1984) 531- 555.

Jayme, Erik, The Rome Convention on the law applicable to contractual obligations (1980), in: Sarcevic, Petar (ed), International Contracts and Conflicts of Laws, A Collection of Essays, London 1990, 36 - 50 (cited: International Contracts).

id, Ausländische Rechtsregeln und Tatbestand inländischer Sachnormen, in: Gedächtnisschrift Albert A. Ehrenzweig, Heidelberg 1976, 35 - 49 (cited: GS Ehrenzweig).

id, Haustürgeschäfte deutscher Urlauber in Spanien: Horizontale Wirkungen er EG-Richtlinien und internatonales Vertragsrecht (zu OLG Hamm 1.12.1988 - 4 U 12/088), in: IPRax 1990, 220 - 222.

id, "Timesharing-Verträge" im Internationalen Vertrags- und Verfahrensrecht, in: IPRax 1995, 234 - 236.

id, Zur Anwendung ausländischer Verbotsgesetze durch den Supreme Court von Kalifornien, in: IPRax 1986, 46 - 48.

Juenger, Friedrich K., American and European Conflicts Law, in: Am J Comp L 30 (1982) 117 - 133.

Junker, Abbo, Die zwingenden Bestimmungen im Internationalen Arbeitsrecht, in: IPRax 1989, 69 - 75.

id, Schadensersatzpflicht bei einem Verstoß gegen ein ausländisches Embargo, in: JZ 1991, 699 - 702.

id, Die freie Rechtswahl und ihre Grenzen, in: IPRax 1993, 1 - 10.

id, Vom Citoyen zum Consommateur - internationales Verbraucherschutzrecht, in: IPRax 1998, 65 - 74.

Kahn, Ellison, International Contracts III, in: 20 BML (1990) 35 - 38, International Contracts VI, in: 20 BML (1991) 147 - 150.

id, Conflict of Laws, in: 1991 ASSAL 580 - 593.

Karrer, Pierre A./Arnold, Karl W., Switzerland's Private International Law Statute of December 18, 1987 - The Swiss Code on Conflicts of Laws and related Legislation, Deventer, Bosten 1989 (cited: Switzerland's Private International Law Statute).

Kay, Herma Hill, Theory into Practice: Choice of Law in the Courts, in: Mercer L Rev 34 (1983) 521 - 592.

Kaye, Peter, The New Private International Law of Contract of the European Community, Aldershot, Brookfield USA 1993 (cited: The New Private International Law).

Kegel, Gerhard, Internationales Privatrecht, 7th ed, München 1995, 6th ed, München 1987, 5th ed, München 1985, (cited: IPR edition).

id, Die selbstgerechte Sachnorm, in: Gedächtnisschrift für Albert Ehrenzweig, Heidelberg 1976, 51 - 87 (cited: Die selbstgerechte Sachnorm).

id/Seidel-Hohnveldern, Ignaz, Zum Territorialitätsprinzip im internationalen öffentlichen Recht, in: Festschrift für Murad Ferid, München 1978, 233 - 278 (cited: FS Ferid).

id, 'Vaterhaus, Traumhaus. Herkömmliches IPR und Hauptthesen der amerikanischen Reformer, in: Festschrift Günther Beitzke, Berlin, NY 1979, 551 - 573 (cited: FS Beitzke).

id, Die Rolle des öffentlichen Rechts im IPR, in: Festschrift für Ignaz Seidl-Hohenveldern, Köln 1988, 243 - 278 (cited: Die Rolle des öffentlichen Rechts).

id, The Rôle of Public Law in Private international Law: German Report, in: Basle Symposium on the Rôle of Public Law in Private International Law, Klein (ed.), Bâle et Francfort-sur-le-Main 1991, 29 - 62 (cited: The Rôle of public law).

id, Diskussionsbeitrag zu Kreuzer, in: Zum Deutschen und Internationalen Schuldrecht, Schlechtriem, Peter/Leser, Hans G. (eds), Tübingen 1983, 111 (cited: Schechtriem/Leser).

Keller, Max, Schutz des schwächeren im internationalen Vertragsrrecht, in: Festschrift für Frank Vischer, Zürich 1983, 175-188 (cited: FS Vischer).

Keller, Max/Siehr, Kurt, Allgemeine Lehren des Internationalen Privatrechts, Zürich 1986, (cited: IPR).

Kohte, Wolfhard, Verbraucherschutz im Licht des europäischen Wirtschaftsrechts, in: EUZW (1990) 150 - 156.

Kleinschmidt, Peter, Zur Anwendbarkeit zwingenden Rechts im internationalen Schuldvertragsrecht unter besonderer Berücksichtigung von Absatzmittlerverträgen, Dissertation, München 1985 (cited: Anwendbarkeit).

Knüppel, Norbert, Zwingendes materielles Recht und internationale Schuldverträge, Dissertation, Bonn 1988 (cited: Zwingendes materielles Recht).

Kösters, Friedrich, Die Anwendung ausländischer Eingriffsnormen im französischen Recht, Dissertation, Münster 1991 (cited: Anwendung).

Kratz, Brigitte, Ausländische Eingriffsnorm und inländischer Privatrechtsvertrag, Dissertation, Frankfurt, Bern, NY 1986 (cited: Ausländische Eingriffsnorm).

Kren, Jolanta, Die Behandlung der schwächeren Partei im schweizerischen internationalen Vertragsrecht unter Berücksichtigung der deutschen Rechtsordnung, in: ZVglRWiss 87 (1988) 48 - 70.

Kreuzer, Karl F., Ausländisches Wirtschaftsrecht vor deutschen Gerichten, Heidelberg 1986 (cited: Ausländisches Wirtschaftsrecht).

id, Erklärung eines generellen Vorbehalts zu Art. 7 Abs. 1 des Übereinkommens vom 19.6.1980 über das auf vertragliche Schuldverhältnisse anzuwendende Recht? in: IPRax 1984, 293 - 295.

id, Parteiautonomie und fremdes Außenwirtschaftsrecht in: Zum Deutschen und Internationalen Schuldrecht, Schlechtriem, Peter/ Leser, Hans G (eds), Tübingen 1983, 89 - 111 (cited: Schlechtriem/Leser).

Kropholler, Jan, Internationales Privatrecht, 3rd ed, Tübingen 1997 (cited: IPR).

id, Das kollisionsrechtliche System des Schutzes der schwächeren Vertragspartei, in: RabelsZ 42 (1978) 634 - 661.

Kuyper, Pieter Jan, The European Community and the US Pipeline Embargo: Comments on Comments, in: GYBIL 27 (1984) 72 - 96.

Lando, Ole/Hoffmann, Bernd, von/Siehr, Kurt, European Private International Law of Obligations, Tübingen 1975 (cited: see the authors).

Lando, Ole, The EC Drafts Convention on the Law applicable to Contractual and Non-Contractual Obligations, in: RabelsZ 38 (1974) 6 - 55.

id, Contracts, in: International Encyclopedia of Comparative Law, Lipstein, Kurt (ed), Vol. III, Private International Law, Chapter 24, Tübingen 1976 (cited: Contracts).

id, New American Choice-of-Law Principles and the European Conflict of Laws of Contracts, in: Am J Comp L 30 (1982) 19 - 36.

id, The Conflict of Laws of Contracts, in: Rec des Cours 189 (1984 VI) 229 - 408.

id, The EEC Convention on the Law Applicable to contractual obligations, in: CMLR 24 (1987) 159 - 214.

Lasok, D./Stone, P. A., Conflict of Laws in the European Community, Abingdon, Oxon 1987 (cited Conflict of Laws).

Leflar, Robert A., American Conflicts Law, 3rd ed, Indianapolis 1977 (cited: American Conflicts Law).

id, Choice-Influencing Considerations in Conflicts Law, in: NY UL Rev 41 (1966) 267 - 327.

Lehmann, Rolf, Zwingendes Recht dritter Staaten im internationalen Vertragsrecht, Dissertation, FfM, Berlin, NY 1986 (cited: Zwingendes Recht).

id, Eingriffsnormen dritter Staaten und die deutsche IPR Reform, in: ZRP 1987, 319 - 321.

Leible, Stefan, Rechtswahlfreiheit und kollisionsrechtlicher Verbraucherschutz, in: JBJZRW (1995) 245 - 269.

Lipstein, Kurt, General Principles of Private International Law, in: Rec des Cours 135 (1972 I) 99 - 226.

id, Conflict of Laws 1921 - 71, The way ahead, in: 31 (1972 B) CLJ 67 - 120.

id, Comments on Arts 1 to 21 of the Draft Convention in: European Private International Law of Obligations, Lando/v. Hoffmann/Siehr (eds), Tübingen 1975, 155 - 169 (cited: Comments).

id, Inherent Limitations in Statutes and the Conflict of Laws, in: ICLQ 26 (1977) 884 - 902.

id, Harmonisation of Private International Law by the E.E.C., Lipstein, Kurt (ed), London 1978 (for citation see contributors).

id, Conflict of public Laws - Visions and Realities, in: Festschrift für Imre Zajtay, Graveson, Ronald/Kreuzer, Karl/Tunc, André/Zweigert, Konrad (eds), Tübingen 1982, 357 - 378 (cited: Conflict of Public Laws).

id, Öffentliches Recht und internationales Privatrecht, in: Internationales Privatrecht, Internationales Wirtschaftsrecht, Holl, Wolfgang/Klinke, Ulrich (eds), Köln, Berlin 1985, 39 - 54 (cited: Öffentliches Recht).

id, Conflict of Laws and Public Law, in: United Kingdom Law in the 1980's, Volume 8, E.K. Banakas (ed) 1988, 38 - 58, (cited: Conflict of Laws).

id, Characterization, in: International Encyclopedia of Comparative Law, Lipstein, Kurt (ed), Vol. III, Private International Law, Chapter 5, Tübingen 1999 (cited: Characterization)

Lorenz, Egon, Die Rechtswahlfreiheit im internationalen Schuldvertragsrecht - Grundsatz und Grenzen, in: RIW 1987, 569 - 584.

id, Das Objektive Arbeitsstatut nach dem Gesetz zur Neuregelung des Internationalen Privatrechts, in: RdA 1989, 220 - 228.

Lorenz, Werner, Vom alten zum neuen internationalen Schuldvertragsrecht, in: IPRax 1987, 269 - 276.

id, Kollisionsrecht des Verbraucherschutzes: Anwendbares Recht und internationale Zuständigkeit, in: IPRax 1994, 429 - 431.

Lowe, A Vaughan, International Law Issues Arising in the 'Pipeline' Dispute: The British Position, in: GYBIL 27 (1984) 54 - 71.

id, Extraterritorial Jurisdiction, The British Practice, in: RabelsZ 52 (1988) 157 - 204.

Lüderitz, Alexander, Internationaler Verbraucherschutz in Nöten, in: IPRax 1990, 216 - 219.

Magnus, Ulrich, Englisches Kündigungsrecht auf deutschem Schiff - Probleme des internationalen Seearbeitsrecht, in: IPRax 1991, 383 - 386.

Mankowsky, Peter, Strukturfragen de internationalen Verbrauchervertragsrechts, in: RIW 1993, 453 - 463.

id, Wichtige Klärungen im internationalen Arbeitsrecht (zu BAG, 29.10.1992 - 2 AZR 267/92), in: IPRax 1994, 88 - 98.

id, Auswirkung ausländischer (nigerianischer) Zoll- und Einfuhrbestimmungen auf einen See-Versicherungsvertrag, Anmerkung zu OLG Hamburg, Urteil vom 6.5.1993, in: RIW 1994, 688 - 692.

id, Timesharingverträge und internationales Vertragsrecht, in: RIW 1995, 364 - 370.

id, Art. 34 EGBGB erfaßt § 138 BGB nicht! in: RIW 1996, 8 - 12.

id, Strukturfragen des Internationalen Verbraucherrechts, Zugleich Anmerkung zu BGH 19.3.1997 - VIII ZR 316/96, RIW 1997, 875 ff, in: RIW 1998, 287 - 291.

Mann, Frederik A., Proper Law and illegality in private international law, in: 18 BYIL (1937) 97 - 113.

id, Conflict of Laws and Public Law, in: Rec des Cours 132 (1971 I) 107- 196.

id, Contracts: Effect of Mandatory Rules, in: Harmonisation of private international Law by the E.E.C., Lipstein, Kurt (ed), London 1978, 31- 37 (cited: Effects).

id, Anmerkung (zu BGH, Urteil vom 22.6.1972 - II ZR 113/70), in: NJW 1972, 2179.

id, Eingriffsgesetze im Internationalen Privatrecht, in: Festschrift für Eduard Wahl, Heidelberg 1973, 139 - 160 (cited: FS Wahl).

id, Sonderanknüpfung und zwingendes Recht im Internationalen Privatrecht in: Festschrift für Günther Beitzke, Berlin, New York 1979, 607 - 624 (cited: FS Beitzke).

Martiny, Dieter, Der deutsche Vorbehalt gegen Art. 7 Abs. 1 des EG-Schuldvertragsübereinkommens vom 19.6.1980 - seine Folgen für die Anwendung ausländischen zwingenden Rechts, in: IPRax 1987, 277 - 280.

id, Internationales Vertragsrecht zwischen Rechtsgefälle und Vereinheitlichung, in: ZEuP 95 (1996) 67 - 88.

Mäsch, Gerald, Rechtswahlfreiheit und Verbraucherschutz, Dissertation, Berlin 1993 (cited: Rechtswahlfreiheit).

Max-Planck-Institut, Kodifikation des deutschen Internationalen Privatrechts - Stellungnahme des Max-Planck-Instituts für ausländisches und internationales Privatrecht zum Regierungsentwurf von 1983, in: RabelsZ 47 (1983) 495 - 690.

Meessen, Karl M., Extraterritoriality of Export Control: A German Lawyer's Analysis of the Pipeline Case, in: GYBIL 27 (1984) 97 - 108.

Mentzel, Ralph, Sonderanknüpfung von Eingriffsrecht im internationalen Vertragsrecht, Dissertation, München 1993.

Morris, J. H. C., Statutes in Conflict of Laws in: Festschrift für Kurt Lipstein, Multum non Multa, Feuerstein, Peter/Parry, Clive (eds), Heidelberg, Karlsruhe 1980, 187- 204 (cited: Statutes).

Morscher, Thomas, Staatliche Rechtssetzungsakte als Leistungshindernisse im internationalen Warenkauf, Dissertation, Basel 1992 (cited: Rechtssetzungsakte).

Morse, C. G. J., Contracts on Employment and the E.E.C. Contractual Obligation Convention, in: Contract Conflicts, North (ed), 1982, 143 - 173 (cited: Contract Conflicts).

id, The EEC Convention on the Law Applicable to Contractual Obligations, in: (1982) 2 YB Eur L 107-171.

id, Consumer Contracts, Employment Contracts and the Rome Convention, in: 41 ICLQR (1992) 1 - 21.

id, England, in: Public Policy in Transnational Relationships, Mauro Rubino-Sammartano, C.G.J. Morse (eds), Supplement 2 (June 1997), The Hague, London, Boston (cited: Public Policy England).

Mülbert, Peter, Ausländische Eingriffsnormen als Datum, in: IPRax 1986, 140 - 142.

Münchener Kommentar zum Bürgerlichen Gesetzbuch, Band 10, Einführungsgesetz zum Bürgerlichen Gesetzbuche, Internationales Privatrecht, 3rd ed, München 1998, authors: Einführung: - Sonnenberger, Art(s) 27 - 30 und 34: - Martiny (cited: MünchKomm/author).

Neels, Jan L., Geooroofdheid van 'n kontrak en openbare beleid in die internasionale privaatreg, in: 1991 TSAR 694 - 701.

Neuhaus, Paul H., Die Grundbegriffe des internationalen Privatrechts, 2nd ed, Tübingen 1976 (cited: Grundbegriffe).

id, Der schweizer IPR-Entwurf - ein internationales Modell? in: RabelsZ 43 (1979) 277 - 289.

Neumayer, Karl, Anmerkung (zu BGH RabelsZ 25 (1960) 645 - 649), in: RabelsZ 25 (1960) 649 - 657.

id, Die Notgesetzgebung des Wirtschaftsrechts im internatioalen Privatrecht, in: BerDGesVöR 2 (1958) 35 - 59.

Niederer, Werner, Einführung in die allgemeinen Lehren des internationalen Privatrechts, 3rd ed, Zürich 1961 (cited: Einführung).

North, Peter, The E.E.C. Convention on the Law Applicable to Contractual Obligations, in: JBL (1980) 382 - 387.

id, Contracts Conflicts, The E.E.C. Convention on the Law Applicable to Contractual Obligations: A Comparative Study, North, Peter M. (ed), Amsterdam, NY, Oxford 1982 (cited: author Contract Conflicts).

id, The E.E.C. Convention on the Law Applicable to Contractual Obligations (1980): Its History and Main Features in Contract Conflicts, North (ed), 3 - 24 (cited: Contract Conflicts).

id, Die Anwendung ausländischen öffentlichen Rechts im englischen IPR, in: IPRax 1988, 257 - 258.

id, Private International Law Problems in Common Law Jurisdictions, Dordrecht, Boston, London 1993 (cited: Private International Law Problems).

Overbeck, Alfred, von, Der schweizerische Entwurf eines Bundesgesetzes über das Internationale Privatrecht, in: RabelsZ 42 (1978) 601 - 633.

id, Contracts: The Swiss Draft Statute compared with the E.E.C. Convention in: Contract Conflicts, North (ed), 1982, 269 - 294 (cited: Contract Conflicts).

id, Das neue schweizerische Bundesgesetze über das Internationale Privatrecht, in: IPRax 1988, 329 - 334.

Peterson, Courtland H., Moderne amerikanische IPR-Theorie, in: Internationales Vertragsrecht und internationales Wirtschaftsrecht, Holl, Wolfgang/ Klinke, Ulrich, Köln, Berlin 1985, 77 - 90 (cited: Moderne amerikanische IPR-Theorie).

Philipp, Allan, Mandatory Rules, Public Law (Political Rules) and Choice of Law in the E.E.C. Convention on The Law applicable to Contractual Obligations, in: Contract Conflicts, North (ed), 1982, 81 - 109 (cited: Contract Conflicts).

id, Recent Provisions on Mandatory Laws in Private International Law, in: Festschrift für Kurt Lipstein Multum non Multa, Feuerstein, Peter/Parry, Clive (eds), Heidelberg, Karlsruhe 1980, 241 - 249 (cited: Recent Provisions).

Piehl, Hansjörg, Ausländische zwingende Vorschriften und deutsches Schuldstatut, in: RIW/AWD 1988, 841 - 843.

Plender, Richard, The European Contracts Convention: The Rome Convention on the Choice of Law for Contracts, London 1991 (cited: The European Contracts Convention).

Püls, Joachim, Parteiautonomie: Die Bedeutung des Parteiwillens und die Entwicklung seiner Schranken bei Schuldverträgen im deutschen Rechtsanwendungsrecht des 19. und 20. Jahrhunderts, Dissertation, Berlin 1995 (cited: Parteiautonomie).

Raape, Leo/Sturm, Fritz, Internationales Privatrecht Band I, 6th ed, München 1977 (cited IPR).

Radtke, Rolf, Schuldstatut und Eingriffsrecht, in: ZVglRWiss 84 (1985) 325 - 357.

Reese, Willis L. M., American Choice of Law, in: Am J Comp L 30 (1982) 135 - 146.

Rehbinder, Eckard, Zur Politisierung des Internationalen Privatrechts, in: JZ 1973, 151 - 158.

Remien, Oliver, Außenwirtschaftsrecht in kollisionsrechtlicher Sicht, Zur internationalen Reichweite von Aus- und Einfuhrverboten, in: RabelsZ 54 (1990) 431 - 480.

Reichelt, Gerte, Beachtung zwingender Bestimmungen im österreichischen IPRG. Ansätze richterlicher Rechtsfortbildung zu § 1 öIPRG, in: ZfR 29 (1988) 82 - 88.

Reithmann, Christoph/ Martiny, Dieter, Internationales Vertragsrecht, Das Internationale Privatrecht der Schuldverträge, 5th ed, Köln 1996 (cited: Reithmann/Martiny/author Internationales Vertragsrecht).

Rinze, Jens, The scope of Party Autonomy under the 1980 Rome Convention on the Law Applicable to Contractual Obligations, in: JBL (1994) 412 - 430.

Roth, Wulf-Henning, Zur Anwendung der §§ 134 und 306 BGB bei Importverboten, in: IPRax 1984, 76 - 79.

id, Verbraucherschutz über die Grenze (Anmerkung zu BGH 26.10.1993), in: RIW 1994, 275 - 278.

id, Zum Verhältnis von Art. 7 Abs. 2 und Art. 5 der Römer Schuldvertragskonvention in: Internationales Verbraucherschutzrecht, Schnyder, Anton/ Heiß, Helmut/ Rudisch, Bernhard (eds), Tübingen 1995, 35 - 51 (cited: Schnyder/Heiß/Rudisch).

Sandrock, Otto, Bedeutung des Gesetzes zur Neuregelung des Internationalen Privaterechts für die Unternehmenspraxis, in: RIW 1986, 841 - 855.

Sandrock, Otto/ Steinschulte, Fritz Peter, Handbuch der internationalen Vertragsgestaltung, Band 1, Heidelberg 1980 (cited: Handbuch).

Sarcevic, Petar, International Contracts and Conflicts of Laws, A Collection of Essays, Sarcevic, Petar (ed), London 1990 (cited: author International Contracts).

Savigny, Friedrich Carl, von, System des heutigen römischen Rechts Vol VIII, Berlin 1849.

Schäfer, Martin, Eingriffsnorm im deutschen IPR- eine never ending story? in: Festgabe Otto Sandrock, Iusto Iure, Heidelberg 1995, 37 - 53 (cited FG Sandrock).

Schiffer, Jan, Normen ausländischen öffentlichen Rechts im Internationalen Handelsschiedsverfahren, Dissertation, Köln, Berlin, Bonn, München 1990 (cited: Normen).

id, Sonderanknüpfung ausländischen "öffentlichen" Rechts in der internationalen Handelsschiedsgerichtsbarkeit, in: ZverglRWiss 90 (1991) 390 - 443.

Schnyder, Anton K., Das neue IPR-Gesetz - Einführung in das Bundesgesetz vom 18. Dezember 1987 über das Internationale Privatrecht (IPRG), 2nd ed, Zürich 1990 (cited: Das neue IPRG).

id, Wirtschaftskollisionsrecht, Sonderanknüpfung und extraterritoriale Anwendung wirtschaftsrechtlicher Normen unter besonderer Berücksichtigung von Marktrecht, Zürich 1990 (cited: Wirtschaftskollisionsrecht).

id, Ausweichklausel und Verbraucherschutz - Herausforderung des Schweizer Internationalprivatrechts, in: Schnyder, Anton/Heiß, Helmut/Rudisch, Bernhard (eds), Internationales Verbraucherschutzrecht, Tübingen 1995, 57 et seq (cited: Schnyder/Heiß/Rudisch).

Schubert, Mathias, Internationale Verträge und Eingriffsrecht - Ein Beitrag zur Methode des Wirtschaftskollisionsrechts, in: RIW 1987, 729 - 746.

Schulte, Dieter, Die Anknüpfung von Eingriffsnormen, insbesondere wirtschaftsrechtlicher Art, im internationalen Vertragsrecht Dissertation, Bielefeld 1975 (cited: Eingriffsnormen).

Schultsz, Jan C., Dutch Antecedents and Parallels t Article 7 of the EEC Contracts Convention of 1980, in: RabelsZ 47 (1983) 267 - 283.

Schurig, Klaus, Kollisionsnorm und Sachrecht, Habitilation, Berlin 1981, (cited: Kollisionsnorm).

id, Zwingendes Recht, Eingriffsnormen und neues IPR, in: RabelsZ 54 (1990) 217 - 250.

id, Lois d'application immédiate und Sonderanknüpfung zwingenden Rechts oder Mystifikation? in: Internationales Vertragsrecht und internationales Wirtschaftsrecht, Holl, Wolfgang/Klinke, Ulrich, Köln, Berlin 1985, 55 - 76 (cited: Lois).

id, Die Gesetzesumgehung im Privatrecht - Eine Studie mit kollisionsrechtlichen und rechtsvergleichenden Aspekten -, in: Festschrift für Murad Ferid, Frankfurt 1988, 375 - 422 (cited: FS Ferid).

Schwander, Ivo, Einführung in das internationale Privatrecht, Erster Band: Allgemeiner Teil, 2nd ed, St. Gallen 1990 (cited: IPR AT).

id, "Lois d'application immédiate, Sonderanknüpfung, IPR-Sachnormen und andere Ausnahmen von der gewöhnlichen Anknüpfung im Internationalen Privatrecht", Dissertation, Zürich 1975 (cited: Lois).

id, Zur Rechtswahl im IPR des Schuldvertragsrecht in: Festschrift für Max Keller, Forstmoser, Peter/Heini, Anton et al (eds), Zürich 1989, 473 - 484 (cited: FS Keller).

Siehr, Kurt, Normen mit eigener Bestimmung ihres räumlichen-persönlichen Anwendungsbereichs im Kollisionsrecht der Bundesrepublik Deutschland, in: RabelsZ 46 (1982) 357 - 382.

id, Domestic Relations in Europe: European Equivalents to American Evolutions, in: Am J Comp L 30 (1982) 37 - 71.

id, Ausländische Eingriffsnorm im inländischen Wirtschaftskollisionsrecht, in: RabelsZ 52 (1988) 41 - 102.

id, Parteiautonomie im Internationalen Vertragsrecht, in: Festschrift für Max Keller, Forstmoser, Peter/ Heini, Anton et al (eds), Zürich 1989, 485 - 510 (cited: FS Keller).

id, Entwurf des schweizerischen Bundesrates zum Bundesgesetze über das IPR, in: RabelsZ 47(1983) 342 - 348.

Soergel, Bürgerliches Gesetzbuch, Mit Einführungsgesetz und Nebengesetzen, Band 10: Einführungsgesetz, 12th ed, Stand: 1996, Stuttgart, Berlin, Köln, Art(s) 27 - 34: - von Hoffmann, 11th ed, Stand: 1984, Stuttgart, Berlin, Köln, vor Art 7: - Kegel (cited: Soergel/von Hoffmann; Soergel/Kegel 11th ed).

Sonnenberger, Hans J., Internationales Privatrecht/Internationales öffentliches Recht, in: Festschrift für Kurt Rebmann, München 1989, 819 - 838 (cited: FS Rebmann).

Spiro, Erwin, The general Principles of the Conflict of Laws, Cape Town, 1982, (cited: General Principles).

id, Autonomy of the parties to a contract and the conflict of laws: illegality, in: XVII CILSA 1984, 197 - 210.

Staudinger, J. von, Kommentar zum Bürgerlichen Gesetzbuch, mit Einführungsgesetz und Nebengesetzen, 12th ed, Berlin 1998, Einl., Art(s) 27, 30, 32, 34: - Magnus, Art(s) 29, 36: - Reinhart (cited: Staudinger/author).

Sturm, Fritz, Die allgemeinen Grundsätze im schweizerischen IPR-Gesetzesentwurf, eine kritische Analyse, in: Festschrift für Rudolf Moser, Beiträge zum neuen IPR des Sachen-, Schuld- und Gesellschaftsrechts, Zürich 1987, 3 - 23 (cited: FS Moser).

Taupitz, Jochen, Kaffeefahrten deutscher Urlauber auf Gran Canaria: Deutscher Verbraucherschutz im Urlaubsgepäck? in: BB 1990, 642 - 652.

Tiemann, Volker, Eine Anknüpfungsleiter für das Wirtschaftskollisionsrecht, Dissertation, Bielefeld 1993 (cited: Anknüpfungsleiter).

Triebel, Volker, The Choice of Law in Commercial Relations: A German Perspective, in: 37 ICLQ (1988) 935 - 945.

Ungeheuer, Christina, Die Beachtung von Eingriffsnormen in der internationalen Handelsschiedsgerichtsbarkeit, Dissertation, FfM, Berlin, NY 1995 (cited: Beachtung).

Vagts, Detlev F., The Pipeline Controversy: An American Viewpoint, in: GYBIL 27 (1984) 38 - 53.

Van der Kessel, D.G., Praelectiones Juris Hoderni and Hugonis Gratii introductionem ad jurisprudentiam hollandicam Vol I (translated into Afrikaans by P van Warmelo and others, Amsterdam, Cape Town, 1961), (cited: Praelectiones).

Van Rooyen, J. C. W., Die Kontrak in die Suid-Afrikaanse Internasionale Privaatreg, Cape Town 1972 (cited: Die Kontrak).

Viejobueno, Sonia, Private International Law rules relating to the validity of international sales contracts, in: XXVI CILSA 1993, 172 - 210.

Vischer, Frank, Kollisionsrechtliche Parteiautonomie und dirigistische Wirtschaftsgesetzgebung, in: Festschrift für Max Gerwig, Juristische Fakultät der Universität Basel (eds), Basel 1960, 167 - 191 (cited: FS Gerwig).

id, Internationales Vertragsrecht, Bern 1962.

id, The Antagonism between legal security and the search for justice in the field of contracts, in: Rec des Cours 142 (1974 II) 1 - 70.

id, Zwingendes Recht und Eingriffsgesetze nach dem Schweizerischen IPR-Gesetz, in: RabelsZ 53 (1989) 438 - 461.

id, General Course on Private International Law, in: Rec des Cours 232 (1992 I) 9 - 256.

id, Connecting Factors, in: International Encyclopedia of Comparative Law, Vol. III, Private International Law, Lipstein, Kurt (eds), Chapter 4, Tübingen 1999 (cited: Connecting Factors).

Vischer, Frank/Planta, Andreas, von, Internationales Privatrecht, 2nd ed, Basel, FfM 1982 (cited: IPR).

Vitta, Edoardo, The Impact in Europe of the American "Conflict Revolution", in: Am J Comp L 30 (1982) 1 - 18.

Voet, Johannes, Commentarius ad Pandactas, The Hague 1698 - 1704, (cited: Commentarius).

Voet, Paul, De Statutis earem concursu, Amsterdam 1661, (cited: De Statutis).

Voser, Natalie, Die Theorie der Lois d'application immédiate im Internationalen Privatrecht, Dissertation, Basel, FfM 1993 (cited: Lois d'application immédiate).

id, Current development: Mandatory rules of law as a limitation on the law applicable in international commercial arbitration, in: 7 Am Rev Int'l Arb 319, LEXIS-NEXIS Academic Universe - Document, (1996) 38 pages.

Weber, Helmut, Das zwingende an den zwingenden Bestimmungen im internationalen Arbeitsrecht, in: IPRax 1988, 82 - 85.

Wengler, Wilhelm, Die Anknüpfung zwingendes Schuldrechts im internationalen Privatrecht - eine rechtsvergleichende Studie, in: ZvglRWiss 54 (1941) 165 - 212.

Williams, Patrick Ross, The E.E.C. Convention on the Law Applicable to Contractual Obligations, in: 35 ICLQ (1986) 1 - 30.

Zimmer, Daniel, Ausländisches Wirtschaftsrecht vor deutschen Gerichten, in: IPRax 1993, 65 - 69.

Zweigert, Konrad, Nichterfüllung auf Grund ausländischer Leistungsverbote, in: RabelsZ 14 (1942) 283 - 307.

Table of cases

English cases

(Including other common law countries)

Antares (Nos 1 and 2), The [1987] 1 Lloyd's Rep 424

Attorney-General for the United Kingdom v Wellington Newspapers Ltd [1988] 1 NZLR 129 (CA New Zealand)

Attorney-General (UK) v Heinemann Publishers Australia (1988) 165 CLR 30 (High Court Of Australia)

Attorney-General of New Zealand v Ortiz [1984] AC 1 (CA and HL)

Banque des Merchands des Moscou (No 2), Re [1954] 1 WLR 1108

Boissevain v Weil [1950] AC 327; [1950] 1 All ER 728 (HL)

British Nylon Spinners v Imperial Chemical Industries Ltd [1955] Ch 37; [1953] Ch 19 (CA)

Brodin A/R v Seljan 1973 S.C. 213 (Outer House, Court of Session)

Coast Lines Ltd Hudig & Veder Cartering NV [1972] 1 All ER 451

De Béeche v South American Stores Ltd [1935] AC 148; [1934] All ER Rep 284

De Wutz v Hendriks (1824) 2 Bing. 314

Dynamit A/G Rio Tinto Co [1918] AC 260 (HL)

Emery's Investment Trust, Re [1959] Ch 410

English v Donnelly 1958 SC 494; (1959) SLT 2 (Court of Session Scotland)

Euro-Diam Ltd v Brathurst [1990] 1 QB 1; [1988] 2 WLR 517; [1988] 1 Lloyd's Rep 228 (CA); [1987] 2 All ER 113

Foster v Driscoll [1929] 1 KB 470 (CA); [1928] All ER Rep 130

Grell v Levy (1864) 10 CB (NS) 73

Golden Acres Ltd v Queensland Estates Pty Ltd [1969] QdR 378

Government of India v Taylor [1955] AC 491

Helbert Wagg & Co Ltd, Re [1956] Ch 323; [1956] 1 All ER 129; [1956] 2 WLR 183

Hollandia, The [1983] 1 AC 565; [1982] 3 WLR 111 (HL); [1982] 2 QB 872 (CA)

Howard v Shirlstar Container Transport Ltd [1990] 1 WLR 1992 (CA)

Huntingtdon v Attril (1893) AC 150 (PC)

International Trustee for the Protection of Bondholders Act, Re v [1937] AC 500; [1937] 2 All ER 621 (HL); [1936] 3 All ER 407 (CA)

Irish Shipping Ltd v Commercial Union Assurance Co plc [1991] 2 QB 206 (CA)

Ispahani v Bank Melli Iran [1998] Lloyd's Rep. (Bank) 133 (CA)

Kahler v Midland Bank Ltd [1950] AC 24 (HL); [1949] 2 All ER 621

Kay's Leasing Corporation v Fletcher (1964) 116 CLR124

Kleinwort, Sons & Co v Ungarische Baumwolle Industrie AG [1939] 2 KB 678; [1939] 3 All ER 38 (CA)

Kursell v Timber Operations & Contractors Ltd [1927] 1 K.B. 298 (CA)

Lemanda Trading Co v African Middle East Petrolium Co [1988] 2 WLR 735; [1988] QB 448; [1988] 1 All ER 513

Libyan Arab Foreign Bank v Bankers Trust Co [1989] 3 All ER 252; [1989] QB 728

Machender v Feldia AC [1967] 2 QB 590

Metliss v National Bank of Greece and Athens S.A. [1957] 2 QB 33; [1957] 2 All ER 1

Metropolitan Water Board v Dick, Kerr & Co [1918] AC 119 (HL)

Missouri Steamship Co, Re (1889) 42 Ch D 321

Mitsubishi Corporation v Alafonzos [1988] 1 Lloyd's Rep 191

New Brunswich Railway Co v British & French Trust Corporation Ltd [1939] AC 1; [1938] 4 All ER 747 (HL)

Oppenheimer v Cattermole [1976] AC 249

Peter Buchanan Ltd v McWey [1954] AC 516 (Supreme Court of Ireland)

Playa Larga, The [1983] 2 Lloyd's Rep 171 (CA)

Ralli Brothers v Compaia Naviera Sota y Aznar [1920] 2 K.B. 287 (CA)

Regazzoni v KC Sethia (1944) Ltd [1958] AC 301 (HL)

Rossano Manufacturers Life Insurance Co Ltd [1963] 2 QB 352

Rousillon v Rousillon (1880) 14 Ch D 351

Royal Boskalis Westminster NV v Mountain [1999] QB 674 (CA)

Royal Exchange Assurance Corp v Vega [1902] 2 KB 384 (CA)

Sayers v International Drilling Co [1971] WLR 1176; [1971] 2 L'loyds Rep 105; [1971] 3 All ER 63 (CA)

Sing Batra v Ebrahim The Times, 3 May 1977 (CA)

Soleimany v Soleimany [1999] QB 785 (CA)

State of Norway's Application (Nos 1 and 2, Re [1987] QB 473 (CA); [1990] 1 AC 723 (HL)

St. Pierre and Others v South American Stores (Gath and Chaves) Ltd and

Chilean Stores (Gath and Chaves) Ltd [1937] 3 All ER 349
Toprak v Finagrain Compagnie Commerciale Agricole et Financière S.A. [1979] 2 Lloyd's Rep 98 (CA)
UCM v Royal Bank of Canada [1983] AC 168; [1982] 2 WLR 1039; [1982] 2 All ER (HL)
United City Merchands (Investments) Ltd v Royal Bank of Canada [1982] QB 208, 228
United States of America (US) v Inkley [1989] QB 255 (CA)
Vita Food Products Inc v Unus Shipping Co Ltd [1939] AC 277 (PC)
Williams & Humbert Ltd v W & H Trade Marks (Jersey) Ltd [1986] AC 368
Zivnostenska Banka v Frankmann [1950] AC 57; [1949] 2 All ER 671

German Cases

RG 10.5.1884 RGZ 12, 34
RG 5.11.1898 RGZ 42, 295
RG 26.5.1900 RGZ 46, 112
RG 2.12.1903 RGZ 56, 179
RG 22.12.1916 Cruchot Vol 61 (1917) 460
RG 19.10.1917 RGZ 91, 46
RG 13.11.1917 RGZ 91, 260
RG 28.7.1918 RGZ 93, 182
RG 26.9.1919 JW 1920, 138
RG 30.9.1919 RGZ 96, 282
RG 17.19.1919 RGZ 97, 6
RG 21.10.1921 NiemeyersZ 1924, 452
RG 2.5.1923 RGZ 107, 174
RG 3.10.1923 RGZ 108, 241
RG 9.2.1926 JW 1926, 2169; IPRespr 1926/27 Nr. 16
RG 10.3.1927 JW 1927, 2287; IPRespr 1926/27 Nr. 17
RG 24.6.1927 JW 1927, 2288; IPRespr 1926/27 Nr. 15
RG 4.4.1929 IPRespr 1929 Nr. 31
RG 26.10.1928 JW 1929, 244; IPRespr 1928 Nr. 20
15.2.1930 IPRespr 1930 Nr. 13
RG 28.3.1930 JW 1932, 591; IPRespr. 1931 Nr. 7
RG 1.7.1930 IPRespr 1930 Nr. 15
RG 17.10.1930 JW 1931, 928; IPRespr 1931 Nr. 9
RG 27.4.1936 IPRespr 1935-44 Nr. 468
RG 18.5.1936 RabelsZ 1936, 385; JW 1936, 2085

RG 17.6.1939 RGZ 161, 296
BGH 17.12.1959 BGHZ 31, 367; NJW 1960, 1101
BGH 21.12.1960 BGHZ 34, 169; NJW 1961, 822
BGH 19.4.1962 IPRespr 1962-63 Nr 163; WM 1962, 601; MDR 1962, 563
BGH 1.7.1963 IPRespr 1962/63 Nr. 30; WM 1963, 938
BGH 24.5.1962 NJW 1962, 1436; MDR 1962, 719
BGH 28.1.1965 IzRespr 1964/65 Nr 68; DB 1965, 512
BGH 18.2.1965 BGHZ 43, 162
BGH 22.6.1972 BGHZ 59, 82; NJW 1972, 1575
BGH 30.11.1972 BGHZ 60, 14
BGH 12.7.1973 NJW 1973, 1609; BGHSt 25, 208
BGH 16.4.1975 BGHZ 64, 183; NJW 1975, 1220
BGH 8.4.1976 VersR 1976, 678
BGH 29.9.1977 BGHZ 69, 295
OLG Hamm 7.2.1977 NJW 1977, 1594
BGH 29.5.1979 NJW 1979, 2613
BGH 21.10.1980 NJW 1980, 157
BGH 23.10.1980 RIW 1981, 194
BGH 25.5.1981 NJW 1981, 1898; IPRax 1982, 69
BGH 11.3.1982 BGHZ 83, 197
BGH 8.6.1983, IPRax 1984, 91
BGH 8.2.1984 IPRax 1986, 154
BGH 6.5.1985 BGHZ 94, 262, 265
BGH 8.5.1985 BGHZ 94, 268; IPRax 1987, 110
BGH 11.7.1985 BGHZ 95, 256
BGH 16.11.1987 BGHZ 102, 204
OLG Hamm 1.12.1988 IPRax 1990, 242
BAG 24.8.1989 IPRax 1991, 407; BAGE 63, 17
BGH 20.11.1990 JZ 1991, 719
BGH 26.2.1991 WM 1991, 576
BAG 24.3.1992 NZA 1992, 1129
BGH 20.10.1992 NJW 1993, 194; RIW 1993, 156
BAG 29.10.1992 IPRax 1994, 123; BAGE 71, 297
OLG Hamburg 6.5.1993 RIW 1994, 686 et seq
OLG Düsseldorf 8.9.1993 NJW 1994, 1074
BGH 26.10.1993 RIW 1994, 154; BGHZ 123, 380
BGH 27.1.1994 BGHZ 125, 27; JZ 1994, 725; NJW 1994, 858
LG Detmold 29.9.1994, IPRax 1995, 249
BGH 17.11.1994 BGHZ 128, 41; WM 1995, 124
BGH 19.3.1997 RIW 1997, 875; NJW 1997, 1697

South African cases
(Including other Roman-Dutch law countries and the Netherlands)

Berman v Winrow 1943 TPD 213

Bishop & others v Conrath & another 1947 (2) SA 800 (T)

Cargo Motor Corporation Ltd v Tofalos Transport Ltd 1972 (1) SA 186 (W)

Commissioner of Inland Revenue v Estate Greenacre 1936 NPD 225

Commissioner of Taxes, Federation of Rhodesia v McFarland 1965 (1) SA 470 (W)

Compagnie Européenne des Pétrols SA ca Sensor Nederland BV, Pres Arr-Rechtsbank s' Gravenhage (Den Haag) 17.9.1982, RabelsZ 47 (1983) 141

Farbenfabriken Bayer AG v Bayer Pharma (Pty) Ltd 1963 (1) SA 699 (Federal Supreme Court of the Federation of Rhodesia and Nyasaland, FSC)

Guggenheim v Rosenbaum (2) 1961 (4) SA 21 (W)

Henry v Branfield 1996 (1) SA 244 (D)

Herbst v Surti 1991 (2) SA 75 (Z)

Improvair (Cape) v Establissements Neu 1983 (2) SA 138 (C)

Jones No & others v Borland SSC & others 1969 (4) SA 29 (W)

Kassim v Gumran & another 1981 Zimbabwe LR 227

Laconian Maritime Enterprise Ltd v Agromar Lineas Ltd 1986 3 SA 509 (D)

Murata Machinery Ltd v Capelon Yarns (Pty) Ltd 1986 (4) SA 671 (C)

Ocean Commodities Inc v Standard Bank of SA Ltd 1978 (2) SA 367 (W)

Pretorius v Pretorius 1948 (4) SA 144 (O)

Pretorious & another v Natal South Sea Investment Trust Ltd 1965 (3) SA 410 (W)

Priestly v Clegg 1985 (3) SA 955 (T)

Standard Bank of SA Ltd & another v Ocean Commodities & others 1980 (2) SA 175 (T)

Standard Bank of SA Ltd v Efroiken and Newman 1924 AD 171

Standard Bank of South Africa v Ocean Commodities 1983 (1) 276 (A)

Taylor v Hollard 1886 (2) SAR 78

Timms v Nicol 1968 (1) SA 299 (R)

Swiss Cases

BGE 39 II 73 (1913)
BGE 39 II 640 (1913)
BGE 42 II 179 (1916)
BGE 42 II 379 (1916)
BGE 43 II 225 (1917)
BGE 44 II 163 (1918)
BGE 45 II 41 (1919)
BGE 60 II 294 (1934)
BGE 61 II 242 (1935)
BGE 62 II 108 (1936)
BGE 64 II 88 (1938)
BGE 67 II 215 (1941)
BGE 68 II 203 (1942)
BGE 72 I 267 (1946)
BGE 74 II 224 (1948)
BGE 76 II 33 (1950)
BGE 79 II 87 (1953)
BGE 80 II 45 (1954)
BGE 80 II 49 (1954)
BGE 80 II 53 (1954)
BGE 81 II 227 (1955)
BGE 82 I 196 (1956)
BGE 83 II 312 (1957)
BG 28.5.1957 SJZ 54 (1958) 218
BG 5.7.1957 SJZ 56 (1960) 43
Commercial Court at Zurich 9.5.1968 SJZ 64 (1968) 354
BGE 91 II 44 (1965)
BGE 95 II 109 (1969)
BGE 102 II 143 (1976)
BGE 107 II 489 (1981)
BGE 109 II 65 (1983)
BGE 109 III 52 (1983)
BGE 111 II 175 (1985)
BGE 111 II 352 (1985)
BGE 118 II 348 (1992)

Abbreviations of journals and reports

AC	Law Reports, Appeal Cases
AD	Appellate Division
All E R	All England Law Reports
Am J Comp L	American Journal of Comparative Law
Am J Int L	American Journal of International Law
Ann Inst Dr int	Annuaire de l'Institute de Droit international
ASSAL	Annual Survey of South African Law
BAGE	Entscheidungen des Bundesarbeitsgerichts
BB	Betriebsberater
Ber D Ges Völk R	Berichte der Deutschen Gesellschaft für Völkerrecht
BGE	Entscheidungen des schweizerischen Bundesgerichts
BGHZ	Entscheidungen des Bundesgerichtshofs in Zivilsachen
Bing	Bingham New Cases, Common Pleas Reports
BML	Businessman's Law
British YB Int L	The British Year Book on International Law
Ch/ Ch D	Law Reports, Chancery Division
CILSA	Comparative and International Journal of Southern Africa
CLJ	The Cambridge Law Journal
CLR	Commonwealth Law Reports (Australien)
Clunet	Journal du droit international privé et de law jurisprodrunce comparée
CMLR	Common Market Law Reports
Cruchot	Journal du droit international
DB	Der Betrieb
ELR	European Law Reports
EuZW	Europäische Zeitschrift für Wirtschaftsrecht
EwiR	Entscheidungen zum Wirtschaftsrecht
FSC	Federal Supreme Court of the Federation of Rhodesia and Nyasaland
German YB Int L	German Yearbook of International Law- Jahrbuch für internationales Recht
Harv L Rev	Harvard Law Review
IBL	International Business lawyer
ICLQ	International and Comparative Law Quarterly
Int Encyclopedia	International Encyclopedia of Comparative Law
Int L Q	International Law Quarterly
IPRax	Zeitschrift für International Privatrechtliche Praxis

IPRespr	Die Deutsche Rechtsprechungspraxis auf dem Gebiete des Internationalen Privatrechts
IzRespr	Sammlung der deutschen Entscheidungen zum interzonalen Privaterecht
J Cons P	Journal of Consumer Policy – Consumer Issues in Law, Economics and behavioural Sciences
JBJZRWiss	Jahrbuch Junger Zivilrechtswissenschaftler
JBL	Journal of Business Law
JW	Juristische Wochenschrift
JZ	Juristenzeitung
KB	Law Reports, King's Bench
LJ Ch	Law Journal Reports, Chancery
Lloyd's Rep.	Lloyd's List Law Reports
LMCLQ	Loyd's Maritime & Commercial Law Quarterly
LQR	Law Quarterly Review
LT	Law Times Report
LR (Zimbabwe)	Zimbabwe Law Report
MDR	Monatsschrift für Deutsches Recht
Mercer L Rev	Mercer Law Review
MLR	Modern Law Review
NiemeyersZ	Niemeyers Zeitschrift für internationales Recht
NJW	Neue Juristische Wochenschrift
NJW-RR	Neue Juristische Wochenschrift Rechtsprechungsreport
NPD	Natal Provincial Division
NY UL Rev	New York University Law Review
NZA	Neue Zeitschrift für Arbeitsrecht
NZLR	New Zealand Law Review
QB	Law Reports, Queen's Bench
QdR	Queensland Reports
RabelsZ	Rabels Zeitschrift für ausländisches und internationales Privatrecht
Rec des Cours	Recueil des Cours – Collected Courses of the Hague Academy of International Law
RdA	Recht der Arbeit
Rev Crit	Revue critique de droit internaional privé
Riv dir int priv proc	Rivista di Diritto Internazionale Privato et Processuale
RGZ	Entscheidungen des Reichsgerichts für Zivilsachen
RIW	Recht der Internationalen Wirtschaft
SA	South African Law Reports
SALJ	South African Law Journal
SC	Session Cases Reports
SC	Supreme Court Reports (Cape of Good Hope)

Schw Jb Int R	Schweizer Jahrbuch für Internationales Recht
SJZ	Schweizerische Juristen Zeitung
TPD	Transvaal Provincial Division
TSAR	Tydskrif Vir Die Suid-Afrikaanse Reg
Va J Int L	Virginia Journal of International Law
Van L Rev	Vanderbilt Law Review
VersR	Versicherungsrecht
WLR	Weekly Law Reports
WM	Wertpapier Mitteilungen
YB Eur L	European Yearbook of International Law
ZEuP	Zeitschrift für Europäisches Privatrecht
ZfA	Zeitschrift für Arbeitsrecht
ZfR	Zeitschrift für Rechtsvergleichung
ZHR	Zeitschrift für Handelsrecht
ZRP	Zeitschrift für Rechtspolitik
ZverglRWiss	Zeitschrift für vergleichende Rechtswissenschaften

Peter Lang · Internationaler Verlag der Wissenschaften

Ulla Liukkunen

Cross-Border Services and Choice of Law

A Comparative Study of the European Approach

Frankfurt am Main, Berlin, Bern, Bruxelles, New York, Oxford, Wien, 2006.
290 S.
Internationalrechtliche Studien. Herausgegeben von Ulrich Magnus. Bd. 45
ISBN 978-3-631-55964-2 · pb. € 56,80*

This multidisciplinary study explores cross-border services from the viewpoint of private international law. It takes a fresh approach to this field of law and reflects on the multiple facets of the Europeanisation of conflicts rules in commercial law, consumer law, company law and labour law, confronted with the challenges of globalisation. The book examines, for instance, the interaction between different fields of law that has been enabled by the means of conflicts rules. Also studied are the present challenges of the conversion of the Rome Convention into a Community instrument. The author focuses on a broad spectrum of problems caused by the fragmentation of conflicts law in Europe and seeks a way towards better coherence. With legal comparisons, an EU and US comparison included, the study seeks to provide a broader understanding of the characteristics of the Europeanisation of the conflict of laws.

Contents: Cross-border services · Private international law · Legal comparison · EU · EC law · Fragmentation of law · EU and US comparison · Commercial law · Consumer law · Labour law · Company law · Human and fundamental rights

Lightning Source UK Ltd.
Milton Keynes UK
UKHW021252170722
405967UK00009B/90

9 783631 551769